MYTHOPOESIS

MYTHOPOESIS

Mythic Patterns in the Literary Classics

by Harry Slochower

Wayne State University Press   Detroit, 1970

Published simultaneously in Canada
by The Copp Clark Publishing Company
517 Wellington Street, West
Toronto 2B, Canada

Library of Congress Catalog Card Number: 96-11337

International Standard Book Number: 0-8143-1511-9

First paperback reprint, September, 1973

Waynebook number 35

To my daughter Joyce

Contents

Illustrations

Acknowledgments

I AM INDEBTED to the Bollingen Foundation which helped further these studies.

Many of the ideas in this book were stimulated by discussions with my students at Brooklyn College, The New School, The William Alanson White Institute and Drew University.

I am grateful for permission to quote from articles of mine which appeared in the following publications:

American Quarterly II:3 (Fall, 1950): "*Moby Dick*: Myth of Democratic Expectancy." Copyright, 1950, Trustees of the University of Pennsylvania.

The Chicago Jewish Forum (Fall, 1951): "Hebrew Myth of a Chosen God."

Complex (Fall, 1950): "Freudian Motifs in Moby Dick"; (Spring, 1952), "Oedipus: Fromm or Freud."

Drew Gateway (Winter, 1954): "The Divine Comedy as Mythopoesis."

Grune & Stratton, Inc.: "Psychoanalysis and Literature," in *Progress in Clinical Psychology*, IV (1960).

International Record of Medicine, 171 (December, 1958): 761: "The Book of Job: Its Symbolism and Psychoanalytic Process."

Manas (August, 1961), "Man's Creative Potential."

Yale French Studies (Spring, 1948): "The Function of Myth in Existentialism"; (December, 1949), "André Gide's *Theseus* and the French Myth."

And I also wish to make acknowledgment to the following for permission to reprint:

Basic Books Inc., Publishers, New York: from Chapter 9, Volume IV; from Chapter 21, Volume V of *The Collected Papers of Sigmund Freud*, edited by Ernest Jones, M.D.

Gioia Bernheim and Edmund R. Brill: The material in note 3, Appendix VI is from *The Basic Writings of Sigmund Freud*, translated and edited by Dr. A. A. Brill, copyright 1938 by Random House, Inc. Copyright renewed 1965 by Gioia B. Bernheim and Edmund R. Brill.

The Clarendon Press, Oxford: Dante, *Convivio*, trans. W. W. Jackson (1947); Euripides, *Bacchae*, 2d ed., trans. E. R. Dodds (1960).

J. M. Dent & Sons Ltd.: Dante, *De Monarchia*, Temple Classics edition (1947).

The Dial Press, Inc.: *The Short Novels of Dostoevsky*, Introduction by Thomas Mann (1945).

Farrar, Straus & Giroux, Inc.: *The Golden Ass of Apuleius*, trans. and Introduction by Robert Graves. Copyright 1951 by Farrar, Straus & Young, Inc.; Theodore Reik, *Ritual: Four Psychoanalytic Studies*. Copyright 1946 by Grove Press, Inc.

Harcourt, Brace & World, Inc.: *Heinrich Heine: Paradox and Poet*, Vol. II: *The Poems*, ed. and trans. Louis Untermeyer (1937); Carl Sandburg, *The People, Yes* (1936).

The Hogarth Press Ltd.: Freud, *Collected Papers*, ed. James Strachey, Vol. V (1950).

The Hogarth Press Ltd., Sigmund Freud Copyrights Ltd., and The Institute of Psycho-Analysis: Freud, *Standard Edition*, rev. and ed. by James Strachey, Vol. IX: "Creative Writers and Day-Dreaming" (1959), Vol. XVIII: *Group Psychology and the Analysis of the Ego* (1955), Vol. XXI: "Dostoevsky and Parricide" (1961), Vol. XXII: *Moses and Monotheism* (1964).

Liveright Publishing Corp.: Freud, *Group Psychology and the Analysis of the Ego*, *Standard Edition*, Vol. XVIII (1955).

W. W. Norton & Co., Inc. and Routledge and Kegan Paul Ltd.: Freud, *Totem and Taboo*, *Standard Edition*, Vol. XIII (1955).

Philosophical Library: Jean-Paul Sartre, *Existentialism*, trans. Bernard Frechtman (1947).

Random House, Inc., Alfred A. Knopf, Inc.: Albert Camus, *The Myth of Sisyphus and Other Essays*, trans. Justin O'Brien (1959); *The Complete Greek Drama*, ed. W. J. Oates, and Eugene O'Neill, Jr. (1938 and renewed 1966); Dostoevsky, *The Brothers Karamazov*, trans. Constance Garnett (1950); Freud, *Moses and Monotheism*, *Standard Edition*, Vol. XXII (1964); André Gide, *Two Legends: Oedipus, Theseus*, trans. John Russell (1950); Goethe, *Faust*, trans. Bayard Taylor; Franz Kafka, *The Trial*, trans. Willa and Edwin Muir (1937); Thomas Mann, *Doctor Faustus*, trans. H. T. Lowe-

Porter (1948), *Joseph and His Brothers,* trans. H. T. Lowe-Porter (1948), *The Magic Mountain,* trans. H. T. Lowe-Porter (1927 and renewed 1955); Otto Rank, *The Myth of the Birth of the Hero* (1959); Jean-Paul Sartre, *No Exit and Three Other Plays,* trans. Stuart Gilbert.

The Society of Authors as the literary representative of the Estate of Laurence Binyon: Dante, *The Divine Comedy,* trans. Laurence Binyon (1947).

The Viking Press, Inc.: Cervantes, *The Ingenious Gentleman Don Quixote de la Mancha,* trans. Samuel Putnam. Copyright 1949 by The Viking Press, Inc.

Preface

Mythopoesis: The Tradition of Creativity

THIS BOOK IS based on the persuasion that, despite the agonizing conflicts and inhibiting forces of our day, man's creative impulse can be quickened by looking back towards the tradition of creativity embodied in mythopoesis from the Book of Job to *Joseph and His Brothers*.

Ours is an alienated and an alienating era. This condition is not only attributable to dislocations in our socio-economic relations. The hunger for bread is gradually being met by the development of technology which is liberating the energies of our natural resources. But there is a deeper hunger which is not being satisfied by these achievements. It is the hunger to be oneself, to be creative.

The present holds a special threat to individual autonomy. The fateful question today is this: How do I prevent my self from being flattened by the system, the machine, "integrated" with the party, the committee, the organization? How can I feel and say "*I* exist?" This burning question is opened up to Mitya Karamazov in his prison cell. "You wouldn't believe," he tells his brother Alexey,

> how I want to live now, what a thirst for existence and consciousness has sprung up in me within these peeling walls . . . . And I seem to have such strength in me now, that I think I could stand anything, any suffering, only to be able to say and to repeat to myself every moment, "I exist." In thousands of agonies—"I exist!" I'm tormented on the rack—but I exist! Though I sit alone in a pillar—"I exist!"

Today, the individual, particularly the creative artist, writer, and scientist, feels himself to be in a kind of prison, the prison of impersonal authorities. The problem of creativity is immense in our time because of the difficulty of identifying with creative models. The egalitarian fashion, supported by the standard of mechanical uniformity, discourages the emergence of "personalities" who kindle our enthusiasm by virtue of what they are.

"Identification," in our day, is molded by forces which make for a coordination in which the individual feels left out and alone. Our "communication media" foster an automatic response from the viewer. Radio and television inform, evaluate, and interpret, even supply us with ready-made imagery and feelings. Automation "integrates" to the point of wiping out indigenous folk-roots and folkways, stamping out personal insignia. It makes for little and hollow men, for Mr. and Mrs. Zeroes, for dead salesmen, for the naked and the dead. Over all rules the organization man who puts everything into a uniform.

The hope that technical power with its resultant increase of material goods and leisure would bring gladness of heart is withering away. Indeed, many feel that these very "goods" tend to increase spiritual and emotional tensions. Thermonuclear energy could turn deserts into gardens, but it can also turn gardens into deserts. Here, contemporary man faces an impersonal power of incalculable and universal dimension, a diabolical power that could be unleashed by a single individual pushing a gadget. Gadgets ride man today, conditioning the feverish rhythm and directionless pace of his life. They determine his "other-directed" needs and wants, distorting his personal needs and wants.

Some react to this situation by passive withdrawal, others by the rage of the angry young men and the defiant beatniks. Where the individual can find no organic attachments to the demands of the day, he tends to succumb to the devil's two major temptations: lethargy and dullness or violence and frenzy.

Are these the sole alternatives open to us? To become part of the "mass-cult," to merge with what Ernst Toller called the *Massemensch?* Or else vainly to seek the blessed isles which are surely becoming extinct? Both of these alternatives are at odds with the kind of life we hope for and dream about, are at odds with what ancient prophets, seers, artists, poets and mythmakers have envisioned.

The machine and leisure in themselves cannot be held responsible for our spiritual "malaise." It is true that the corruption of our economic-social-political relations contributes to the corroding of our motives, to the reigning attitude of "what's in it for me?" However, on a deeper level, the difficulty is nurtured by our obsession with the immediate present, the latest fashion, the *nunc et stans*. But, by itself, "news on the hour" can offer no direction, no purpose or goal. It produces what Thomas Mann once called "futurism without a future." It has no future because—and this anticipates the argument of the book—it lacks the vision of values created in the past by our living mythic tradition. Without such a basic platform, the satisfactions of technology are not humanly adequate. We remain restless, nervous, irritable.

This study points to an alternative identification that could counteract this gloomy outlook, an identification with the symbolic values of our mythic heroes as fashioned in the outstanding literary classics. This mythic hero is not the average, nor the common denominator of humanity. Neither is he the aristocratic individual disconnected from what is common to man. He is close to the *elemental* sources of life, but represents them in their higher, wider and deeper phases. In the study and "imitation" of mythic heroes, of Job, Prometheus, Oedipus, Virgil and Dante, of Don Quixote, Hamlet, Faust, Mitya Karamazov, and Captain Ahab, yes, even of contemporary heroes, of Nexö's Pelle, Thomas Mann's Joseph and Gide's Theseus, lies the hope for the revival of creativity.

According to Greek legend, Memory was the Mother of the Muses. Mythology draws on our oldest memories, and it has always fascinated the common man, as well as the artist, writer and thinker. In the form of a picture, a story or a song, myth touches on man's basic relation to his world and fellow men, on his original roots, his future possibilities and destiny. Myth has cast a spell on the very ages which denied or opposed it. Like the severed head of Orpheus, it "goes on singing even in death and from afar."[1]

The perennial appeal and vitality of mythic thinking stem from the fact that it makes us feel that in all civilizations men face analogous situations, undergo similar experiences. Myth draws on these underlying correspondences which inevitably make for One World. Men, writes William E. Hocking, "must loyally remember. . .if only to retain their identity. . .must be united in their sense of destiny to which their journey points." Myth supplies "a symbolic memory and a symbolic hope, and an allegorized account of the perils of the way."[2]

In sum: the myth unfolds the living chain which connects the recurrent recognition scenes of the human drama. They assure us that we are not strangers and alone in the world.

MYTHOLOGY AND MYTHOPOESIS

The subject matter of this study is not the myth as such, nor the mythologies, such as we have in Ovid, Hesiod and others which relate the adventures of gods, titans and heroes, giving us multiple variations of plots. This book deals with mythopoesis. It examines those myths which have seized the imagination of our classical writers who then transformed the various mythological accounts into a single, unfied work of art. Mytho-*poesis* (from the Greek *poiein*, meaning to make, to create) *re*-creates the ancient stories. And, while mythology presents its stories as if they actually took place, mythopoesis transposes them to a symbolic meaning. Indeed, *the mythopoeic works examined in this study arose when the literal account of the legend could no longer be accepted.* They arose *in periods of crisis, of cultural transition,* when faith in the authoritative structure was waning. It is at this juncture that our great prophets and artists would redeem the values of the past and present in their *symbolic* form, transposing their historic transitoriness into permanent promises.

The modern revival of the myth began in the nineteenth century, that is, at the very time when technology threatened to wipe out ancient folkways. In our own day, the theme has again fired the imagination of artists from Picasso to the surrealists, and of writers from Proust, Joyce and Thomas Mann to Kafka, Sartre, Cocteau and Faulkner. It penetrates our cultural areas, from anthropology, philosophy and religion to criticism and psychology in the work of Malinowski, Cassirer and Tillich, of Spengler and Toynbee, of I.A. Richards and T.S. Eliot, of Freud, Jung and Reik. The revival of myth in our time is an attempt to satisfy the human need for relatedness to fellow-travelers on our common journey.

The myth addresses itself to the problem of identity, asking "who am I?" And it proceeds to examine three questions that are organically related: "Where do I come from?", "Where am I bound?", and "What must I do now to get there?" In mythic language, the problems deal with Creation, with Destiny and with the Quest.

In his *Life of Reason*, George Santayana makes the pithy observation that those "who cannot remember the past are condemned to repeat it." The living myth would not restore the dead past, but would *redeem* its living heritage. The myth also contains *the tradition of re-creation.* Unrest, disquiet and revolt are as much part of man's history as is the tradition of idolatry. The culture hero in mythopoesis *chooses* his tradition, rejects the stultified in favor of the creative roots in the past. His choice of tradition is a recollection of man's native genius. By aligning himself with the high levels of the past, man gains the dignity of belonging without becoming depersonalized.

The myth is of particular import for the modern artist who feels himself estranged from the divisiveness and uniformity of our age.

Many have responded by removing themselves to a pure esthetics, to a no-man's land of abstract fancy. But this purist realm is itself an expression of the very specialization against which it is directed, and it addresses itself and communicates to a specialized audience. The myth offers the artist a theme which sounds a basic motif and thus makes it possible for him to return to his world-wide audience.

The myth is a power by which men live. And this power can be used for good or evil. Mythic symbols can represent an ideal or an ideology. The fateful import of the myth for our day stems from the fact that it is pivotal to the idea of One World. It can determine whether this world is to be one of unity and totality or one of uniformity and totalitarianism, whether the powers of man are to be freed or shackled.

The living, humanized myth is not given, but must be won:

> "What from your father's heritage is lent,
> Earn it anew, to really possess it!"
>
> (Goethe, *Faust I*)

This depends partly on historic pressures which can quicken or drain a myth. But it also depends on the vision and the will to realize it.

At this moment, we seem to be rushing towards an abyss. Yet, we can draw comfort from the story of mythopoesis, from its long-range perspective which enables us to see beneath and beyond the dust of the hour. It assures us of the never-extinguished genius of man which needs to be remembered and reactivated. Our own time records such memory in Nexö's *Pelle the Conqueror*, Malraux's *Man's Fate* and *Man's Hope*, Gide's *Theseus*, and Thomas Mann's *Joseph and His Brothers*. In each, the tradition of a rebellious quest is pitted against a paralyzing tradition.

This study centers in Western mythopoesis. It touches on Oriental mythology and presents the residue of the Eastern myth of the Earth-Mother in *The Brothers Karamazov*. The literary works selected are not equal in scope, artistic structure and resonance. *Oedipus* and *Hamlet* have more universal echo than *Moby Dick* and *The Trial*; *The Brothers Karamazov* and *The Magic Mountain* have a broader canvas than Gide's *Theseus* and Sartre's *The Flies*. *The Divine Comedy* is more structured than *Don Quixote*. What they all have in common is that each sounds the perennial motifs of human nature, its origin, quest and destiny. This is their universal relevance. But each speaks this universal language in its particular dialect. Every epoch has its own myth which provides the center of its life, gives the tone, manner and rhythm to its existence, permeates its institutions and thought, its art, science, religion, politics, its psychology and its folkways—that is, *the myth organizes the values of its epoch.* The literary form of the myth preserves its symbolic values which transcend the drossy historical surface. "The old myths," a writer states,

> the almost forgotten myths of antiquity were stories we can no longer believe, as stories, but we may still discover in these ancient intuitions the thread of an undying vision . . . in these days of crumbling institutional forms and beliefs, and in the agony of a desperation which finds no peace or promise of peace in the world we know, we may begin to hear our own voices as almost the cry of disembodied intelligence, demanding its spiritual rights. And then, perhaps, we shall begin to make a new sort of alliance with the world, on terms which acknowledge and declare, first of all, the humanity of the human race.[3]

NOTES

1. Carl Kerenyi in *Essays on a Science of Mythology* by C. G. Jung and C. Kerenyi (New York, 1949), p. 5.
2. *Goethe and the Modern Era* (Chicago, 1949), pp. 279-280.
3. "The Dynamics of Change," *Manas*, Vol. XIV, No. 8. The methodology of this study is indebted to Ernst Cassirer. His notion of "serial order" postulates the question "what are the conditions according to which one element is arranged and connected with another?" rather than pursuing the abstract philosophical quest for the characteristics which are common to various elements. What is sought are analogous correspondences. In this system, "each separate form gains its meaning purely from the position which it occupies, where its content and import are marked by the wealth and the individuality of relations and implications through which it is connected with the other human forces, and finally with their totality." The unity which is achieved thereby is not of materials, but "a functional unity" of the creative process. The productive promise in this method is that it permits us not only to establish the relationship between existing entities, but also to envisage the relationship between what exists and what is possible. For a discussion of Cassirer's functional approach, see my essay "Ernst Cassirer's Functional Approach to Art and Literature" in *The Philosophy of Ernst Cassirer*, The Library of Living Philosophers, VI (Evanston, Illinois, 1949), 631-661.

   Cassirer's functional unity is similar to Silberer's functional symbol-phenomena. In Silberer's psychoanalytic approach, the important element in images is not the content, but the form of the mind's functioning.

   Put another way, this study attempts to do justice both to the universal

17

schema of the myth and to its temporal or story-sequence, with the literary form picturing its moving face. Stated in terms of the classical Four Causes, one might say that the mythic pattern provides the formal and the final cause, while the historical content operates as the material and efficient cause.

Introduction

MYTH AND REALITY

THE WORD *myth* is derived from the same root as *mystery* and *mystic*, and the Oxford dictionary defines it as a "purely fictitious narrative." The philologist Max Müller called myth a disease of language. He traced its origin to the circumstance that primitives used the same name for different objects and different names for the same object, and he concluded that mythology was the result of the ambiguous meaning of words. In *Das Leben Jesu* (Stuttgart, 1905), David Friedrich Strauss separated the truth of Jesus' teachings from the mythical accounts of his personality. Machiavelli supported his counsel that a prudent ruler has to be "a great feigner and dissembler" by referring to the myth of Achilles, who was educated by the centaur Chiron so that he might know his beastly as well as his human nature. While Machiavelli's intent was to destroy false myths about human nature, George Sorel's *Reflections on Violence* advocated the use of fictions to set loose primitive mass forces in a class war, arguing that, to dominate people, we must give up truth in favor of myths.[1]

On the other hand, writers from Wilhelm Wundt to Franz Boas have shown that myths are not freely "made," but represent a folk product expressing the collective labors, emotions and genius of peoples. They are either composite productions, such as the epics of the ancient Orient, or, where they have been molded into mythopoesis by an individual artist, they rest on a long tradition. (Even Blake's "private" myths grow out of Greek, Christian, and his own tradition.) The ancient stories are retold, rewritten, and transmitted as people find in them analogies to their own situation and destiny. In this sense, myth is not something invented or fancied. It is rather *a pictorial hypothesis* about the nature of man. While myths do not have existence, they enter the realm of *reality* in that they enable us to explain and predict events in the empirical world.[2]

19

Myth and Science

In popular usage, myth and science exclude each other. However many thinkers and scholars see them as closely related. Freud regarded the mythological view of the world as "nothing other than psychological processes projected into the other world." And, in a letter to Albert Einstein, he wrote:

> It may perhaps seem to you as though our theories are a kind of mythology. . . . But does not every science come in the end to a kind of mythology like this? Cannot the same be said today of your own Physics?[3]

Ernst Cassirer, a student of mathematical physics, states that science begins with mythic perception. His *Philosophy of Symbolic Forms* (New Haven, 1953-1957) also shows that the beginnings of science, as of art, language, writing, and philosophy lead us back to the stage when they are rooted in mythical images and expressions.

Following Cassirer, Susanne K. Langer's studies in symbolic logic emphasize that both science and myth deal with symbolic transformation (discursive in one and non-discursive in the other). She calls myth a primitive and indispensable forerunner of metaphysical thought. Langer further points out that modern science also deals with fictions— such as zero and infinity, square roots of negative numbers, incommensurable lengths, fourth dimensions, imaginary numbers—which have relevance to reality. In his eloquent essay "Science and Human Values" (*The Nation*, December 29, 1956), J. Bronislawski elaborates the point that such scientists as Copernicus, Kepler, and Newton felt their laws to be metaphors and symbols, which "are as necessary to science as to poetry." Science, he writes, "is the search for unity in hidden likenesses," and mass, time, magnetic moment are symbolic concepts. In sum, "thinking as we understand it is made possible only by the use of names or symbols."

Historically, myth and science often went hand in hand. Frazer (*The Golden Bough* [New York, 1929]) sees a form of science in the magical practices of early man, in that the primitive believed "in a certain established order of nature on which he can surely count, and which he can manipulate for his own ends." To be sure, primitive man errs in his notion of the nature of this order, and when he finds that his predictions do not come about, he "throws himself humbly on the mercy of certain great invisible beings . . . to whom he now ascribes all those far-reaching powers." At this point, religion supersedes magic.[4] And, when the religious belief in a variable and irregular succession of events proves unsatisfactory, man turns to the assumption that natural events operate

20

with constant regularity. This scientific stage is won by exact observation of the phenomena themselves and not, as in magic, by a false analogy of the order in which ideas present themselves to the mind. Yet, this newly won scientific ground does not drive out mythic thinking. The Greeks, for example, were firmly pledged to the scientific method; still, their literature and philosophy were filled with mythic imagery. Even as Plato rejected the myth in his political theory, he made extensive use of it in his Dialogues and created his own myth, the Demiurge of *The Timaeus*, in his natural philosophy.

The relationship between myth and science may also be seen in mythopoesis: Dante attempts to hold his realms together by an exact triadical scheme; Mark Schorer's analysis of Blake indicates the scientific aspects of his mythic symbolism, and Lewis Mumford has shown that *Moby Dick* blends science and mythic imagination; Thomas Mann's *Doctor Faustus* carries mathematical symbolism over into mythic musicology.

At the same time, there remain significant differences between the two realms. Science gets its universal laws by abstracting from particular phenomena, reducing them to precise univalent formulae. Mythic symbolism, on the other hand, is pictorial—the fire of Prometheus, the snakes of Orestes, the ketonet of Joseph—and is by nature inexact and ambivalent.[5] Furthermore, where science is neutral to human values, mythic thought views nature as friendly or hostile. Science and myth are further distinguished by their concepts of causation. In science, no theory can explain the final "why"; that is, scientific method precludes a final hypothesis which may not be questioned. But the myth assumes a basic "it is," to which there is no "why." Spinoza stated that a scientific definition consists in determining what a thing is not (*omnis determinatio est negatio*). The mythic vision, however, would enclose the whole.

Myth and Religion

Myth and religion jointly answer man's need for collective identification and the feeling of his intimate relation to the world. Mythic and religious motifs are nearly indistinguishable in primitive and Oriental mythology. They are also closely interconnected in the mythopoesis of Greece and Rome, in *The Divine Comedy* and *Don Quixote*. Religion also penetrates modern mythopoesis, such as Racine's *Phædre*, Rabelais' *Gargantua*, Goethe's *Faust*, Wagner's *Ring*, Melville's *Moby Dick*, the poetry of William Blake, Dostoyevsky's *The Brothers Karamazov*, the work of James Joyce, Franz Kafka and Thomas Mann.[6] Myth and religion are differentiated from other cultural forms by their anthropomorphic orientation and their normative approach. Their interest is, not the universe, but man, not pure objective data, but what contributes to man's welfare.

While myth and religion have never been completely divorced, Western mythopoesis, beginning with the Book of Job and Greek tragedy, separates itself from religion to the extent that it does not acknowledge a supernatural authority to which man must surrender. Even as the hero in mythopoesis must learn to curb his rebelliousness, he remains a hero only if he does *not* completely submit. This is connected with the *immanent* character of the myth, which distinguishes it from those religions which emphasize the transcendental nature of salvation. Because the mythic hero never fully surrenders or recants, he cannot achieve complete redemption and his problem cannot be resolved by heavenly grace.[7]

MYTHOPOESIS: A DRAMA IN THREE ACTS WITH AN EPILOGUE

This study interweaves two basic perspectives: the *historic* and the *recurrent*.

On the historic level, each mythopoeic work is viewed as the center which unifies the multiple cultural forms of its era, organizing its art, psychology, philosophy, religion and social currents.

Intertwined with the historic level—and this is the second major thesis—is a universal pattern. The Ariadne thread which runs through all mythopoesis is a *structural unity* that consists of *the analogous stages* in the development of the mythopoeic heroes from Job to Thomas Mann's Joseph and Sartre's Orestes. This unity takes on the form of *a drama* in three acts, followed by *an epilogue*. By implication, this pattern constitutes the nature of the human journey itself, is characteristic for the unheroic as well as for the heroic, obtains for the individual and for society.

The Drama begins with a *First Act* of communal harmony. In the *Second Act*, this harmony is disturbed by the emergence of the hero who sets out on his *Quest* which entails a challenge to his group. The *Quest* is pivotal for the mythopoeic drama. *For, it is through his challenge and revolt that the hero can become a creative agent of his community.* This creative impulse moves the hero towards the *Third Act*. This is a kind of "Homecoming" through which a new harmony is reached. However, the harmony attained carries within itself the earlier moments of dissidence and contains the seeds of a renewed conflict. This determines the *Epilogue* which makes for *the tragic residue* in the mythopoeic drama.

The functional unity in this dramatic structure constitutes the link in all-human development, even as its individual expressions vary in polar and dialectic rhythms. Throughout, the hero's quest aims at the recreation of the One Human World which presumably once existed and which might be approximated in the future. Thus, the mythopoeic journey could release the ageless springs of human creativity.

Act I: Creation or Eden

Mythology speaks of an initial state of blissfulness, called Eden or Paradise, Islands of the Blessed, Elysium or the Golden Age. Here man was at home, at one with nature and his group. In mythopoesis, however, this first act no longer exists, but is only a nostalgic "memory."

Act II: The Quest—Homeleaving or Expulsion of the Hero

Act II begins with the "birth" of the hero, who is set out or invites expulsion by his authoritative powers. In primitive mythology, the hero does not stand in opposition to his community, but carries out his task in conformity with its traditional symbols. However, almost from the beginning, the nature of the hero is ambiguous. Franz Boas has shown that in the role of the Transformer, American legends present him at once as a culture hero and as an irresponsible trickster, intent on gratifying his personal desires. In either case, he transgresses against what the group regards as a natural or sacred order, violates a taboo by peering into forbidden mysteries. He becomes "the dangerous child." In Nietzsche's language, the hero *must* commit a crime. The crime is usually one of commission: He steals the fire, becomes a parricide, commits incest. In the case of some heroes—Job, Hamlet—the crime is one of omission. In others—Kafka's Joseph K., Mann's Castorp—the character is arrested or arrests himself, not for what he has done or has deliberately planned to do, but for his unconscious wish to do something that is prohibited.

The consequence of the mythic crime is the hero's fall and his Journey.

The Journey is a central experience in all the great myths. It takes the form of a descent into Hell (in the myths of Krishna, Zoroaster, Osiris, Baldur, Adonis, Bacchus, Hercules, Mercury, Odysseus), or of a symbolic entry into the "dark night of the soul" (Jesus, Aeneas, Dante, and every modern mythic hero). In pre-Renaissance mythopoesis, the journey has a definite, fixed goal, and we know—even if the hero does not—that the wanderer will be brought home at last. Homecoming is assured because, in his very rebellion, the hero represents the reigning symbols of his group. In the modern myth, where the individual would free himself more radically from his community, the journey takes on an indefinite character, and the homecoming is tenuous, as in *Don Quixote, Hamlet, Faust, Moby Dick*, and in the work of Kafka and Thomas Mann.

Act III: Destiny—Re-creation or Homecoming

The fall of the hero is not final. Jessie L. Weston (*From Ritual to Romance* [New York, 1957]) has shown that, even in the early vegetation cults, the important element is not the worship of the dead, but the restoration to life.

In primitive and Oriental mythology, rebirth generally constitutes return to the identical earlier form, an analogy to the never-varying order of the seasonal changes. In Western mythopoesis, rebirth depends on the extent to which the quest results in the hero's own questioning of his deviation. The furies which pursue Orestes, Oedipus and Dante, Don Quixote and Ahab are, in this sense, self-inflicted punishments. This self-questioning holds the promise of the hero's transformation.[8] Through it, he comes to recognize the *symbolic* values which are present in the very tradition he has violated. He is thereby moved to recast the function of his demon and realign himself with the wider interests of his group. In this way, he can become a *culture* hero. He now sees his supra-individual relation as complementing and fulfilling his individuality. Reintegration lies *beyond* individual autonomy. Return is not to the earlier starting point, for the hero's rebellion has re-created the authoritarian mode, has quickened and transformed its earlier sluggishness. In this sense, the culture hero acts for the others, becomes the instrument of social salvation, and his sacrifice makes him a blessed figure. Such sanctification comes to Oedipus in Colonus, Virgil in Latium, Don Quixote in La Mancha, Hamlet in Horatio's final prayer.

This has become possible through the hero's knowledge and consciousness. He now reaches a higher form of acceptance, one which follows from having made his *own* choice. This choice makes for responsibility and ethics. In sum, the victory of the mythopoeic hero is the victory of consciousness and of social morality.

Epilogue: Tragic Transcendance

In *The Myth of the Birth of the Hero* (New York, 1959), Otto Rank points out that all mythic heroes go through certain stages:[9]

> The hero is the child of most distinguished parents, usually the son of a king. His origin is preceded by difficulties, such as continence, or prolonged barrenness, or secret intercourse of the parents, due to external prohibition or obstacles. During the pregnancy, or antedating the same, there is a prophecy, in the form of a dream or oracle, cautioning against his birth, and usually threatening danger to the father, or his representative. As a rule, he is surrendered to the water, in a box. He is then saved by animals, or by lowly people (shepherds) and is suckled by a female animal or by a humble woman. After he has grown up, he finds his distinguished parents, in a highly versatile fashion takes his revenge on his father, on the one hand, is acknowledged on the other, and finally achieves rank and honors.

Rank's scheme may be transposed into naturalistic-psychological terms: The child's distinguished parents point to the hero's exceptional sources; the difficult conception suggests the obstacles in the way of the creative process. As a potential hero, the son is "the dangerous child" and a threat to the father. This is sensed by the father, or, in mythic language, is told him by an oracle, dream or prophecy. The father's natural love for his child prevents him from removing his son and he orders someone to expose him. But the child is saved by animals or humble people, that is, by "nature" or "the folk."

The Rankian scheme ends with the success of the hero. It applies to many primitive and Oriental myths, fairy tales and some religio-mystic systems in which all problems are resolved in a paradisiac finale.[10]

Mythopoesis, however, precludes such a resolution. Since its final reference is to the reality character of the human condition, it only unfolds the successful *tempering* of the conflicting relations. On the other hand, the tertiary phase of the hero's reintegration incorporates the critical approach in the quest; indeed, it is conditioned by his maintaining this critique: Job, who questions the ways of the Lord, is uplifted, not the Friends who urge submission; Oedipus, who retains his "tyrannical" personality becomes the Savior-figure, not the just and kindly Theseus; Hamlet, not Horatio, emerges as "a noble heart"; Thomas Mann's ravaged Judah, not his comfortable Joseph, receives Jacob's blessing in Egypt.

The living character of mythopoesis appears in the never-ending need of the dissident hero to galvanize his state towards reshaping its tradition. The heroic quest is not eliminated but *assimilated*.

Here lies the *revolutionary* leaven of mythopoesis. To be sure, the myth contains a conservative fibre which makes for idolatry of the past. However, it would also preserve another kind of tradition—*the tradition of freedom*—expressed in the myths of Dionysus and Prometheus where the hero is pledged to a *futuristic* tradition.

In this interplay between preservation and challenge, the mythic quest is inherited and passed on. Prometheus is carried forward by Hercules, Oedipus by Polyneices, Don Quixote by Sancho Panza, Hamlet by Fortinbras and Horatio, Ahab by Ishmael, Nexö's Pelle by Morton, Joyce's Earwicker by Shem-Shaun, Mann's Joseph by Judah. Mythic transcendence does not allow for a paradisiac ending, and reconciliation in the mythopoeic drama is on a tragic plane.

MYTHOPOESIS AND PSYCHOLOGY

"It had occurred to me long ago," Ferenczi writes, "that for any useful writings on individual psychology we have to go not to scientific literature, but to belles-lettres."[11]

In recent years, there has been a growing preoccupation on the part of writers with the depth implications of literature. At the same time, more and more psychoanalytic criticism has turned towards an examination of the arts. Following the pathfinding work of Freud, Rank, Hanns Sachs, Ferenczi, and Jung, we have had the contributions to this problem by Kris, Jones, Marie Bonaparte, Ella Sharpe, Reik, and, more recently, D. E. Schneider, Kubie, Kanzer, Phyllis Greenacre, Bergler, Eissler and others.

Concern with unconscious motivation in the arts is a relatively modern phenomenon. The impetus came with the Renaissance conception of the "free" individual whose inner self was regarded as the crucial factor determining his destiny. Whereas Orestes' Erinyes and Dante's Lucifer were external physical powers, the Renaissance interiorized such powers, as in Marlowe's Mephistophilis, Hamlet's Ghost, and Faust's Grey Women. More explicit recognition of unconscious conflicts appeared in Diderot's *Rameau's Nephew*, in the writings of the German Romanticists and in Wagner's music drama. For Dostoyevsky, Chekhov, Artzybashev, and Andreyev, the lacerated Russian personality became the central problem. Finally, the theme of psychological alienation may be said to be the leitmotif of twentieth century writing.[12] Structurally, the impact of psychoanalysis on literature produced styles that tend toward "free association."[13] In impressionistic, expressionis-

tic and surrealistic art (Joyce is the most extreme example in literature), form was freed from the logic of syntax and grammar.

Manifold Motivation in Art

Ernst Kris stressed the point that in analyzing a creative work we
need to consider not only the unconscious drives, but also the conscious
and preconscious powers in the writer's personality, as well as his social
conditioning. Some literary critics focus on the technical forms of a
work. A rounded psychoanalytic interpretation needs to examine the
interrelationships among these various aspects. Very little is revealed,
for example, by noting that Shakespeare's Hamlet has an oedipal
burden. For his Hamlet is not Sophocles' Oedipus. Furthermore, Shakespeare does not give us a living person, but a dramatic-poetic figure,
produced by his particular language. To understand the specific motivations of *Shakespeare's* Hamlet, we need to analyze *his* idiom and
imagery, and *his* historic framework. Neglect of the technical, esthetic
and social categories can give us only an impoverished general psychological type, applicable at once to the Hamlet of a great writer and that
of his imitators.

It is well known that Freud thought artistic attainment as "psycho-
analytically inaccessible to us," that psychoanalysis has to lay down
its arms before artistic genius and the problem of artistic technique.
Indeed, Freud expressed envy of poets who, he said, "discovered the
unconscious" before he did, and who "salvage from the whirlpool of
their emotions the deepest truths to which we others have to force our
way, ceaselessly groping among torturing uncertainties." And one may
add that more can be learned about the concrete dynamics of psychological processes from *Hamlet, The Brothers Karamazov, The Magic
Mountain* and *Joseph and His Brothers* than from many psychoanalytic
texts.

In the dramatic style of his case presentations, Freud was himself
something of an artistic "story-teller," and *The Interpretation of
Dreams* has recourse to metaphoric analogies.[14] The basic affinity between literature and psychoanalysis is this: both are concerned with
human motives and both deal with them as expressed in language and
gesture. Psychoanalysis is a science to the extent that it can predict
human behavior on the basis of primary principles. But it is also an art.
The sensitive analyst may get his deepest insights not so much from
the content of a patient's productions, as from his tone, the use of metaphors and imagery. The analyst can also sense the secret import of a

patient's communication from his "body-language," his gestures and other physical movements. In both psychoanalysis and literature, "style" is the final method of communication and is the clue to the underlying motif behind the multiple "voices." A psychoanalytic examination of art must therefore consider the formal aspects, must pay attention to the dramatic sequence—how, when, where and to whom a character speaks.[15]

The limitations of most psychoanalytic criticism arise from its failure to give due weight to these factors. It has been particularly deficient in evaluating the crucial relationship between form and "meaning" in art. It treats a poetic work and its characters as "a case study," thereby reducing the rich sensuousness and individuation of the dramatic process in the literary arts to a thin psychological category.[16] The style and form of a literary work—that which distinguishes it from a critical argument—has been virtually ignored.

Bergler on Literature as Pathology

Edmund Bergler's *The Writer and Psychoanalysis* (New York, 1950) may be taken as a representative example of the extremes to which the disregard of literary form may lead. Bergler argues that writers are *ipso facto* neurotic. He focuses on the pathological processes in a writer's *life* and projects them into his *work*. Bergler sees writing as the result of oral, anal-sadistic syndromes in the writer's personality and states flatly: "Normal people just don't feel impelled to write." This method commits the genetic fallacy in that it identifies the writer's biographic sources with his literary product. Furthermore, it does not distinguish between the writer (a *living* person) and his poetic characters (his *symbolic* figures). Moreover, two positive factors are left out in this analysis: The *creative* nature of literature and *the joy* it gives both the creator and his audience. Indeed, Bergler is not primarily concerned with the creative writer as such, stating that it is "immaterial, for psychological evaluation, whether he is a good or bad writer." And, where Freud speaks of "the pleasure of the writer in creation," Bergler states that "the man who suffers" and "the man which [!] creates are one and the same."[17]

The focus on genetic factors neglects the specific element which defines a work of art, namely, *the transformation* of these factors. Many psychoanalytic examinations reveal that an artist's work exhibits oral-anal-oedipal derivatives which have been repressed. But *repression does not explain art*. In the artistic process, such drives are transformed into something which is not orally wet, anally smelly, and not oedipally incestuous and murderous. Art and the artist cannot be understood solely by the method of analytical reduction. The artist embodies and expresses not only the genetic-pathological "background"; he also employs the "forward-" tendencies and intactness of his ego.

Symbolism and Distortion

Ernst Cassirer has developed the thesis that symbolism is central in human culture or, in his striking formulation: man is a symbolical animal.[18] Cassirer's notion that symbolism is the differentiating characteristic of human life is shared by such philosophers, psychologists and anthropologists as Russell, Piaget, Wertheimer, Köhler, Korzybski and Devereux. Symbolic transformation allows man to transcend the immediacy of experience, to convert memory of the past and vision of the future into present possession. In an essay on "The Distortion of the Symbolic Process in Neurosis and Psychosis," (*Journal of the American Psychoanalytic Association*, I [1953], 59-86), Lawrence S. Kubie writes of the symbolic capacity as "the unique hallmark of Man" and notes its function as "a bridge." Kubie confines himself to showing this function in the field of psychology. But it also pertains to art. The arts present the universal through the particular. Thereby they bridge or mediate between the concept and the precept, thought and sensuousness, the object and the subject, fact and fancy. The writer, in particular, acts as a mediator in establishing "communication"—communication among his multiple characters, as well as between them and his audience. Form itself expresses this bridging function: its sensuous imagery carries "unlawful" discharges, held in check by the grammar of language.[19]

Bergler makes a valid point in speaking of the criminal motivation in writing. Art deals with crime in that it presents a drama in which characters violate a convention, undergo conflict and crisis. He is also right in stating that a writer must present such crime as having a degree of legitimacy if the "villains" are not to be mechanical stereotypes. Now, such legitimacy is an expression of a writer's sensitivity to "the other side." Nietzsche called man *das kranke Tier*—the sick animal. And, in the work of Thomas Mann, this "sickness" constitutes "the honorable" in man, for it sensitizes him to the value-element in the opposition and, in the case of the artist, makes possible his attempt to mediate among his different characters. But, by its very nature, this is an unstable bridge and renders the symbolic process a borderline activity.[20] (In passing, it should be noted that the general psychoanalytic meaning of symbols—in distinction to the esthetic—is that in the former "one member of the equation is repressed into the unconscious," as Ferenczi puts it in his essay "The Ontogenesis of Symbols" [*Sex in Psychoanalysis*]. Rank and Sachs make the same distinction.) Thus, the symbolic process is subject to a greater degree of distortion and may, as Kubie pointed out, fixate the emotional disturbance. That is, man's sensitivity, expressed in his symbolic vision, can become the condition for neurosis and psychosis. Animals are less vulnerable because they do not respond to symbols but to signs (Pavlov's bell and food). And, whereas signs are fixed and unambiguous, symbols are variable and ambiguous in their meaning. In other words, precisely because man is a symbolical animal, he is especially vulnerable to neurotic distortions. Man, Kubie stated, would not develop a neurosis or psychosis "without those very symbolic potentialities which are essential to his highest psychological development."[21]

The symbolic view also introduces an element of the tragic. Unlike science, philosophy and religion, art does not pretend to offer final resolutions or precise answers. As noted, the symbolic vision reveals the legitimacy of alternate possibilities. But all action calls for *choice*, the selection of some particular way (as when we vote, we can choose only one candidate), thus forcing us to negate the validity of an alternate choice. Here is the inevitability of the tragic sense of life, of what Malraux once called *La Condition Humaine (Man's Fate)*.

Integrative Function of Art and Literature

Freud called myths "secular dreams," the day-dreams of young peoples. He saw a correlation between the mentality of early man and the unconscious mind, particularly of childhood. In this context, Freud saw the neurotic proclivities in the artist. In "Creative Writers and Day-Dreaming" (St. Ed., Vol. IX [London, 1959]) he indicates that day-dreaming gratifies the artist's archaic wishes in imaginary form. Artistic creation has its origin in a desire to discharge a private burden. The artist, like any other person who has unsatisfied longings, "turns away from reality and transfers all his interest, and all his Libido too, on to the creation of his wishes in the life of phantasy from which the way might readily lead to neurosis." The art of the dramatist, Freud also notes, consists in decomposing his inner self into the various characters of the play, embodying his self in each of the characters and his ontogenetic self through the phylogenetic forms of the myth. In "Relation of the Imposter to the Artist," Phyllis Greenacre speaks of the artist's "special disturbances in the sense of identity and reality." These follow from the heightened sensibility and imaginativeness with which the artist is endowed and perhaps even more from the fact that the writer splits his over-all identity into the multiple characters which he creates. This attests to the breadth and strength of his ego, but it also makes for a delicate balance among the elements in his ego.

This situation can lead to neurosis. However, Freud shows that, while the artist at first separates himself from his audience in his imagination, he finds his way back to reality through telling his story to and sharing it with others. What tends to counteract a neurosis in the case of the artist, Freud goes on to say, is probably that his constitution is endowed "with a powerful capacity for sublimation and with a certain flexibility (*Lockerheit*) in the repressions determining the conflict." In this manner, art provides "a path from phantasy back again to reality." This way back is available to the "true artist" who knows how to elaborate his daydreams, "so that they lose their personal note." For, the artist "possesses the mysterious ability to mould his particular material until it expresses the ideas of his phantasy faithfully." Because he can exercise "flexibility" of the repressions, the artist derives pleasure not only from the discharge, but also from the mastery of his emotions, achieved by employing the rules operative in technique, design and structure.

This aspect of literature and art contains a "curative" ingredient. There is a crucial distinction between a crime committed in fantasy and a crime committed in a literary work. Whereas the neurotic would gain his goal in imagination, the artist wins it by *embodying* his fantasy in particular concrete objects, thereby setting *limits* to the fantasy. (John Crowe Ransom calls art "the world's body" and Yeats speaks of "the thinking of the body.") The symbolism of art is *immanent*. An artist, Cassirer points out, does not merely "feel"; he externalizes what he feels and imagines in visible, audible, tangible modes. He works not simply "in a particular medium—in clay, bronze or marble—but in sensuous forms, in rhythms, in color patterns, in lines, in plastic shapes."[22] Shakespeare illustrated this aspect of the poetic imagination in *A Midsummer Night's Dream*:

> And, as imagination bodies forth
> The forms of things unknown, the poet's pen
> Turns them to shapes, and gives to airy nothing
> A local habitation and a name.

And Goethe summed it up in the opening scene of *Faust II*: "Am farbigen Abglanz haben wir das Leben."

Art is furthermore an act of construction: it organizes its material and thus expresses emotion in a disciplined way. At the same time, art contains an element of freedom. This factor is inherent to its symbolic functioning which presents life as a mobile, dynamic process, transforming our passions into "a free and active state."[23]

Writing as a Function of the Ego

In "Dream-Work" (*The Interpretation of Dreams*, St. Ed., Vols. IV and V [London, 1953]), Freud assigns "final significance" not to the importance of symbols, but "to the utterances of the dreamer," that is, to his associations. Now, there is a rough analogy between a dreamer's symbols and a writer's fantasy, and between a dreamer's associations and the writer's elaboration of his poetic or fictional creations. However, "associations" in the literary work are not "free." Insofar as the work has structure, design and form, the "associations" are *organized*.[24] This is dictated by the fact that the writer has an audience to whom he wants to communicate. That is, the writer is both the dreamer and the one who associates to and structures the associations to his dream. Form organizes the inchoate fantasy material and its elaboration into a coherent unity. And, it is precisely by structuring "the dream-work" of his characters that a writer produces a work of art. In a brief, but penetrating chapter on "Freud and Modern Philosophy" Abraham Kaplan writes that, for Freud,

> Not Narcissus but Pygmalion is the true artist. He is in love not with his own image, but with a creation having a form, movement, and substance— in a word, a life—of its own. . . . Art is the triumph of the pleasure principle and the reality principle acting in concert . . . Freud poses the challenge of providing an esthetics which does equal justice to both inspiration and skill, inner idea and outer expression, latent content and manifest form—in short, to both wish and reality . . . the unifying conception which binds together these two moments of the esthetic . . is the symbol.[25]

Herein lies the integrative function of literature and art. A character in literature becomes integrated to the extent that the writer develops him towards sensing the nature of his hidden motivations and the disintegrating effect of yielding to his immediate drives. As is the case in the psychoanalytic process, "catharsis" takes place by substituting the symbolic act for physical acting out. A few quick examples: Sophocles' Oedipus in Colonus repeats the violation of the Mother, but does it only symbolically; similarly, Dante on the Earthly Paradise with Beatrice, and Goethe's Faust with Helena. Form in art also helps to integrate the writer. Through his work, the writer at once discharges psychic tensions and controls the discharge by the ramparts of the formal design.[26]

The basic link between psychoanalysis and literature consists in the function of language. Sapir calls language primarily a vocal actualization of the tendency to see reality symbolically. Language has wrought the humanization of the primitive myth by the symbolic and evocative nature of the metaphor. In the pre-literary myth, the word was synonymous with the dreaded object and primitive man felt himself in the grip of vague, undefined mythic demons. Mythopoesis *names* these demons. Thereby it *externalizes* them, thus converting them into the partly known. The amorphous, indeterminate and undefined becomes formed, determined and defined. This element constitutes a degree of freedom by which, as Ernst Cassirer puts it, mythic fate and guilt become natural necessity and moral guilt. In Aeschylus' Oresteia, Athena states that the function of speech is "to free man from the bondage of irrational fears." In the words of Theodor Reik, such reactivating has "a freeing and cathartic, a 'telling' effect."

To be sure, art is sublimation, and sublimation begins with a narcissistic libido. Yet, in *The Ego and the Id* (St. Ed., Vol. XIX [London, 1961]), Freud suggests the possibility of widening this libido towards "another aim."[27] The writer is also in contact with the wholesome aspects of his own ego and with those of his characters. In this sense, we can say that there cannot be a totally unhealthy artist or art-work.[28]

In his *Neurotic Distortion of the Creative Process* (Lawrence, 1958), Lawrence Kubie, like Kris, places major stress on the creative role of preconscious processes. But, in his attempt to counter the position that the unconscious is the source of creativity, Kubie calls it "our straitjacket" and assigns it a warping and destructive function: "Where unconscious influences play a dominant role the creative process in science or art becomes almost identical with the neurotic process." Kubie's over-all argument is that normality and creativity depend on whether the conscious-preconscious alliance is dominant over the unconscious.

The thesis presented here is that normality and creativity are endangered where there is a preponderence of any *one* of these three powers, and that their functioning is conditioned by the harmonious interplay among them. Seen as a whole, the creative process entails three stages: It begins with "prelogical experience," or the primary process of the fantasy or inspiration. It becomes a formal work through the secondary process in which the fantasy is elaborated and organized.

In this phase, writing is a function of the ego in its preconscious-conscious alliance. However, in the final creative product, the original fantasy is not totally repressed or destroyed, but continues to exert a nutritive pressure, even as it is held in check by the controlling forces of the ego.

Psychoanalytic Differentiation Between Myth and Mythopoesis

Psychoanalytic theory has dealt with myth and mythology, but has not clearly differentiated them from mythopoesis. Writers on the subject[29] hold that the function of the myth is to *adapt* the individual to the group. The myth is seen as binding repressed instinctual impulses, thereby warding off feelings of guilt and anxiety. Referring to the myth of Prometheus, Arlow writes that it represents the stage of

the overwhelming impact of the fear of retaliation . . . pointing to the desirability of establishing internal prohibition and condemnation in order to ward off punishment and castration.[30]

Mythopoesis develops from mythology, never wholly loosens itself from the genetic base, and it does "warn" against a rebellion, which does not "remember" its social sources and keep in mind its societal needs. Indeed, structure and form—the ego element in mythopoesis—check the wish for immediate gratification. Art is a social and socializing force and a character in mythopoesis becomes *a culture hero* precisely by assuming a sense of responsibility towards the *living* and *creative* forces in his society. To this extent, mythopoesis also exercises an adaptive function.

However, this function is primarily characteristic for those historic scenes where the ruling powers are in a position to impose acquiescence to and "identification" with their own special interests. This holds for some primitive societies, Oriental kingdoms, and for subsequent varitions of totalitarian regimes.

Now, the argument of this book is that the adaptive function is nearly *reversed* in mythopoesis, beginning with the Gilgamesh epic and the Persian myth,[31] and more markedly in Western mythopoesis from the Book of Job to Mann's Jacob and Joseph. In the *re*-creation of the myth by outstanding individual artists, the hero's quest becomes *a critique* of the existing social norms and points to a futuristic order which is envisaged as integrating the valuable residues of the past and present. And the argument of this study is that it is precisely this rebellious function which renders the hero *redeemable*—shown most pointedly in *Oedipus in Colonus*.

Moreover, if one centers the adaptive approach in terms of the audience, the author of the art work should be included as part of this audience. Indeed, our artists and mythmakers represent the high level of their society. Now, their "point of view" does not lie only in the manifest "what," that is, the content of the plot. More crucial is the "how," their imagery, metaphor and symbolism which determine the richness and stature of the characters. And, it is the relative power and fullness of the writer's delineation which give us his *artistic sympathy* and *identification*. Marlowe, for example, condemns his Doctor Faustus to hell fire for his social infractions. Yet, even as Marlowe's historic scene did not permit his Faustus to be saved, the art of the drama unmistakably reveals that Marlowe bleeds for his hero. Similarly, while Dostoyevsky calls Alyosha his "hero" or his "future hero," it is the rebels—Mitya, Ivan and even Smerdyakov—who are drawn with greater power. Such artistic identification is illustrated in all mythopoeic works, beginning with the Book of Job.

The phenomenologic and metapsychological distinction between myth and mythopoesis hinges on the historical development from tribalism to hierarchic class societies which is accompanied by the evolution towards greater consciousness, individuation and the emergence of the rebel as hero. In many instances, the author may feel himself to be a violator, as in the case of Dante, Dostoyevsky and others. At any rate, such "violation" is a necessary quality of the hero. And, it is his rebellious acts which constitute the necessary condition for the emergence of creative values. Our mythopoeic authors do not merely "explain" the world to which their heroes are to "adapt." Their function is not to "support" their society. In indirect and oblique ways, that is, through their art form, they would transform it by identifying with the hero who would change the world.

The distinction between myth and mythopoesis can also be seen by noting the varying import of mythic powers in each. In the primitive myth and Oriental mythologies, the elements *are* divine powers; in mythopoesis, they become *verbalized symbols* of these powers. The myth which was primarily ritual did "adjust" the individual to the existing authority—the chieftain, Pharaoh, King etc. It also served as a defense against his chaotic drives and narcissistic tendencies. But, it is precisely this form of adaptedness that was used to place the individual in the service of established mores, ideologies and institutions, that is to say, what Francis Bacon called "the idols of the tribe," a function which is today filled by our mass media as Jacob Arlow suggests.[32]

Still, intrapsychic conflicts and conflicts with the world of reality persist. That is, these powers succeed only in keeping the conflict from bursting all bounds. At most, one gets used "to not getting used", as Thomas Mann's Hans Castorp puts it in *The Magic Mountain*.

The concept of "adaptation," as applied to the myth is undistributed. It transposes the function of the ritualistic and religious myth to all types of myth, including mythopoesis. It neglects to note the progression from primitive and Oriental mythology to Western mythopoesis in which history enacts a transformative function through which the old myths are re-created by our great artists. Here, the decisive role of the hero is to counter that identification and "adaptation" which acquiesces in and supports the status quo.[33] The mythopoeic hero would cleanse the stables of the state in which "there is something rotten" and would awaken and quicken the creative powers in his society. In mythopoesis, identification with the hero, who is engaged in the transvaluation of old values, works counter to idolatry and to identification with the stagnant society. His labors hold forth a futuristic promise in which "adaptation" to and "identification" with also refer to the rebellious act.[34]

Freud foreshadows the argument presented here. His brief formulations on the myth include the notion that the myth enables the individual to emerge from the group. (*Group Psychology and the Analysis of Ego*, pp. 69-143.)

Freud's Dramatic Structure

In the Freudian drama, Eden has but a shadowy existence, limited to the child's security in the mother's womb. Man's actual history begins with the domination of the father, followed by his murder. Now, whether this is understood as an actual historic event or as an hypothetical human paradigm, the crucial relevance of this theory to mythopoesis is the transformation of this murder into a *symbolic* act. According to Freud, this transformation takes place in totemism where the totem is killed and eaten, and revered as the protecting ancestral spirit of the clan. This substitution of the symbol for the act makes possible the control of the libidinal urges.

Here lies the futuristic horizon in Freud's schema. In his essay on "Freud and the Future," (*Essays of Three Decades* [New York, 1947]) Thomas Mann writes that the work of the founder of psychoanalysis contains "hidden seeds and elements of a new and coming sense of our humanity . . . of a wiser and freer humanity," and makes him "the pathfinder towards a humanism of the future" which may one day lead to "the resolution of our great fear and our great hate." Mann reminds us that Freud once called his theory of dreams "a bit of scientific new-found land won from superstition and mysticism," and likened his labor to a "reclamation work like the dredging of the Zuyder Zee." Writing to Einstein, Freud himself expressed this hope in the statement that "within a measurable time," and depending on "the growth of culture," there may be an end to the waging of war.

While Freudianism labors toward humanizing and controlling the dark powers in man's archaic heritage, it regards the irrational unconscious as "the larger circle . . . the true psychic reality," whose *daemonic power*" is immortal.[35] For Freud, "the Devil" is ever-present, personified in the "repressed unconscious instinctual life" (*Interpretation of Dreams*).

As we have seen, mythopoesis also has its tragic residue. But, since it envisages a first act of harmony, peace and unity, it can have a third act in which these are restored on a higher, more complex level. This re-creation of an approximate Golden Age in which the bad authority is converted into a good authority appears in every mythopoeic work from the Book of Job, Aeschylus' *Eumenides* and Sophocles' *Oedipus in Colonus* to Goethe's *Faust*, Dostoyevsky's *The Brothers Karamazov*. Nexö's *Pelle the Conqueror*, Gide's *Theseus* and Thomas Mann's *Joseph and His Brothers*.

Archaic Heritage and the Individual

Mythopoesis pictures the recurrent phases of human action and passion in their variant historic and individual forms. A similar dynamic relationship between the recurrent and the unique is also characteristic of Freudian strategy.

Freud's theory of the primal horde has been interpreted by some critics to mean that for Freud, man is doomed to repeat a pattern which has its prototype at the beginning of his history. But a close reading of Freud's clinical observations and presentation of specific case material makes it clear that he considers the archaic heritage as a kind of poetic picture which indicates *a general inherited tendency* that can be modified and varied according to particular family and individual experiences. The unconscious memory that "once upon a time" men had a mother they desired, a father they killed, brothers with whom they quarreled, does not predetermine the recurrence of such relationships.

To my mind, the import of Freud's theory in *Totem and Taboo* (St.

Ed., Vol. XIII [London, 1955]) is that of a symbol, rather than as a statement of pre-historical precedent.[36] Freud calls it "only a *hypothesis*" which postulates that the emotional life of human beings shows the same essential characteristics and stages. And in psychoanalytic treatment of individuals, we find this same *predisposition* to reenact the primal crime. This predisposition exists today as it did at "the beginning":

> since all human beings go through the same experiences, at least in their earliest years, they also react to them in the same way.

And, while these reactions need not be "re-acquired," they do need, as Freud states in *Moses and Monotheism* (St. Ed., Vol. XXII [London, 1964]), to be "awakened" by some traumatic experience to become operative in the life of the individual.

Similarly, Freud's thesis that the development of the individual is "an abridged repetition" of racial evolution ("ontogeny recapitulates phylogeny") is modified by his *historical and social* perspective. To begin with, the memory of "psychical antiquities" is received by the individual in the form of his *specific family mores* which differ with varying historical cultures and particular social settings. The social drive, Freud notes, may have "the beginnings of its development in a narrower circle, such as the family."[37] It is sometimes overlooked that the libido contains a social drive which Freud likens to Plato's Eros:

> Libido is the energy which keeps the members of the group together . . . the energy . . . which can be composed under "love" to people, parents, ideas, humanity, objects.

Freudian individual psychology is also social psychology:

> In the individual's mental life someone else is invariably involved, as a model, as an object, as a helper, as an opponent, and so from the very first Individual Psychology is, at the same time, Social Psychology as well—in this extended but entirely justifiable sense of the word.[38]

One of the most neglected strains in Freudian doctrine is its historical outlook which modifies its substantive thought. Herbert Marcuse's *Eros and Civilization* is the first major study which indicates the hidden role which historical change plays in Freud's metapsychology. In "Why War" (St. Ed., Vol. XXII [London, 1964]) Freud states that "for incalculable ages, mankind has been passing through a process of evolution and culture," and in his preface to Theodor Reik's *Ritual* (New York, 1949), he suggests that the Oedipus complex too may have had stages of development, and that the study of prehistory may enable us to trace them out. Investigation suggests that life in the human family took a quite different form in those remote days from that with which we are now familiar. (pp. 3, ff.)

Central to psychoanalytic theory, writes Abraham Kaplan, is the plasticity of impulse and the range of its socially conditioned expressions. . . . Psychoanalysis postulates constancy, not fixity—a regularity of pattern, not recurrence of the elements composing the pattern from case to case. . . . What is insisted upon is only that the variability is not endless. It occurs within limits, and it is these, rather than a fixed 'essence,' that make for discernable regularities. (*The New World of Philosophy*, pp. 136-137)

The criticism that Freud failed to see the impact of social forces loses its point when we bear in mind that, for Freud, repression is not self-imposed by the individual, but is generated by society, primarily through the family. Hence, the individual cannot be understood apart from an analysis of social pressures. As Kaplan puts it: where Kant focused on the superego, Nietzsche on the id, Dewey on the ego, Freud would show their interrelation and the effect of culture which provides the setting and significance of moral action.

HISTORY AND THE TIME-TABLE OF MYTHOPOESIS

In *Essays on a Science of Mythology*, Carl Kerenyi distinguishes between two levels of mythology. There are the *archai*, or first principles, "to which everything individual and particular goes back and out of which it is made, whilst they remain ageless, inexhaustible, invincible in timeless primordiality." However, man can experience the *archai* only through a historic prism, in the form of a definite culture and tradition which speak in the manner of a certain people. In the "Prelude" to his Joseph cycle, Thomas Mann makes a similar distinction between the "bottomless . . . well of the past" and "provisional origins." The latter are man's "conditional beginnings." They

form the first beginnings of the particular tradition held by a given community, folk or communion of faith; and memory, though sufficiently instructed that the depths have not actually been plumbed, yet nationally may find reassurance in some primitive point of time and, personally and historically speaking, come to rest there. (*Joseph and His Brothers* [New York, 1948], p. 3)

39

Mythology may be said to present a picture of reality through a story, painting, etc. Commenting on proposition No. 2 of his *Tractatus-Logico Philosophicus* (London, 1961), Ludwig Wittgenstein states that, in order to discover whether the picture is true or false, we must compare it with reality.

If we view the myth as a picture, then the reality behind it is the concrete social-historic life which conditions each of the culture-myths. For each age shapes the old myths in accordance with the needs and character of its climate. The story of mythopoesis receives its vitality from history, from the mark of time, place and atmosphere. Attention to the historic roots of mythology and mythopoesis can rescue its living relevance from the romantic view in which mythology is an ineffable universal.

The myth would present the complete man. But historic fissures have limited or warped this total view. Aristotle had warned against this function of the myth. In the 11th book of his *Metaphysics*, he stated that myths (such as that the heavens are gods and that the Divinity encompasses the whole of nature) have been brought forward by legislators "for the purpose of winning the assent of the multitude, and enforcing the utility that is urged in favour of the laws, and of general expediency." The mythic pattern thus shows a rhythmic swing between such historic ideology and the universal archetype. Its uses are benign and malign; they appear in the dual forms of Zeus-Nimrod, Jacob-Cronos, Rebecca-Rhea, Abel-Cain.

There is a need to de-romanticize the myth, to rescue its living relevance from the oceanic night of the romantic conception which views it as an eternal fixed substance, unaffected by empirical forces and the clash of interests. This study will attempt to show the extent to which the historic scene and social hierarchical divisions define each of the poetic myths and give expression to their partisan "ideology." Indeed, such pressures tend to distort the mythic import, moving it towards mysticism or a parody of the myth.

However, historic ideologies never completely eliminate the universal vision. Every age has its prophets and artists who transcend the boundaries of their era towards the all-human. Their symbolic creations at once give central focus to the culture of their time and connect them with what Goethe called "the truth, the old truth" present in all our culture myths.

The dramatic structure which characterizes the literary myth also appears in the historic development of mythopoesis itself. Here, primitive and Oriental mythology serves as a kind of an idealized Edenic first act. Mythopoesis proper begins with the Hebrew Book of Job and Greek tragedy, which center in the second act—the emergence of the rebellious hero, his expulsion and quest. In *The Divine Comedy*, we reach a third act of homecoming in a divine kingdom, followed by the epilogue in *Don Quixote* which questions the reality of the hero's reintegration.

The major emphasis in Renaissance mythopoesis—*Hamlet, Faust, Moby Dick*—is the renewal of the quest. This quest differs from the Hebrew and Grecian in that the modern hero is more alienated from his group. In *The Brothers Karamazov*, the quest assumes an Eastern quality. Here, there is greater belief in the possibility of homecoming, for its hero has the memory of the Pan-Slavic Mother Goddess who incorporates the values of communality and of equality.

In the contemporary era, we move towards the third act of reintegration in the notion of One World. But here the question arises whether this world is to be a living organic unity or a deadening uniformity alternating with a desolate loneliness. The hope is expressed by Thomas Mann's Joseph story and, in a narrower compass, by Nexö's *Pelle the Conqueror* and Gide's *Theseus*. More characteristic of our immediate present are the doubts over this promise. We find them again in the representative work of Thomas Mann, in the figures of Joseph and Judah, and more explicitly in *The Magic Mountain* and *Doctor Faustus*, as well as in the work of Franz Kafka and the existentialists. Here is the epilogue to the historic unfolding of mythopoesis.

NOTES

1. Here, Sorel reversed Plato who sought to free politics from the conservatism of mythic tradition. At the same time, Plato feared the wild and unrestrained in the Dionysian element of the myth.

2. Freud, Rank and Ricklin have indicated that wish-fulfillment occupies a dominant place in the happy ending of the fairy tale. We are not disturbed by these tales because we know that the hero will triumph in the end. Myth, on the other hand, takes account of the obstacles and recalcitrances in the objective world which introduce a tragic element. Where the fairy tale presents the hero in pure opposition *to* the world, the myth sees him involved *within* the world with which he attempts to be reconciled.

   Yet, fairy tales and utopias are also rooted in social history. In his study of Utopias, Ernst Bloch shows that they bear the stamp of their historic epochs. This is more apparent in the case of legends and folk tales where the hero has a definite geographic locus and has more limited powers, and where he is shown as a carrier of tribal tradition. But, in contrast to the myth, his affilia-

41

tion and import are national, rather than universal, as seen in the legends of Charlemagne, King Arthur, William Tell, Frederick Barbarossa, Napoleon. According to Franz Boas, folk tales, legends and myths sometimes blend into one another, for example in the Northwest coast of America. See Franz Ricklin, *Wishfulfillment and Symbolism in Fairy Tales*. Nervous and Mental Disease Monograph Series No. 21 (New York, 1915).

3. *Psychopathology of Everyday Life*, St. Ed., Vol. VI (London, 1960); *Group Psychology and the Analysis of the Ego*, St. Ed., XVIII (London, 1955), 114-115; *Collected Papers*, V (London, 1950), 283.

4. R. R. Marrett and others hold that religion does not follow magic, but that both are aspects of the same pattern. Frazer and Taylor tend to blur the difference between the primitive and the civilized mind, underestimating their varying historical levels. On the other hand, theories such as those of Levy-Brühl, which regard them as completely opposed, wipe out their historical continuity.

5. Such ambivalence may be seen in the meaning of some words: the Greek *eschatos* means both highest and lowest, the Latin *altus* both deep and high.

6. See my essay, "The Use of Myth in Kafka and Mann," in *Spiritual Problems in Contemporary Literature* (New York, 1957).

7. The religious symbol is moral and sacred, specific and undeviating; in mythopoesis, the symbolic meaning is multivalent.

8. The psychological process involved here is well suggested by Henri Bergson in *The Two Sources of Religion and Morals* (New York, 1954). He writes of "the disturbance which is the passage from the static to the dynamic," and of the image which rises to the surface in the course of this agitation. Where the agitation is futile, the image will be only hallucination. But, in the case of artistic and psychical transcendence, the disturbance will contain "a systematic rearrangement looking toward a higher unity: the image is then symbolic of what is being prepared, and the emotion is a concentration of the soul in the expectation of a transformation." Here, transcendence becomes possible because the agitation is not indulged in, yielded to and "enjoyed." (Translation by Francis Fergusson.)

9. Lord Raglan's *The Hero* (London, 1936) restates Rank's thesis. For Raglan, the most striking features are the attempt on the hero's life at birth. Neither Rank nor Raglan place the erotic relation with the mother in the foreground. However, in *Das Inzest-Motif in Dichtung und Sage* (2d ed.; Leipzig und Wien, 1926), Rank draws on numerous literary works to illustrate incest-motifs in mother-son, father-daughter, sister-brother relations.

10. Thus, the final stage of the mystic way, as outlined by Evelyn Underhill (*The Essentials of Mysticism* [London, 1920]) is absolute attainment of Truth. In Blake, it is "Innocence," with the added wisdom of "Experience."

11. *Sex in Psychoanalysis* (New York, 1956), p. 15.

12. In modern art, the organic connection which art once had with work, politics and ethics has been loosened, and art is regarded as an autonomous, specialized activity. In Thomas Mann, the artist becomes a white or black magician, divorced from reality. However, as Phyllis Greenacre ("The Relation of the Im-

postor to the Artist," *Psychoanalytic Study of the Child*, XIII [New York, 1958], 521-541) points out, the artist is distinguished from the counterfeiter in that the former knows that he counterfeits and why.

13. In Ernst Kris' formulation: "Creative artists of our day are wont to use free association as a training ground for creative thinking or as an independent mode of expression, and some among the surrealists have assigned to their work the function of thus making explicit what had previously been implicit." *Psychoanalytic Explorations in Art* (New York, 1952), pp. 25, 30.

14. E. S. Tauber and M. R. Greene, *Prelogical Experience* (New York, 1959).

15. Schneider makes this point. However, his analytic categories are not clear and, in his analysis of writers and painters, Schneider does not apply his own principle. Daniel E. Schneider, *The Psychoanalyst and the Artist* (2d ed.; New York, 1954).

16. Irving Howe argues that such impoverishment is inherent to the use of the psychoanalytic method. The case is quite the reverse. Psychoanalysis is peculiarly concerned with the individual manifestations of a psychological law, and not simply with "archetypes." Howe's point is valid with respect to the sociological approach to literature. It is in the nature of sociology to view processes in "large curves." Irving Howe, *Modern Literary Criticism* (New York, 1959).

17. According to Bergler, writers concern themselves "exclusively with abnormal human reactions." They do not depict reality, but unconsciously select those segments which are needed for their defensive efforts. The writer is "the most anti-social human being conceivable," does not want to communicate, but writes "solely to solve an inner conflict." To be able to produce, the writer must think that he gives to himself out of himself, that he is the autarchic personality, combining mother and child. It would seem to follow that to cure a writer's "block," the analyst must try and get the writer to regress towards the infantile delusion of omnipotence.

18. Cassirer's Kantian attachment sometimes leads him to suggest that the human mind *creates* reality and that man is "in a sense constantly conversing with himself."

19. Kant's *Critique of Judgment* argues for this function of art which mediates by the "third faculty," Imagination.

20. In Mark Kanzer's formulation:

> ". . . the essential ingredients of art take their origin in the psychological sphere that has as its purpose not the perpetuation of sleep, nor yet the achievement of reality testing, but rather the fascinating and all-important area of choice between both tendencies. Art draws part of its sustenance from a dream, but only part; the remainder comes from a portrayal or reality that keeps attention riveted to the waking world. In this sense, the mental state of the artist is close to that of the neurotic, and also to the analysand under the influence of transference." "Contemporary Psychoanalytic Views of Aesthetics," *Journal of the American Psychoanalytic Association*, III (1957), 514-524.

21. In a subsequent paper, "The Fundamental Nature of the Distinction Between

Normality and Neurosis," Kubie modifies this position, stating that the symbolic process makes possible our great cultural achievement, and he sees the evolvement of neurosis only "through a distortion of the symbolic process." *Psychoanalytic Quarterly*, XXXIII (1954), 167-204.

22. Truth in art is what Heidegger calls "apophantic," in that it *shows* its truth, rather than proves it.

23. Ernst Cassirer, *An Essay on Man* (New Haven, 1944), pp. 23-26.

24. See G. Kepes' *Language and Vision* (Chicago, 1951) and H. Read's *The Nature of Literature* (New York, 1956). In non-objective art, there is the trend toward retransposing the object into the fantasy.

25. Kaplan, *The New World of Philosophy* (New York, 1961), pp. 136-137. Cf. Harry Slochower, "Symbolism and the Creative Process of Art," *American Imago*, Vol. XXII (Spring-Summer, 1965).

26. In terms of Ernst Kris' application of ego psychology to art:
    "We are no longer satisfied with the notion that repressed emotions lose their hold over our mental life when an outlet for them has been found. We believe rather that what Aristotle describes as purging enables the ego to re-establish the control which is threatened by dammed-up instinctual demands. The search for outlets acts as an aid to assuring or re-establishing this control, and the pleasure is a double one, in both discharge and control." *Psychoanalytic Explorations in Art*, pp. 25-30.
    For a modification of this position, see Ernest G. Schachtel's *Metamorphosis* (New York, 1959), pp. 237-448.

27. See Herbert Marcuse's brilliant study, *Eros and Civilization* (Boston, 1955), which argues that Freud's metapsychology allows for the possibility of a nonrepressive sublimation.

28. Edward Glover has well formulated this point:
    "Whatever its original unconscious aim, the work of art represents a *forward* urge of the libido seeking to maintain its hold on the world of objects. Its instinctual compromises are not the result of a pathological breakdown of the repressive system. Rather it acts as an auxiliary device to maintain the efficiency of repression. It is in the truest sense a sublimation, and consequently obviates the need for self-punishment." *Freud or Jung* (New York, 1950), p. 185.

29. *The Psychoanalytic Study of Society*, Vol. III, ed. Warner Muensterberger and Sidney Axelrad (New York, 1964).

30. J. A. Arlow: "Ego Psychology and the Study of Mythology," *Journal of the American Psychoanalytic Association*, IX (1961), 383.

31. See Appendix I, "Primitive and Oriental Mythology."

32. Cf. Erich Kahler, "The Persistence of Myth" in *Out of the Labyrinth* (New York, 1967), pp. 41-51.

33. In *Ego Psychology and the Problem of Adaptation* (New York, 1958), Heinz Hartmann uses "adaptation" to cover both social compliance and attempts to change the social environment. He distinguishes between a passive "*state of*

adaptedness," which may be regressive and *"the process of adaptation"* which may be progressive involving the individual's changing and adapting the environment to "human functions." In this discriminatory use of "adaptation," Hartmann leaves some room for the function of mythopoesis, especially when he notes that individual adaptation "may clash with the adaptation of the species." (pp. 12-32)

34. Tarachow (in *The Psychoanalytic Study of Society,* III, 11) also notes that myths may be "maladaptive and rebellious," but this point is not developed.

35. However, Marcuse's *Eros and Civilization* interprets Freud's metapsychology as offering a basis for a free culture and society.

36. Ernest Jones states that it is "a gross misunderstanding" to say that Freud dated "the whole genesis of culture from a single event." He points out that some of our eminent anthropologists support Freud's theory. He cites Clyde Kluckhohn, among others, who wrote him: "I am convinced that the essential universality of the Oedipus complex and of sibling rivalry are now established by the anthropological record." *The Life and Work of Sigmund Freud,* III (New York, 1957), 328 f. For a recent evaluation of Freud's theory, see Derek Freeman: "Totem and Taboo. A Reappraisal," *The Psychoanalytic Study of Society,* IV (New York, 1967), 9-34. While Freeman argues that for Freud the killing of the father was an actual historic event, he supports Freud's psychic hypothesis. That Freud at least wavered on whether he regarded the killing as an actual event, appears in his calling it "only a hypothesis . . . a 'Just-So-Story,' as it was amusingly called by a not unkind English critic [the anthropologist R. R. Marrett]; but I think it is creditable to such a hypothesis if it proves able to bring coherence and understanding into more and more new regions." (*Group Psychology and the Analysis of the Ego,* p. 122.)

37. *Group Psychology and the Analysis of the Ego,* pp. 1-3 and chapter 4.

38. *Collected Papers,* V, 96, 74, 286. In this emphasis, Freud approaches Marx. In *Neue Folge,* he states that the strength of Marxism lies not in its conception of history, but in its perceptive indication of the influence which economic relations have on man's intellectual, ethical and artistic attitudes. See the chapter "Clash and Congruence Between Marx and Freud" in my *No Voice Is Wholly Lost* (New York, 1945; paperback edition: *Literature and Philosophy Between Two World Wars* [New York, 1964]).

Erich Fromm and others have charged that Freud's androcentric theory (the domination by the father) is refuted by the research of Bachofen and his followers on the existence of societies ruled by "mother-right." Now, to begin with, the term "mother-right" is misleading since (as Engels observed) in many matrilineal societies there are no rulers or ruled, but each sex contributes its share, with leadership held by the most able.

More telling are the findings of Bronislaw Malinowski. Malinowski showed that among the Trobriands, the wish was not to kill the father and to sleep with the mother, but to kill the maternal uncle and to sleep with the sister. He sets forth a number of important variables, not considered by Freud: the distribution of power within the family, the pattern of descent, inheritance and succession, the residence of parents and children, and the transmission of skills. Yet, despite these modifications, he found that Freud's essential thesis was valid, concluding that "Freud's theories not only roughly correspond to human psychology . . . they follow closely the modifications in human nature brought about by various constitutions of society." (*Sex and Repression in Savage Society* [London, 1949], p. 81.)

A. L. Kroeber also accepts Freud's account to the degree that the incest drive and incest repression are operative in the psychic process. See A. L. Kroeber, "Totem and Taboo: An Ethnological Psychoanalysis," *American Anthropologist*, XXII, 48-55 and his "Totem and Taboo in Retrospect," *American Journal of Sociology*, XLV, 446-451.

Freud's more basic methodological strategy refers to *the symbol of authority*. This point is made by Ralph Linton. Oedipal attitudes, he notes, are directed at any figure—father or mother's brother—who assumes this function (*Culture and Mental Disorders* [Springfield, Illinois, 1956]). In any case, even if Freud's theory is not altogether valid for early history, it is clearly relevant to Western societies in which the father is the dominating figure.

The Hebrew Memory of a
Chosen God
The Book of Job

Why did the Holy One, blessed be He, choose Israel? Because . . . Israel chose the Holy One, blessed be He, and His Torah.

—Midrash
Numbers Rabba

MYTHOLOGY OCCUPIES a minor place in the Hebrew pantheon.[1] Myths did not take root in the popular mind of the Jews partly because their history did not favor the formation of a settled folk-tradition and because the Hebraic injunction against the making of "graven images" of God worked against the representation of mythic powers in pictures and stories. To be sure, the figure of Job was an old folk memory.[2] Still, the specific *Hebraic* quality of Job, as presented in the Book of Job, is shaped by the very absence of a cohesive folk-life and by the admonition against the portrayal of God through imagery.

The only Biblical theme which has been molded into a mythopoeic work is the story of Job. Like the Oriental legends, the *Iliad, Odyssey* and the Germanic *Niebelungenlied*, it is a folk product, the work of multiple authors. It is also a folk memory reaching back into a distant past. Job is mentioned by Ezekiel as a man of piety. He appears in the Epistle of James, in Arabic and other literature. There is an earlier Babylonian poem (*Ludlul bel nimequi*) dealing with the suffering of a pious king which has been called the "Babylonian Job." However, it is not the specific story of Job, but the *question* he propounds that has become an organic part of the universal myth. We find it among the psalmists (37, 49, 73) and the prophets, notably Jeremiah:

> Wherefore doth the way of the wicked prosper?
> Why are they at ease that deal treacherously?

The question is asked by later mythic heroes, from Prometheus, Oedipus and Hamlet to Ivan Karamazov, Kafka's Joseph K. and Mann's Jacob.

Traditional Exegeses

Commentators generally treat the Book of Job as a religious poem. Job is seen as a man whose righteousness is tested by suffering. When he demands to know the reason for his punishment, he is told that man cannot know the ways of God. He is finally redeemed through humble acceptance of God's mystery. In this view, Job's affliction becomes a "false arrest," of the type experienced by Kafka's characters. It implies that man is originally or natively guilty, that he can be delivered only by divine grace.[3]

This religious interpretation aligns the book with the Oriental and Christian myth, but fails to bring out its *Hebrew* character, specifically that of the post-exilic, post-prophetic era.[4] In the religious myth, man's suffering on earth may be compensated for by a physical or spiritual after-life, and the suffering of innocents becomes a condition for the eventual happiness of all mankind. But, as Father Kissane points out, these interpretations do not fit the Hebrew poem.[5] Job does not believe in a paradisiacal after-life—a notion developed only later in the Book of Wisdom—holding that "man dieth . . . and riseth not."[6] Sheol is but a shadowy domain where all souls, guilty and innocent, survive without distinction. Nor can Job find solace in the idea that he is punished for the sins of his ancestors. Indeed, the notion of tribal guilt had been shattered by the prophets. "Everyone," Jeremiah writes, "shall die for his own iniquity." Ezekiel states: "The son shall not bear the iniquity of the father, neither shall the father bear the iniquity of the son." The only "Hebraic" theme which remains in this approach is that of the Jew who suffers simply because he is a Jew.

This interpretation runs into a number of difficulties. To begin with, *it ignores Job's revolutionary indictment* which comprises the body of the book, and implies that Job's position at the end is the same one he held at the beginning. Furthermore, if Job is uplifted because he accepts God as an unfathomable mystery, then the Friends should have been rewarded even more, for this is their persistent argument. Yet Yahweh condemns the Friends.

The difficulties of the religious exegesis, which comes to a *credo quia ignorabimus*, have led to a second line of interpretation, represented by Morris Jastrow. His main thesis is that the book is not a unity, but a composite production and one of gradual growth. The older book contained a protest against the prophets' assurance that the world is governed by a just and merciful power. Later additions and amplifications attempted to controvert the older book in the interests of Jewish orthodoxy. According to Jastrow, the protesting Job of the discussions and the pious Job of the Prologue and Epilogue cannot be reconciled.[7]

The argument of this study is that the Book of Job, despite its composite character, contains a unified statement of the Hebrew myth, if approached as a drama in which Job and his God are developing characters. It will attempt to show that the Book breaks the long chain of the Oriental religious myth in that it introduces the category of *choice* which renders the character both heroic and guilty, and he is *redeemed because of his guilt*. It takes the step from collective to individual responsibility while maintaining supra-personal standards. However, even as it moves away from Eastern impersonality and mystic identification, it does not quite affirm the Greek and Western notions of personality, freedom and the rebellious quest.

Folk-Memory

The universal character of the Book has its roots in the post-exilic period of Jewish life. This historic base conditions the nature of its hero, his mythic crime and rehabilitation.

The decisive experience of the Hebrews was their forty years of desert life. The "waste-howling wilderness" (Deuteronomy) formed their conception of a nomadic or transcendent God and their notion of freedom.[8]

> In the stark solitude of the desert where nothing changes, nothing moves (except man at his own free will), where features in the landscape are only pointers, landmarks, without significance in themselves—there we may expect the image of God to transcend concrete phenomena altogether. Man confronting God will not contemplate him but will hear his voice and command, as Moses did, and the prophets, and Mohammed. (Frankfort *et al.*, *Ancient Man*, p. 372.)

However, the development of urban life and the formation of the kingdom introduced a luxurious court-life, the employment of Hebrew slaves and a life of ease for the wealthier classes.

It was against such life of adulation and self-indulgence that the prophets levelled their scorn, excoriating social injustice and inequality of wealth. Some, such as Hosea, held up the past as an ideal, the time when Israel lived in tents. They spoke out against pagan rituals of lustration, insisting that only the personal moral act and "thoughts of the heart" could bring purification. God, according to Jeremiah, will put His law in men's "inward parts, and will write it upon their heart." He wanted no ritual sacrifices, writes the psalmist:

> Thou hast no pleasure in burnt offering . . . A broken and contrite heart, O God, thou wilt not despise.

The Hebrews developed their concept of the deity while journeying through the desert. Thus, Yahweh became a wandering, restless God.[9] Later, under the influence of Moses and the prophets, the tribal conception of Yahweh is transformed into a single God ruling over the whole world. He was not a local Baal, but a universal God who could not find corporeal representation in graven images. Totemism therefore never became part of Hebrew ritual. Yahweh is now conceived as a Father-God. Where the Oriental and Graeco-Roman myth regarded the God incomplete without the Goddess (who is generally his mother—or sister-wife), the Hebrews stressed the all-sufficiency and sternness of the patriarchal God. This may account for one of the distinctive features of the Hebrew myth—the absence of the incest theme.[10]

Hebrew monotheism stood for one humanistic, moral world. In Egypt, monotheism meant "imperialism in religion"(Breasted), whereas in Israel it was a morality of freedom. It answered the condition of a people whose freedom was constantly restricted, whose country was, in Heine's phrase, a "portable fatherland." It was this spirituality and universalism, coupled with the idea of individual responsibility, which made "the Jew" the center of attack by "Blood and Soil" Nazism.[11]

Throughout, Yahweh retained the characteristics of disquiet and unrest. In Thomas Mann's formulation, Abraham chose to serve "The Highest," that is, one God for all, one of "Geist" who could not be confined or limited.[12] In terms of the mythic vocabulary, the Hebrew God was one whose creation required constant re-creation, that is, He was a God of the Quest. The Messianic idea does not envisage a finished paradise, but calls on man to continue "the act of creation." This is the critical meaning of the term "the chosen people." God chose to protect those who would not bow down to anything less than the highest. This means, as Willa Cather put it, that the Jews were the chosen people in that they were *the people who chose*. In this sense, the Hebrew myth becomes the myth of the chosen God.

Job as a Mythic Hero

The crucial phase of the mythic hero begins when he is "set out" without apparent cause. This question recurs in mythopoesis. We find it

50

in Oedipus, who insists that "in nature" he was not evil; in Hamlet, who states that his is "unpregnant" of the cause for his "bad dreams," in Ahab, who does not understand why the whale bit off his leg; in Ivan Karamazov's question, why do the innocent suffer; in Kafka's Joseph K. who is arrested "without having done anything wrong."

Early in the Book, Job asks: "Why is light given to man whose way is hid, and whom God hath hedged in?" Here, Job sounds the protest against God for having infused man with infinite desires and imposed numberless obligations upon him, but has not given him the powers to carry them out. "What is man," Job asks, "that thou shouldest magnify him, and . . . try him every moment?"—a cry echoed by Goethe's Faust.

And Job goes beyond this general indictment: He wants to know wherein *he* erred as an individual, and the main body of the Book consists of Job's insistent demand to be told wherein he transgressed. In this question and in Yahweh's final response, we have the nature of both Job's mythic crime and his redemption. To understand the dialectic complex of this problem, we need to analyze the work as *a drama*.

The Book of Job is a ballad, that is, a story in dramatic form. As such, the various characters—Elohim, the Satan, Job, the Friends, Elihu and Yahweh—are externalizations of the development *within* Job.

Act I: Tribal Harmony

The exact date of the Book is uncertain, but scholars agree that it belongs to the post-prophetic era. It is therefore relevant to ask: Was Job of the Prologue "perfect and upright" in the light of the values stressed by the prophets?

The Book begins with a picture of tribal harmony. Job lives in peace with his family and his community, fears God and avoids evil. Yet, Job's piety appears primarily in that he does not violate the laws set down in "the books"; he performs the required rituals, offering sacrifices for his sons on the possibility that they may have sinned. The author speaks of Job's "great household," of his exceptional "substance"—sheep, camels, oxen—which makes him "the greatest of all the men of the east." He gives to the poor, but has enough left to wash his "steps with butter." And Job *gloried* in his favored position. In chapter 29, he recalls the days

> When I washed my steps with butter,[13] and the rock poured me out rivers of oil . . .
> The young saw me, and hid themselves: and the aged arose, and stood up.
> The princes refrained talking, and laid their hand on their mouth.
> The nobles held their peace. . . .

This was the time when he "sat chief, and dwelt as a king in the army," enjoyed ease, "safety," "rest" and "quiet." What is even more telling, Job appears indifferent when his animals, servants and children are killed. Is this the attitude of a "perfect and upright" man? Does it not rather suggest that there is something rotten in the land of Uz belying its outer harmony?

Job's crime is not in the nature of an active violation, such as that of Prometheus. His is the passive crime of contentment and self-satisfaction with his superior status. His failing lies not in his wealth, but in his *attitude*—that wealth is his due, and that it is proper to indulge in pompous enjoyment of the power it gives him. In Elihu's later formulation, Job enjoyed the comforts of the table.

Now, sluggishness of the soul is a crime in the eyes of the God envisioned by the prophets. This God calls for a hero who does not rest comfortably in the present, but who peers back towards the mysteries of creation and carries the burden of future re-creation, one who has knowledge of the abyss, experiences homelessness and nomadic wandering, one who is aware of man's infinite obligations. The Job of the Prologue knows little of these things. Paul Weiss speaks of Job's psychological, moral and social suffering ("Job, God and Evil," *Commentary*, VI, No. 2 [August, 1948], 144-151.) One must add that his suffering is related to his crime of psychic lassitude, moral smugness and social insensitivity to existing disparities. Not until he is personally afflicted does he begin to lament, insisting on *his* rights and his righteousness.

But, it is urged, does not Elohim of the Prologue Himself speak of Job as "a perfect and upright man, one that feareth God and escheweth evil?" However, we must examine the nature of the Lord in the Prologue. Paul Weiss calls attention to His callousness in permitting the Satan to kill Job's flocks, servants and children, that is, to destroy those who, unlike Job, are not involved in the trial at all, but are innocent bystanders. Is not Elohim here as insensitive and complacent in the use of His power as Job is? Now, Elohim to whom Job appears perfect and upright must be differentiated from the Voice of Yahweh which addresses Job at the end.[14] As will be shown, the latter does not "judge" Job with the same standards by which he is declared upright at the beginning. That is, *the God of the Book, like its hero, also undergoes dramatic development.*

Traditional Guides: The Friends

Job's moral state in the Prologue may be gathered from the fact that his position is apparently the same as that of the Friends.[15] The three

Friends represent the approach of the average man who is guided by the stock answers contained in "the books." They argue *ad hoc* that Job is guilty since he is being punished—a striking analogy to the case of Kafka's Joseph K. whose "friends" (Fräulein Bürstner, the advocate, his uncle) take it for granted that the very questioning by officials indicates that Joseph K. must have done something wrong. The Friends constitute the "chorus," reduced from the discriminating Greek voice to a crowd-attitude. They are "cabalists," uncritical followers of traditional theology, holding fast to that "which wise men have told from their fathers," and advising Job to heed their teachings (7,15). They are calculators who believe that by unquestioning surrender, man will be rewarded. Thus, their stand amounts to a *quid pro quo* business theology. Essentially, they de-dignify the Hebrew God viewing Him in terms of mystery, miracle and authority. And, as in the case of Dostoyevsky's Grand Inquisitor, they have no faith in moral freedom. Man, they believe, is impure by nature and is but a "worm" before God. Their "secret," like the Inquisitor's, is that they do not believe in God, setting themselves up as the final judges of Job's guilt. Their passive acceptance amounts to an irreligious repudiation of the dynamic nature of Yahweh. Indeed, it is not clear whether they are Hebrews.[16]

Yet, the author does allow dramatic justification for some of their arguments. Eliphaz charges that Job did not give water to the weary, withheld bread from the hungry, and respected the rich. Bildad indirectly suggests Job's sinful state when he refers to the iniquities of his children. Above all, since their stand is one which Job once shared, they represent the dramatic hurdle he must overcome before he can be uplifted.

Act II: Expulsion and Rebellion

The punishment heaped upon Job may be likened to the expulsion of the Hebrews from the fleshpots of Egypt into a barren wilderness. Job loses his possessions, is stripped of his status, and is driven out into the dark night of his soul. He is set out from his Eden-like state of security and comfort, separated from his fellowmen by the Cain-mark of physical wounds, social loss and spiritual anguish. His life becomes a psychic journey through a desert-existence, in quest of an answer to the question which Jews have asked throughout the ages: *Eli, Eli, lama sabachtani?* As in the case of Aeschylus' Prometheus—who likewise remains in one spot throughout the drama—the journey is one of the mind and the emotions. In both, the dramatic "action" consists in the change of tone in the lament and argument, in the speeches of the various characters. This makes for a fluctuating rhythm and pace, at times quiet, at times whirling and torrential like the elements.

Job's trial is his "experience" which galvanizes him into "revolution." Not until he is reduced to the elemental level of human existence, placed on an equal footing with the lowest, is Job awakened to consciousness. His false security which had blunted his critical and imaginative faculties is shattered, and he is catapulted out of his settled and sated condition towards a dynamic challenging attitude. Job's suffering is not only a punishment; it is also, and first of all, *a guide* to his higher self. It prods and harries him into his integrity. His refusal to accept the Friends' conception of God as a mysterious and miraculous authority defines the assertion of this self.

Job's new character emerges through his debate with the Friends.[17] His opening words strike a despairing, self-denying note, voicing the temptation to regress towards pre-natal security. He curses the day on which he was born, even wishes he had not been conceived. Job proceeds to argue in the causal, legalistic manner characteristic of the Friends. He wants his grief "weighed" and his calamity balanced. Yet, almost at once, he insists on his right to question: "Therefore I will not refrain my mouth; I will speak in the anguish of my spirit; I will complain in the bitterness of my soul" (7). He turns from the Friends to God and asks to "see" and "reason" with Him, "as a man pleadeth for his neighbour," that he might know his transgressions. He passes from the theme of the injustice done him to the general proposition that God's world is one where the wicked prosper and the just are a laughing stock. As to the Friends, their uncritical belief in God's ultimate justice stamps them as "miserable comforters . . . forgers of lies . . . physicians of no value," and their "wisdom" will die with them (10-16).

Job's *impatience marks the birth of his ego*. It appears in *his own* realization that he had *not* been perfect and upright. Job recalls the iniquities of his youth. He now sees that his righteousness was "put on . . . and it clothed me," that he had only scorn for those who suffered from "want and famine" (13,29,30). He now indicts those who, through greed and violence "turn the needy out of the way," and the condition in which they who tread the winepresses suffer thirst. Job admits that he may have hidden "mine iniquity in my bosom," in fear of "the great multitude" and "the contempt of families" (24,31). To be sure, these are admissions not to wilful or conscious acts, but to what Job may have done in his ignorance.[18]

The most direct statement of Job's rebirth appears in chapters 13 and 27. They contain Job's declaration of moral independence in which he insists on holding his "own ways," though he may burn for it:

> Though he slay me, yet will I trust in him:[19] but I will maintain mine own ways before him.
>
> He shall also be my salvation: for a hypocrite shall not come before him . . .
>
> Behold now, I have ordered my cause; I know I shall be justified.
>
> Who is he that will plead with me? for now, if I hold my tongue, I shall give up the ghost.

And later, in his reply to Bildad:

> God forbid that I should justify you: till I die I will not remove mine integrity from me.
>
> My righteousness I hold fast, and will not let it go: my heart shall not reproach me so long as I live . . .
>
> For what is the hope of the hypocrite though he hath gained, when God taketh away his soul. . . .

Job's "patience," as Gersonides points out, lies in his steady belief that when God had tried him, he would "come forth as gold" (23). Indeed, Job affirms God more passionately in his state of affliction than he had in his state of complacency.[20]

The Herald: Elihu

Like Dante, Job feels himself lost in a dark forest. God "hath fenced up my way that I cannot pass, and He hath set darkness in my paths." The Friends are the "rational" guides whose traditional wisdom helps Job only in making him aware that he must go beyond it. They are followed by Elihu and by Yahweh.

It is generally held that Elihu merely recapitulates the arguments of the Friends.[21] However, this contention is not borne out by the text. To begin with, Elihu's wrath is kindled not only against Job, but also against the Friends "because they had found no answer, and yet had condemned Job." Furthermore, where they excoriated Job for voicing his grievance, Elihu calls on him to "speak, for I desire to justify thee." He is a younger man who claims to be speaking "in God's stead." (His name means "My God is he.") God, he says, communicates to man by dreams and illness, through which He "openeth the ears of men, and sealeth their instruction." In this manner, God warns man, and thereby gives him an opportunity to provide against what may be forthcoming, that is, allows *human choice*. (Prometheus similarly says that man can anticipate the future through dreams.) Job himself spoke earlier of the dreams through which God terrifies him at night (7). But, Elihu charges, Job did not realize his social shortcomings, did not come to the aid of the oppressed who "cry out by reason of the arm of the mighty." Instead, he indulged in a life of ease and luxury, enjoyed the comforts of the table.[22]

Elihu's role as herald or messenger of the Lord appears in that he offers the definition of God which Yahweh gives of Himself at the close: The union of wisdom and power, manifested in His creation and purposeful manipulation of the elements. He speaks of God's voice which "roareth" and "thundereth," foreshadowing Yahweh's speeches "out of the whirlwind."

Act III: Recognition Scene—Yahweh

Nearly all critics are of the opinion that the speeches of the Lord do not answer Job's question. Kissane's view is representative of this position:

> The implication in the First Speech is that the suffering of the just, like all the phenomena of the universe, enters into the scheme of Divine Providence; but the motive of God's action in an individual case remains a mystery. The aim of the Speeches is not to penetrate this mystery, but to show that man is to accept God's will with humility and resignation, without questioning the propriety of God's action . . . the writer teaches that suffering is not always the result of sin (Dialogue), and . . . that it is not due to God's want of knowledge of the just man's distress, nor want of power to intervene on his behalf. But in neither case does the writer give any *positive* solution of the problem. (*Book of Job*, p. xxix)

This view raises several questions. If man must accept God's will with humility and resignation, why does not the Lord continue to punish a recalcitrant Job? Why does He bother to appear and challenge him to "answer?"

Yahweh speaks of Himself as encompassing the whole universe. This has led Horace Kallen to see in him a "God of indifference," akin to the Greek Moira, and in the Book "a Greek tragedy."[23] But, unlike the Aristotelian *Nous*, Yahweh is not an "unmoved mover," and does not view physical and human nature as belonging to the same order of things. On the contrary, this is a patriarchal deity of will and purpose. His rule is not one of cosmic neutrality, but of *choice*. Yahweh is concerned about man's welfare, singles out Job, comes and speaks to him with dramatic passion and in *human* terms, as he did to Adam, Eve, Noah. In the end, he *discriminates* between Job and the Friends.

In his first speeches, Yahweh emphasizes His power and wisdom, and it is to be noted that Job reacts to them with *a sullen response*. Called upon to answer, he states:

> Once have I spoken, but I will not answer again;
> Yea, twice, but I will proceed no further.

Yahweh then introduces a new motif. He now adds that *Job can save himself*:

> Then will I also confess unto thee
> That thine own right hand can save thee.

Job remains silent and answers only after Yahweh proceeds to speak of Behemoth and the Leviathan.

Yahweh first speaks of Behemoth, the land animal, as having been created at "the beginning," together "with thee." He dwells at greater length on Leviathan, the sea monster, emphasizing the fact that he will not allow himself to be subdued: One cannot "play with him as with a bird;" he does not supplicate or "speak soft words;" one cannot "press down his tongue with a cord," lead him by the nose, for he will not permit himself to be made into "a servant for ever."

These passages have been interpreted as arguing that if the Lord rules such mighty creatures, then how can a man stand up to him? However, I would suggest a supplementary meaning: If an animal such as the Leviathan, won't let himself become enslaved, how much less should man submit, he who is made in God's image? Yahweh states that the skin of these animals cannot be penetrated by arrows. Now, the human skin *is* penetrable, and its "openness" is associated with man's greater sensitivity—the very quality that makes him receptive to the spiritual nature of the Hebrew God and renders him creative.[24] For, Yahweh speaks of Himself not only as the archer, but also as *the rain which fructifies the land* to the extent that its "skin" is penetrable:

> Who hath cleft a channel for the waterflood,
> Or a way for the lightning of the thunder;
> To cause it to rain on a land where no man is . . .
> To satisfy the desolate and waste ground,
> And to cause the bud of the tender herb to spring forth.

In this sense as well, Yahweh should be distinguished from Elohim of the Prologue. Where the latter appears indifferent to the fate of Job's animals, servants and children, Yahweh speaks of His animal creations, particularly the war-horse, with something of an artist's pride in his creations. And, he has faith in Job's human powers, calling on him to gird himself like a man, assuring him that he can be saved by his "own right hand."[25]

One of the crucial features of the mythic hero is his acting as a scapegoat for society. Prometheus endures for mankind, Oedipus and Orestes suffer for the Greek *polis*, the trials of Hamlet, Goethe's Faust, Gide's Theseus and Thomas Mann's Joseph are finally in the interests of social welfare. Job, on the other hand, appears to be concerned only about himself.

To be sure, the Book does not reach the degree of socialization voiced by Deutero-Isaiah. Still, in the course of his psychic journey, Job moves towards a powerful indictment of social wrong and exploitation. In chapter 24, he speaks of those who carry the sheaves and go about hungry, who work the winepresses, yet suffer thirst:

> There are that pluck the fatherless from the breast,
> And take a pledge of the poor;
> So that they go about naked without clothing,
> And being hungry they carry the sheaves;
> They make oil within the rows of these men;
> They tread their winepresses, and suffer thirst. . . .

In chapter 30, he talks of men

> . . . gaunt with want and famine;
> They gnaw the dry ground, in the gloom of wasteness and desolation. . . .
> In the clefts of the valleys they must dwell,
> In holes of the earth and of the rocks.

In the following chapter, Job champions the human rights of the slave:

> Did not He that made me in the womb make him?
> And did not One fashion us in the womb?

Commenting on such passages in the Book, Isaac Mendelssohn writes that Job is the first in the ancient Near East who "raised his voice in a sweeping condemnation of slavery as a cruel and inhuman institution, irrespective of nationality and race."[26] At the end, Job forgives the Friends who had calumniated him, and gives his daughters inheritance along with his sons, thereby going beyond the old patrilineal law.

The Psychic Process of Job's Redemption

This chapter argues that Job's "redemption" comes about through a change in his personality. And, I want to suggest that this change is analogous to a psychoanalytic process if we view the Friends, Elihu and Yahweh as developing aspects of his ego. This process is dramatized in Job's debates with these characters in the course of which he relives the intellectual and emotional experience of his "guilty" past.

At the beginning, we find Job at home, amidst family and friends, enjoying his material possessions and social status. Following his "breakdown," we see him lying or sitting. He then begins to "talk."[27]

The crucial stage in Job's growing awareness is reached in the speeches of Elihu which follow his debate with the Friends.

In his final answer to the Friends, Job casts a last nostalgic glance back to "the days of my youth," when young and old, the poor and wealthy paid him homage. In the next chapter, Job admits that he *may* have committed many sins.

> If I have walked with vanity . . .
> If my heart have been enticed unto a woman . . .
> If I did despise the cause of my man-servant . . .
> If I have withheld aught that the poor desired . . .
> If I have made gold my hope
> If after the manner of men I covered my transgressions,
> By hiding mine iniquity in my bosom—
> Because I feared the great multitude. . . .

At this point, Job becomes ready for Elihu's revelations to which he makes no rejoinder.

Elihu begins by rebuking the Friends for not meeting Job's argument. He then states that God also communicates with man by dreams, "though man perceiveth it not." Elihu then points to Job's central sin: his life of ease amidst the comforts of the table. In a vague way, Job had known what Elihu makes explicit. He spoke earlier (7) of God scaring him "with dreams," terrifying him "through visions," and of the iniquities he may have hidden in his bosom. Finally, Elihu prepares Job for the revelation imparted by Yahweh.

Yahweh is the all-sufficient, unfathomable "giant," whom Job had been asking for an answer and who at last tells him what his "talk" comes to. He is at first a threatening disturbing father figure to Job. Job feels himself condemned by Yahweh, proved "perverse," although he thinks himself innocent. Job likens Yahweh to the archer who shoots his arrows into him, breaches and cleaves his reins, gnashes him with his teeth:[28]

> I was at ease, and He broke me asunder;
> Yea, He hath taken me by the neck, and dashed me to pieces;
> He hath also set me up for His mark.
> His archers compass me round about,
> He cleaveth my reins asunder, and doth not spare;
> He poureth out my gall upon the ground,

> He breaketh me with breach upon breach;
> He runneth upon me like a giant.

Towards the end, Yahweh also appears as creator and nourisher, as the power that brought Job out of the womb, poured him out "as milk," clothed him "with skin and flesh" (10). And Job's attitude toward God is correspondingly ambivalent. Like Ivan Karamazov, he rejects God's world as unjust, and like him, he accepts God himself. Ahab too addresses his "fiery father" with ringing defiance, yet begs him to "come in thy lowest form of love, and I will kneel and kiss thee."

Job is rewarded for his critical examination and the God who had been a total mystery, reveals Himself and talks to Job. Before, Job had only "heard" of God through the precepts handed down by tradition. But what Job wanted was to "see" him: "Lo, He goeth by me, and I see Him not;" After Job has gone through his ordeal, the wish is granted, and he says to Yahweh:

> I had heard of Thee by the hearing of the ear;
> But now mine eye seeth Thee.

The speeches of Elihu and Yahweh are a dramatization of what Job has come to "see" in the course of his psychic development. In this process, Job is shocked into life, that is, to a critical attitude towards his God and himself. At the end, he accepts Yahweh. But, unlike the Friends, he does so only after he has passed through the revolt by reason and the stages of emotional understanding. With Prometheus, Job rebels only against the father who seems to act arbitrarily and tyrannically, but affirms Him when His power is directed by wisdom. Above all, Job can accept the God who reproves the uncritical Friends, just as Job had hoped:

> He shall surely reprove you,
> If ye do secretly show favor.

Stated summarily, *Job is redeemed precisely because he has refused to accept an irrational authority*, because he has insisted on maintaining his own ways without losing faith in a substantive principle. Job persists in making his own choice and, to this extent, is his own instrument for salvation. In these several ways, the Book of Job redeems the ancient prophetic temper by symbolic representation.

Epilogue

The value placed on the critical approach precludes a paradisiac Third Act in the Hebrew Myth—Moses too was not to enter the Promised Land. Even as the Hebrew God developed from the tribal to the cosmic deity, he retained the restless features of the desert- and volcano-God. He is the whirlwind who dislocates Job. In turn, Job is rehabilitated because he exhibits the qualities of the God of the whirlwind. In this connection, history takes on a new function. Mircea Eliade points out that while time is a factor in Greek mythopoesis, it is only with the Hebrews that *historical time* plays a vital role, that they were the first "to discover the meaning of history as the epiphany of God. . . ."[29]

This note introduces an element of mystery into the Book of Job. The poem belongs to a time when the myth had not yet emancipated itself from its magic-religious layers. The Hebrew God is *a will*, that is, a force which cannot be grasped by logic. Yahweh's appearance has an apocalyptic character, his language has a tone of sublimity, is more incantatory than reasoned. Job had demanded complete justice. But, Yahweh asks him:

> Where wast thou when I laid the foundations of the earth?
> Hast thou commanded the morning since thy days began. . . .

The individual comes into a world "given" to him in order and sequence so that, already at birth, he owes an infinitude of debts. Man cannot know the bottomless well of the past, the ultimate why and how of creation, but only some of its implications.

However, this is less an anticipation of the doctrine of grace than a statement of the quest proper to those who have chosen to follow a God who is not content with creation and preservation, but insists on dynamic recreation.[30] This makes for tragic heroism. The Book does close with Job restored to his former greatness. Yet, his restitution is not without its tragic residue—his servants and children are dead, and cannot be replaced by those given him. Moreover, this reward is out of rhythm with the tone of the Book, and with the story of "The Wandering Jew," of a people whose history, as Erich Kahler puts it, *begins* with exile, given over to the loneliness of the quest. In the words of H. and H. A. Frankfort:

> Nowhere in the literature of Egypt or Babylonia, do we meet the loneliness of the Biblical figures . . . Saul . . . David . . . men in terrible isolation facing a transcendent God: Abraham trudging to the place of sacrifice with his son, Jacob in his struggle, and Moses and the prophets. (*Ancient Man*, p. 371.)

This loneliness appears in the characters of Franz Kafka and Sholem Asch, in Joyce's Bloom, Mann's Naphta and Jacob, makes itself felt in Proust's Swann.

Yet, this alienation is also the promise of a creative future. Thorstein Veblen speaks of the Jew as "a disturber of the intellectual peace . . . a wanderer in the intellectual no man's land, seeking another place to rest, further along the road, somewhere over the horizon. . . . never complacent nor contented." Similarly, for Jacques Maritain, Judaism "bars slumber, it teaches the world to be discontented and restless as long as the world has not God; it stimulates the movement of history."[31] It is in this sense that the Book of Job is a *statement of the symbolic value of exile,* that is, the value of spiritual rebellion, which is a concomitant of the exiled condition. In a basic sense, the *Book of Job is a dramatic statement of the religious attitude.*

Jewish characters in modern literature, far removed from Job's memory of his origins, have become too "civilized" to insist on their own ways, or too "sensitive" to challenge the hidden or open accusations of their alleged guilt. The historic fate which has deprived the Jew of a folk base hangs over these characters—Lessing's Nathan, Proust's Swann, Kafka's Joseph K., Mann's Naphta.

However, Thomas Mann's later epic of Jacob and Joseph is a contemporary reaffirmation of the Hebrew myth and its universal import. This work was conceived and executed even as Hitlerism attempted to reduce the Jew to dust and ashes. This very attempt served as a shock which roused in many the memory of their tradition, making possible the heroic resistance by the Warsaw ghetto and the Israeli war of liberation.

There remains the perennial mythic import of the Book—its homily on the living value of the critical conscience. Historic circumstances have produced perhaps an over-accentuation of this faculty in the Jew. Yet, criticism is a function of the spirit itself. "Spiritually," Maritain writes, "we are all Semites." Transposed into human affairs, the Book is a warning against the self-sufficiency of folk interests. For the prophets, Amos in particular, the Jew was nearly synonymous with mankind in its higher strivings. The author of the Book speaks of Job, not as a Hebrew, but as "a man." And Job becomes truly human and alive through his quest and questioning, for the God he chose to follow is a God of The Quest. In this sense, the Book is a link in the mythic tradition of freedom from Aeschylus' Prometheus to Thomas Mann's Jacob.

NOTES

1. See Angelo S. Rappoport, *Myth and Legend of Ancient Israel* (London, 1928), Vol. I; H. and H. A. Frankfort *et al., The Intellectual Adventure of Ancient Man* (Chicago, 1946). S. H. Langdon (*The Mythology of All Races,* Vol. V

THE BOOK OF JOB

[Boston, 1931]) considers the following stories specifically Jewish: The Tables of the Law, Sodom and Gomorrha, the Egyptian Plagues, Balaam and the Ass, Jonah and the Whale, Samson and Delilah. But none of them has become the subject of a major mythopoeic work.

2. Morris Jastrow states that "from an early age, Job has become a popular figure among the Hebrews." (*The Book of Job* [Philadelphia and London, 1920], p. 46). According to William F. Albright (*From the Stone Age to Christianity* [Baltimore, 1940]), the name of Job first appears in an Egyptian list of Palestinian chieftains (about 2000 B.C.). See Shalom Spiegel's article, "Noah, Daniel and Job" in *Louis Ginsberg's Jubilee Volume* (New York, 1945), pp. 305-355.

3. According to the Talmudic view (quoted in Dr. Victor E. Reichert's *Job* [The Soncino Press, 1946], p. 223), Job shows "the virtue of resignation." Moses Buttenwieser (*The Book of Job* [New York, 1925]) sees the Book as teaching that finite man "cannot fathom the infinite wisdom of God, or comprehend the mystery of his Rule."

Carl Jung (*Answer to Job* [London, 1954]) follows the traditional view that Job is guiltless. But he makes two startlingly new points: Job finally recognizes that Yahweh is an amoral, antinomical God who is impervious to moral considerations. However, Jung argues that, in the end, Yahweh becomes conscious that the victim, Job, stands morally higher than God, his victimizer. To catch up with man, Yahweh has to become human and regenerate himself. This intention, according to Jung, is fulfilled in Christ's life and sufferings. The basis for Jung's diatribe against Yahweh is his disparagement of the Father Imago, primarily representing Power, in favor of the compassionate Mother Imago.

4. The "Babylonian Job" accepts God's ways as unfathomable, asking "How can mortals learn the way of a God?"

5. *Book of Job* (New York, 1946).

6. All quotations follow the King James version.

7. Jastrow (*The Book of Job*) not only denies any connection between the defiant and the resigned Job, but sees none between the sympathetic Friends and their later harsh judgments of Job, and none between the God of the Prologue and the God in the discussions. Yahweh's speeches are said to be independent compositions which have no bearing on the central theme.

8. For an elaboration of this historical element, see William Irwin and H. and H. A. Frankfort in *The Intellectual Adventure of Ancient Man*.

9. Sinai, where the law was given, is encircled by the desert. From here, the Jews wandered to Kadesh, in the wilderness of Zin. (See Jack Finegan, *Light from the Ancient East* [Princeton, 1946].) W. F. Albright denies a fixed nomadic tradition in early Israel, arguing that mass nomadic movements were not possible because the desert would not sustain them. (*Archaelogy and the Religion of Israel* [Baltimore, 1942]). On the other hand, Th. H. Robinson argues for their nomadic ancestry and W. O. E. Oesterley holds that the Feast of Passover

was originally a nomadic Moon-festival. (See S. H. Hooke, *Myth and Ritual* [London, 1933].) Theodor Gaster (*Thespis* [New York, 1950]) refers to frequent allusions in the Old Testament to the seasonal ritual and to the detailed description in the Mishnah of an elaborate rain-making ceremony. Yet, fertility rites found no central place since the uncertain life of an exiled people offered no basis for feeling a bond between nature and man. Indeed, there are no nature myths in the Hebrew tradition. "Those who served Yahweh must forego the richness, the fulfilment, and the consolation of a life which moves in tune with the great rhythms of earth and sky." H. and H. A. Frankfort, *Ancient Man*, pp. 343 ff.

10. Prior to the time of Job, Hebrew theology was laden with elements of Babylonic mythology where the Earth-Mother is the creatress of mankind. Even later, when the Semitic myth identifies Yahweh with the Rain-and Thunder-God, Adad, he is still associated with the Canaanitish Mother-Goddess Ash-tart-Anat. (See S. H. Langdon, *The Mythology of All Races*). Isolated instances of the incest theme remain: the cabalistic story of the Messiah as issuing from incest; Noah and his daughters; Judah and Tamar. What may be the reasons for the minor role of incest in the Hebrew myth? Was the taboo "naturally" adhered to because of the need to keep intact the unity of a people which was threatened in many other ways? Is the God-Father self-sufficient because all-containing? Does his spirituality forbid his mingling with an "earth-"mother? Is this why woman is pictured as the temptress (Lillith, Delilah, Job's wife)? To be sure, the "female" element of love is not altogether absent in the Hebrew Father-God. Hosea (11) writes of God's "tenderness." The Psalmist speaks of his "tender mercies" (103, 145). The element of comfort is more prominent in modern Jewish writers, notably Franz Werfel and Sholem Asch.

11. This point is developed by Ernst Cassirer in his essay "Judaism and the Modern Political Myths," *Contemporary Jewish Record* (April, 1944).

12. Cf. my study, *Thomas Mann's Joseph Story. An Interpretation* (New York, 1938).

13. Jastrow translates: "When my guests washed in cream."

14. The point is strengthened by the fact that the text uses various terms for the Lord. According to Kissane (*Book of Job*): "In the Prologue, Job, his wife, the messenger and Satan use the name *Elohim* for God; in the Dialogue the names used are *El* (55), *Eloah* (41), *Shaddai* (31), and *Elohim* (6), all of which were employed in the patriarchal age. The writer himself, in the narrative passages, uses the name Yahweh, which indicates that he is an Israel-ite." *Elohim* (Job's term) is used at times in the sense of "Judge," a name not reserved for the Lord, as when God tells Moses to speak to Aaron in his office as *Elohim*. One should also note the Lord's active role in Job's affliction. In Goethe's *Faust*, the Lord mentions Faust only after Mephisto (who is differentiated from "the true sons" of God) speaks derogatorily of man. In the Book, the Satan (who is included among the sons of God) does not censure man,

but speaks of "going to and fro in the earth." Thereupon, the Lord challengingly brings up the case of Job, stating that he is perfect and upright. Thus, it is the Lord who provokes the Satan towards proposing that Job be tried, and sets up the situation which leads to the massacre of his household and to his plight.

15. Kissane cites various authorities for holding that the lines "I will teach you by the hand of God. . . . This is the portion of a wicked man with God" are spoken by Bildad in his third speech where he is "quoting Job's words spoken to those who, in former days, were perplexed by the prosperity of the wicked. Job's earlier views coincided with those of his Friends, which he now so vehemently rejects." *Book of Job*, pp. 166, 163.

16. Gersonides and Jastrow say flatly that they are not Hebrews.

17. Job does not begin his lament until the Friends appear. Their unspoken acceptance of his punishment seems to rouse Job against them.

18. In chapter 10, Job distinguishes between "wickedness," which is deliberate flouting of God's will, and "sin," which is due to ignorance. Kissane calls attention to a similar distinction made in Numbers, the Psalms, Leviticus and elsewhere between "sins of ignorance," "errors," or "hidden sins" and "sins committed with a high hand." In the Prologue, Job speaks of the possibility that his sons may have cursed God "in their hearts."

19. Jastrow states that this line must be translated as: "Though he slay me, I tremble not." This makes Job's challenge even stronger.

20. In chapters 36 and 37, Job characterizes the nature of God in the way in which Yahweh defines himself at the end.

21. According to Kissane, only a few critics, Budde and Cornill in particular, maintain that Elihu's chief contribution is "that suffering is an effective instrument in God's hands, leading man to the knowledge of himself, of the evil propensities within him." *Book of Job*, p. xxxix.

22. The text is somewhat corrupt here, but according to Kissane, a literal translation reads: "And He hath enticed thee from . . . the comfort of the table full of fatness." It also suggests that Job has been partial to the wealthy and powerful. *Book of Job*, pp. 247, 248.

23. *The Book of Job* (New York, 1918). Kallen interprets Yahweh as analogous to the *deus ex machina* of Euripides and argues that only "moral indifference can be genuine justice" and that Job is comforted by Yahweh's very indifference. Kallen's view of Yahweh fits the earlier conception of the Hebrew God as a nature power, that is, neutral to moral issues. A different analogy to Euripides could be drawn in that he too presented revolutionary characters who insist on their personal choice. However, whereas his *deus ex machina* device was meant to disparage the Greek god, the author of the Book treats Yahweh with unreserved awe.

24. Cf. Northrup Frye, *Fearful Symmetry, A Study of William Blake* (Boston, 1962).

25. In the Greek version, Yahweh says to Job:

> "Despise not my chastisement!
> Dost thou think I would have revealed myself
> Were it not that thou mightest be proven righteous!"

(Quoted by Moses Buttenwieser, *The Book of Job*, p. 62.) Albright suggests that the Hebrew God is both "jealous" over his sovereignty, as well as "zealous" for the well-being of his people. The dual meaning is also present in the German word *Eifer-sucht*.

26. *Slavery in the Ancient Near East* (New York, 1949).

27. It is to be noted that the main "action" of the Book consists of "talking." These talks are between Job and only one character at a time— one of the Friends, or Elihu or Yahweh. When he is not responding to the arguments of the Friends, Job lapses into ruminations about his past.

28. Dr. Reichert points out that the word "reins" is "metaphorical for the most sensitive and vital part of the body." Job also speaks of God's "rod" (9) which terrifies him, of God, the "lion" who hunts him.

29. *The Myth of the Eternal Return* (New York, 1954), p. 104.

30. According to S. R. Driver (*An Introduction to the Literature of the Old Testament* [New York, 1903], p. 418), "Redeemer" is used to denote "a deliverer, not from sin, but from affliction and wrong not due to him."

31. *True Humanism* (2d ed.; New York, 1954); *Freedom in the Modern World* (London, 1935).

Greek Mythopoesis
The Blessed Crime
Aeschylus, Sophocles, Euripides

ACCORDING TO HESIOD's version of the first or Golden Age of Man, men lived "without cares or labor . . . never growing old, dancing and laughing much; death to them was no more terrible than sleep. They are all gone now, but their spirits survive as happy genii" (Transliteration by Robert Graves). And in Plato's *Timaeus*, Critias states that when Solon was in Egypt, one of its priests told him:

> You do not know that there formerly dwelt in your land the fairest and no-blest race of men which ever lived, and that you and your whole city are descended from a small seed or remnant of them which survived. . . . For there was a time, Solon, before the great deluge of all, when the city which now is Athens was first in war and in every way the best governed of all cities, and is said to have performed the noblest deeds and to have had the fairest constitution of any of which tradition tells, under the face of heaven . . . excelled all mankind in all virtue . . . preserved from slavery those who were not yet subjugated, and generously liberated all the rest of us.

Freud speculates (*Moses and Monotheism*) that Greek mythology drew on the memory of an ancient glory, possibly that of Minoan and Mycenean culture.[1] With the development of a mercantile and monetary economy, based on a growing slave market, the memory of this splendor was growing dim. It is at this point that the idea of Greece's golden age is redeemed symbolically in its mythopoesis.

The mythic view was native to the Greeks. They viewed nearly everything on a mythic plane—from flies and asses to men and gods, from the seasonal cycle to human birth and death, from the idea of number, space and time to religion, philosophy and the arts. Poetry, in particular, was mytho-poesis to them (Werner Jaeger points out that the Greeks had no word which exactly corresponds to "literature.") The poet was a "maker," combining the functions of teacher, prophet and interpreter. His art was part of *Paideia,* and *Paideia* encompassed the whole of man in his varied relations. The unitary quality of the myth fitted the compact Greek world which was then the anchor of civilization. And, it fitted in with the *polis* which embraced the citizen's entire activity, integrating his politics, art, science, philosophy and religion.

The Greek myth, like all myths, had a historic-social function. George Thomson and Henri Frankfort have shown that it was used to further social-political interests and for that reason the tyrant Peisistratos gave the mythic rituals official sanction, instituting them as part of the Dionysian festival. In George Thomson's formulation, the Achean Olympus "was the mythical mirror of social reality."[2] His *Studies in Ancient Greek Society* presents interesting material on the social genesis of the Moirai. These supreme powers (they also rule over Zeus) represented social authority in everything except their immortality. Thomson traces the original meaning of the Moirai to "portion" of wealth, or "division" of labor, representing man's "share" and "lot" or fate. In Plato, they are associated with the "spinners" of destiny— Clotho, Atropos, Lachesis—who spin man's lot at the moment of his birth.

Like the spinners of destiny, the Moirai are female powers, and probably connected with mother-right in Indo-European pre-history. As such, they have a democratic, egalitarian function and the "lot" used to guarantee equal, impartial distribution. The Moirai, Thomson writes

> stood for the authority of ancestral custom, which determined each man's birthright . . . . [They] originated as symbols of the economic and social functions of primitive communism—the sharing of game, the sharing of booty, the sharing of land, the sharing of labour between the clans; that is to say, they grew out of the neolithic mother-goddesses, who, emanating from the female elders of the matriarchal clan, symbolized the collective authority of countless generations of ancestresses. (*Ancient Greek Society,* pp. 337, 339.)

When Greece passed from tribalism to the city state and its slave system, the Moirai were displaced or joined by Ananke (Necessity) which was to reconcile men with slavery.[3]

The period of the merchant princes also witnessed the emergence of political democracy.[4] Its effect appears in Aeschylus where the tyrant Zeus of *Prometheus Bound* becomes a just ruler in the fragments of *Prometheus Unbound* and the stern Erinyes of the Oresteia are transformed into the kindly Eumenides. Summary vengeance is abandoned for trial by jury, which considers not the act alone, but the individual's motive and his subsequent change of heart. Orestes tells the Furies:

> . . . Look, how the stain of blood
> Is dull upon mine hand and wastes away,
> And laved and lost therewith is the deep curse
> Of matricide . . .
> How oft since then among my fellow-men
> I stood and brought no curse. Time cleanses all—
> Time, the coeval of all things that are.[5]

Apollo and Dionysus

Winckelmann characterized Hellenic art as exhibiting "noble simplicity and quiet grandeur" (*edle Einfalt und stille Grösse*). Erwin Rohde and Friedrich Nietzsche saw this as the "Apollonian" face of Greece, standing for restraint and reason, for equilibrium and order.[6] This aspect has been stressed in our own day by Edith Hamilton who identifies it with the Western temper.

In *The Greeks and the Irrational*, E.R. Dodds has modified and corrected this sharp contrast between the "rational" religion of Apollo and the "irrational" religion of Dionysus. According to Dodds, there is evidence in the *Iliad* that Apollo was originally an Asiatic and that there were shamanistic elements in the cult of Apollo.[7] In his *Dionysus, Myth and Cult*, Walter F. Otto states that the worship of Dionysus was older than that of Apollo but adds that their two worlds coexisted and were interdependent.[8] Dodds tends to support this approach, pointing out that Apollo was simultaneously the patron of scientific medicine and of healing by prayer and incantation. Each, he writes, ministered "in his own way to the anxieties characterized by a guilt culture. Apollo promised security . . . Dionysus offered freedom. . . ." (*The Greeks and the Irrational*, p. 76).

While it is therefore inaccurate to use "Apollo" and "Dionysus" as representing clearly demarcated historic stages or as sharply divided categories, they might be employed as *symbolic* representations in the relative weight traditionally accorded to Western "Apollonian" light and reason in contrast to Eastern "Dionysian" unrestraint and ecstasy.

In any case, the Hellenic period did attempt to cleanse the myth of primitive magic and Oriental religious mystery, to naturalize it by science and humanize it by ethics. For Protagoras, *man*, not God, was the measure of things. The authority of the priesthood was replaced by the authority of a critical dialectic.[9] With the pre-Socratic philosophers, Moira and Nemesis became Substance and Causality which were subject to scientific analysis. Socrates' basic assumption was that truth and justice can be found by critical examination. Ernst Cassirer has shown that for Greek philosophy, the same laws govern nature (Kosmos), logic (Logos) and morals (Dike). Its substantive thinking converted chronological beginnings into philosophic priorities, the mythic "once upon a time" into first principles. Where the Hindu Brahma saw only the ephemeralness of existence, Greek substance emphasized *the law* in change. And the Greek thinkers sought to find this law in philosophy, physics and art.[10]

This principle is applied in Aristotle's *Poetics.* Poetry, it states, is more philosophical than history in that the poet "imitates" an action which is not unique, but has archetypal representation. Similarly, art effects a "catharsis" by revealing that the outcome was not an accident of history, but has the character of universal necessity: the hero's fall is not due to "vice or depravity," but to "frailty" (*hamartia* or faulty insight), that is, to inadequate knowledge of the order of things. Thus, we may interpret Aristotle as saying that knowledge of necesssity purges man of pity (which comes from feeling that the unfortunate event was avoidable) and of fear (which comes from not knowing the nature and source of the threat).

The principle was also applied in the Greek theatre, which fused all the arts—drama, acting, dancing, poetry, designing, song. It presented myths, that is, stories which were universally known, performed in an open amphitheatre large enough to hold the entire Athenian citizenry. The actors wore masks indicating their representation of generic characters ("the King," "Priest," etc.) and the chorus summed up the inevitability of the action in a "doxology." Inevitability was further indicated by the use of the "analytical technique," or what Schiller called "tragic analysis," in which the tragic ending was determined by events preceding the opening of the dramatic action.

However, the necessity of the action did not preclude individual choice and responsibility. As *an art*, Greek tragedy presented the law of Moira through particular individuals and events. In Gerhard Nebel's formulation, the infinite was given finite form and the tragic process became "the definition of the indefinite." Aeschylus, Sophocles and Euripides dealt more or less with the same mythic stories involving Oedipus, Electra, Antigone, Orestes, etc. Yet, each dramatist gave the various figures differentiating characteristics, which provided the basis for the shift from tribal to individual guilt, and from "Fate" to human choice. And, as we shall see in discussing Aeschylus' Prometheia, the hero was not only fated to accept; he was also fated to rebel.

The union of necessity and freedom brought a reorientation in the function of the oracle. The mythic curse and blessing still operated; but to be effective, they had to be renewed by *an individual act* of *hybris* or *arete*. The oracle did not simply pronounce an inevitable happening. It became *a warning voice*, calling attention to *the tendencies* of an individual or a family to perform certain acts. The fate of Odysseus and his companions is not sealed in the *Odyssey*. They are warned by the oracle that *if* they slay the cattle of Helios, they will perish. This "if" corresponds to the hypothesis in science, pointing to elements in a character which predispose him to act in a certain way. And, *knowledge of his predisposition* gives the individual an opportunity to provide against such acting out.[11]

The Greeks were the first to see the dialectic relationship between necessity and freedom. It is clearly stated in Plato's myth of Er at the end of *The Republic* (Book X): The distaff of Necessity spins around with uniform velocity, accompanied by the song of sirens producing a single harmony. The Fates chant to their music—Lachesis sounds the events of the past, Clotho of the present, Atropos of the future. And Lachesis, the daughter of Necessity, declares that man's destiny is not allotted, but shall be *chosen* by him: "The responsibility lies with the chooser. Heaven is guiltless." And Socrates continues:

> and for this reason, above all others, it is the duty of each of us diligently to investigate and study . . . that science which may haply enable a man to learn and discover . . . as to be able to discriminate between a good and an evil life, and according to his means to choose, always and everywhere, that better life, by carefully calculating the influence which the things just mentioned, in combination or in separation, have upon real excellence of life.

This means that *man can choose his fate*, or as Heraclitus put it: "Man's character is his fate." When Clytemnestra tries to shift the blame for the murder of Agamemnon "to the old Avenger," the Chorus indignantly exclaims:

> Thou guiltless of this murder, thou!
> Who dares such thought avow?

Dionysus

Greek culture had emerged from primitive and Eastern civilizations which left their mark. The traditional picture of Greek serenity ignores the fact that, except for the relative tranquility in the brief cultural flowering between the Persian and Peloponnesian wars, Greek history is filled with war and civil war. These historic incidences help explain why the Greeks also felt the power of an older, primitive god, Dionysus.

In *The Birth of Tragedy*, Nietzsche stressed the Dionysian *Rausch* or ecstasy in Greek drama. In our own time, Jane Harrison has analyzed Greek tragedy in terms of the primitive ritual, and George Thomson has found remnants of totemism in Greek history. This suggests that the Greeks *needed* Apollonian form to control the rage of their Dionysianism, that their stress on law was to meet the threat of disorder and unrestraint.

Greek tragedy arose, not out of the Apollonian, but out of the ancient Dionysian cult. Where Apollo was associated with light and with the aristocratic patriarchal Olympus, Dionysus derived from the dark Chthonic underground and from the democratic matriarchy.[12]

The worship of Dionysus had the character of rapture, associated with his companions, the raging maenads.[13] To be sure, the function of the ritual was to promote fertility of the soil.[14] However, its temper was one of rebellious defiance. In Euripides' *The Bacchae*, Dionysianism is the underground storm which breaks up the stratified intellectual civilization of Pentheus.[15]

Jane Harrison (*Ancient Art and Ritual* [London, 1913]) argues that the art of tragedy has its origin in the ritual vestiges of tribal initiation and is connected with the seasonal ritual. Applied to mythopoesis, this approach can be helpful in directing attention to the *literary* ritual, that is, to the dramatic language, form and structure through which the myth is humanized. However, the limitation of the seasonal approach lies in its failure to consider the distinction between the year-god and the human personality. For primitives, almost wholly at the mercy of natural powers, the seasonal rhythm was the pattern for life of man as well. Mythopoesis breaks with this static rhythm. It connotes that by the use of knowledge and the tool, man can control the forces of nature and thus become a *culture* hero. Just as Hellenic art moved from rigid archaic figures towards the human body, so it reshaped the seasonal rhythm of the old myth into the human act. To give two brief examples: The Oresteia begins with the death of the king and queen and the mangling of Orestes. It ends with a "higher" replacement of the old king and queen (by Apollo and Athena) and the rebirth of Orestes. This process is foretold by the Chorus in *Agamemnon*:

> List! on my soul breathes yet a harmony,
> From realms of ageless powers, and strong to save!

and by Clytemnestra:

> As saith the adage, *From the womb of Night*
> *Spring forth, with promise fair, the young child Light.*

Similarly, Sophocles' Oedipus tragedy begins with the winter scourge of Thebes and closes with the promise of peace and security.

The development of the chorus also indicates the emergence of this element. Through music and the dance, the chorus expressed that which was hidden, was supra-individual and supra-rational. In Greek tragedy, the chorus generally (though not always) consists of the most distinguished members of the community, but is not the sole spokesman, as it may have been in its beginnings. For, now we get "the second actor," the leader of the chorus. With the introduction of the mythic hero, we get the condition for conflict, or *drama* proper.

The Dionysian myth unleashed the savagery of primitive subterranean forces. At the same time, its very frenzy served, as Dodds points out, to bring psychological release: "it purged the individual of those infectious irrational impulses . . . it relieved them by providing them with a ritual outlet." Thus, in Euripides' *The Bacchae*, Dionysus is "the cause of madness and the liberator from madness." The Apollonian attempted to control these powers by form and order. In Greek mythopoesis as a whole, "Dionysus" and "Apollo" interacted in a dialectic rhythm.

In his study of the Doric Temple, Max Raphael shows that the equilibrium of the Doric column is not achieved by the "compromise" of the Roman arch, but by tension and stress, producing a delicate balance between the horizontal and the vertical.[16] In Greek mythopoesis, harmony is likewise won by strain and strife. Greek cosmogony is crowded with patricide and incest. With the help of his mother, Gaia, Kronos castrates his father, Uranus, and later swallows his own children; Zeus who is saved by Rhea's ruse, dethrones his father, Kronos, and is in turn challenged by Prometheus; Oedipus kills his father, and Orestes, his mother. Equally pervasive is the theme of incest between mother-sister and son-brother, as between Orthos and Echidna, Oedipus and Jocasta, Gaia-Rhea and Uranus-Cronos. Fratricide and infanticide appear in the stories of Atreus, who slays his brother's children and serves them to their father at a banquet; Medea kills her sons; Agamemnon sacrifices his daughter; Oedipus is exposed on the mountain by his parents. It is to be noted that in the mythological stories such acts are committed with full knowledge, whereas in mythopoesis, they are covered and take on a more symbolic character. As noted, here *a*

73

character becomes heroic only after he has violated some primary ta-boo. Nietzsche refers to the Persian belief that a wise man is born of incest, and the same idea is found in the Hebrew legend of the Messiah. Thomas Mann's *The Holy Sinner* treats the medieval story of Gregory, who is born of the union between a brother and sister, later marries his mother, and subsequently is elected Pope. Infringement of established rules is a condition for the development of the heroic in mythopoesis.

Greek mythic thought exhibits the same dialectic principle with respect to the relation between the aristocratic and democratic forms and between the matriarchic and patriarchic values. Historically, Greece was developing towards the patriarchy; yet, its memory of the matriarchy was never wholly submerged.[17] The most dramatic example of this principle of conservation is Athena: In Homer, she is Odysseus' guiding hand and counters the wrath of Poseidon. And, while she argues for the greater importance of the father in *The Eumenides*, it is *her* vote which is decisive in acquitting Orestes.[18] The crucial role of the mother-goddess is later revived in Christianity and Greek orthodoxy.

The entrance to Apollo's temple at Delphi bore the inscriptions: "Nothing too much" and "Know thyself." The first summed up the ideal of moderation (*sophrosyne*), echoing the argument of Plato's *Republic* that justice is the harmonious interplay among the various powers in the individual and society. The second inscription, "Know thyself," pointed to man's need to recognize the tendency of one or the other of his powers to overreach itself. For the Greeks, beauty also lay in the harmonious proportions of the *human* body, in contrast to the rigid forms of animals, griffins, demons of the archaic period. Its keynote of *flexibility* was connected with the political aim of the *polis*. The Oresteia ends with Athena's chant that

> . . . gracious powers on earth
> Henceforth be seen to bless the life of men.

This prayer was briefly voiced during the Periclean period. But soon, the slave system and the imperialism of the city state brought conflict of authorities. "The middle way" which is "dearest unto God," of which the Chorus sings in *The Eumenides*, was being disturbed. By the time of Euripides the "Apollonian" was defied and the "Dionysian" came to the fore.

AESCHYLUS' PROMETHEIA

The legend of the fire-bringer belongs to the earliest folk-traditions. In primitive stories, fire is brought by an animal or wrested by a giant. In Greek mythology, it is stolen by a titan.

According to Hesiod, Uranus named those who tended to "over-reach" themselves "titans." Fire has been connected with the titanic because of its elemental savagery and because it too "overreaches" itself.[19] In Greek thought, fire was considered an ambivalent force. Heraclitus called it the Logos or basic Substance whose "life" depended on the very material it destroyed.[20] Pliny saw it as an active agent in the work of human ingenuity:

> Fire takes in sand and gives back, now glass, now silver, now minium, now various kinds of lead, now pigments, now medicines. By fire stones are melted into bronze, by fire iron is made and mastered, by fire gold is produced, by fire that stone is calcined which, in the form of cement, holds our houses over our heads. (*Natural History*, xxxvi)

Pliny concluded by calling fire a "measureless and implacable portion of nature," asking whether it should rightly be called "destroyer or creator."

According to legend, Aeschylus was involved in the Eleusian and Dionysian mystery rites. Of the Greek tragedians, he stood closest to the primitive and religious mode and his style shows greatest restlessness. The action of *The Persians* is dominated by mythic powers in whose hands man is an object of their passion and will.

The central character of *Prometheus Bound* is a titan, surrounded by figures who are either allegorical, such as Power and Force, or divine missionaries, such as Hephaesthus, Oceanus and Hermes. (Io is a human character; but her story is secondary to the main theme.) The *Oresteia* is dominated by the Tantalus curse of ancestral guilt and retribution.

Despite these features, it is misleading to interpret Aeschylus as a religious mythicist. For, as we shall see, his Prometheia relies less on supernatural than on human power.

Aeschylus' Prometheus is the first culture hero in mythopoesis. He develops from an intransigent rebel to a hero who is mindful of the powers above (Zeus), the powers below (Themis, his Earth-Mother), and of his ties with man. In the older versions, Prometheus was doomed to defeat.[21] Hesiod saw in Prometheus' rebellious action the cause of human toil. In other accounts, it brought evil into the world, such as the box of Pandora which let sorrow, sickness and labor loose in the world. Aeschylus recast these ancient legends in naturalistic, human terms, transforming Moira into a character to whom Zeus too is subject (even he will be dethroned "by his own folly").[22]

In *The Birth of Tragedy*, Nietzsche stated that the core of the Prometheus myth is the necessity of the titanic individual to commit a crime. But only in the Greek version is the crime directed against a god. And, where Job is punished for what he neglected to do and Oedipus for what he did without conscious knowledge, Prometheus suffers from an active crime, committed with full awareness. He tells the Leader of the Chorus: "With open eyes, with willing mind, I erred." He knows what he did and is ready to face the consequences. In Oriental mythology, the past determines the future. In Aeschylus' Prometheia, knowledge of the future determines the present.

Act I: Harmony with Parental Authority

The Prometheia refers to an initial and to a final state of harmony between Prometheus and Zeus:

> Often to me my mother Themis (or call her Earth, for many names she hath, being one) had foretold in oracles what was to be, with warning that not by might or brutal force should victory come, but by guile alone.

When the titans tried to make themselves "lords by force," Prometheus supported Zeus in his struggle with them. But later Zeus became a tyrant who, as the Chorus proclaims, "unlawfully rules," wanting to blot out the whole human race.

"Prometheus" means "fore-knowledge." From his mother, he knows the future, knows the secret which conditions Zeus' fate—that if Zeus marries Thetis, he will be dethroned. It is this "if" which constitutes the dramatic conflict of Aeschylus' poetic version. The gloom of the opening setting in which Prometheus is bound to the rocks in a winter-bitten gorge where no human voice can reach him, where he is to waste his strength in ceaseless lamentations, is lightened by Prometheus' fore-knowledge of ultimate reconciliation.

The drama opens with the hero set out, bound "in never-yielding fetters." Yet, from the beginning, there is promise of rescue by natural and human powers. In his opening chant, Prometheus invokes, not magical forces, but the elements: the "air divine," the "swift-winged winds," the "river-fountains," the "ocean waves," his "mother earth" and the "all-discerning orb o' the sun." Moreover, he has the sympathy of all the characters in the drama, with the exception of Zeus' lackeys: Power, Force, and Hermes. Even Hephaesthus, who uses his art of fire to bind Prometheus, does this against his will and he groans for the titan's pangs.

Act II: The Crime—Freedom from Fear

Prometheus displayed extraordinary courage in stealing fire from Zeus. Yet, as he is riveted to the rocks, he is gripped by fear "in whatever approaches." But, as he *speaks* of his act and becomes aware of its character, he regains courage. Aeschylus transposes the gift of fire into the psychic power of consciousness that removes the old fear of dark authorities.

Before he gave mankind "understanding and a portion of reason," Prometheus tells the Leader of the Chorus, the people were in a womb-like state:

> like children . . . seeing they saw not, and hearing they understood not, but like as shapes in a dream they wrought all the days of their life in confusion . . . like the little ants they dwelt underground in the sunless depth of caverns.

"Understanding" and "a portion of reason" are more than reflective thought. By *sophia* or "wisdom," the Greeks understood *practical application* of knowledge. Prometheus taught man "to discern the seasons by the rising and the obscure setting of the stars." He gave them understanding of their rituals, "of the altar-flames that before were meaningless." No longer would they need to propitiate a capricious "seasonal god," but could predict and provide for the workings of the natural phenomena. He revealed the technique for coping with disease, taught the use of "the secret treasures of the earth . . . copper, iron, silver, gold." In this context, fire becomes a technical-social lever for freeing human power, *a tool* which raises man from the animal towards the human stage.

Prometheus' "reason" went beyond the rational meaning of language; he "found the subtle interpretation of words half heard or heard by chance, and of meetings by the way." He even penetrated into the realm of the unconscious as revealed in dreams:

> From dreams I first taught them to judge what should befall in waking state.

At the same time, Prometheus stressed the value of tradition: "I taught them the grouping of letters, to be a memorial and record of the past, the mistress of the arts and mother of the muses." Prometheus thus combined bold re-creation of the human heritage with piety towards its valuable residue. In sum, "all human arts are from Prometheus."

The Journey

Prometheus attempted to free man from "the disease of tyranny." Now, he himself is a titan who had once been Zeus' ally; hence, the dramatic need for introducing the story of Io, a human victim. Unlike Prometheus, Io is an innocent sacrifice, and her fate presents the case for Prometheus in more human terms than his own story.

77

Io had been Hera's priestess in Argos and she became the double target of Zeus' desire and of Hera's jealousy. Stung by the gadfly, pursued by the spectre of Argus, she is driven "weary and famished," over land and water. The physical journey of "the wandering virgin of sorrows" is the counterpart of Prometheus' psychic journey.

Prometheus is punished for having committed a deliberate act; Io is punished although she seems to have done no wrong. Yet, she too is not free from guilt. Aeschylus recreates the legend to suggest that Io "wished" Zeus' passion for her. Before the God's desire is made manifest, Io is stirred by "Wild, perturbing wonders," and dreams that she is being exhorted to satisfy Zeus' yearning for her:

> For always in the drowsy hours of night
> I, sleeping in my virgin chambers, saw
> Strange visitations pass, and as they passed
> Each smiled and whispered: O sweet-favored girl,
> Why cherish long thy maiden loneliness,
> When love celestial calleth? Fair art thou,
> And thronèd Zeus, heart-smitten with desire,
> Yearns from his heaven to woo thee. Nay, sweet child,
> Disdain him not.

This is Io's "oracle," a warning of her desires. Here, again punishment fits the crime. As the fire-bringer is fettered by the fire-god Hephaesthus, so the passion of Io's dreams results in the "madness" which smites her brain "as a fire," and her animal desires are requited by her transformation into a heifer.[23]

The case for Prometheus is also made by the contrasting figure of Hermes who attempts to persuade Prometheus to divulge the secret knowledge of the conditions under which Zeus might be dethroned. He argues that there is no "profit" in his stand, and threatens that his body will be encased in the fiery rock and that Zeus' ravening eagle will feast on his liver. But Prometheus declares: "There is no fear in me," and that there is

> no torment or contrivance in the power of Zeus to wring this utterance from me, except these bonds are loosened.

He will not grow "woman-hearted . . . It is not in my nature." He tells Hermes: "I will not barter my hard lot for your menial service."

In Aeschylus' poetic version, Prometheus is punished not merely because he gave fire to man. (Conceivably, Zeus might recover, or mankind might lose the material substance of fire.) What Prometheus bequeathed is the fire of revolt, the spirit of defiance, that is, man's freedom from fear. Once set free, this power can never be lost, and with it ultimate victory over tyrannical authority is certain. In the magnificent lines of Prometheus' final chant, he sings of freedom as self-determination:

> Ay, let the lightning be launched
> With curled and forked flame
> On my head; let the air confounded
> Shudder with thunderous peals
> And convulsion of raging winds;
> Let tempests beat on the earth
> Till her rooted foundations tremble;
> The boisterous surge of the sea
> Leap up to mingle its crest
> With the stars eclipsed in their orbs;
> Let the whirling blasts of Necessity
> Seize on my body and hurl it
> Down to the darkness of Tartarus,—
> Yet all he shall not destroy me!

Here, Job's implicit insistence on self-determination is made explicit by Prometheus.

The Chorus approximates the people who shelter the hero. "Fear nothing" are the first words of the Chorus, and it goes on to assure Prometheus that the peoples of East and West are with him:

> Lo, all the land groans aloud;
> And the people that dwell in the West
> Lament for thy time-honored reign
> And the sway of thy kindred, Prometheus;
> And they who have builded their homes
> In holy Asia to the wail
> Of thine anguish lament.

The sympathy of the Chorus is for the plight of Prometheus, but his defiance frightens it. The Leader of the Chorus even advises him to "Abandon vaunting pride and seek wise counsel." Still, after he and Io have stated their case, the Chorus identifies itself with his stand:

> Better I deem it to suffer
> Whate'er he endures; for traitors
> My soul abhorreth, their shame
> I spew from my heart as a pest.

When, at the close of the drama, Prometheus is hurled down, the Chorus sinks with him, chooses to share his fate.

Hybris

Emerson called Prometheus the Jesus of Greek mythology, in that he freely chose to sacrifice himself because of his love for man. (An ancient vase painting shows Prometheus with pillars piercing his chest.) Yet, like all mythopoeic heroes, Prometheus is guilty. His mythic guilt lies in the titan's tendency to overreach himself. Above all, it lies in his uncompromising attitude, in being as intransigent as his adversary, Zeus. A more subtle aspect of overreaching consists in the fact that Prometheus never asks himself whether mankind is ready to use fire for its own good. The point is made by the Chorus:

> Their weakness hast thou not discovered,
> Their feeble blindness wherein
> Like dreaming shadows they move?

The Erinyes similarly accuse Apollo in *The Eumenides*:

> For thou too heinous a respect didst hold
> Of man, too little heed of powers divine

As a whole, the work of Aeschylus celebrates freedom of will. The Leader of the Chorus urges Electra and Orestes in *The Choephori*: "Take fortune by the hand and work thy will." And, in *The Eumenides*, Apollo encourages Orestes:

> Have thou too heed, nor let thy fear prevail
> Above thy will.

But the Chorus also sees the threat in its misuse. It declares in *The Choephori* that of all the things to fear the greatest is "the aweless soul" in man. That is, Aeschylus' drama sees the need to control the rebellious temper. Io's fire spends itself in her wanderings, Prometheus becomes a culture hero by curbing his fiery demon. Aeschylus affirms freedom of will, and at the same time points to its limiting determinants.

The mother of Prometheus seems to bear no relation to his stealing the fire. But it is through her that he finds the strength to confront Zeus' wrath. From her, he knows the secret by which Zeus can lose honor and throne, and that, in the end, Zeus will implore him for his friendship.

In his essay on the Prometheus legend, "The Acquisition of Power over Fire," Freud points out that primitive man

could not but regard fire as something analogous to the passion of love. . . . The warmth radiated by fire evokes the same kind of glow as accompanies the state of sexual excitation, and the form and motion of the flame suggest the phallus in action.

In stealing Zeus' fire, Prometheus took the secret of his power. (In one version, Prometheus secretly made his way to the Olympian hearth and hid the flame in a hollowed-out stalk.)[24]

In mythology, the gratification of sensual desires is a special privilege of the gods, in particular of Zeus, who possesses unlimited sexual power. Zeus punished Prometheus by binding him to a rock where a vulture fed on his liver. Freud states that in ancient times the liver was regarded as the seat of all the passions and desires. Prometheus' punishment thus fits his crime: he is reduced to infantile helplessness and his organ of desire is eaten away.

By assigning a *cultural* use for fire, Prometheus urged renunciation of instinctual desires. This aroused resentment in instinct-ridden humanity, which could therefore welcome Zeus' retaliatory action. However, Prometheus did not keep the fire to himself, but passed it on to man. He is rewarded for this by the daily renewal of his liver. This, Freud writes, is the second reaction of primitive man to the blow struck at its instinctual life. Following the punishment of the criminal, "comes the assurance that, after all, he has done nothing irreparable."

Act III: Reconciliation

From fragments (available in Latin translation by Cicero and Accius) it may be assumed that *Prometheus Bound* was followed by *Prometheus Unbound* and *Prometheus the Fire-Bringer*. After thousands of years, Prometheus is readmitted to Olympus and he reveals his secret that Zeus can avoid his downfall by wedding Hera instead of Thetis. The two antagonists have abandoned their inflexible positions and are reconciled. As in the Book of Job, the Prometheia rejects the narrow tribal god, but reaches an understanding with a god who approximates a universal deity. The agency of change is time which "teaches all things." Prometheus is delivered after many thousands of years and Io is restored after wanderings over Europe and Asia. Here, Zeus also plays a role. In foreswearing Thetis and delivering Io from torment, Zeus contributes to Prometheus' ultimate deliverance.

Epilogue

Prometheus is rescued by Hercules, the son of Zeus' union with a mortal woman, Alcmene. That is, he is rehabilitated, not by a god, but by a god-man.[25] In turn, the deliverer must engage in his "Twelve Labors" and serve as woman-man to Omphale. Once again, the hero has the task of cleansing the stables of the rotten state.[26]

THE NUCLEUS OF MYTHOPOEIC DRAMA:
SOPHOCLES' OEDIPUS

Become who you are after you have learned it.

—Pindar

In Greek mythology, Oedipus is subject to an inexorable Moira or "Fate" which completely predetermines his acts. This approach has been carried over into the interpretation of Sophocles' Oedipus dramas. Gerhard Nebel's *Weltangst und Götterzorn* is a religious formulation of this view. Sophocles' *Oedipus* is seen as expressing the inscrutable decree of "the angry God" before whom Oedipus incurs guilt no matter what he does. His very attempts to circumvent fate only hasten its fulfilment.

A more analytical approach is that of the Cambridge School, which examines the myth in terms of its ritual. Here, the fortune of Oedipus is viewed as the ritual of the seasonal god whose dismemberment is "the winter" preceding the rejuvenation of the city he represents. In *The Idea of a Theater* (Princeton, 1949), Francis Fergusson achieves perceptive results by applying this method to Sophocles' text. Yet, Oedipus' individual choice is not shown as affecting this ritual, and his character is reduced to an "analogue" in a general tragic rhythm.

Erich Fromm's interpretation (*The Forgotten Language* [New York, 1951]) explains the Oedipus myth as marking the transition from democratic matriarchy to authoritarian patriarchy. Fromm makes a much needed contribution towards de-romanticizing the myth by suggesting its social-historic basis. But here, too, the character of Sophocles' Oedipus itself is not considered.

Now, general categories, such as the legendary curse, the seasonal rhythm and the historic scene are necessary but not sufficient conditions for explaining a character in an art-work. This chapter proposes to indicate that Sophocles' work, like all mythopoesis, shows the interplay between "the gods" (or Moira) and the individual personality.[27] A careful reading of the text bears out the Freudian thesis, at least to the extent that it reveals Oedipus' *tendencies* towards incest and patricide; finally, that Oedipus' heroic and prophetic qualities are bound up with his guilt.[28]

Like Shakesleare's *Hamlet*, Sophocles' Oedipus drama begins by focusing on the social disease. Indeed, in Sophocles, it is more than the underlying situation in the drama. As a representative and king of the state, Oedipus identifies himself with its plight and concentrates his entire effort to rid it of the burden no matter what the cost be to himself.

In this respect, the ancient Oedipus is much less concerned with his personal welfare; he feels himself more a part of his Greek *polis* than Hamlet of his Danish state.[29]

At the same time, Sophocles presents Oedipus not as an average man or as an anonymous "King," but as a personality who measures up to the Greek notion of an eminent character. The Priest of Zeus calls him "the first of men" and Oedipus refers to himself as "renowned of all." And we learn that he has *earned* his exceptional stature. Like Prometheus, Oedipus is not a speculative thinker. He is a philosopher-king whose concern is with the city and its people. In solving the riddle of the sphinx, he showed himself to be wiser than the seer Teiresias. Furthermore, he exhibited bravery at the Crossroads and in confronting the sphinx. Finally he has shown himself a successful ruler. As he had once saved the city, he is now ready to do so again regardless of the consequences to himself. Unlike Hamlet, Oedipus has already proved himself, has succeeded in replacing his predecessor as king, husband and father. He expresses no doubts as to his ability to set things right. In all this Oedipus appears as a strong individual. As such, his character is necessarily a function of his "fate."

Oedipus' Mythic Crime

From Oedipus' own account of what transpired before the plague strikes the city, we learn the following:

During a banquet at Polybus' court, Oedipus was taunted by a man "full of wine"[30] with not being the son of Polybus and Merope. The attempts of the king and queen to reassure Oedipus fail to dispel the doubts raised in his mind, especially as the story "still crept abroad with strong rumor." Thereupon, he sought clarification from the oracle. The latter did not answer his question. Instead, it "set forth other things, full of sorrow and terror and woe; even that I was fated to defile my mother's bed . . . and that I should be the slayer of the sire who begat me." Although he was still uncertain, Oedipus fled from Corinth so as to avoid contact with Polybus and Merope.

On his flight, Oedipus met a man, old enough to be his father. Although the oracle had foretold that he would kill his father, Oedipus did not stop to ask who this man was, but killed him. To be sure, Oedipus was first assaulted by the old man; still, he was able to kill not only his assailant, but "every man of them."

Oedipus next faced the sphinx. Presumably, he knew that the one who could answer its riddle would become king and be rewarded with the queen as a wife. One may then say that when Oedipus confronted the sphinx, he was offering himself as a candidate for both. And, in the queen, he met a woman who was old enough to be his mother. Yet, though the oracle had also spoken of his marrying his mother, Oedipus accepted Jocasta as his wife without inquiring into her past. Nor did he reveal anything of his own past to her or anyone else. Oedipus admits that he had heard of how the king met his death. Yet, he never mentioned to anyone the adventure in which he killed an old man (who presumably was dressed as a king).

Oedipus Brings His Birth to Light

Oedipus' patricide and incest precede the opening of the drama. The work itself unfolds the process by which Oedipus becomes aware of these acts. He gets to know himself, or, in his own words, brings "his birth to light."

When the play begins, the Eden-like peace and well-being which Oedipus brought to the city and which he himself enjoyed are gravely disturbed by drought and pestilence. There is something rotten in the state of Thebes, and its people have come to ask their ruler to rid them of their plight. Now, Oedipus knows all this. "Oh my piteous children, known, well known to me are the desires wherewith ye have come . . . So that ye rouse me not, truly, as one sunk in sleep." Indeed, he tells the Priest that he identifies himself with the disease which has seized the city: ". . . my soul mourns at once for the city, and for myself, and for thee." Oedipus has anticipated the cry for help and sent Creon to ask Phoebus by what deed or by what "word" he might deliver the town. Creon reports that Phoebus bids them banish the man who slew Laios. However, nothing is said about where the murderer is to be found, and Oedipus sets himself the task to unravel "the dim track of this old crime," in order "once more to make dark things plain." He calls on the people to help him find the slayer of Laios. In the end, however, Oedipus accomplishes the task mainly by his own efforts and questionings.

Early in the drama, Oedipus' choice of words hints at his own entanglement, of which he is as yet unaware. He declares that he will uphold Laios' cause, "even as the cause of mine own sire." He tells Creon that his effort to "dispel this taint" is not in behalf of some "far-off friend, no, but in mine own cause." Oedipus speaks of the slayer's "hidden guilt," and without any apparent reason suggests the possibility that the murderer might be "an inmate" of his own house, adding that in such a case, "I may suffer the same things which even now I called down upon others."

Further indirect confessions of Oedipus' "hidden guilt" appear in the precipitate manner he adopts as he accuses others of the crime. When Teiresias at first refuses to divulge the secret, Oedipus calls him "basest of the base . . . a scheming juggler . . . a tricky quack" and declares that he helped plot the murder. Following the blind seer's revelation, Oedipus at once turns the charge against him and Creon. Before Creon has a chance to utter a word, Oedipus calls him "the proved assassin" and demands his death. The deep irony in this situation is that Oedipus' discernment as a social seer and his ability to govern the city are at the price of blindness to his own involvements. Like Hamlet and Ahab, Oedipus shifts the guilt to the world and to others.[31]

The method by which Oedipus discovers the secret of his birth is analogous to the psychoanalytic process if we may regard Teiresias, the Herdsman, Jocasta, Creon and Theseus as aspects of Oedipus' self.

The first act in Oedipus' drama of personal unfolding is his summoning of Teiresias. The ancient blind seer knows the past and future and is said to be "most like our lord Phoebus." Teiresias was present at Oedipus' birth, and it is he who prophesies to him: "This day shall show thy birth . . ." He and the old Herdsman hold the secret of Oedipus' past and both at first resist his efforts to unravel it. When Oedipus continues to press him, Teiresias finally tells him:

> . . . *thou* art the accursed defiler of this land . . . I say that thou hast been living in unguessed shame with thy nearest kin . . .

To this, Oedipus reacts with an anger that seems irrelevant to the accusation. He merely warns Teiresias: "Dost thou think that thou shalt always speak thus without smarting?" It is as though Oedipus had not been listening. Only later, and not until Teiresias speaks of "the parents who begat thee," is Oedipus ready to *hear*. As though struck for the first time by the possibility of his involvement, he asks: "What parents? Stay . . . and who of men is my sire?" But Oedipus is not yet altogether prepared to accept the revelation of his past. He dismisses the seer in the hope that "when thou hast vanished, thou wilt vex me no more." But the past cannot be banished. Teiresias replies: "I will go when I have done mine errand, fearless of thy frown: for thou canst never destroy me!"

Jocasta is the second act in Oedipus' drama of self-recognition. If Teiresias knows the past and future, Jocasta would ignore the past as having no bearing on the future. Ferenczi calls her the pleasure principle within Oedipus. Jocasta knew, of course, about her son's ankles and should have been struck by her husband's swollen feet. And, although she noticed that Oedipus' "form was not greatly unlike" Laios', she married him without making any inquiries. (Oedipus and Jocasta seem to have entered into a kind of mutual "conspiracy" of not questioning each other about themselves). Now as the past begins to intrude upon and disturb the present, she urges Oedipus to ignore it all:

'Tis best to live at random, as one may . . .

And, as the Messenger is about to reveal Oedipus' relation to Polybus, she cries out desperately:

Regard it not . . . waste not a thought on what he said . . . 'twere idle . . . forbear this search . . . Mayst thou never come to know who thou art.

Above all, she would have him disregard the oracle's incest prophecy. It is the voice of his mother who became his wife, that is, the voice of her who carries his past over into the present, which stirs Oedipus' memory. When she mentions that Laios was killed "at a place where three highways meet," he calls out:

What restlessness of soul, lady, what tumult of the mind hath just come upon me since I heard thee speak.

At this point, he recalls his past and tells the story of his life from the time when he was taunted at the house of Polybus to his encounter at the meeting of the three highways.[32]

From this point on, the process of Oedipus' self-revelation assumes less hidden form. Attention has been called to his harsh treatment of Teiresias. Oedipus shows the same temper towards the old Herdsman who saved his life as an infant. In his attitude towards these father-figures, Oedipus is committing symbolic patricide. This "oedipal" tendency in his character is furthermore made plain in his reaction to the news that Polybus is dead. At this stage, Oedipus still regards himself as his son. He is aware of the love Polybus had for him, even suggesting that possibly the king "was killed by longing for me." We can understand that Oedipus should be relieved at the Messenger's news, for now he cannot become Polybus' slayer. But what is astounding is that Oedipus shows *only relief*. He does not utter a single word of sorrow. In his exchange with the Messenger, Oedipus merely expresses curiosity as to the cause of Polybus' death. (In passing, it should be noted that Oedipus interprets Polybus' death as possibly a fulfillment of the oracle, saying that if he was killed by longing for Oedipus, then "indeed, I should be the cause of his death.")

Following the revelation of the Messenger (another old memory), Oedipus announces: "The hour hath come that these things should be finally revealed." He brushes aside Jocasta's pleading to disregard it all as "idle." This time, Oedipus turns his character as "Tyrannos" towards bringing his "birth to light," regardless of the consequences. Following the Herdsman's disclosures, Oedipus at last beholds "the whole truth." He now realizes that he had acted blindly, that his eyes had looked without seeing.

The most dramatic instance showing that Jocasta and Oedipus are not mere objects of "Fate" or of an "angry God" are their acts of *self-punishment*. Whereas in Homer guilt is determined by the gods and even Aeschylus' Prometheus, Io and Orestes suffer mainly at the hands of heavenly or underground powers, Sophocles' Jocasta and Oedipus punish themselves. Oedipus acknowledges his guilt in words as well. This curse, he cried earlier, "was laid on me by no mouth but mine own!" To be sure, within the framework of Greek mythology, this curse is sent by some power above man:

> Apollo, friends, Apollo was he that brought my woes to pass, these my sore, sore woes.

But Oedipus adds:

> The hand that struck the eyes was none save mine, wretched that I am!

The Chorus agrees:

> These things were even as thou sayest.

Earlier, the Second Messenger declared that the ills of the house of Labdacus were "wrought not unwittingly, but of purpose. And those griefs smart most which are seen to be of our own choice." Later, he reports that as Oedipus smote his eyeballs, he uttered the following:

> No more shall ye behold such horrors as I was suffering and working! Long enough have ye looked on those whom ye ought never to have seen, failed in knowledge of those whom I yearned to know—henceforth ye shall be dark!

In these lines Oedipus recognizes that his act was at once one of *fate* and *character*, or in his words, of "suffering and working." Not only does Oedipus condemn himself; he also determines what his punishment is to be—exile from the *polis*—perhaps the severest penalty for a Greek citizen and king:

> . . . hide me somewhere beyond the land, or slay me, or cast me into the sea, where ye shall never behold me more!

Oedipus' Incest Guilt

The theme of incest is particularly prominent in Oriental legends, with patricide in the background. Sophocles' Oedipus drama is the first major literary myth in which the two themes are directly interwoven although here too incest appears as the greater crime.

In his essay on the Oedipus myth, (*The Forgotten Language*) Erich Fromm would counter Freud's interpretation by showing that the attitude toward authority, not sexual desires, is the central theme of the myth. Like Voltaire, though for different reasons, Fromm would relegate the incest-motif to a minor place. He argues that

> the myth can be understood as a symbol not of the incestuous love between mother and son but of the rebellion of the son against the authority of the father in the patriarchal family; that the marriage of Oedipus and Jocasta is only a secondary element, only one of the symbols of the victory of the son, who takes his father's place and with it all his privileges.

Fromm also stresses that "there is no indication whatsoever in the myth that Oedipus is attracted by or falls in love with Jocasta." As to this, it should be noted that generally Greek tragedy did not treat the theme of "falling in love" as a specialized activity. Love, together with beauty, goodness and truth were parts of an organic cluster making up the whole man. Furthermore, as Freud indicates, we are dealing here—more so than in *Hamlet* and *The Brothers Karamazov*—with a more suppressed and covered drive. And, as pointed out before, in attempting to answer the sphinx Oedipus applies for the queen as well, knowing that she "goes with the throne" (to use Fromm's formulation). Fromm does not explain Oedipus' unquestioning acceptance of Jocasta as his wife, despite her age, despite the prophecy of the oracle, and despite his uncertainty whether Merope was his mother. Nor does he consider the lines spoken by Jocasta to Oedipus which Freud calls "the key to the tragedy and the complement to the dream of the death of the father":

> But fear not thou touching wedlock with thy mother. Many men have so fared in dreams also: but he to whom these things are as naught bears his life most easily.[33]

Fromm would strengthen his interpretation of *Oedipus the King* by arguing that the father-son conflict is also present in *Oedipus in Colonus* (between Oedipus and his sons) and in *Antigone* (between Creon and Haemon). This conflict is present in these dramas, although it may be questioned whether the father-son opposition in *Antigone* is as much in the foreground as is the devotion Antigone exhibits towards her brother's memory. However, towards the end of the essay, Fromm modifies his thesis. Here, he states that it may be "doubtful" whether patricide or incest is dominant in *Oedipus the King*, though he still insists that the former is central in *Antigone*. He also qualifies his hypothesis that *Oedipus the King* exemplifies the victory of the partriarchal system over the matriarchal by saying that it is a "blend" of the two. But he maintains his thesis that the incest motif is secondary.

Now, the passages cited make it evident that Oedipus feels at least as guilty in having married his mother as in having killed his father. Teiresias, Creon and the others also refer to both acts as constituting Oedipus' crime. And, it is significant that Oedipus punishes only that organ with which he had beheld (as he puts it) "such horrors as I was suffering and working," with which he had "looked on those whom ye ought never to have seen . . ."—clearly pointing to his incest guilt. It is the marriage-rites that wrought "the foulest shame among men" which Oedipus bewails first and foremost:

> O marriage-rites, ye gave me birth, and when ye had brought me forth, again ye bore children to your child, ye created an incestuous kinship of fathers, brothers, sons,—brides, wives, mothers,—yea, all the foulest shame that is wrought among men!

The difficulty of Fromm's position is that it cannot explain the guilt Oedipus feels over having married his mother, a guilt which is at least as great as that over having slain his father.

Towards the end of the chapter, Fromm writes of the all-important place occupied by the Eumenides, the earth-goddesses, in the Oedipus myth. He argues that Oedipus' patricide expresses his connection with the mother-goddesses through whom he is redeemed. At the end, Oedipus finds rest in the grove of the Eumenides, that is, he is "brought back to the place he belonged, to the mothers." To reinforce his point regarding the mother-aspect of the Eumenides, Fromm draws a suggestive parallel between them and the Mothers in Goethe's *Faust*, underscoring the "dread" and "awful" aspect which is ascribed to them in both works.[34]

Fromm, however, does not consider why the sight of the Eumenides should produce dread, nor does he attempt to integrate this aspect of the Mothers with his thesis as a whole. As a matter of fact, it would seem, ironically enough, that the point Fromm makes here provides additional support for the central importance of the incest element in Sophocles' Oedipus myth. For, Oedipus' relation to the Eumenides renews—on another level—his contact with Jocasta. Indeed, the horror expressed at his daring to approach their forbidden grove is similar to that voiced at his earlier violation. That is, Oedipus' attempt to penetrate the hidden abode of the Earth-Mothers *repeats his incest* with his biologic mother. To be sure, Oedipus is now more aware of what he is doing, and readily heeds the call of the Chorus to respect "the customs of the land" and withdraw. Above all, there is this crucial difference: His "return to the mother" now takes place, not on a literal, but on *a symbolical level.*[35] And there is this further difference: where actual incest was coupled with patricide, symbolic incest is followed by cooperation with a surrogate father, Theseus.

Otto Rank sees the symbolic import of the Oedipus legend as the attempt of the individual "to be neither father nor son, but simply Self." In the primitive myth, Oedipus was "a phallic vegetation spirit, an offspring of the earth-mother whose son was also her husband." Incest is the means whereby the individual tries once more to be reborn through his own mother. As a whole, the Oedipus legend would solve

> the mysterious question of the origin and destiny of man . . . not intellectually, but actually returning into the mother's womb.

However, Rank apparently does not mean an actual return, for he goes on to state:

> This happens entirely in a symbolic form, for his blindness in the deepest sense represents a return into the darkness of the mother's womb, and his final disappearance through a cleft rock into the Underworld expresses once again the same wish tendency to return into the mother earth.[36]

The supreme import of the incest-patricide theme in Sophocles' dramas lies in its symbolic transformation through which Oedipus becomes a sanctified figure. His final resting place serves as a blessing to the community, a defense, "better than many shields, better than the succouring spear of neighbours." His very acts of *hybris* express a heroic temerity to gain knowledge of his sources, to wrest from nature the secret of human creation. But, the criminal violator is turned into "a prophet" only after *he repeats these acts symbolically.*[37] Like other heroes in mythopoesis, Oedipus enacts his journey into the underworld twice, once in physical indulgence, the second time, in symbolic recreation. In this transformation, physical blindness (as later in Goethe's Faust, Melville's Ahab and Mann's Joseph in the pit) becomes prophetic vision. The man who committed patricide and incest comes to Colonus "as one sacred, and pious, and fraught with comfort for this people."

From this perspective, Oedipus' *hybris* does not lie, as many critics hold, in his rashness, impatience, or even in the excesses of his wrath, with which Creon charges him. For we note that Oedipus retains this intemperance in Colonus, in his treatment of Polyneices and Creon. The Greek character remains the same in both phases. What has changed is the direction and the plane in which his energy is expended. In Colonus,

Oedipus turns his "Tyrannos" character against filial ingratitude and Creon's tyrannical rule.

Act III: Rehabilitation

Sophocles' Oedipus makes a complete revolution from a blessedness given him by nature to one earned by him through his journey to the underworld. He begins as a royal son, that is, one blessed in social status. He is next blessed with an extraordinary rescue as an infant, is endowed with the blessed knowledge to solve the riddle of the sphinx, becomes king and experiences the highest blessing of all (at least according to Freud)—union with the mother. At this point, he is roused by a social disease which turns out to be interwoven with his own crime. Oedipus becomes aware that he had lived in self-indulgence, which is equated with blindness to the societal aspects of the self. He learns the need to tame Dionysian excess, learns that "patience is the lesson of suffering" as "of a noble mind." Oedipus gets to know himself in his generic alignment and names himself as belonging to "the race of Labdacidae." As Jocasta is replaced by the Eumenides, the kindly Earth-Mothers, so is Laios replaced by Theseus, the kindly surrogate father. The king offers Oedipus shelter and establishes him as a citizen in the land. He too has known exile and wrestled with dangers in foreign lands. "Never, then," he tells Oedipus, "would I turn aside from a stranger, such as thou art, . . . for well know I that I am a man, and that in the morrow my portion is no greater than thine." Likewise, Oedipus' own collective representation has been widened. The Theban Oedipus becomes the benefactor of Athens, then embodying the democratic state. Sophocles was born in Colonus. *Oedipus in Colonus*, presumably Sophocles' last drama, is a kind of "homecoming" for the poet as well.

The passing of Oedipus, characterized as "above mortals wonderful," has something of that mystery and sublimity suggested in Yahweh's appearance before Job. Here, too, there is an uproar of the elements, followed by the hero's rehabilitation. For the death of Oedipus is in the nature of an epiphany. Summoned by the god, the blind man becomes guide to others, "beckoning the others onward." Like Jacob and Aeneas, Oedipus ends his days "on foreign ground, the ground of his choice." Like Moses, he is buried in a secret place.

Oedipus' transformation is not a change in his basic character, but only of its function. The acts of slaying Laios and marrying Jocasta were done without examining the realities of the situation. Oedipus continues to exhibit intemperance in his treatment of Teiresias, Creon, the

Herdsman and his son. But in these instances, his acts are directed by the passion for the truth and in the interests of the community. To be sure, the redemption appears in part as a mysterious event, as it does in the Book of Job. Yet, in both, it is conditioned by the knowledge the characters gain about themselves. Oedipus now realizes that "in knowledge is the safeguard of our course."

Epilogue: Reaffirmation of Revolt

In Colonus, Oedipus seems to reverse himself in the matter of admitting his guilt. Although, in replying to Creon's attacks, he speaks of "myself-wrought woes," he tells the Chorus that his acts, at least, "have been suffering rather than doing." He demands to know how "in *nature*" was he evil?

> I, who was but requiting a wrong, so that, had I been acting with knowledge, even then I could not be accounted wicked; but, as it was, all unknowing went I—whither I went—while they who wronged me knowingly sought my ruin.

And reiterating the point later:

> I have suffered misery, strangers,—suffered it through unwitting deeds, and of those acts—be Heaven my witness!—no part was of mine own choice . . . they whom I slew would have taken mine own life: stainless before the law, void of malice, have I come unto this pass!

Yet, even as Oedipus is protesting his innocence, he is at the same time giving a *hypothetical justification* of his acts, disregarding the fact that he did not know that he was "but requiting a wrong."

These passages again indicate that Oedipus retains his rebellious character in Colonus. The point is supported by the opening setting of which we are told that it contains not only the grove of the conciliatory Eumenides, but also that of Prometheus, "the fire-fraught god." The view that Sophocles accepts the law of the Moirai and that such acceptance brings Apollonian calm not only underrates the *Dionysian process* through which harmony is reached, but ignores the fact that Oedipus *earns his sanctification partly by his violations.*

The *hybris* element in Oedipus' character carries over into Colonus, as shown in his bearing towards Polyneices. Here, Oedipus nearly re-enacts the way of Cronos who, having emasculated his father Uranos, in turn swallows his own sons. Even in Thebes, Oedipus is strangely indifferent to his sons' welfare. While he begs Creon to watch over his daughters, he adds: "Take no care on thee for my sons; they are men."

To be sure, when Oedipus was later banished, the sons took no steps to prevent it. Yet their father's wrath is out of all proportion to this crime of omission. When Polyneices appears in Colonus as a wretched suppliant, Oedipus calls him "a murderer," invokes curses that he die by "a kindred hand," and prays that the strife between the brothers may never end: "I call the paternal darkness of dread Tartarus . . . I call the Destroying God, who hath set the dreadful hatred in you twain."

Oedipus, like other heroes in mythopoesis, is redeemed *because* of his questioning. But, whereas Job's crime is mainly one of omission and Aeschylus' Orestes acts more at the behest of the god than his own nature, remaining a passive sufferer, Oedipus' failing is shown to be a function of his character. (Oedipus' sons, too, are said to have been "moved by some god and by a sinful mind.") Sophocles breaks with the older notions of an impenetrable Moira and of tribal guilt by introducing individual choice and responsibility to the point where *fate* and *character* are in dynamic balance.

THE EPILOGUE OF GREEK MYTHOPOESIS: EURIPIDES

The tragedies of Sophocles approximate the third act of the Greek mythopoeic process. Despite its reactivization of strife among Oedipus and his sons, Sophocles' last work ends on an epiphanic note of resurrection and peace, with the "Apollonian" gaining mastery over the "Dionysian."

Writers from Aristophanes to August Wilhelm Schlegel and Friedrich Nietzsche have charged that Euripides undermined the aristocratic Apollonian myth. Aristophanes specifically took Euripides to task for attempting to destroy the ancient religious beliefs and for presenting the ignoble passions of common people. Likewise, Nietzsche criticized Euripides for bringing the "mass" on the stage and replacing the dignified demi-god by "bourgeois mediocrity." In our own time, A. W. Verrall has written of *Euripides the Rationalist*, (Cambridge, England, 1895) who "stood up to answer the Sphinx." Euripides subjected the Gods and the Moirai to a scathing critique, showing that they use their power immorally or blindly, that they act arbitrarily—*ex machina*—using hocus-pocus trickery.

To appreciate Euripides' position towards the Greek myth, we must examine the social changes which were taking place in the Greece of his time. The age of Euripides saw the disintegration of the city-state through civil strife and war. It was a period of territorial expansion, of increased slave labor and what Aristotle called the "limited slavery" of the poorer aliens, and of the lowered position of women. Law and justice were displaced by discord, poverty, and the violation of individual rights.

Euripides was an opponent of Athenian imperialism and, with the Sophists, a critic of the state. His work pictures the eclipse of the aristocratic Apollonian myth which had become a class ideology, and in which the individual had become a puppet in the hands of the "gods." Hence, the characters of Euripides act less as individuals than as products of social pressures. In the end, he shows them rebelling against being pushed around by external forces, a rebellion that is expressed in Dionysian frenzy. That is, Euripides revives the worship of Dionysus, the primitive Eastern god, to counteract the Western Apollo who had become hollow and unscrupulous. We see this most directly expressed in *Medea* and *The Bacchae*.

Jason, a traditional Greek hero, had once exhibited daring and valor, had wrested the Golden Fleece from the monster and won Medea, who was descended from the sun-God. In Euripides, Jason has become careful and calculating. He would banish Medea, who is now a "barbarian" to him, and marry Creusa, daughter of the king of Corinth. He does this not out of changed feelings towards Medea nor out of passion for Creusa, but because he has become "prudent," desires comfort and security. He admits to Medea:

> 'Tis not because I loathe thee for my wife . . . 'tis not because I am smitten with desire for a new bride . . . Nay, 'tis that we—and this is most important —may dwell in comfort . . . and that I might rear my sons as doth befit my house.[38]

In *Antigone* and elsewhere, Sophocles had decried the "excessive" pursuit of money, and the Chorus in *Medea* laments that "Order and the universe are being reversed . . . honor is found no more." The Greek hero who had once engaged in the quest of the Golden Fleece has become a slave of gold. Greece is turning towards an ingrown nationalistic endogamy. Jason tells Medea:

> Thou received more than ever thou gavest. . . . First thou dwellest in Hellas, instead of thy barbarian land, and hast learnt what justice means and how to live by law.

Euripides displays his subtlety in showing the dialectic relationship between the two forces. Out of her love for Jason, Medea had deceived her father and slain her brother. By her union with the Greek hero, she had gained something of a new ego. But, when Jason himself betrays

94

his Grecian values, Medea turns her newly found ego against his false state, in which women are poor relations. Her resurrected Circean frenzy is the answer to a Moira which had become a static formula.

In *The Bacchae*, such calculating prudence turns Pentheus against another Eastern figure, Dionysus, who has come to waken "all that faint and stray." Pentheus' rationalistic temper rejects the Dionysian mystery, calling the story of his second birth "blasphemies," mocking the new God as a "girl-faced stranger," an "Eastern knave," a "trickster . . . praying on our maids and wives." He suspects that the Dionysian gathering of the Theban women "to wild and secret rites" is for the purpose of making love. Dionysus must be met with "an iron hand," and he would quell his "music" by interning the god within walls.

The transformation of the stratified Apollonian into a raging Dionysianism also appears in *The Bacchae*, where Pentheus himself becomes a participant of the new worship. Pentheus becomes vulnerable to the irrational forces precisely because he had overstressed reason. He, who had jeered at Dionysus' female figure, dresses as a Bacchanal, eager to witness his rites. The words he suddenly hears himself speak are the voices he had attempted to still.[39] His rationalistic self is "blinded" so that he can witness the forbidden, "holy and fearful" rites of his mother which he had characterized as "love" rites:

> They lie there now, methinks—the wild birds caught,
> By love among the leaves, and fluttering not!

The incest motif is sounded when Pentheus declares that

> I am their king,
> Aye, their one Man, seeing I dare this thing!

Euripides, who is charged with having destroyed the myth, actually reintroduced its more primitive ritual in diction and style.[40] His criticism of the gods is never applied to Dionysus or Eros. In *The Bacchae*, Dionysus appears as the conglomerate God who fuses the qualities of Zeus and Prometheus. He is called the "Lord of Many Voices" who unites music and laughter, prophecy, dance and prayer, the aristocratic and democratic, the "immaculate" and the "Living Fountain," the sacrificer and the sacrifice:

> Yea, being God, the blood of him is set
> Before the Gods in sacrifice, that we for his sake may be blest.

The womanly figure of Dionysus, worshipped by the band of Eastern maidens wearing fawn-skins, brings back "the soul of that dead life of old."

The age of Euripides marks the breakdown of an old culture. War-frenzy is replaced by nature-frenzy, the *ex machina* deities by a wild divinity. Its effect has an "underground" character and people are moved to join Dionysus without knowing why. With Dionysus,

> God's child hath come, and all is overthrown! . . .
> . . . with a great wind . . .
> Blowing to beautiful things,
> On, amid dark and light,
> Till Life, through the trammelings
> Of Laws that are not the Right,
> Breaks, clean and pure, and sings
> Glorying to God in the height!

Yet, the epilogue in the work of Euripides is not a simple return to the pre-Aeschylean period. Medea and Agave are extreme *Western* reactions to an inflexible and deteriorated Apollonianism. Here, as in Franz Werfel's "The Goatsong" (*Bocksgesang*), the primitive underground explodes into "tragedy" (*tragos oidos*). Euripides saw the productive possibilities of Dionysian frenzy, especially the cathartic value of its ritual. But he also feared the destructiveness which it set loose. If Jason's self is sterile and smug, Medea's is threateningly alive, caring for nothing except its blind feelings of limitless revenge. Hers, too, is destructive of the self. Medea kills her innocent sons, the only possessions which tie her to life. She punishes Jason according to the primitive notion of ancestral guilt—she kills his offspring. The "revolution" devours its own children. Except for the chorus, Euripides' Bacchic women deny their womanliness and contradict their motherly and familial ties: Medea kills her children and Agave tears off the head of her son. Euripides indicates his reservations over resurrecting Dionysianism by making Pentheus the dismembered god and sacrifice who evokes our pity and fear. Like Aeschylus and Sophocles—though with different emphasis —Euripides saw the need to curb Dionysian passion with Apollonian reason.

NOTES

1. M. P. Nilsson's *History of Greek Religion* (2d ed.; New York, 1949, p. 42) likewise shows that the great cycles of Greek myths belong to the main centres of Mycenean culture, that "their richness and fame are in direct correspondence with the importance of the towns in Mycenean times."

2. Nilsson writes that religious festivals served to weld the citizen to the "market." He points out that "panegyrics" means both "festival" and "market," and that festivals were popular in part because they offered the only opportunity

Book of Job, Plate 17, "I have heard of thee with the hearing of the Ear
but now my Eye seeth thee" by William Blake
(facsimile edition, Detroit Institute of Arts)

Oedipus Consulting the Sphinx
by J. A. Ingres (Louvre, Paris)

for many men to eat roast beef. According to Thomson, the Delphic priesthood became the religious stronghold of the aristocracy, and the priestly clan of the Branchidae at Miletus owed their power to the skillful manipulation of oracles. Cf. George Thomson's *Studies in Ancient Greek Society* (New York, 1949), pp. 163, 637.

3. Aristotle noted that under the oligarchy, "the poor were enslaved by the rich, they and their wives and children. . . . All land was in the hands of a few men." Thomson states that Ananke, is connected with Douleia or slavery. He refers to a painting of the Orphic underworld in which Sisyphus is watched over by Ananke, a slave driver. Under Orphism (which developed with the urban revolution), the older hylozoism, in which the body was an organic part of the soul, is replaced by a dualism with hope lying in separation from the evil world. Yet, the Orphic doctrines of love and unrestraint were a rebellion against *sophrosyne* or contentment in the mean, and against Ananke.

4. The rule of the merchant prince towards the end of the seventh century B.C. encouraged science, but also emphasized the importance of money, giving rise to the new "money-mad" kings who were called tyrants. This provided the basis for the story of the Phrygian king Midas, who turned all he touched into gold, and for the old legend of Gyges, whose gold ring made him invisible and gave him the power to penetrate everywhere. Cf. George Thomson, *Aeschylus and Athens* (New York, 1950), pp. 85 ff., 215 ff.

5. *The Complete Greek Drama*, ed., Whitney J. Oates and Eugene O'Neill, Jr. (New York, 1938). Subsequent quotations are from this edition.

6. Johann J. Winckelmann, *Kunsttheoretische Schriften* (Baden-Baden, 1962-66); Erwin Rohde, *Psyche* (1891-94, English translation, 1925); Friedrich Nietzsche, *Birth of Tragedy* in *The Philosophy of Nietzsche* (New York, 1927).

7. E. R. Dodds, *The Greeks and the Irrational* (Berkeley and Los Angeles, 1966), pp. 68-76.

8. Walter F. Otto, *Dionysus, Myth and Cult* (Bloomington and London, 1965), pp. 53, 65, 142, 203. Otto states:

    "Apollo shared the Delphic festival year with Dionysus. . . . The pediments of the temple of Apollo portray on one side Apollo with Leto, Artemis, and the Muses, and on the other side Dionysus and the thyiads, in short, the raging God. . . . A vase painting of about 400 B.C. shows Apollo and Dionysus in Delphi holding out their hands to one another." (p. 203)

9. The Greek gods were not transcendental powers, but mixed in human affairs, often in sordid ways. Aside from their immortality, they were superior to humans only in the range of power and the intensity of passion. The democratization of the myth appears in the institution of the Council of the Four Hundred by the side of the Council of the Areopagus. In Aeschylus' *Eumenides*, it is this court, with Athena (rather than Zeus, Apollo or the Erinyes) casting the deciding vote, which acquits Orestes. For a development of this point, see G. Thomson's *Aeschylus and Athens*, pp. 89 ff.

10. Pre-Socratic philosophy and science were not pure theory. Philosophy was "love of wisdom," and the Milesian school, as well as Heraclitus, engaged in natural research. They attempted to give a naturalistic explanation of man and his world by reducing substance to one or several of the elements. In poetry and drama, the earth is generally singled out. A Homeric hymn sings to "the Earth Mother":

> "O Universal Mother, who dost keep
> From everlasting thy foundations deep
> Eldest of things, Great Earth, I sing of thee!"

Aeschylus paid tribute to the earth, the mother of Prometheus. In his *Eumenides*, the Pythian Priestess names "the prophet-mother Earth" as the first of the Gods.

11. Where, as in the Oresteia, the tribal curse is the main reference, the character is more a passive victim than a hero. Orestes is saved by the intervention of Apollo and Athena.

12. According to Thomson, the cult of Dionysus developed from the totemic clan during the later phases of tribal society. This suggests that the cult goes back to *group* worship connected with the mother deity. Dionysus is shown almost everywhere surrounded by a chorus of women. Dionysus himself (at least after the fourth century B.C.) appeared with long hair and flesh-tints. His drapery had a soft texture and he wore the *kothornos*, the high boot, used principally by women; also the *krokotos*, a woman's over-mantle and the *mitra*, a woman's head band. Cf. *Mythology of All Races*, Vol. I (Boston, 1916); G. Thomson's *Aeschylus and Athens*, p. 442.

13. In this guise, Dionysus is more than the bull of the dithyrambic contests. He is the pupil of Silenus, and the god whose last gift was the grape. As the center of a chorus dressed as goats, he is a satyr figure with phallic associations.

14. The Dionysian ritual was connected with the Chorus which accompanied the God. Hence, Nietzsche rejected Schlegel's view that the Greek chorus was an "ideal spectator," a passive Apollonian observer, as well as the notion that it represented the viewpoint of "the people" against that of the ruling class. Tragedy, Nietzsche argued, arose out of the Dionysian chorus and was at one time nothing else but this chorus. Hence, it could not be an ideal spectator, even as Greek tragedy struggled towards an Apollonian world.

15. Dionysus is connected with the underground. In one version, he is the son of Persephone and receives the surname of Chthonios; in another, he is the son of Semele, the name given to Chthonia by the Phrygians. Cf. Carl Kerenyi's *The Gods of the Greeks* (London and New York, 1951). For a detailed, scholarly discussion of Dionysianism, its nature, religion, especially as it appears in the *Bacchae* of Euripides, see E. R. Dodds, *Euripides: Bacchae* (2d ed.; New York, 1960).

16. *Der Dorische Tempel* (Augsburg, 1930). Cf. Helene Deutsch, *Apollo and Dionysus* (New York, 1969).

17. Olympus is dominated by the father-god, not admitting the chthonic mother

deities or Dionysus. When Odysseus meets Agamemnon in Hades, he observes that the counsel of women has brought ruin to the house of Atreus. Odysseus himself is held captive by Calypso, tempted by Circe and the Sirens, threatened by Scylla and Charybdis. Yet, at the end, his rehabilitation depends on the faithfulness of his wife Penelope.

18. To be sure, Athena herself has no mother, and in the patriarchal state, she becomes a valorous masculine figure. The use of the snake symbol in connection with Athena is a further illustration of the principle that the heroic depends on violation: From ancient times, the snake has been regarded as immortal, owing to its ability to renew itself by casting off its slough. In the figures of Demeter and Athena, the snake first appears as the protector of the house. However, in the Oresteia snake-worship takes on an ambivalent meaning. On the one hand, it is associated with the tradition of tribal revenge—the Erinyes take the form of snakes and Orestes along with his mother are likened to snakes. Now, the avenging Erinyes are not eliminated, but are *converted* into the merciful Eumenides (the Greek term "Eumenides" is sometimes used to designate both the dark and the light powers), and Orestes has a change of heart and is acquitted. The Erinyes yield to the persuasive plea of Athena who is herself a snake-goddess (Phidias' statue of Athena in the Parthenon shows a little snake curled at the goddess' feet).

19. The association of the titanic with fire was extended to the sun, conceived as a male god. In the case of the Minotaur, to whom seven boys and seven girls were periodically sacrificed, the sun assumed the character of a cruel father.

20. Theophrastus' treatise *On Fire* makes this idea explicit:
    "Fire can not only generate itself but extinguish itself. . . . The other elements are self-subsistent, they do not require a substratum. Fire does. . . . Speaking generally fire is always coming into being. . . . It perishes as it comes into being. As it leaves its substratum it perishes itself. That is what the ancients meant when they said that fire is always in search of nutriment. They saw that it could not subsist of itself without its material." (Quoted in B. Farrington's *Greek Science*, II (Pelican edition), 25-26.

21. Other rebellious titans are also unredeemed: Atlas has to bear the heavens on his head and hands; Minoitios is struck by lightning.

22. He omits Hesiod's version—Prometheus' creation of man and how he tricked Zeus into choosing the bones wrapped in gleaming fat. All translations are by Paul Elmer More as revised by Oates and O'Neill in *The Complete Greek Drama*.

23. Io also plays the role of Prometheus' future "mother." As Themis' prophetic powers gave Prometheus assurance of his ultimate delivery, so Io's union with Zeus results in the birth of Hercules, who is to free Prometheus.

24. Sigmund Freud, *Collected Papers*, Vol. V (London, 1950). In his *Trauma of Birth* (New York, 1950), Otto Rank interprets the fire of the hearth as mother warmth.

25. Freud points out that it is Hercules who extinguishes the fire which Prometheus set loose. Hercules subdues the water-serpent (the hydra of Lerna) by fire, burning off its immortal head. Freud sees in the myth "the reaction of a later epoch of civilization to the circumstances in which power over fire was acquired." Hercules, nearer to man than the titan Prometheus, practices the control of fire.

26. For a note on the Prometheus of Shelley and of Goethe, see Appendix II.

27. Sophocles does not refer to the legendary curse according to which Pelops cursed Laios with childlessness or with death at his child's hands in retaliation for Laios' having carried off Pelops' son. This is confirmed by the Delphic oracle which pronounces that Laios is doomed to be killed by his son.

      On the other hand, Sophocles introduces several features which he uses to re-create the ancient legend: the plague in Thebes, Creon's report of the oracle pointing to the murderer of Laios as the cause of the city's plight, and the Messenger who brings the news of Polybus' death.

28. Cf. Mark Kanzer's "The Oedipus Trilogy," *The Psychoanalytic Quarterly*, Vol. XIX, No. 4 (October, 1950), also his "On Interpreting the Oedipus Plays" in *The Psychoanalytic Study of Society*, ed.; Muensterberger and Axelrad (New York, 1967).

29. By the time of Strindberg's *The Father*, the personal issue occupies the center. The Captain's discontent is pictured as his own with only the barest hints of its social determinants.

30. Translations of *Oedipus the King* and *Oedipus in Colonus* by R. C. Jebb in Oates and O'Neill, *The Complete Greek Drama*.

31. As in the case of Ahab, Oedipus' public stature is contradicted by his personal defeat. Both are "marked" men, Ahab with his maimed leg, Oedipus with his swollen foot. Exposure was common practice among the Greeks. On this basis, A. J. Levin has argued that Oedipus' "Fate" was "a life of wrath and vengeance" for what was done to him as an infant ("The Oedipus Myth in History and Psychiatry," *Psychiatry*, XI, [1948]). Levin's point is well taken with regard to the initial wrong done Oedipus and to its historic condition. But in Sophocles there is no reference whatsoever to Oedipus' knowledge that Laios had ordered his ankles pierced. The theme of the diseased foot and its blessed function also appears in *Philoctetes*, with Neoptolemus approximating the role of the Herdsman. And, as Oedipus becomes the surety for peace in Athens, so Troy cannot be conquered and harmony reestablished without Philoctetes.

32. The number three is a pervading motif in the play (we also find it in *The Divine Comedy, Don Quixote, The Brothers Karamazov*). According to Jocasta, Oedipus was three days old when he was exposed on the mountain; the sphinx's riddle refers to three stages in man's life; the plot revolves about the relationship among the two parents and their son; Oedipus calls on his "three-fold help against death" (Athena, Artemis, Phoebus); he speaks of himself as "accursed in birth, accursed in wedlock, accursed in the shedding of blood!," as "thrice wretched" through marriage-rites which "created an incestuous kinship of fathers, brothers, sons—brides, wives, mothers."

Similarly, in Aeschylus' Oresteia: Zeus, the Deliverer, is called the Third; Orestes speaks of three motives for carrying out his task and of a "deep third draught of rich unmingled blood" which shall drain the house; the Erinyes ask Orestes three questions (whether, how and why he killed); Clytemnestra deals Agamemnon three blows.

The number three is indeed central to Greek mythology as a whole. According to it, the world is divided into three parts, ruled by a three-fold goddess or by three mother goddesses (the sea, the night and the earth). There are three main goddesses—Hera, Demeter, Hestia. Rhea produces three great son-gods—Zeus with his lightning, Poseidon with his trident, Hades with his head turned back to front. There are three Moirae (Clotho, Lachesis, Atropos), three Gorgons and (whenever their number is mentioned) three Erinyes. The number is, of course, pivotal in the ritual process of the year-god (Birth, Mangling, Rebirth).

33. In terms of the "manifest" content, Oedipus first killed his father and then married his mother. Yet, in Oedipus' own account of the oracle's portent and in nearly all of his later references, he *mentions the incest ahead of the patricide*. This reversal corresponds to the psychological sequence in the Freudian scheme.

34. The Eumenides are called "the dread goddesses . . . the daughters of Earth and Darkness." The Chorus trembles to speak their names and passes them by "with eyes turned away." When it discovers that Oedipus has entered their "untrodden grove," it warns him: "too far thou goest—too far! . . . retire— withdraw! . . . leave forbidden ground. . . ." When Thesus witnesses Oedipus' disappearance at the end, he is seen "holding his hand before his face to screen his eyes, as if some dread sight had been seen, and such as none might endure to behold. And then after a short space, we saw him salute the earth and the home of the gods above, both at once, in one prayer."

35. The symbolical transformation also appears in that the Eumenides are called "maidens" and their number is plural. Oedipus' relation to his daughters may have some bearing on this point. At the close of the first drama, he says that his one wish is not to be parted from Antigone and Ismene, begotten "at the sources of his own being!" He begs Creon: "Ah, could I but once touch them with my hands, I should think that they were with me, even as when I had sight. . . ." He predicts, as well as bewails, that they will remain unwed: "The man lives not, no, it cannot be, my children, but ye must wither in barren maidenhood." Oedipus' last words, addressed to his daughters, speak of the love they had from him, "as from none beside." We know that, in the myth, Antigone's most intense devotion is for her brother Polyneices.

For textual support of this interpretation, and a critique of Fromm's position, see Helen H. Bacon's "Woman's Two Faces: Sophocles' View of the Tragedy of Oedipus and His Family" in *Science and Psychoanalysis*, Vol. X (New York, 1966); see also her "The Shield of Eteocles" in *Arion* (Autumn, 1964).

36. Rank's view (as summarized in Theodor Reik's *Dogma and Compulsion* [New York, 1951]) is that the sphinx and the mother were once one. Later, the orig-

inal *violation* of the mother was replaced by a *conflict* with the sphinx and still later into an *intellectual* contest. For Rank, the sphinx episode represents a "doubling" of the rape of Jocasta, introduced in the course of repression and mythic stratification.

For Theodor Reik, "the slaying of the Sphinx is originally the killing of the totem." Later, it became the rape of the mother. Hence the duplication of the father-image and the mother-image in the figure of the Sphinx. Thus, the legend as we now have it is a condensation in which the slaying of the father and the violation of the mother are compressed into a single act of which the sphinx is the victim.

37. For an analogy in the Christian myth, cf. *John* 3.5.3. To Nicodemus' question, can a man "enter a second time into his mother's womb, and be born"! Jesus answered: "Verily, verily, I say unto thee, Except a man be born of water and Spirit, he cannot enter into the Kingdom of God."

While Oedipus has a human "flaw" (*hamartia*), there is a religious element in his epiphany: he receives "grace" in a divine form, is accorded immortality —perhaps because his suffering was supra-human. Antigone, by contrast, is drawn more as representing human suffering and human love (for her father and brother). She voices no self-pity and does not ask for nor does she get any "reward."

38. Translation of *Medea* by E. P. Coleridge in *The Complete Greek Drama*, ed., Oates and O'Neill.

39, E. R. Dodds (*Euripides: Bacchae*, p. 172) calls it "a psychic invasion. . . . The god wins because he has an ally in the enemy's camp: the persecutor is betrayed by what he would persecute—the Dionysiac longing in himself."

40. Dodds, *Bacchae*, p. xxxvii.

The Catholic Vision of
Divine Harmony
The Divine Comedy

THE MEDIEVAL ERA provided favorable ground for mythic thought in
that Catholicism and feudalism offered a unifying reference for the religious, cultural and social life of man. Christianity had systematized the
Hebrew idea of a universal God and the Stoic principle of world citizenship. Its theology taught that all men belonged to one human race,
having a single origin, ruled by one God and church, subject to one
truth and love through which "Everyman" could find salvation. Philosophically, this doctrine was expressed in "realism" (the reality of universals); ritualistically, in group worship, enacted in the communal
love feast (*agape*); socially and economically, in the international perspective of feudalism.

Christianity was a response to the disintegration of Graeco-Roman
civilization. Disillusionment with secular authority led to hope in a
divine Prince who would establish the City of God in which justice and
harmony would abide. Nor was this ideal simply otherworldly. Christian thought attempted to correct Platonism by connecting the ideal
with the real, ethics with existence. Christ was conceived as both real
and transcendental, and the church as the incarnation of the Christian idea. Transposed into social-economic thought, this meant that all
men were to be treated as children of God and were to enjoy what
Karl Kautsky called "communism of consumption."

In actual practice, however, one social-economic group dominated
and exploited another. This disparity between the ideal and the real
brought forth a protest which based itself on the gospels. It pointed to
the Christ who drove the money changers from the temple, who rejected the three temptations of property, wealth and the political

church, and who opposed the Pharisee's notion of law as the final authority. St. Luke expressed the class hatred of the downtrodden. This note was continued by St. Augustine, who held that there must always be an unbridgeable gulf between church and state, and by later figures, such as Joachim di Fiore, who complained that "they adorn the altars and the poor suffer hunger." It appeared in Christian chiliasm and mysticism. These continuous, if sporadic, movements of social protest indicate that the Middle Ages did not enjoy the unity which Henry Adams and T. S. Eliot have ascribed to this period. In its feudal system, all possessions were held as imperial fiefs and the power of the ruling hierarchy was declared to be derived from God. St. Paul had stated in Romans:

> Let every soul be subject to the higher authorities. There is no authority that is not from God, and the existing authorities are appointed by God . . . Wherefore he that opposeth the authorities resisteth the ordinance of God . . . ye shall pay them taxes; for they are the functionaries of God.

This directive was systematized some twelve centuries later by Thomas Aquinas. To be sure, Aquinas argued that divine creation made for fundamental equality, unity and order in the world where God's love "works good to all things." Yet, his *Summa* was a grand argument for mediation and compromise. It attempted to join Aristotle and Christian thought, reason and faith, natural and divine law, state and church. It taught that inner security depended on acceptance of one's assigned place in the religious and social order. It sanctioned the social inequality in feudalism by pointing to its counterpart in the divine hierarchy of the theologic scheme. Aquinas even found casuistic grounds for defending "just" usury. Thus, the church attempted to combine two seemingly contradictory positions: it held that this world was essentially sinful and that it was good, since it was created by God. St. Augustine made a distinction between evil enacted by man and as used by God for good. In his *Confessions*, evil is an "eclipse" of the good.[1]

THE DIVINE COMEDY AS MYTHOPOESIS

The approach to *The Divine Comedy* as mythopoesis conceives Dante's epic as a fusion of religious doctrine and esthetic imagery, both centering in the Catholic vision of divine harmony. This notion deviates from the view of Croce, who would separate Dante's teaching from his poetry. More generally, it runs up against the thesis—vigorously argued by Joseph Haroutunian—that Christian theology and the mythic perspective are incompatible.[2]

Haroutunian rejects the position of Ernst Cassirer which couples mythical and religious feeling, and he criticizes Reinhold Niebuhr along with other thinkers who hold that "religion seeks mythically to grasp life in its unity and wholeness." Referring to Athanasius' statement in *Contra Gentes*, "such then is their mythology,—far be it for us to call it religion," Haroutunian flatly asserts that "according to the church, mythology and Christian theology exclude one the other."

The basis of Haroutunian's position is the doctrine that Christianity rests on a particular historic event: the life of Christ. In his brilliant study, *The Crisis of Faith*, (New York, Nashville, 1944) Stanley Romaine Hopper calls the historic Incarnation of Jesus Christ the "Archimedian point" with which it proposes "to lift the whole world." He adds that "conceding to an event in history a character of eternal significance is indeed paradoxical—at least to the reason." For Arnold Toynbee, too, Christianity attains its deepest spiritual meaning from

> the interpretation of the future coming of the Saviour or Messiah as the future return to Earth of an historical figure who had already lived on Earth as a human being.[3]

(This motif was later adopted in the legends of the Second Coming of King Arthur and of Emperor Frederick Barbarossa.)

Now, Haroutunian argues that this belief gives Christianity a unique temporal mission which is obscured or swallowed by the concept of mythic universality. For the myth speaks not of historic existence but of symbolic reality in which figures and events are only analogous to one other. It follows that in the mythic schema, Christ is *like* other heroes who precede and follow him. Here, the mythopoeic faculty emphasizes human imagination. The Church, on the other hand, "has made a radical distinction between the revelation of God in Jesus Christ and the products of human imagination embodied in ethnic mythologies." Its truth, revealed once and for all, at a particular time, teaches that man was made in God's image, not God in man's image. This means that God the Father "is not an imaginary person after the likeness of a human father." To see Christianity merely as one historical function of a universal process is therefore "a source of weakness rather than strength." Niebuhr and Tillich, who interpret Christian doctrine as particular myths, give us the deepest symbolism, but they confuse Christian faith and revelation with religious and mythopoeic vision. The doctrine of *imago dei* is not a variation of a theme common to mythical anthropologists, but "constitutes a unique understanding of man, in and through Jesus Christ." The belief that God created the world *ex nihilo*, that not until Jesus Christ appeared was God's truth proclaimed, has its authority in the Bible and the Church and depends not on vision but on faith. "The Church says, *credo*, not *video, ut intelligam*." Summing up, Haroutunian states:

> If myths are products of man's common imagination under the influence of a dimension of the empirical world . . . if they embody timeless truths about man and surroundings; if they are illustrations of a common religious principle such as sympathy . . . then Christian doctrines are not myths.[4]

Indeed, Haroutunian's thesis implies other disparities between the Christian and mythic outlook, particularly on the question of guilt.

The myth does not speak of sin, but of crime. And mythic crime is "original" only in that the hero, by his very nature of being a hero, *must* commit a crime. And what he violates is not a heavenly decree, but a taboo set up by what Cassirer calls "the society of life." Moreover, his revolt is beneficent to the extent that it overthrows a tyrannical or recharges a lethargic authority. The mythic hero thus becomes a blessed figure *by virtue* of his rebellion. In mythopoesis, the basic task of the hero is to uncover his original sources, *to discover who he is*. In Catholic doctrine, this attempt to find the First Cause is an attempt to be akin to God, and is therefore sinful. Here, the heroic way lies not in expression and fulfillment of the self, but in self-denial, obedience, and faith, with man gaining will and knowledge to the extent that he participates in God's love. And man's love for God should take precedence over social, familial and fleshly attachments. Whereas in mythopoesis the hero's rebellion is an element in his ultimate rehabilitation, redemption in the Catholic scheme is possible only by a *complete* change in the hero's sinful nature. And he earns his redemption, not so much by what he has learned, as by the rite of communion, by revelation and grace. Finally, where Catholic doctrine offers the possibility of a paradise, the myth disallows such a happy ending.

Of mythopoesis since the Book of Job, *The Divine Comedy* is closer to religious doctrine than to literature. Not that its poetic scope is narrow.[5] In his monumental study of Dante, Karl Vossler calls his epic "an international folk song," the only poem, besides *Faust*, in which "all culture and the entire world" are absorbed and re-created in a single work of art. Indeed, the epic sums up some thirteen centuries of Christianity, the history of Italy and Florence, dramatized through the author's personal experiences in love and politics.

However, by Dante's time, the firm medieval-Catholic tradition which had provided unifying reference for the cultural and practical life of men was being challenged by Protestantism in religion, by nominalism and individualism in philosophy, by nationalism in politics, and

106

by commercial capitalism in economics. In Dante, Jacques Maritain states, "age-old Christendom was singing its last song." Precisely at this point, a great writer summons up his poetic genius and religious persuasion to present the supra-historical or symbolic reality of the Catholic idea. Like other mythopoesis, *The Divine Comedy* is the poetic re-creation of a glorious past.

Now, as noted, symbolic transformation is a deflection from belief in literal existence. Hence, it can be said that *Dante saves the mythic reality of the Catholic idea precisely by such deviation from and transposition of historic dogma*. In doing this, the poet, to be sure, blunts its uniqueness. But he also enriches its import by indicating its affinity with other mythopoeic works. In *Myth and Ritual in Christianity*, Alan W. Watts argues that Christianity acquires the dignity of myth to the extent that it is not restricted to its historical uniqueness. That Christ is *man*, not *a* man, Watts writes, means "that the Incarnation of God is not something which comes to pass in a single particular individual alone," and his release of pre-Christians in Hell "particularly suggests the timeless and mythological character of Christianity." Indeed, Watts thinks that "Christianity began to die in the moment when theologians began to treat the divine story as history." Yet, there is much evidence that nearly every Christian ritual has a precedent in pre-Christian mythology and legend.[6]

Even as Arnold Toynbee highlights Christ's historic existence, he sees Christ as part of a universal pattern (a kind of Rankian hero):

> Jesus is the babe born to a royal heritage—a scion of David or a son of God Himself—who is cast away in infancy . . . finds no room in the inn and has to be laid in a manger, like Moses in his ark or Perseus in his chest. In the stable He is watched over by a wolf and Cyrus by a hound; he also receives the ministrations of shepherds, and is reared by a foster-father of humble birth, like Romulus and Cyrus and Oedipus. Thereafter He is saved from Herod's murderous design by being taken away privily to Egypt, as Moses is saved from Pharaoh's murderous design by being hidden in the bulrushes, and as Jason is placed beyond the reach of King Pelias by being hidden in the fastness of Mount Helio. (*A Study of History*, p. 222.)

We also have the recurrent motif of the Journey: Jesus' withdrawing into the wilderness for forty days, following his baptism by John, his later withdrawal into "the high mountain apart," and his subsequent descent.

Dante's Deviations in Theology

Dante is generally thought of as a faithful disciple of traditional Christian doctrine, although there is a dispute as to whether he is a follower of St. Augustine or of Aquinas. Dante consistently follows the Thomistic doctrine that there are transitional spatial stages between the world of nature and the hereafter, and that sin and hell are part of the divine scheme. Yet, Dante deviates from Catholic doctrine.[7] His heretical temper manifests itself in his attitude towards the temporal claims of the papacy and the relation between church and state.

Dante regarded ideal politics as emanating from ideal ethics (an implication of his method which deduces the higher from the lower). Now, Dante follows the Roman-medieval tradition which viewed politics as a natural activity of all citizens. And, whereas Aquinas declared theology to be the queen over the empire, Dante wrote that it was only "the dove," and that *state* rule was the remedy "against the malady of sin" (*De Monarchia*, II,12;III,4). Hence, he extolled Virgil for upholding a supra-national world organization, centered in Rome, and Henry VII for working towards a polyphonic world state.

To be sure, Dante saw that man, in his helplessness, needed the authority of "two suns," both the state and the church, to regulate his terrestrial and his spiritual life.[8] But unlike Aquinas, who taught that the state must be subordinated to the church, Dante saw them as independent entities. This is the evangelical idea when Rome

> Was used to have two suns, by which were clear
> Both roads, that of the world and that of God.
>
> (*Purgatorio*, XVI)[9]

At that time, the church did not engage in worldly political affairs, its property was then held in common and used not "for one's kin, nor yet some viler soul," whereas today

> Walls that were once an abbey now conceal
> A den of thieves. (*Paradiso*, XXII)

The "two suns" now intrude on each other's orbits and the papacy has become a "shameless harlot" mating with political despotism (Purgatorio, XXXII).[10]

Dante's most dramatic deviation is *his assumption of a God-role* in the epic. The author places himself in the center of the divine process, as the prototype of mankind's fate. He—not Christ—descends to hell. He and he alone makes the complete journey and is accorded the unique grace of being allowed to enter Paradise while still alive.[11] Dante sets himself up as the supreme judge, determining who is guilty, who is to be in hell, who is to pass on to purgatory and heaven. And these decisions rest, not on revelation, but on Dante's *personal preferences.*

In his role of supreme arbiter, Dante celebrates pagan philosophers and poets as noble and divine, despite the fact that they had not been baptized. Virgil, in particular, becomes "Guide, master, lord." He is accorded equal status with Jesus and Mary in that Dante gives him a similar existential reality, and makes him as indispensable to the success of his journey as are St. Bernard and Mary.[12] Dante pays tribute to Aristotle as the master "of them that know," and to Homer as *poeta sovrano.* The *Convivio* states that following Beatrice's death, Dante sought consolation in Boethius and Tully who directed him "to the love, that is to the study, of this most gentle lady, Philosophy." Cato is declared to be more worthy "to symbolize God" than any man on earth—this although Cato committed the sin of suicide. In *Purgatorio* (XXVIII), Matilda suggests that the Earthly Paradise is like the Golden Age of which the ancients sang:

> They who in old time dreaming poetized
> Of the felicity of the Age of Gold
> On Helicon perchance this place organized.

The "memory" which Dante invokes in the second canto of the *Inferno* goes beyond Biblical revelation, when he calls on the "Muses" and "high Genius" for the power to reveal "memory, that errs not." Finally, Dante admits into Paradise heathens of both pre-and post-Christian eras: the Trojan Ripheus, Emperor Trajan, and the declared enemy of Christianity, Siger of Brabant. Indeed, the Symbolic Eagle declares that some non-Christians shall be nearer to Christ on the day of judgment than many who cry out his name.

Even more telling is the place the poet chooses to accord Beatrice. As Maritain puts it: Dante has the "brazen audacity" to exalt a certain girl "as the incarnation of theological knowledge, in whose eyes the humanity and the divinity of Christ are mirrored," simply because in his life, Dante's "flesh burned for her."[13] We should add that in the *Commedia*, Dante "forgets" that Beatrice was a married woman and transfers to her the religious imagery of the Virgin.[14] This unorthodox "chivalric" treatment of Beatrice has implications for Dante's attitude towards art, his conception of sin in the *Inferno* and of salvation in the *Paradiso.*

Dante's Deviations in His Conception of Art

Christian doctrine before Dante allows but peripheral value to poetry. Augustine accepted only the "non-material" art of music as a Christian form. In the Middle Ages, poetry was generally regarded as a pagan heritage. Scholasticism denied that it had a cogitive function and Aquinas held it to be below reason. He characterized metaphors as a defection from truth, quoting the Greek saying that poets are liars. The Middle Ages and Aquinas believed in a literal hell and heaven.

Dante is the first great Catholic writer to break with this tradition in that he distinguishes between existence and its symbol. The *Commedia* presents demons and angels as *likenesses*. The *Inferno* associates Greek mythic furies with Christian devils and demons. In *Purgatorio* (VI), Christ is addressed as "O highest Jove," and the *Paradiso* begins by invoking the "good Apollo" as an aid in describing the heavenly realm.

Dante's deviation also appears in his "four-fold" interpretation—literal, allegorical, tropological, anagogical.[15] His work would not only teach the fixed meaning of church doctrine, would not only give its moral and spiritual teaching, but would also be allegorical. And, allegory, he explains, as derived from the Greek and Latin, means diverse, varying. Its form of treatment is "poetic, fictive, descriptive, digressive, transumptive . . . by way of example." The *Convivio* (II,i) admits that theologians, "to be sure, take this sense otherwise than poets," and that he is using the allegorical "as the poets use it." (In the *Paradiso* we are told that to speak of things which are beyond the bonds of human sense, we must be satisfied with using "the example.") Dante's endorsement of the method "by way of example" makes his work translatable. In sum, Catholicism becomes mythopoesis in *The Divine Comedy* through Dante's deviation from orthodox theology and orthodox esthetic doctrine. These deviations are embodied in the art of the epic.

In his *Mimesis*, Erich Auerbach illustrates the realism of Dante's beyond: The eternal realms contain earthly frenzy, anger, action and passion. In Georg Lukacs' formulation (*Theorie des Romans*), Dante makes the transcendent immanent. Even the *Paradiso* is studded with metaphorical likenesses of the invisible and intangible, employing musical and planetary images to suggest the immateriality of the vision. His work as a whole presents man's problems in a highly personal form.

Charles Williams (*The Figure of Beatrice* [London, 1943].) distinguishes between the use of imagery ("the Way of Affirmation") and the renunciation of all images ("the Way of Rejection"). He shows that the two ways are intertwined in Dante and that the meaning of his work is gathered into what the *Convivio* terms "one simple substance." Dante does not stop at philosophic and religious sublimation of the passions. He *redirects* their frustrations into the sensuous sphere of his art. His poem thus *reasserts* the adventure of sensuous living and expresses the symbolic fulfillment of his self. This approach can help us see that *Dante's three realms coexist in each one*: Elements of paradise are foreshadowed in hell and the heavenly realm affirms the beauty of the body. His work receives its *dramatic* quality from the tension between the inchoateness of human existence and the peace of divine reality. This tension is present everywhere. It is at its greatest in the first and third realms, least in the middle kingdom where the poet gives freer expression to mythic analogies and to Italian legend and folktale.

As noted, for Christianity, redemption is possible only if the sinner undergoes absolute repentance. Dante follows this precept to the extent that the people in his *Inferno* are doomed to eternal punishment because they remain uncontrite. But Dante's *poetic attitude* tells a different story: The poet evinces sympathy, even admiration for some of his sinners. They know the consequences of their action (they suffer for it), yet insist on their ways. Farinata, Capaneus, Odysseus, Ugolino, above all, Francesca and Paolo, do not ask to be taken out of hell. They *accept* the result of their character, and one might say that Dante views them *as sacrifices to a doctrine*.

Dante argues against pride, excessive love and power. Yet, even doctrinally, he regards them as distortions of divine love. A strong will is superior to a good will. (Those with a good will are placed in the lowest Paradise.) But the crucial test, I repeat, is Dante's esthetic attitude. The poet pours more of his sensuous passion into the love which moves the rebellious sinners than into the love which moves the sun and other stars. As artist, Dante allows more "grace" to Francesca than to Beatrice. Indeed, as Charles Williams points out, the love which Dante finally affirms is itself a *restless* power: it *moves* man.

Beatrice and the City

Dante's epic contains the first extended love story in Western mythopoesis. Vossler remarks that Dante is among the first to counteract the depreciation of women, taught by the Greeks, Ovid and the church. But the new element in Dante is his linking woman with the city, state and God. The poet relates the fate of Beatrice to the fate of the community, likening her death to the scourge which descends on the city: "How doth the city sit solitary, that was full of people! how is she become a widow." When the *Convivio* (I, III) states that its author is

> a vessel without sail and without rudder, driven about upon different ports
> and shores by the dry wind that springs out of dolorous poverty,

the tone and some of the imagery are similar to those used in complaining that Italy has no government, no peace, is without a pilot in a storm, denuded by priests, growing fat from filth and gain.

Dante's work is the first to raise sex-love to the existential plane of politics and religion. In Graeco-Roman mythopoesis, women are important primarily in their relation to the *polis*. (In Aeschylus, Zeus' passion for Io and Aegisthus' for Clytemnestra are a sub-theme.) Oedipus wins Jocasta as a reward for ridding the city of its blight; Medea is outraged because she is rejected as coming from a barbarian land; the love of Virgil's Dido for Aeneas is intertwined with her social role of founding a city. In traditional Christianity, the Virgin remains inaccessible as a woman and sex love is a hindrance to the pure love of God. Dante is the first major writer to celebrate love for a particular woman and to see in it the kernel of social and religious love, the first whose hero is redeemed through the intercession of a woman. In the manner of the Orpheus legend where the beloved is resurrected by word and song, and of Novalis' "Hymns to the Night" in which the poet apotheosized his dead beloved, Dante resolved to write of his departed Beatrice "what hath not before been written of any woman."[16] Beatrice's passing produced what Vossler characterizes as "the germ of a poetic world of Christian mythology."

Act I: Eden

For Dante, the Golden Age of universal peace and love of truth is at the root of man (*l'umana radice*), the source of his innocent beginnings. In the life of mankind, it is the memory of our communal mother (*commune madre*); in the life of the individual, it is the nursery stage, the time of "our true first speech"; historically, it was ancient Rome and Florence, the age of the "two suns," when property was held in common and there was concord, simplicity, chastity.[17] And, the poet invokes these memories to counteract the schism and corruption of his day.

In his letter to Can Grande (*The Letters of Dante* [Oxford, 1920], p. 202), Dante states that the *Commedia* was undertaken, not for the sake of speculation, but "for a practical purpose." The work, with its demons, minotaurs and angels, its hell, purgatory and heaven, has been called a "vision." But medieval man believed such visions to have physical existence, and Dante's art makes them visible, audible and tangible. Unlike the allegorical figures in Bunyan or the thin shadows in Kafka,

Dante and Virgil by Eugene Delacroix (The Bettmann Archives)

Faust, Marguerite and Mephistopheles in the Street,
lithograph illustration to Goethe's *Faust*
(Dept. of Graphic Arts, Harvard College Library)

Dante's characters are sensuous people and his journey into the realm of the dead becomes an experience in the realm of the living. *The Divine Comedy* deals with man in nature. We know the lament of Francesca and Farinata, the storms and flames which lash and scorch the sinners, know their anguish and restlessness, the torment of their loneliness. We also know the hope of the repenting sinners in purgatory and get a sense of the overwhelming gladness of those who are in paradise. The author who writes about the other world is alive and can view it only in its likeness to the living world. If *The Divine Comedy* is to be taken seriously, then its other life must be relevant to our life, the only kind we know.

Act II: The Mythic Crime

The starting point of *The Divine Comedy* is the same as that in other mythopoesis: There is something rotten in the state. The point is restated in the *Paradiso* (XI), where sin consists in being insensitive (*insensata cura dei mortali*) to abiding values:

> Distracted mortals! of what paltry worth
> Are the arguments whereby ye are so prone
> Senselessly to beat down your wings to earth!
> One wooed the Law, one the Aphorisms, one
> Coveted the priesthood, and another pressed
> Through force or fraud to acquire dominion;
> One plunder, and one business, quite possessed;
> One in the pleasures of the carnal sty
> Grew weary; another in his own ease caressed . . .

Dante's charge is directed to Everyman, but his examples are historic and contemporary. Sin is so recent in the poem, Mark Van Doren remarks, that the author can name the sinners, locating them in Italian-Florentine politics.

Now, the world of sinners includes Dante, who has gone astray. And this happened, not "originally," but "midway the journey of this life," when he *became aware* of being lost (*mi ritrovai*—"came to myself").[18] The *selva oscura* where he is lost is at once the general situation of man, of Italy and Florence, and the darkness in Dante's own life. But what was Dante's personal sin?

Beatrice's specific charge is that Dante neglected her for some little girl (*pargoletta*):

> Thou oughtest not to have stooped thy pinions downward
> To wait for further blows, or little girl,
> Or other vanity of such brief use. (Longfellow's translation).

Nowhere does Dante summon up as much pity and sympathy as he does for the carnal sinners with whom Hell proper begins.

Dante's sensuous burden is foreshadowed in the very first canto where the Leopard, the Lion and the She-Wolf bar his path. These animals are interpreted as having political meaning or as representing Incontinence, Violence and Fraud. I would suggest that two of them also refer to Dante's own carnal demon.

The poet mentions the Lion briefly and concentrates on the Leopard and the She-Wolf. They are described in imagery which alludes to quick, unsteady movements and alluring seductiveness. The Leopard, "light and swift of limb," is the animal with the gay skin (*gaietta pelle*), the She-Wolf is "That restless beast," lean and full of cravings (*tutte brame*). Dante is finally stopped by the She-Wolf, which drives him back "To where the Sun is silent." Virgil says of this female animal that "Her craving maw never is satisfied," that after feeding, she is hungrier than before. Again, in *Purgatorio* (XX), Dante curses the "she-wolf of old" that preys more than all the other beasts, whose hunger is unappeasable. The quality of restlessness, of insatiability also appears in the wind and tempest metaphors of the carnal sinners in Canto V. Through such figures, *the author relives their sins symbolically*. His very intemperate denunciations point to his affinity with the sinners. And, in depicting their punishment, Dante also experiences symbolical atonement for his own sins. Dante's vicarious acceptance of punishment, meted out to others, is a well-known device for displacement of personal guilt.[19]

Dante's elevation of sin as a moral condition for redemption appears obliquely in his attitude towards those who were neither virtuous nor immoral. They live in Ante-Hell, for even "deep Hell refuses them." Virgil comments that besides such, "the sinner would be proud," for he at least made a choice, although a bad choice. In contrast to their realm, Hell is made part of the divine order, the inscription on its door reading

> Me did Divine Authority Uprear;
> Me Supreme Wisdom and Primal Love Sustain.

Those in Hell are better off than the forlorn spirits in Ante-Hell who "never were alive," who acted "without infamy and without praise." Virgil and Dante pass them by in contempt.

The poet's identification with those assigned to the Inferno begins in that part of Limbo which he reserves for his favorite non-Christians. Although they have not been baptized and hence have no faith, they suffer no pain, but are placed in what Zimmer calls a "sort of idyllic,

Elysian lobby." Among them are the "four great shades," Homer, Horace, Ovid and Lucan. Dante is proud to join them and feels exalted when he sees other "great spirits," such as Hector, Aeneas, Caesar, Brutus, Aristotle and Plato.

The Pattern of the Inferno: Paolo and Francesca

It is generally acknowledged that Dante imparts the greatest intensity, vividness and dramatic realism to the *Inferno*. Where Aquinas says very little about hell, Dante devotes a third of his epic to it.

The distinguishing character of suffering in hell is that here man has no hope of ever emerging from it. And there is no hope because there is no love. In the formulation given by Dostoyevsky's Father Zossima, hell is the suffering of loneliness which comes from the inability to love.

The Canto dealing with the carnal sinners Paolo and Francesca is deservedly renowned for its poetic quality and it is pivotal for establishing Dante's principle of *contrapasso*,—that a man shall be punished wherewith he sins.

In life, the two lovers allowed the storm of their passion full sway and their punishment consists in having to experience this passion, and this passion alone, forever:

> To and fro, down, up . . . in helpless flight,
> Comforted by no hope ever to lie
> At rest, nor even to bear a pain more light.

Forever, they are to be whirled by "The abysmal tempest that never can sleep," smitten and driven by the warring wind and the billowing sea.

From a strict view, the punishment meted out to the lovers exceeds their crime. For a few hours of unpermitted passion, Paolo and Francesca are given over to an eternity of torment. Yet, what Dante intends to show is that *their act is a way of living which carries over into the life pattern as a whole.* Dante's moral-esthetic strategy consists in *essentializing* both the good and the evil act. For all its realism, his art does not aim at the three-dimensional fullness that we find, say in Tolstoy, but goes out for the essence—in medieval language, the "quiddity"—for the pure "reality" which underlies the appearance of actuality. In *Purgatorio* (XXI), Dante tells us:

> The live appeared living and dead the dead.
> Not better he who saw the actual deed
> Saw than I, stooping, all beneath my tread.

His characters are at once sensuous beings in time and space, and lead what Hegel called a "changeless existence." We are, Auerbach observes, "in an eternal place, and yet we encounter appearance and concrete occurrence there." He formulates Dante's method by calling it "the absolute realization of a particular earthly personality in the place definitely assigned to it," which "constitutes the Divine Judgment." The individual, concrete appearance of passion is viewed in its intrinsic substance.

This approach appears in Dante's treatment of Paolo and Francesca. Dante reduces the hours of their specific indulgence to *the principle of indulgence,* and they are made to experience their passion *to the exclusion of everything else.* This is specialization, and specialization is hell for man who wants to be a complete human being. By being endlessly repeated, the love of Paolo and Francesca becomes at once agonizing restlessness and monotonous sameness. Hell is the monotony and futility in changeless repetition, its "law and quality" ever remaining the same (*Inferno* VI).

This, then, is the "practical" import of the poem: It warns us that once we have established a certain way of life—of indulging, falsifying, betraying—we are driven to repeat it. Once we have established our character, it becomes our fate. Capaneus cries out: "What I was alive, that I am dead" (XV). According to this pattern, the punishment of the sinners consists in their having to repeat their transgressions forever: The heretics are divided, the avaricious assail one another, the flatterers are immersed in filth, the envious have their eyelids sewn, etc.

Charles Williams indicates the relation of the Paolo-Francesca scene to the larger theme of communality in the *Commedia.* The deeper meaning of their adultery is that it shuts out the public, communal aspect of the self. In *Purgatorio* (XIV), Guy del Duca bewails the fact that man sets his heart there where he must separate himself from his consorts:

> O gente umana, perchè poni il core
> là v' è mestier di consorto divieto?[20]

In self-indulgence, man deprives himself of fulfilling his whole being, and this, Williams notes, is "possible to all lovers, married or unmarried, adulterous or marital." The evil of mutual indulgence lies in that it is "bound too soon to become two separate single indulgences." This holds for Dante's lovers as well as for Tolstoy's Vronsky and Anna Karenina. They too begin with a concealed kiss; they too shut themselves off and are shut off from their city; in time, they develop hatred of each other's indulgence, are in hell while they are alive. The supreme achievement of hell, writes Williams, "is to make interchange impossible." All the sinners in Hell are "without regard for the City. Farinata is the pride of the citizen in his house or his party held more passionately close than the City . . . the usurers make private profit out of the City. . . ."

Yet, to repeat the point made earlier, while Dante the religious thinker condemns such sinners, Dante the artist makes the most renowned of them—Francesca, Farinata, Cavalcante, Ulysses, Ugolino—attractive, even heroic. Again, his treatment of the Paolo-Francesca story may serve as a prototype. When Dante hears their wailings, he begs Virgil that he might speak with them. Their transgression rouses him, not to indignation, but to tears, as he considers

> How many sweet thoughts and what longings fain
> Led them into the lamentable pass![21]

His identification is such that—like the lovers who that day read no further in their book—Dante too goes no further in his book, but swoons, "like a body falling dead."

It is noteworthy that Dante does not dwell on the sinful acts of his major figures. In his *Life of Dante*, Michele Barbi points out that the poet reevokes that which has nothing to do with their being in hell. This is especially the case with Ugolino: " . . . not the act of betrayal performed and suffered by Count Ugolino, but the cruel mode of his death," is what Dante places in the foreground. And, we are wrung with grief by Dante's account of how the father stood helplessly while his little sons vainly begged for food and then saw them starve to death.

Dante evinces a similar attitude towards Farinata, whom he calls *magnanimo*, and Capaneus, whom he calls "that great spirit." Farinata lies in a burning coffin, scorched by flames, and Capaneus is charred by a fiery rain. Yet, both are undaunted and unbent. Farinata rises up in front of Dante "As if of Hell he had a great disdain." The poet grants them something of the stature of Aeschylus' Prometheus and Milton's Satan. Likewise, Dante's account of Cavalcante fills us with deep pity, as we hear him sorrowing in the belief that his son is dead. "We cannot," writes Erich Auerbach,

> but admire Farinata and weep with Cavalcante. What actually moves us is
> not that God has damned them, but that the one is unbroken and the other
> mourns so heart-rendingly for his son and the sweetness of the light.
> (*Mimesis*, p. 200.)

And, in the story of Ulysses, Dante pays homage to the adventure of earthly experience. Even in hell, Ulysses insists that nothing

> Could conquer the inward hunger that I had
> To master earth's experience, and to attain
> Knowledge of man's mind, both the good and the bad.

The *Inferno* can thus be viewed as both an expression of and a check on Dante's own drives. The check is felt in his anger at the sinners and expressed formally in the severe, mathematical architecture of the poem. As Karl Vossler puts it, these are the ramparts with which Dante would dam up the raging tides within himself.[22] Yet, the very rigidity of the design points to the power of the emotional storms within.

In *Purgatorio* (X), we are told "Think of the sequel." The sequel of establishing a sinful pattern is to repeat it eternally. Yet, Dante seems to be saying that to learn what sin is, we must experience it. In this connection, it is relevant to note that Virgil and Dante are helped by Antaeus and Satan in their journey through hell. (They are taken by Antaeus into the deep of the Ninth Circle and are enabled to leave the inferno by clinging to Lucifer's fell). Nearly as much as in Goethe's *Faust*, the devil helps man to achieve the realm of clarity. Dante had first attempted to reach the mountain of purgatory by a direct short route. But, stopped by the She-Wolf, he was forced to take a roundabout passage, had to traverse the hellish terrain to find his way to the earthly and divine paradise.

Purgatory: Visual Recognition

Purgatory is still the world of sinners. But in the inferno they were *made* to suffer, whereas here they *desire* to suffer: The proud want to be humbled, the gluttons to be famished, the slothful to be in restless motion. One extreme is to be purged by its *converso*, by another extreme. Yet—and here again the attractiveness of sin is obliquely acknowledged—to prove themselves capable of withstanding its seductiveness, *they must expose themselves to the temptation of sinning*: the unchaste practice chastity amidst the fire and heat of glowing flames; the gluttons sing as they weep from hunger:

> That appetite they followed with such heat,
> Holy again through hunger and thirst shall be.
> The scent that from the apple comes so sweet
> And from the sprinkling of the leaves with spray
> Fires us with craving both to drink and eat.

That is, in purgatory, *man becomes aware of sin by re-experiencing it symbolically.*

In the inferno, awareness was obscured by hell's murky grey. But purgatory is lit up by the sun, objects are shown in soft colors (*dolce color*), and *sin becomes visible*. It is here that the angel inscribes the letter P on Dante's forehead; only here do the seven deadly sins become

visible. Suffering in purgatory does not have the stark physical character
of the inferno and is more suggestive of mental suffering.[23] What had
been lived through physically is now lived through symbolically.

In *Purgatorio* (XXVII), Dante calls sleep a state

> . . . which often will apprize
> Of things to come, and ere the event foreknow.

Charles Williams calls attention to the fact that only in purgatory does
Dante sleep and that only here does he cast a shadow. Hell is too disturbing for sleep and too murky to allow for a shadow. It is in the midway realm of purgatory that sleep and dream enable Dante to achieve
awareness, what Dante calls *amore d'animo*. The psychological process is also suggested by the circumstance that here Dante *journeys backwards*. By moving *against* the stream (Lethe), memory of guilt is
washed away. Dante advises those guilty of Envy that their bad conscience may be removed by "The stream of memory down-flowing . . ."
(*per essa scenda della mente il fiume*). By alternate sleep and wake-
fulness, Dante moves backwards towards remembering and reordering
his past.

From Virgil, Dante learned that love is

> . . . the seed of virtue pure
> And of all works deserving chastisement.

and that "natural" love, which is always free from error, is to be distinguished from love "of the mind," which may become excessive or distorted love (*Purgatorio*, XVII, XVIII). Dante is also told that he can
master sinful desires "of the mind" by proper exercise of the free will.
With the removal of guilt, there is left only the memory of the better
self which Dante recovers by drinking from the waters of Eunoë. Having been purified, Dante becomes freed of the memory of original sin
and achieves the highest form of freedom of the will. Virgil declares
that Dante is now his own master and can be left to go the rest of the
way without him.

Act III: Return to Origins

One of the supreme ironies of *The Divine Comedy* is that precisely
at this point, Dante becomes a "child" again. When he beholds Beatrice,
Dante turns to Virgil for help

> With such trust as a child that is afraid
> Or hurt, runs to his mother with his pains.

But the father-guide is gone and Dante faces Beatrice alone, like "a child" confronted by "a mother." Whatever self-knowledge and self-esteem Dante had gained vanish, as he stands before Beatrice in fear and confusion, "letting gush the sighs and tears." He confesses his basic sin, which he calls enslavement to momentary pleasures—*le presenti cose:*

> Weeping I said: "Things of the passing day,
> Soon as your face no longer on me shone,
> With their false pleasure turned my steps away."

Dante's *le presenti cose* correspond to the Mephistophelian bed of sloth or the denial of the quest. But neither Faust nor any other hero in mythopoesis renounces his crime as completely as Dante does. When Beatrice continues to upbraid him, charging that he paid attention to girls, Dante accepts the rebuke in the manner of children (*fanciulli*):

> As boys that dumb with shamefastness remain,
> Eyes to ground, listening to their faults rehearsed,
> Knowing themselves in penitence and pain,
> So stood I . . .

Beatrice, who had been his wished-for beloved now becomes his *mamma*.

In the *Convivio*, Dante writes that

> the supreme desire of everything, and that first given by nature, is to return
> to its source; and since God is the source of our souls . . . to him this soul
> chiefly desireth to return (IV, 12).

And, when Dante is asked in *Purgatorio* (II) why he is taking the journey, he replies that he may thereby achieve a return:

> . . . per tornare altra volta
> La dove son, fo io questo viaggio.[24]

Unlike Job, Prometheus and Oedipus, Dante makes no decisions of his own, but follows his trusted guides from Virgil, Statius and St. Bernard to Lucy, Leah, Matelda, Beatrice and the Virgin Mary.

When Dante reaches the Earthly Paradise on Purgatory, his purification is completed. Why, then, it has been asked, is it necessary for him to go on to Paradise? Adam had to forsake Eden because he desired knowledge of good and evil before he was ready for it. But Dante had already learned the consequences of false choice, had become his own master. What need then for further instruction and purification? Vossler calls Paradise "the heavenly reflection of the peaceful and visionary piety" of Dante's childhood. But if it is no more than that, then Dante has learned nothing from his journey.

However, Dante has passed through the plane of knowledge which the *Convivio* calls "the ultimate perfection of our soul, in which consists our ultimate felicity."[25] And Dante himself suggests that return to infancy is neither possible nor desirable. His *De Vulgari Eloquentia* begins with an attempt to justify the replacement of Latin by Italian as a literary medium. At first, Dante defends "vulgar" speech as the natural "mother-tongue" which infants imitate from their nurses. But he goes on to argue in behalf of *ideal* speech, one that is "illustrious, cardinal, courtly, and curial."

Gertrude Leigh thinks that Dante succeeded in transforming his sensual desires into spiritual channels. In his *Goliath* (New York, 1938), Borgese also argues that Dante sublimated the failures in his personal life by projecting a religious and universal realm. Indeed, Dante's life as a whole shows a series of basic deprivations and estrangements: He lost his mother when he was only a small child; his father became a usurer; his wife, Gemma Donati, was chosen for him by his father (Dante never mentions her in his work); he felt himself rejected by Beatrice; he was frustrated in his political efforts as a Florentine and Italian, and he died in exile.

Dante himself lends support to the thesis that his work is a symbolic compensation for his wordly failures. He tells us in the *Convivio* that the loss of Beatrice led him first to philosophic, then to religious love. However, I would suggest that we need to examine elements of Dante's carnal passion *within* his invocation of heavenly love. Dante's temperament did not allow for peace in sublimations. He remained proud, arrogant and rebellious to the end. And both the *Vita* and the *Commedia* offer clues that Dante did not succeed in curbing his sensual nature.

Sex and Love

Dante's *Vita Nuova* (Rosetti translation) states that his love for Beatrice sprang from ideal boyhood feelings and that it retained this quality nine years later when he was eighteen. When he was nine years old, "the glorious Lady" of his "mind" seemed to him a heavenly figure,—

> so noble and praiseworthy that certainly of her might have been said the words of the poet Homer, "She seemed not to be the daughter of a mortal man, but of God."

When he saw her again nine years later, he had a dream about this "daughter . . . of God," in which Dante's "master" appears, "a lord of

terrible aspect," enveloped by "a mist of the colour of fire." He has the
sleeping lady in his arm, and holds Dante's heart, "burning in flames."
The master bids the lady eat Dante's heart and then "it seemed to me
that he went with her up towards heaven." Whereupon, "such a great
anguish came upon me that my light slumber could not endure through
it, but was suddenly broken."

The implicit rivalry between Dante and his "master" over the lady,
as well as the inevitability of Dante's renunciation ("When Love was
shown me with such terrors fraught") are made explicit in a sonnet,
written after Beatrice's death. Here, "the Eternal Sire" is seized by
"a sweet desire" for Beatrice's "lovely excellence" and thence bids her
"to Himself aspire":

> Beatrice is gone up into high Heaven,
> The kingdom where the angels are at peace ; . . .
> For from the lamp of her meek lowlihead
> Such an exceeding glory went up hence
> That it woke wonder in the Eternal Sire,
> Until a sweet desire
> Enter'd Him for that lovely excellence,
> So that he bade her to Himself aspire:
> Counting this weary and most evil place
> Unworthy of a thing so full of grace.

(Rosetti translation)

From that night on, the natural functions of his body began "to be vexed
and impeded." There follows a second dream in which the master bids
him "compose certain things in rhyme . . . And thus she shall be made
to know thy desire."[26] Having written the sonnet, Dante begins to be
harassed by doubts whether his master is good or evil and concludes
that he can only commend himself to Pity. But Dante's ambivalent
feeling towards him becomes clear when he calls Pity "mine enemy."[27]

In the meantime, other "Beatrices" came his way. One with whom

> . . . dwells the counterpart
> of the same Love who holds me weeping now.

There was another, called Pietra (addressed in the poem "To the Dim
Light"), who "stone-like" refused his love. Dante would have it that
these other women were "a screen for so much love" he felt for Beatrice;
but it is also possible that the love for the Lady of his "mind" was a
screen for so much passion he felt for more accessible women. (In the
Commedia, Dante admits shamefacedly to having paid attention to
such, and in the Vita, he speaks of "the unsteadfastness of mine eyes.")

Dante did not regard asceticism as an ideal. In *Paradiso* (XIV), Solomon hopes for the resurrection of the body:

> When flesh is glorified and sainted state
> Shall be re-clothed, our persons in esteem
> Shall be more pleasing, being then complete . . .
> For the organs of the body shall acquire
> Strength to support all that may most delight.

Dante's three dreams in *Purgatorio* (IX, XIX, XXVII), contain a similar erotic-esthetic configuration.

Stirred by "something of Adam," Dante first dreams that an eagle snatches him up into the fiery sphere.

> We approached and were arriving at a spot
> Whence, there where first to me a gap appeared
> Like in a wall some crack that it hath got,
> I saw a gate . . .

Here stands "a guardian," with a countenance "such as I could not sustain," who bids them halt and declare their will, after which Dante "mounts" the three steps towards the gate. Next, Dante dreams of the sweet Siren who leads mariners astray with her wiles. She is promptly confounded by another figure, "a lady in whom was holiness."

Dante has the third dream when he is about to behold Beatrice on the Earthly Paradise. Virgil tells him that first he will have to pass through a "womb of flames," which is the "wall" between him and Beatrice. Dante is terrified and troubled like a child until he is reassured. Dante then dreams of Leah, who sings while she gathers flowers, and of Rachel, who sits before the mirror which reflects her beautiful eyes. As Dante beholds Beatrice at the topmost step, he feels the mighty power of ancient love (*d' antico amor senti la gran potenza*). Beatrice accuses him of seeking girls and forgetting the great "pleasure" her own "fair limbs" presented to him. As he is drawn into the dance of the star-nymphs and led up to the Gryphon's breast, he sees Christ reflected in Beatrice's eyes. At this point, he is stirred by "thousand desires, hotter than flame":

> Thousand desires, hotter than flame, constrained
> The gaze of mine eyes to the shining eyes
> Which on the Gryphon only fixed remained.

In the midst of Dante's recognition scene with Beatrice, the harlot turns her wanton eyes on him, as she is about to mate with a towering giant. Dante's meeting with Beatrice amidst "the living green of the divine forest" (XXVIII) is in the mythic tradition of the union between the mother-sister-goddess and the son-brother-hero, here clothed in Christian imagery.

The term "ancient" recurs in these Cantos (*antico amor, antica fiamma, selva antica, l'antica madre*; Beatrice's self is called *se stessa antica.*) But the ancient love which Dante feels in the ancient forest for Beatrice's ancient self cannot be Eden, for it is experienced by one who knows the temptations of sin. This dialectic carries over into the *Paradiso* where Beatrice has to reprove Dante for continuing to find the "sacred flame" solely in her eyes:

> She spoke to me: "turn now and listen anew!
> Not only in my eyes is Paradise."

Here again, Dante mixes religious and sexual allusions: Led by Beatrice, Dante sees a ladder standing erect (*eretto*), reaching up towards the Heavenly Rose, where he is to resolve his passionate desires (*Solvi il tuo caldo disio*). The Saints reach up to touch the Virgin, with their flame, in the manner of a child stretching his arms when he has milked the mother's breasts; the angels descend into and reascend the divine Rose, like bees "which deep into the flowers retreat" (XXIII, XXXI). The emotions of the Sixth Beatitude are expressed in terms of the May breeze which stirs the sweet winds, impregnate with grass and flowers. Beatrice appears "amid a cloud of flowers . . . Clothed in the colour of a living flame." Charles Williams and Allen Tate have helped correct the view that Beatrice "represents theology" by pointing out that the love which Dante expresses for her in *Purgatorio* includes the passion he felt for the bodily charms of the girl he saw in the streets of Florence.

The fiery wall which stands between Dante and Beatrice is roughly analogous to the pestilential fire which Oedipus is called upon to put out before he can gain Jocasta, and to the ring of fire which Siegfried must penetrate to reach Brunhilde. Dante's meeting with the mother-figure takes place only after Virgil, his father-mentor, has left. In *The Magic Mountain*, Castorp approaches his Beatrice on Walpurgisnight only after he has dismissed Settembrini, his Virgilian guide.

The three realms suggest three psychic powers in varying proportions: In the *Inferno*, primitive, anti-social acts predominate; in *Purgatorio*, the ego, or the operation of the will gains mastery; in the *Paradiso*, the psyche is integrated.

Here again, the function of the ego appears in Dante's art which molds the underlying erotic fantasies into their symbolic forms.

Epilogue

Dante's epic ends with the light-simile *stelle*, in contrast to the sombre *umbras* of Virgil's *Aeneid*, and the author called his work a *Commedia*, to indicate its happy resolution. As noted, the doctrine of grace precludes final tragedy in the Christian religion.

Yet, *The Divine Comedy* does contain the tragic residue of mythopoesis. In his essay, "The Symbolic Imagination" (*Kenyon Review* [Spring, 1952]), Allen Tate has noted this element by distinguishing between the hero and the author. He points out that after Dante has ended the poem, he still faces the *human* task and fails "in the sense that he will have to start over again when he steps out of the poem." Tate also questions that we are to suppose the hero actually attains the Beatific Vision. The vision in the poem, he writes, "is imagined, it is *imaged*; its essence is not possessed. . . . Perhaps the symbolic imagination is tragic in sentiment, if not always in form, in the degree of its development." In *De Vulgari Eloquentia*, Dante himself states that "the style which we call tragic appears to be the highest style."

The disparity between existence and reality appears in the social order of Dante's *Paradiso* itself. In early Christian doctrine, God's love is equally distributed to everyone at all times. In Dante's paradise, God, "the Prime Equality" (XV), distributes his love *unequally*. The first Canto announces this theme by declaring that the glow of God's glory penetrates more in some regions and less in others. There is "disparity" (XV) in heaven: Some souls are placed in lower, others in higher heavens. (Even new-born infants, saved by baptism, are placed in varying orders.) Apart from the spaceless and timeless Empyrean, where all are united in one heavenly rose, Paradise consists of hierarchical orders. *Dante's Heaven thus reconstructs the medieval feudal system where everyone was to accept his assigned station.* That is, Dante's poem spiritualizes the very historic system which was the basis for his political dissidence.

Yet, here too, Dante evinces his criticism of this structure. This is manifested directly in his inclusion of heathens and declared enemies of Christianity in his Catholic Heaven, and more subtly in the Canto dealing with Piccarda and Constanza. Piccarda had been forced by her brother to leave the cloister and accept a political marriage. Yet, Santayana points out, she is placed in the lowest Paradise of the Inconstant Moon although she had broken her vows *unwillingly*. When Dante asks her whether she wishes for a higher sphere, she replies that such desire is impossible, for our peace lies in His will. The hierarchical order is itself an expression of the diversity of God's grace (XXXII).[28] The case of Piccarda shows that divine justice is exacting. Love is administered, not by the tender Mother-Goddess, as in Eastern Orthodoxy, but by God the Father and the Son. Dante retains the hierarchy of the patriarchal scheme. (Even Beatrice is, for the most part, a "masculine sage," as Vossler calls her, an "angelic creature under the hood of a doctor of theology.")

Peace on Earth

From Virgil, Dante learned that social-political peace was a condition for spiritual harmony. A terrestial paradise must precede the heavenly peace which Dante finds in Paradise.[29] How deeply Dante felt about this emerges from the prayerful lines in *De Monarchia* (Book I):

> Whence it is manifest that universal peace is the best of all those things which are ordained for our blessedness. And that is why there rang out to the shepherds from on high, not riches, not pleasures, not honors, not length of life, not health, not strength, not beauty, but peace. For the celestial soldiery proclaims, 'Glory to God in the highest; and, on earth, peace to men of good will.' Hence, also, 'Peace be with you' was the salutation of him who was the salvation of man.[30]

In *Purgatorio* (XV), Virgil told Dante that sharing increases the things shared and later he heard Beatrice's "We are" (*Ben sem*) countering the Siren's song, "I am." Dante saw Florence and Rome, the city and the church, corrupted by self-indulgence, torn by strife and treachery. His Paradise is a prayer that earthly divisiveness might be supplanted by universal communality. The heart of his idea was the union of an ethical politics with a practical morality, aiming at a supra-national world. Perhaps Friedrich Engels had this in mind when he characterized Dante as the first international mind of our modern era. Dante seems to be saying, as Santayana puts it, that what mankind was once, that it must become again: "What in his day seemed a dream—that mankind should be one commonwealth, is now obvious to the idealist, the socialist, the merchant." This idea may be one of the reasons for the appeal which Dante has in our day.

Yet *The Divine Comedy* shows the marks of the coming Renaissance in that the main focus is on the hero, Dante, for whose sake the journey takes place (the word "I" is on nearly every page of the poem). His mission is to save himself, rather than the others, who remain where they are.[31] However, this individual emphasis is also expressed in Dante's rebellious spirit. In life, Dante was a dissident, suffering exile from country, friends and family, rather than recant his beliefs. In the famous lines written to a friend:

> Far be it from the preacher of justice, when he hath suffered a wrong, to pay his coin to them that inflicted it as though they had deserved well of him. . . . What then? May I not gaze upon the mirror of the sun and stars wherever I may be? Can I not ponder on the sweetest truths wherever I may be beneath the heaven, but I must first make me inglorious, nay infamous, before the people and the state of Florence? Nor shall I lack bread. (*Letters of Dante*, p. 659.)

The epilogue in *The Divine Comedy* is connected with its transcendent concept of God. In contrast to Job's Yahweh and the Greek deities who can be seen, addressed, and who manifest themselves in the dynamics of natural phenomena, Dante's God transcends the sphere of nature. To be sure, there is grace. But the nature of human desires is such that man is forever tempted by earthly illusions. This precludes a paradisiac finale in Dante's Catholic myth as well. Charles Williams points out that the very last lines of the epic emphasize will, desire and movement:

> Already on my desire and will prevailed
> The Love that moves the sun and the other stars.

In the final analysis, the epilogue follows from the mystery of primary causation. Man, we are told, can know only the effects of the divine plan, but not its cause (in theologic terminology, only the *quia*, not the *propter quid*). In connection with the mystery of the Trinity, Dante is instructed:

> He is mad who hopes that reason in its sweep
> The infinite way can traverse back and forth
> Which the Three Persons in one substance keep.
> With the quia stay content, children of the earth!

While this may also discourage inquiry into temporal maladjustments, it can serve as the basis for the inspiration of the quest. In the beautiful lines from the final Canto, Dante sings of the sweet effect which lasts in memory, even as the cause remains a mystery:

> As he who dreams sees, and when disappears
> The dream, the passion of its print remains,
> And naught else to the memory adheres,
> Even such am I; for almost wholly wanes
> My vision now, yet still the drops I feel
> Of sweetness it distilled into my veins.[32]

127

NOTES

1. Arthur Lovejoy's *The Great Chain of Being* (Cambridge, Mass., 1936) summarizes the ways this problem was handled. The Scotists argued that whatever God willed was good because he willed it and Abelard held that the goodness of the world followed from the fact that it was created by a good and rational deity. Aquinas rejected such necessitarian optimism since it disallowed free will and made the distinction between absolute and hypothetical necessity. At the same time, he stated that "a universe in which there was no evil would not be so good as the actual universe." According to Lovejoy, Aquinas evaded the consequence of the two premises when they led towards admitting the complete correspondence of the possible and the actual.

2. The quotations from Mr. Haroutunian are taken from an unpublished paper he read before the Duodecim Society in November, 1948.

3. Arnold Toynbee, *A Study of History* (New York and London, 1947), p. 223.

4. The historic existence of a figure, by itself, does not prevent its becoming the subject of mythopoesis. The crucial question is whether such a figure is *translatable* into other frameworks. In an essay on "Typological Symbolism in Medieval Literature" (*Yale French Studies*, No. 9), Erich Auerbach argues that "figurative interpretation" in Christian literature attributes a common meaning to causal and chronological events. Thus, an event which preceded Christ is revealed "as a prefiguration of a fulfillment or perhaps as an imitation of other events." Hence, Dante can include the Roman empire of Augustus as a "figure of God's eternal empire." The figurative interpretation derives from the eternal wisdom of God in whose sight "what happens here and now, has happened from the very beginning, and may recur at any moment in the flow of time." In Auerbach's interpretation, the difference between Christian and mythic doctrine is mainly terminological, the Christian God corresponding to the mythic eternal "It is." However, whereas in medieval thought God alone is both the eternal and temporal first cause, in the mythic perspective any figure or period can be "first." In mythopoesis, the imaginative power of man brings forth a reinterpretation, and in that sense, a re-creation of the world.

5. Erich Auerbach's *Mimesis* (Princeton, 1953) points to Dante's range of technical levels, from the elevated antique style to the vernacular realism and the "comic" mood. To Eliot, no poet of similar stature "has been a more attentive student of the *art* of poetry, or a more scrupulous, painstaking and *conscious* practitioner of the *craft*," no poet has the same "width of emotional range." Dante himself recognized the importance of technical skill and style. In *De Vulgari Eloquentia*, he wrote that the tragic style "can never be attained to without strenuous efforts of genius, constant practice in the art and the habit of the sciences." (All quotations from Dante are from *The Portable Dante* [New York, 1947].)

6. Alan Watts, *Myth and Ritual in Christianity* (New York, 1953). Cf. J. M. Robertson, *Christianity and Mythology* (London, 1936), Homer W. Smith, *Man and his Gods* (Boston, 1952), C. O. James, *Christian Myth and Ritual* (London, 1933).

7. Gertrude Leigh's *The Passing of Beatrice: A Study of Heterodoxy* (London, 1932) discusses some of these aspects. In his own time, Dante was neglected or abused by Catholic circles and his *De Monarchia* was burned by an inquisitor. See Ernest Curtius' essay, "The Medieval Basis of Western Thought" in *Goethe and the Modern Age* (Chicago, 1949).

8. Even St. Augustine, for whom the state was the work of the devil, wrote that the earthly city is "its own obvious presence," and the "symbolic presentation of the heavenly city." *Confessions,* Book XV, ch. 2, and *The City of God.*

9. Translations of *The Divine Comedy* are by L. Binyon.

10. Dante is especially scornful of Boniface VIII, whom he calls "the prince of the new Pharisees," consigning him to hell while he was still alive (*Inferno,* XI, XIX, XXVII).

11. This line of thought was suggested to me by Prof. M. J. Benardete. In the *Inferno* (II), Dante raises the question why he is selected to traverse the three realms, though he is "not Aeneas, no, nor Paul," is deemed by himself and others "too weak . . . for this thing." The question is not raised again and is never answered.

12. In *Purgatorio,* Statius declares that he became both a poet and a Christian through Virgil.

13. "Dante's Innocence and Luck," *The Kenyon Review,* XIV, No. 2, 303.

14. Maritain argues that Dante could diverge from Catholic tenets *because* he was "so perfectly sure of his faith," that his very heresies confirm belief, and sees Dante's elevation of Beatrice as due to the poet's naivete which "believes all things." This approach minimizes the implication of the fact, mentioned by Maritain himself, that Dante lived in a time when the old faith was being disputed.

15. For Dante, the literal sense "must come first, being the one which compriseth the others in its significance, and without which the study of the others would be impossible and irrational." Here, Dante shares Aquinas' position that all knowledge has its origin in the senses. For Aquinas, "the phantasm" is "the foundation of intellectual operation" (*On the Trinity,* VI). The "*quiddity* or nature existing in corporeal matter" is "the proper object of the human intellect, which is united to a body" (*Summa,* I, 87). However, Aquinas distinguishes between Theology (or metaphysics) and physics, holding that in the former the intellect frees being from its material trappings and from the imagination: "Therefore although the imagination is necessary for any consideration of divine things according to our status as wayfarer, yet it is never necessary to effect verification in the imagination in the case of divine things" (*On the Trinity,* VI, 2 *ad* 5). See William M. Walton, "Being, Essence and Existence for St. Thomas Aquinas," *The Review of Metaphysics,* III (1950), No. 3.

16. See Kurt Leonhard, *Der gegenwärtige Dante* (Stuttgart, 1950).

17. *De Monarchia,* Bk. I, ch. 4; *Purgatorio* XXVIII; *De Vulgari Eloquentia,* Bk. I, ch. 2.

18. There is a question whether *The Divine Comedy* fully accepts the doctrine of original sin. In *Purgatorio* (XVI), Mark Lombardo tells Dante that the root

cause of all evil is not human nature, but corrupt leadership (*mala condotta*) in the state and church:

> "The evil guidance whereto 'tis enslaved
> Thou seest is that which doth the word corrode,
> Not nature, that in you may be depraved."

And Omberto says that what made him insolent was his family's blood. Gertrude Leigh's *The Passing of Beatrice* argues that Dante denied original sin and held with Aristotle that the seed of nobility is instilled in all men before birth. This made it possible for Dante "to proclaim the divinity of the Roman people, the glory of the Greeks, to declare Aristotle to be divine and Cato to be a symbol of God the Father, to admit pagans, such as Ripheus, into the realm of the blessed."

19. Attention has been called to the wrath which begins with Canto VIII, where Dante wants to see Argenti plunged into the muddy broth and where he enjoys the sight of his being mangled. In Canto XXX, Virgil reproves him for listening "All ears" to the squabbles of perjurers and civic criminals.

20. > "O human people, why the heart confide
> There where fruition ousteth partnership?"

21. In *Purgatorio* (XXIV), Dante repeats the lines he had once written:

> ". . . I am one who hearkens when
> Love prompteth, and I put thought into word
> After the mode which he dictates within."

Dante appears to justify any form of love, so long as it is dictated from "within."

22. *Medieval Culture: An Introduction to Dante* (New York, 1958).

23. Cf. P. H. Wicksteed, *Dante and Aquinas* (New York, 1913). Vossler slurs over the conscious element which is operative in purgatory when he writes that here the sinners "are contending unconsciously against a part of their own ego."

24. > ". . . 'that this place I may see
> Hereafter,' I said, "have I this journey made.' "

Even Vossler notes the infantile nature of Dante's final stage (Santayana suspects that the mystical transformation of Dante's love for Beatrice to philosophy and theology was made possible by some lack of natural manliness in that love). In *Paradiso* (XXI), Beatrice likens Dante to a woman-figure (Semele) and herself to a male god (Zeus). She warns Dante that, were she to smile,

> "Thou would'st be as Semele, when her eyes' desire
> She had, and straightway was to ashes burned."

In *Dante's Drama of the Mind* (Princeton, 1953), Francis Fergusson holds that Purgatory and Paradise are new beginnings for Dante. One should add that he begins each new life as though he had learned almost nothing from the previous one.

25. In *Purgatorio* (XXI), knowledge is called "the natural thirst," and the opening of the *Convivio* repeats Aristotle's dictum that "All men by their very nature yearn for knowledge." Although authority and love are the supreme principles, knowledge is the condition of Love (*Paradiso*, XXVIII).

26. The master now appears as a youth, yet addresses Dante as "My son."
27. There is a remarkable analogy between Dante's dreams and the primitive ritual of sexual initiation. In *Sex and Religion* (New York, 1919), Pierre Gordon writes that among primitive people, ritual defloration is performed by a holy deflowerer. "Obviously, the ritual had to be accomplished by a qualified being endowed with supernatural force . . . Owing to this fact, her entire future sexual activity bore the stamp of divinity." He adds that by a gradual transition, "sexual sanctification had been transformed into sacrificial killing." Dante's dream of Beatrice's death is followed by her actual death.
28. Here, Dante is instructed on the distinction between the free will of man which is relative (though the "most precious" gift God made to man) and the absolute will of God. Aquinas argued that man is free to the extent that his acts are determined not by past but by future life and that he can be regenerated by knowing the consequences of sinning. Yet, since human choices are known to God beforehand and he alone can directly act upon the will, human acts are, in this sense, predestined. Free choice would seem to depend upon grace—it happens to man ("Seizes the soul," as Dante learns in *Purgatorio* [XXI]). In Catholic doctrine, knowledge, bliss and love follow from grace, which is the first principle. Man can only resist "sufficient," but not sanctifying or "efficient" grace, administered by the church. From this, it would appear that guilt and grace—not character—are "fate." It is doubtful how much of this was congenial to Dante's temperament. As noted, there is a question whether *The Divine Comedy* fully accepts original sin. Despite all the instructions Dante receives, he declares that the problem of freedom is incomprehensible (*Paradiso*, XIX).
29. This point was suggested to me by Dr. Roderick Marshall.
30. Peace is the leading motif of the poem: In the *Inferno*, Francesca greets Dante with prayers for the peace denied to her and Paolo; in *Purgatorio* (XXVI), we hear of the angel who came down with the decree of peace, "for ages prayed and wept for." Earlier (V, X), Dante says that he is pursuing peace "From world to world," and is buoyed by the knowledge that he will finally reach a peaceful state. And, as noted, Piccarda speaks the celebrated line "In Sua voluntade e nostra pace" (*Paradiso*, III).
31. Dante's "heroism consists primarily in the fact that he suffers from seeing the plight of others. His own salvation depends on the heavenly, not the social community.
32. See Appendix III for "A Note on Virgil's *Aeneid*."

The Golden Age of
Chivalric Honor
Don Quixote

IN THE THREE CENTURIES which separate *The Divine Comedy* from *Don Quixote*, faith in tradition begins to give way to individual exploration. Dante's way is rigorously fixed by venerable theological law and revelation. In contrast, Quixote does not rely on religious guidance, but draws on his own resources. The Don is the first hero who would prove himself by his personal exploits, who himself chooses to engage in a quest and whose journey has no assigned designation. *Don Quixote* marks the transition from medieval to Renaissance mythopoesis.

For this kind of journey, the novel—and *Don Quixote* is the first major work of this genre—is a particularly fitting form. In contrast to the strict conventions of the Greek drama and the rigid structure of Dante's epic, the novel has a loose organization, permitting a "wandering" journey. The novel arose concurrently with the beginnings of the middle class and pictures its commonplace life in the language of prose. The Prologue to *Don Quixote* suggests this change. A friend advises the author that the grave tone of classical writing and the fantasies of chivalric romances are to be replaced by a colloquial realism and comic overtones:

> . . . there is no reason why you should go begging maxims of the philosophers, counsels of Holy Writ, fables of the poets, orations of the rhetoricians, or miracles of the saints; see to it, rather, that your style flows along smoothly, pleasingly, and sonorously, and that your words are the proper ones . . . without any intricacy or obscurity.[1]

Chivalry

The idea of chivalry was adventure for the sake of adventure.[2] Honor consisted in "pure" service for the Lady who was not present, and the knight's only purpose was to prove *himself* brave, constant and courteous. Ideally, he expected no reward, did not fight for country, profit or God. The Crusades linked the two main chivalric strains—love and war—into a religious pattern. (Earlier, Mohammedanism had joined religion and war in the slogan of "the Holy War.") The chivalric myth was to counteract the knight's merciless cruelty to the enemy and his sexual promiscuity. Service to the feudal lord and to the Lady was transposed into service to God and the Virgin Mary. The knight's courage and courtship were assimilated into Christian chivalry which was to help the needy, weak and oppressed, "the downtrodden, the widow and the orphan" (the Council of Clermont).

However, in his actual historic function, the knight was a member of a highly selected group, did not serve mankind, but the upper hierarchy, for which he was remunerated by grants of land and protection of his castle. Chivalry contributed to the rise of militant feudalism and supported it, as in the case of the Frankish *commendatores* and *caballeri*, and the Teutonic *commutatus*. The knight helped the Frankish rulers resist the invasion of the Vikings, Magyars and Slavs, and helped the Christian kings overthrow the Moorish rule in Spain. Likewise, ideal service to the Lady deteriorated into bigamy and adultery. (The knight was supposed to direct his love towards a married lady.) Knight-errantry became errant passion even as Troubadours and Minnesingers continued to sing of the one true love.

By the time of the Renaissance, chivalry and its international feudal base were no longer a living force in Western Europe and were being supplanted by the national state and middle class commercialism. Artillery fire had made the knight's armor and his personal valor useless. Spain, however, ignored the Western Renaissance. Economically backward and geographically insulated, it had developed no dynamic middle class. Hence, it held fast to its older values, to the memory of its resplendent *conquistadores* and to its Catholic faith. And it clung to the myth of chivalry. The phenomenon was embodied in the *hidalgo* who keeps up the appearance of nobility by shunning work (except sheep industry) as below his dignity. He is represented in the picture of a hungry man who would create the impression that he has dined well by ostentatiously picking his teeth.

Still, by 1600—when *Don Quixote* was being written—even Spain could no longer believe in this medieval myth. The barbers, merchants, the new university students, and the soldiers equipped with modern weapons made the *hidalgo* look foolish. The chivalric idea took on a pseudo-form and became a parody of itself. At this point, Cervantes attempts to save the mythic reality of the chivalric idea by creating the *poetic* figure of Don Quixote.³ His novel attempts to picture *the knight-errant as a complete man* who transcends the specialized qualities of chivalry. Knight-errantry, the author states, is a discipline "that comprises within itself all or most of the others in existence." The knight must be skilled in jurisprudence, astronomy, mathematics, must be a theologian and physician. Unlike the medieval knight, the Don both argues and fights for his idea, is at once a dreamer, philosopher, soldier and god-man.

Cervantes and Don Quixote

Unamuno argues that the greatness of Cervantes' personality is not to be found in his own biography but in the hero of his novel. Yet, the facts of Cervantes' life show both a direct and an ironic relation between the author and his work.

Cervantes and his Don are both poor noblemen whose decline parallels that of Spain; they leave their small villages to become far-wanderers, Cervantes travelling to Italy, Portugal, the Azores and Algiers, Quixote throughout the Spanish peninsula. Neither is successful in meeting practical problems: in his life, Cervantes failed to establish himself as a soldier and public official. (Only in the battle at Lepanto, he is supposed to have shown unusual bravery or perhaps desperation; there is also a story that he refused to name those who tried to help him escape from captivity.) We have an analogy between Quxote's youthful Lady whom he never sees and Cervante's wife, half his age, whom he left shortly after marriage, returning to her only in his old age. Finally, in their last years, both resort to symbolic values: Quixote becomes a visionary knight; Cervantes becomes the poetic creator of the knight.

On the other hand, *Cervantes over-compensates for his personal practical deficiencies by absolutizing Quixote's spiritual assets*: Quixote is poor in material possessions, but rich in generosity; he is physically emaciated, but the bravest of men, never suffering serious disability from his frequent falls; he is an old man, but youthful in his love; he is an unknown *hidalgo*, but becomes famous, the written account of his exploits appearing during his own life. The most prominent over-compensation appears in Quixote's asceticism. Where Cervantes is rumored to have had many love affairs (there are also accounts of his bastard daughter's sordid sexual involvements), the Don's relation to women is one of rigid abstinence. He remains loyal to the Lady he never sees, expending on her his entire love-energy. And he derives his spiritual powers from this asceticism. The novel itself contains an ironic comment on this phenomenon. When the Don returns home, his niece says to him:

> And yet, to think that you could be so blind and foolish as to try and make out that you are a hero when you are really an old man, that you are strong when you are sick, that you are able to straighten out the wrongs of the world when you yourself are bent with age, and, above all, that you are a knight; for, while the real gentry many become knights, the poor never can.

Act I: The Mythic Golden Age

Cervantes' *Don Quixote* transcends historic chivalry, its allusions pointing not so much to actual chivalric figures as to heroes in classical mythology. Its very ideal of the Golden Age is taken from Ovid.[4]

The Don and his squire are in the company of six goatherds who graciously invite them to share their meal, spread on sheepskins. Quixote asks Sancho to seat himself by his side "to see the good that there is in knight-errantry . . . that you may be even as I who am your master and natural lord, and eat from my plate and drink from where I drink; for of knight-errantry one may say the same as of love: that it makes all things equal." After he has stilled his hunger, Quixote begins his celebrated soliloquy:

> Happy the age and happy those centuries to which the ancients gave the name of golden, and not because gold, which is so esteemed in this iron age of ours, was then to be had without toil, but because those who lived in that time did not know the meaning of the words 'thine' and 'mine.' In that blessed era all things were held in common. . . . All then was peace, all was concord and friendship. . . . Thoughts of love, also, in those days were set forth as simply as the simple hearts that conceived them, without any round-about and artificial play of words by way of ornament. Fraud, deceit, and malice had not yet come to mingle with truth and plain-speaking. . . . Maidens in all their modesty . . . went where they would and unattended; whereas in this hateful age of ours none is safe. . . . It was for the safety of such as these, as time went on and depravity increased, that the order of knights-errant was instituted, for the protection of damsels, the aid of widows and orphans, and the succoring of the needy.

Quixote's picture of primitive rustic communality stands in contrast to the sophisticated institution of knighthood and to the chivalric forms in the court epics of *Tristan* and *Parsifal*, of *Orlando Furioso*, the *Nibelungenlied*, and the Spanish *Cid*. The Don does invoke medieval knights—especially Amadis—to teach him how to imitate their deeds, but he does so with occasional irony, as when he refers to their robberies and thefts. He calls attention to the difference between the romantic style of the chivalric books and the "thoughts of love" in his Golden Age which were set forth "as simply as the simple hearts that conceived them, without any roundabout and artificial play of words by way of ornament." Here, life had no "orders," was not organized by rigid ordinances and rituals.[5]

To be sure, this pagan age is welded to a religious function. The novel comes out of a Catholic country, and Cervantes assures the reader that he and his hero are devout Christians. Yet, the memory which Quixote summons up is not of institutionalized Christianity, but *the idea of religion* which can be enacted by men of various faiths. His service calls for no recompense, and reminds one of Spinoza's saying that he who loves God does not expect that God love him in return. Sancho even thinks that his master is "better fitted to be a preacher than a knight-errant," and later suggests that they ought to become "saints." Quixote's reply is that "Chivalry is a religion in itself, and there are many sainted knights in glory."

Act II: The Journey

At the opening, we find Quixote living in harmony with himself and his fellowmen, to whom he is known as Alonzo the Good. It is a womb-like harmony, confined to the tight enclosure of his room which his chivalric books have transformed into a fairy realm, so that he almost wholly forgets "the administration of his estate."

But this Eden, gained by fancy, stands in contrast to the rotten state of the world which Quixote later calls an "iron age," ruled by indolence, arrogance and expediency, by injustice, dishonor, poverty and false pride. As the Don is about to go out on his third sally, he declares to his household:

Today, sloth triumphs over diligence, idleness and ease over exertion, vice over virtue, arrogance over valor, and theory over practice of the warrior's art.

The novel illustrates the truth of Quixote's indictment from the Andres episode at the beginning to the picture of Sancho's "kingdom," Baratria. That both the ideal knights in the cave of Montesinos and Dulcinea, the peerless lady, should be in need of money, and that Don Quixote, the honored knight, should discover holes in his silk stockings, illustrates what Madariaga calls "the melancholy of poverty" in the knight's world. In these "calamitous times," Quixote sees his task

to devote himself to the hardships and exercises of knight-errantry and go about righting wrongs, succoring widows, and protecting damsels . . . favor and aid the weak and needy . . . spare the humble and trample the proud under foot.

His calling, Quixote says, does not permit "easy pace, pleasure and repose—those things were invented for delicate courtiers; but toil, anxiety, and arms." Quixote reasserts the Quest which calls for repudiating Dante's *le presenti cose* and Faust's *Faulbett*.

This infernal state sends Alonzo the Good out from the security of his book-encrusted room to set things right. But, where the medieval knight took a specific direction and for a specific purpose, Quixote wanders anywhere and on principle. And, where the function of the former was restricted to saving a particular king, chieftain or Lady, the Don would liberate the entire Christian world, inspired by love for a Lady he never meets.

Quixote's journey takes him through a realm which he later characterizes as purgatory and in which he *invites punishment* as do the sinners in Dante's middle kingdom. Later, he reaches a kind of earthly paradise in the Cave of Montesinos where he meets his Beatrice, Dulcinea, as well as in the duke's court where he is treated as though he were a real knight and where he again meets Dulcinea in an enchanted shape. Dante goes on from here into the heavenly paradise. In Cervantes' post-medieval setting, Quixote's paradise turns out to be an illusion and the hero returns home to recognize that swine are swine. Still, as we shall see, his journey is not in vain and Alonzo the Good is symbolically saved in the myth of Don Quixote.[6]

Windmills Are Lawless Giants

In his first sally, Quixote continues the fanciful temper he showed at the beginning. He insists that the inn is a castle and that the district prostitutes are ladyships. He is treated like an infant (the girls feed him through a reed) and his behavior (such as his beating the muleteer) is carried out in a kind of somnambulistic state. Upon his return home, he asks Sancho to join him. This is his first realization that he lacks self-sufficiency and that he needs a realistic guide.[7]

Like Shakespeare's Hamlet, who announces in the first act that he plans to put on an antic disposition, Don Quixote states at the beginning of his journey: "I mean to imitate Amadis by playing the part of a desperate and raving madman. . . ." The Don too *knows that he is playing the madman.* Sancho recognizes this when he says that the Don is "a madman with good sense." Quixote himself becomes aware that his attack on the windmills is a moral and social attack on "lawless giants." He tells Sancho:

137

In confronting giants, it is the sin of pride that we slay, even as we combat envy with generosity and goodness of heart; anger, with equanimity and a calm bearing; gluttony and an overfondness of sleep, by eating little when we do eat and by keeping long vigils; lust and lewdness, with the loyalty we show those whom we have made the mistresses of our affections; and sloth, by going everywhere in the world in search of opportunities that may and do make of us famous knights as well as better Christians.

Those very windmills, observes Salvador de Madariaga, "have grown what his wild imagination fancied and seems to have guessed—giants of industry whose hundred powerful arms encircle the world, awe-inspiring powers which work in the night."[8] Quixote's windmills reappear in Faust's Mephistophelian giants who work in the night, in Wagner's dark Nibelungen, and in the myriads of "arms" in the "fallout" of the Hydrogen Bomb.[9] It is mad or foolish to fight windmills, but the temerity to brave dangers is not. The Don is fully aware that "the readiness is all," as Hamlet declares. In the adventure of the fulling hammers, he tells Sancho:

> Supposing that, in place of fulling hammers, this had really been another dangerous adventure, did I not display the requisite courage for undertaking and carrying it through?

The Mythic Crime

In the earliest myths, such as Tammuz-Osiris, to play God means to be God. Beginning with the Grecian myth, the hero only pretends that he is enacting a God-role, realizing that to fulfill his task, he needs the aid of others. Prometheus leans on his mother's foreknowledge and the Chorus, Orestes on Apollo and Athena, Oedipus on Theseus.

Don Quixote would be completely self-sufficient. In Dante, redemption is unthinkable without the church. The Don never seeks its help, placing reliance on himself. He assumes that he alone knows what truth and goodness are—in other words, that he is God and—that he alone knows how they are to be brought about—in other words, that he is also God's minister.[10] Like Spinoza's Substance, he would be his own cause and develop out of his own assumptions. He insists that all must act in accordance with his standards and must do so *without compromise*. Quixote's "crime" lies in his arrogant attempt to replace both God and society. He tells a group of the Holy Brotherhood:

> Who is so ignorant as not to know that knights-errant are beyond all jurisdiction, their only law their swords, while their charter is their mettle and their will is their decrees?

This attitude is criminal or mad in an age when chivalric-religious honor is no longer useful. The Don is not careful or calculating; he insists on justice without regard for practical consequences. A knight-errant, he says, "must uphold the truth though it cost him his life to defend it." Indeed, the Don's "madness" is a deliberate strategy to counteract the "reason" of his time and to remind men of the Golden Age, and its anti-pragmatic values of honor, justice, equality and freedom.

Guides

To become a culture hero, the mythic figure must work not only for, but also with elements of his group. Despite his pretended godlike self-containment, Quixote too relies on guidance—Rocinante, Dulcinea, Sancho, Sansón and Roque.

Rocinante and Dulcinea

As noted, one of the stages of the mythic hero is his rescue by animals or people of humble origin. Among the former is the motif of the horse, found in many myths, from the Oriental novel to Thomas Mann's Joseph.[11]

On the physical level, Rocinante and Dapple provide Quixote and Sancho with the "stature" of a knight and squire on horseback. Sancho is nearly helpless without his Dapple, and Rocinante selects the direction of Quixote's planless journey, the Don letting the horse "take whatever path it chose, for he believed that therein lay the very essence of adventure." Quixote names his humble steed "Rocinante," that is, one that comes "before" all others.

If Rocinante is Quixote's animal guide or "first cause" on the lowest level, Dulcinea is his Platonic guide or entelechy. Like Rocinante, she "accompanies" Quixote throughout, is his silent steady pilot. "God knows," he tells the duchess, "whether or not there is a Dulcinea in this world or if she is a fanciful creation," like the Phyllises, Dianas, Galateas. What matters most is that she is the conception of what

> needs must be, seeing that she is a damsel who possesses all those qualities that may render her famous in all parts of the world, such as: a flawless beauty; dignity without haughtiness; a tenderness that is never immodest; a graciousness due to courtesy and a courtesy that comes from good breeding . . . in short, the ideal of all that is worth while, honorable, and delectable in this world!

Although Dulcinea is of humble origin, she is more to the Don than Helen and Lucretia were to their lovers, her beauty being the realization of "all the impossible and chimerical attributes the poets are accustomed to give to their fair ones." As is the case with Dante's Beatrice, Dulcinea's existence lies in her essence—with this difference: Where Beatrice is a heavenly ideal, Dulcinea is as she "needs must be" on earth. Cervantes transposes Dante's theologic values into the esthetics and morals of chivalry. Since he has become a knight-errant, the Don tells the canon,

> I am brave, polite, liberal, well-bred, generous, courteous, bold, gentle, patient, and long-suffering when it comes to enduring hardships, imprisonment and enchantments.

Here, Cervantes points to the living relevance of his chivalric idea. When Sancho questions his master's service to Dulcinea, the Don replies:

> Do you not know, clodhopper, drudge, scoundrel, that if it were not for the valor she infuses into my arm, I should not have the strength to kill a flea? ... She fights and conquers in my person, and I live and breathe and have my life in her.

Dulcinea is the poem of the book. And when Quixote speaks of poetry, his metaphors are similar to those he applies to Dulcinea. Poetry, he says, is "a young and tender maid of surpassing beauty." Yet, art by itself does not make a poet, but only art combined with nature. Hence, knight-errantry requires more than imagination, must put its art into practice.

But Quixote's "practice" shuns the sexual sphere. Apart from the episodes of the muleteer and Maritornes—and even here the sex act is not consummated—Cervantes keeps male-female involvements in a courtly, decorous key. This motif of chastity is absolutized in Quixote, the Prologue announcing that he is "the most chaste lover and the most valiant knight." The Don never deviates from his abstinence, and his hand, which "no other woman has ever touched," remains pure. ("Quixote," in Spanish, means the piece of armor that protects the thigh.)

Quixote begins like Goethe's Faust. He too is middle aged, unmarried, leading a contemplative life in a room stuffed with books, and he also goes out for a life of experience. Yet, where Faust does allow himself the realistic experience with Gretchen, Quixote remains chaste, and successfully withstands the amorous advances of Altisidora and others.

Sancho: The Folk-Guide

Sancho Panza is the realistic Virgilian guide in Quixote's inferno, his practical sense for compromise balancing the knight's unconditional demands. In Sancho, Cervantes pays homage to the common earthy man, to his steadfastness, loyalty and folk-wisdom. Sancho is fond of using proverbs which the author tells us are "concise maxims drawn from the wisdom and experience of our elders." Sancho's peasant roots also give him a feeling of security and self-respect. When the Don reproves him for refusing to lash himself, Sancho retorts that he is "simply standing up for myself, for I am my own lord." He has no reservations about being able to govern the island, "for I have a soul like anybody else and a body like the rest of them."

The novelist needs Sancho as *the witness* who can verify and lend some creditability to Quixote's visions. Sancho is the bodily corrective of Quixote's spirituality.[12] His earthy and watery personality sustains the airy and fiery knight and prevents his brittle figure from breaking apart. Sancho is a kind of mother-wife to Quixote. Bickerman has noted Sancho's "womanly" aspects: He is soft-hearted, cries readily, is gossipy and noisy, docile, and earthy. His job, Sancho tells Sansón, is "to look after (Quixote's) person and see to keeping him clean and comfortable. . . ." He compares himself to "a piece of land that of itself is dry and barren, but if you scatter manure over it and cultivate it, it will bear good fruit." And he hopes that his master's conversation will bring forth "blessed fruits" in him. Quixote himself says that it is his burden to support Sancho as one "who hath served him faithfully in fertility and abundance." He draws an analogy between the choice of one's wife and the selection of a dependable companion on a journey, one who "must ever be with him, in the bed, at table, wherever he may go."[13]

Sancho has been interpreted as the the reverse of Quixote. But this ignores Sancho's own latent idealism and imaginativeness. While he is sceptical about Quixote's stories of what he saw in the Cave of Montesinos, he is ready to challenge anyone who dares say that his master is a madman. Indeed, Sancho's fantasy is at times even less grounded in fact than his master's. Although he himself has thought up the scheme of Dulcinea's enchantment, he becomes persuaded that the enchantment actually came to pass. When he feels himself borne towards heaven in the duke's mock pageant, his imagination is as rich as was Quixote's in the Cave of Montesinos. For all his sobriety, scepticism and sense for the concrete, Sancho has something of the fiery restlessness of his countrymen who once traversed oceans to found an empire.

Above all, Sancho is loyal. He may think his master stark mad, yet cannot help following him:

> We're from the same village, I've eaten his bread, I like him very much, he's generous to me, he gave me his ass-colts, and, above all, I'm loyal.

He follows the Don not because he really expects to be rewarded with an island, but because he loves him.[14] Like Ahab's Starbuck, he senses his master's "humanities." At the end, he is the one to recognize that in his recantation, Quixote had returned "a victor over himself . . . the greatest victory that could be desired." At the beginning, Sancho exhibits the peasant's psychology of skeptical caution and prejudice, as well as the tendency to believe everything. Through his contact with the Don, Sancho develops an appreciation of Quixote's Golden Age. He learns to depreciate the value of money and property. He tells his wife that while he has brought her no pearls, he has something "of greater value and importance," adding that "there is nothing in the world that is more pleasant than being a respected man, squire to a knight-errant who goes in search of adventures." As for the island, if he does not get it, "my bread will taste as good, and it may be even better, without a governship than if I was a governor."

Towards the end, Sancho approaches Quixote's own anti-pragmatic attitude. His central motivation is also loyalty rather than expediency. Yet, even when he acts without "reason," he rarely leaves solid ground. On the island, he rules "with Solomonic wisdom rather than Quixotic genius," as Entwistle puts it. Sancho cuts through the formalism of the island's feudal bureaucracy and nearly enacts the kind of justice Quixote calls for.

THE SOCIAL MACROCOSM

In the second part of the novel, Quixote learns that Cid Hamete Benengeli has already written a history of his exploits which romanticizes his adventures and makes him appear absurd. *The Don can now see himself as history and society see him.* By this device, Cervantes prepares us for the modification of Quixote's private realm through the entry of *a public witness* which is more inclusive than Sancho. In Part II, Quixote and Sancho enter the social macrocosm, represented by the duke's castle and Sancho's "state" of which he becomes governor. This socialization corresponds to that of Orestes and Oedipus in Athens and Thebes, of Aeneas in Latium, Dante in Paradise, Hamlet and Faust at their courts, Siegfried at Gunther's castle, Mitya Karamazov in court, Mann's Joseph in Egypt.

Act III: The Cave of Montesinos: Eden Regained

At the very point when Quixote's vision has been exposed to public view, the Don undertakes *his most private adventure*, the only one in which *there is no witness* who can either corroborate or refute him. Quixote proposes to enter the Cave of Montesinos to verify the marvelous tales told about its knights. He will penetrate to its bottom, "even it was as deep as Hell . . . an undertaking that is reserved for me . . . that the world may know that there is nothing, however impossible it may seem, that I will not undertake and accomplish." This adventure is analogous to Faust's descent to the realm of "The Mothers."

Quixote is lowered by a rope "into the depths of the horrendous cavern," and upon his return, tells of wonderful experiences: He fell into a profound sleep, and when he awoke, found himself "in the midst of the most beautiful, pleasant, and delightful meadow that nature could create or the most fertile imagination could conceive." His eyes next fell on a sumptuous royal palace where he saw his Dulcinea and Montesinos. Montesinos told him that he and the other knights have waited for him a long time that he "might go back and inform the world of what lies locked and concealed in the depths of this cave." He further learned that Merlin held many of the knights and ladies under a spell. However, Merlin also prophesied that Quixote would come to revive the profession of knight-errantry and that by his favor and mediation, they themselves may be disenchanted. In this adventure, Quixote has his deepest dream, gains the absolute fulfillment of his wishes. He sees his Lady and meets his model forerunners, who accept him as a knight and extol his mission.

Quixote's cave adventure into "those remote regions that are hidden from our sight" is a journey to gain knowledge of his sources, a return to the womb for his "parental" origin. The hero has to delve into these enchanted solitudes alone, only the rope connecting him with the outside human world. As Quixote is lowered, his voice grows fainter and fainter. He returns with his eyes closed, apparently "sound asleep." When he awakens, he gazes about with a bewildered look and asks for something to eat. And his first words are about the Eden-like state he had experienced:

> You have taken me away from the most delightful existence mortal ever knew and the pleasantest sight human eyes ever rested upon.

In this earthly paradise, Quixote saw Montesinos, his "father-model" and Dulcinea, the "mother" of his idea. Here, his mission to free Dulcinea and the world from its present enchantment is sanctioned.

In the cave adventure, Quixote allows his fantasy fullest sway, unimpeded by any audience. Here, he goes *through* the last phase of self-indulgence and thus completes the narcissistic aspect of his self. The "three whole days" spent in the cave prepare his rebirth towards social maturity.[15]

But Quixote's rebirth becomes possible because the reality principle invades his wish. To begin with, his heroes are *historic* prototypes, taken from Carolingian and Arthurian sources. And Quixote sees them not as they were once, but in the state to which they have been reduced in Quixote's own time—in want and in exile. Their sorry state is underscored by the fact that the peerless Dulcinea is obliged to ask for a loan of half a dozen reales.

Disenchantment

In Quixote's next adventure, the Montesinos setting is transposed into the existing social world, the ducal castle, where the Don permits himself to be honored as though he were a real knight. Here, as in the cave, he reaches an earthly paradise, again "sees" his Dulcinea in an enchanted form.

But, this time he realizes that the chivalric idea has degenerated into mock-ritual and pageantry, and active knight-errantry into a theatrical game and hocus-pocus. Quixote enters into this game half-heartedly, ceases to to be a knight and plays the court-fool. He allows himself to become part of an idle world, "leisurely enjoying all the comforts and luxuries." Here, he accepts precisely the kind of ease which he had earlier condemned as invented "for delicate courtiers," embraces the kind of life which threatens the quest of the mythic hero. Quixote's adventures deteriorate to frivolous pranks, such as removing beards from allegedly enchanted ladies, defending the simulated dishonor of the duenna's daughter, battling with cats (here he suffers more serious wounds than when he fought against "giants"). Without Sancho, who has left to assume rule of his island, Quixote is a sad and lonely figure; he has neither a historic nor poetic function. *For the first time, the Don appears in an undignified role.*

His adventures in the cave and at the duchy are the peripety of his journey and the point at which his disenchantment begins. His reversal is foreshadowed in his doubts whether the stories about knights are true, and the Don now questions his cave-adventure. For the first time, Don Quixote exhibits fear. In the braying episode, he flees, without thinking of the danger in which he left Sancho. His confidence is shaken and he speaks of his ultimate defeat.

The change in Don Quixote is further revealed in the advice he gives Sancho on how to rule his island. He, who had been against any compromise, now writes his squire: "Be not always strict, nor always lenient but observe a middle course between these two extremes, for therein lies wisdom." He urges Sancho to lean towards mercy rather than justice and advises him to "consider slowly and deliberately" petitions from beautiful women. And he, who had never doubted who he was, tells Sancho: "You are to bear in mind who you are and seek to know yourself, which is the most difficult knowledge to acquire that can be imagined."

The episode with Sansón Carrasco is a further stage in Quixote's disenchantment. More than any other character in the story, Carrasco seems to make it his life's mission to refute Quixote. While Sansón writes poetry, Quixote's notion of *applying* the claims of poetry strikes him at first as ludicrous, then fills him with envy, especially when Quixote's exploits are written down by Cid Hamete. He does not laugh the knight away, is not amused by him as are the duke and duchess, but grimly proceeds against him. When Quixote insists on sallying forth a third time, despite repeated mishaps, Carrasco hits on the strategy of defeating the Don by entering his realm, becoming a "knight," and forcing Quixote to admit that Dulcinea is not the most beautiful lady. That is, Sansón *would refute the reality of Quixote's vision.* And he would do this, not in the interests of restoring his wits, but out of a bitter "thirst for vengeance."

The passing of chivalry is brought to Quixote's attention by a new type of "knight," Roque Guinart. Roque is a highwayman and his life is also full of strange and dangerous adventures. He, too, is courteous and generous, "better suited to be a friar than a highwayman." Originally, he engaged in this activity to exact personal revenge, but later took up the task to right all kinds of wrongs. Now Roque identifies himself with Quixote, not as a matter of faith, but because he regards him as the most "sensible man in all the world."

But Roque is a Quixote with real enemies and real adventures, and he does not attempt to do everything by himself, but works with his group. He is more merciful than exacting, and he meets injustice by expedient measures, such as providing people with money and safeconducts. He has little to say about ultimate goals, but works for immediate practical results. Don Quixote's silent acceptance of Roque's way constitutes a silent critique of his own functionless knight-errantry.

Swine Are Swine

The meeting with Roque prepares us for the defeat Quixote suffers in the encounter with Sansón. As he lies on the ground, the Don acknowledges that his sorry end was brought about by "presumptuousness." His subsequent plan for a pastoral Arcadia is a weak echo of his original quest. In this effort to achieve an imitation-Eden, he is trampled by bulls. With that, he and Sancho push on "with more of shame than pleasure in their mien." Quixote ceases to idealize his obstacles, calling the bulls "a herd of filthy animals." At this point, the author steps into the story to tell the reader that from now on Quixote calls an inn an inn and not a castle. In his final adventure, he and Sancho are trampled by grunting and snorting pigs. This time, Quixote recognizes that swine are swine, and makes the melancholy observation that Heaven has decreed that a vanquished knight be "eaten by jackals, stung by wasps, and trampled by swine." Unlike Shakespeare's Prospero, who preserves his magic framework, Quixote is shocked back into reality.

On his last return home, Quixote admits the defeat of his historical mission, renouncing the idea that the Golden Age can be brought back into his own time. "In last year's nests," he states, "there are no birds this year." These words express his new insight that a past model cannot be literally transposed to serve different cultural-social foundations. His words take the form of a proverb. They are his final acknowledgment of folk-wisdom.

Parody

From one perspective, Cervantes presents Don Quixote as a parody of a human being. Insisting on a fixed principle, his thrusts, in Thomas Mann's phrase, are "into empty space." Cervantes, who could create a full-dimensioned Sancho, made Quixote a one-dimensional character. Here is Cervantes' own implied reservation over his hero—analogous to Virgil's drawing of Aeneas.

Cervantes' reservation also appears in the fact that Quixote's idealistic attempt to enact justice results in the opposite. He frees dangerous convicts, wrecks funerals and inns, beats innocent servants, smashes Pedro's sole possessions. In the incident with Andres, Quixote makes the lad's master promise to pay Andres what is due him, and then leaves, satisfied that the promised word is sufficient. Not only does Andres' master not pay him, but after Quixote's departure, he mishandles the boy for having complained. When they meet again, Andres begs the knight:

> For the love of God, Sir Knight-errant, if ever you meet me, even though they are hacking me to bits, do not aid or succor me but let me bear it, for no misfortune could be so great as that which comes of being helped by you.

146

Don Quixote belongs to the mythic tradition of the "Fool" who disregards or is unaware of worldly demands and conditions. Such is the foolishness of Buddha, Parsifal, Emanuel Quint, Prince Myshkin and Alyosha Karamazov.[16] These Fool-Figures act without "reason," ignoring practical considerations. Especially in the first half of the book, Quixote approximates the "pure" foolishness of the child which assumes that its imaginative projection is equivalent to the nature of things and that it can remove what it does not like by its magical wish. In these instances, Quixote is a humorous figure.[17] As in the case of Dostoyevsky's Prince Myshkin, Quixote would do away with unjust consequences without inquiring into social causes and without considering the consequences of his own acts.[18]

Reality and Existence

At the beginning, Quixote impresses us as a subjective idealist who would create the world out of his personal idea, or as a Cartesian might argue, "I think, therefore it is." Quixote himself is aware that he is postulating a poetic model and not material existence, that he is not imitating things "as they were but as they ought to have been." Now, Cervantes' hero suffers defeat at the hands of things as they are, but emerges with dignity in refusing to give up the ideal image of things as they ought to be. In a similar way, Faust's inner light is dignified by Goethe, Prospero's magic world by Shakespeare, Wotan's Valhalla by Wagner, Peer Gynt's dreamings by Ibsen, the musical values of Hanno Buddenbrook, Hans Castorp and Andreas Leverkühn by Thomas Mann.[19]

However, *Don Quixote* must be approached from what Americo Castro calls a double perspective. W. H. Auden calls the Don the greatest representation of the Religious Hero in literature in that he is committed to his idea "with absolute passion," pursuing the absolute truth by himself. But Auden slights the other perspective in the novel when he adds that such a religious hero is, in a sense, "not related to others at all."[20] For, alongside his insistence on absolute commitment, Quixote is thoroughly related to others. Where Dante postulates an unbridgeable gulf between existence and essence (the inferno and paradise), Cervantes would join and reconcile them through human effort.

The motif of reconciliation also appears in the introduction of the comic. Cervantes *invites us to laugh at Don Quixote* by presenting the incongruity between his godlike pretentiousness and his human limitations. Yet, this very comic element *socializes and humanizes* his hero. In Dante's "Comedy," there is no laughter, except possibly on the part

147

of God, as he views man's futile effort to extend himself beyond human power. In Cervantes' work, we have *human* laughter. And laughter in turn humanizes. While *The Divine Comedy* dwells on divine love, *Don Quixote* shifts towards man's compassion for man. Dante's Catholic "Comedy" precludes tragedy, postulating a transcendental harmony. Cervantes' novel introduces tragedy into man's earthly function and destiny. At the same time, he softens and socializes man's tragic lot by the comic mode.

In this spirit, Cervantes also democratizes the traditional aristocratic hero. For Quixote, the mark of excellence is character, not station. "They alone impress us as being great and illustrious," the Don tells his niece and housekeeper, "that show themselves to be virtuous, rich and generous." Indeed, the point of the novel is that all can be "knights." It elevates a poor old man into a knight-errant, a peasant into a squire. Rocinante is said to be equal or even superior to Alexander's Bucephalus; the village wench Dulcinea is endowed with the virtues and gifts of the Helens and Didos. Where the picaresque novel regarded the commonplace as something uninteresting, Cervantes' work treats it as containing the elements of excellence.

Waldo Frank holds that Quixote does not convert a single person. This is true in the sense that poetry is not completely translatable into existence. Yet, we have *approximations of conversion.* To begin with, nearly all enter into Quixote's realm of discourse and action, are transformed "into madmen and fools." All the characters derive their legitimacy through the Don—without him, they would cease to have any function in the novel.

In the course of the story, nearly all the characters and the reader develop respect, sympathy and love for the Don. What impresses them most is not so much his courage, nor that he is ready to fight against impossible odds, but that he is *a good man.* "For," the author interpolates at the end,

> as has been stated more than once, whether Don Quixote was plain Alonso Quijano the Good or Don Quixote de la Mancha, he was always of a kindly and pleasant disposition and for this reason was beloved not only by the members of his household but by all who knew him.

And, even as they ridicule his methods, *nobody laughs at the idea* behind them.

Quixote's mission is to free the noble resources which he believes are present in all. And, by acting *as if* goodness, justice and honor are inherent in all, he encourages them to come alive. And here are the practical effects of Quixote's idea: His courteous treatment of the inn-keeper, the prostitutes and others results in their acting in a courteous manner. All sense that his idea is the reservoir of inspiration and hope, of kindness, courage and loyalty, that without it, their life would be a drudge. The students look upon him "with admiration and respect", and as Quixote lies on his death-bed, Sancho begs him:

Ah, master, don't die, your Grace, but take my advice and go on living for many years to come; for the greatest madness that a man can be guilty of in this life is to die without good reason, without anyone's killing him, slain only by the hands of melancholy. Look you, don't be lazy but get up from this bed and let us go out into the fields clad as shepherds as we agreed to do. Who knows but behind some bush we may come upon the lady Dulcinea, as disenchanted as you wish.

The conversion of Sansón is even more impressive. He, who had gone to such extremes to refute the Don's idea, now reverses himself, saying that "the worthy Sancho speaks the truth." At Quixote's death, he is anxious to keep his "madness" alive, and his verses praise the Don as "a gentleman bold." Earlier, he had commented on Cid Hamete's history of Don Quixote: "Little children leaf through it, young people read it, adults appreciate it, and the aged sing its praise."

Towards the end of his life, Quixote declares that he has been "too daring." In this admission, he realizes that no one, however brave, can go it alone. Like Faust, Quixote renounces his superhuman claims and accepts the fact that man must eat dust. But, whereas Faust and other Renaissance heroes fight primarily for themselves, Quixote would be the sacrifice for others. This motive "to live dying," as he puts it, distinguishes him—as Turgenev and Waldo Frank point out—from other mythic heroes, such as Hamlet and Ahab. Quixote's sacrifice has for its aim freedom, justice and peace on earth. Freedom, he tells Sancho

is one of the most precious gifts that the heavens have bestowed on man . . . for the sake of freedom, as for the sake of honor, one may and should risk one's life.

And, in a speech delivered "in such manner and couched in such excel-lent terms that it was quite impossible for the moment for any of those who heard him to take him for a madman," Quixote states that the end of letters is

human knowledge, whose object is to administer distributive justice and give to each that which is his and see that good laws are observed . . . the objec-tive is peace, which is the greatest blessing that men can wish for in this

> life. . . . For the first good news that mankind and the world received was
> that which the angels brought on the night that was our day: "Glory to God
> in the highest, and on earth peace, good will toward men."

Here, Cervantes continues Dante's political philosophy, his hope for
one world of church and state. For the achievement of this goal, Cervantes saw the need of uniting Quixote's idealism with Sancho's realism. Yet, the two are not united but run parallel to each other. In
Spinozistic language, the order and connection of ideas in the one is the
same as the order and connection of things in the other. *Don Quixote*
was published about the same time as *Hamlet*. Here, the perspectives
are no longer parallel, but conflict with each other.

NOTES

1. The translations are from Samuel Putnam's *Don Quixote* (2 vols.; New York, 1949).

2. The chivalric idea has a long history, from the Bushio in Japan and the ancient Beduins of North Arabia to the Teutonic and Frankish orders. The English printer William Caxton gives chivalry a mythic heritage, tracing it back to Adam and Eve. He identifies the archangel Michael as the first knight and claims that chivalry was the earliest divine device for the recovery of the human race from the ruin of the fall. See Hearnshaw's article, "Chivalry," in *The Encyclopedia of the Social Sciences*.

3. Byron's oft-quoted statement that *Don Quixote* laughed chivalry away is there-fore misleading. Quixote is not a knight and must "burnish up some old pieces of armor," fashion a half-helmet out of cardboard and a barber's basin. Quixote himself knows that his horse is a homebred steed, that Sancho is a peasant and Dulcinea a farm-girl of his neighborhood. The figure of an *hidalgo*, ridiculed and beaten, could neither disparage nor glorify the traditional pic-ture of chivalry. This point is developed by Joseph Bickerman, *Don Quixote und Faust* (Berlin, 1929).

4. Quixote's tasks are likened to the labors of Hercules and Jason, his trials to those of Aeneas, his wanderings to those of Ulysses. Analogies are drawn be-tween Quixote and Tantalus, Sisyphus, Ixion; between his demise and the fall of Troy; between his relation to Sancho and that between Castor and Pollux, Orestes and Pylades. The Don's journey through perilous regions is described as a descent into the Orphic shade. References to other legends include Tityus, Silenus, Helen, Pyramus and Thisbe, Zeus and Danae, Actaeon and Diana, Daphne, Perseus, Merlin, Nisus.

5. The irony is that Quixote's soliloquy is delivered after he has fed, not on honey, fruit and water, but on meat and wine. While the herdsmen-theme re-curs in the book (Quixote feasts and fights with herdsmen and wants to become one himself at the end), the novel dwells but little on the role of nature and,

with the exception of the episode of the fulling hammers, is strikingly devoid of nature-descriptions.

6. Cervantes himself suggests that his novel has the character of a seasonal ritual. In the chapter dealing with the end of Sancho's government on the island, he writes that "everything moves in a circle, that is to say, around and around: spring follows summer, summer the harvest season, harvest autumn, autumn winter, and winter spring." Quixote's journey begins in spring-like fancy, followed by a period of "probation" during which he descends into the labyrinth of the Montesinos, "traversing deserts and solitudes." He enjoys a "summer" when he is feted as an honored knight at the ducal palace. His journey culminates in his "fall" in the encounter with the swine, followed by the "winter" of his death. But his death is not final in that his idea is carried forward by Sancho and Sansón Carrasco.

7. The Don retains faith in his idea even after the barber and the curate burn his chivalric books (except for the books of Amadis which are his principal inspiration). The burning of books has as little effect here as it did in Hitlerite Germany. Quixote does *not* need the books as Madame Bovary does to keep her romanticism alive. Hence, she ends as a suicide, none the wiser for her fancies.

8. *Don Quixote* (London, 1940), pp. 2-3.

9. By such transposition, we can also grasp the sense in which Quixote sees a flock of sheep as an army in disguise. And, when we bear in mind the Don's attitude towards the clergy of his day, we can understand why he calls the Benedictine friars a lying rabble and sees in the priests travelling at night "something evil . . . phantoms and monsters from the other world."

10. The religious, Quixote tells Vivaldo,

    "in all peace and tranquillity, pray to Heaven for earth's good, but we soldiers and knights put their prayers into execution by defending with the might of our good arms and the edge of the sword those things for which they pray. . . . Thus we become ministers of God on earth, and our arms the means by which he executes His decrees."

    He has praise for those saints who were valiant and men of arms, such as St. James, the patron saint of Spain; St. Paul, who was "a knight-errant in life"; St. George, who was "a protector of damsels" (he slew the dragon to save the King's daughter) and hence was "one of the best knight-errants that the heavenly militia ever had"; St. Martin, who was even more charitable in giving to the poor than he was valiant.

11. We find it in the Satapatha Brahmana where "the Gods, ascending, knew not the way to the heavenly world, but the horse knew it." It appears in Lucian and in Apuleius' *The Golden Ass*. In the Irish legend of Conn-Eda, the knight lets the animal lead him, and Owain of King Arthur's Round Table is guided by the lion. In the Greek novel, the donkey attains a heroic quality by the quiet patience with which he endures beatings. (See Carl Kerenyi's *Die Griechisch-Orientalische Romanliteratur* [Tübingen, 1927] and Heinrich Zimmer's *The King and the Corpse* [New York, 1948]). In Apuleius, Lucius' transformation

into an ass constitutes punishment. But Robert Graves reminds us that the ass was sacred to the God Set-Typhon:

> "The ass had been so holy a beast that its ears, conventionalized as twin feathers sprouting from the end of a sceptre, became the mark of sovereignty in the hand of every Egyptian deity: and the existence of an early Italian ass-cult is proved by the cognomens Asina and Asellus in the distinguished Scipionian, Claudian and Annian families at Rome. . . . Asses are connected in Western European folklore, especially French, with the mid-winter Saturnalia at the conclusion of which the ass-eared god, later the Christmas Fool with his ass-eared cap, was killed by his rival, the Spirit of the New Year—the child Horus, or Harpocrates, or the infant Zeus . . . there was an eastern European tradition identifying Saturn's counterpart Cronos with the ass. . . . This explains the otherwise unaccountable popular connection between asses and fools." (Introduction to *The Golden Ass of Apuleius* [New York, 1951].)

Thomas Mann's Joseph experiences a rebirth in the pit by the mishap to his donkey Hulda, and it is a donkey which leads him through part of the Egyptian desert. In general, the donkey embodies the wisdom of the lower instincts; in Thomas Mann, there is also a suggestion of the donkey as phallic guidance.

12. Their relation is similar to that of Orestes and Pylades, Leander and Naukleros, Hamlet and Horatio-Fortinbras, Faust and Mephisto, Ahab and Starbuck, Castorp and Joachim, Joseph and his brothers. In particular, the analogy to Mann's *Transposed Heads* suggests itself where Nanda is the body, Schridemann the head. In both, a transposition takes place in which their roles are interchanged.

13. When Quixote insists that Sancho lash himself on his bare back and seat himself on the bare board of the magic horse, Sancho complains that his master wants him to be both pregnant and a virgin.

14. Sancho's faithfulness to Quixote is matched by his devotion to Dapple. Upon giving up his governorship, all he asks for is "a little barley for his gray and half a cheese and half a loaf of bread for himself."

15. As in other mythopoesis (Oedipus, Dante, Faust, Karamazov, Mann's Castorp, Joseph, Grigors) the number three is a recurrent figure: Quixote makes three sallies in all, and leaves for his third sally after spending three days at home; Quixote feasts three days before he goes down into the cave, stays three days with Roque and dies three days after he has made his will; there are three peasant lasses, one of whom Sancho would have him believe is Dulcinea.

16. Variants of this role appear in the simulated foolishness of David, Moses, Cyros, William Tell, and the Hamlet figures of Saxo and Shakespeare. Cf. Otto Rank's *Inzest Motif in Sage and Dichtung*, pp. 264-265.

17. Freud calls humor "the triumph of narcissism." It "refuses to be hurt by the arrows of reality," insisting that "it is impervious to wounds dealt by the outside world." Humor is "rebellious," asserting itself "in the face of the adverse

real circumstances." It "asseverates the invincibility of one's ego against the real world and victoriously upholds the pleasure principle." The humorist plays the part of a superior adult, identifying himself to some extent with the father, "while he reduces the other people to the position of children." *Collected Papers*, V, 217-218.

18. Prince Myshkin also attempts the impossible, knowing that it is impossible, enacting the myth of the sacrifice and atonement for others. Myshkin is the selfless "idiot" who exposes himself and passively accepts suffering; Quixote is the wilful hero who brings about his suffering and insists on being the sacrifice. And, where Dostoyevsky's character would achieve the good by being good, Quixote would change conditions by individual "revolutionary" acts.

19. In the stories of Grisóstomo and Anselmo, Cervantes seems to be saying that one should *not* attempt a literal implementation of the idea. Grisóstomo would also be a knight. But his desire to possess Marcela (his Dulcinea) in flesh and blood results in her death. Similarly, in the story of "One Who Was Too Curious For His Own Good," Anselmo's error is to try and prove the virtue of his lady by presenting her with *real* temptations.

20. W. H. Auden, *The Enchafed Flood* (New York, 1950), pp. 97 ff.

Renaissance Mythopoesis
Hamlet

THE MYTHIC VIEW undergoes an eclipse in the Renaissance. A more critical temper arises and piety for communal standards shifts towards reliance on individual and "private" experience. This shift appears in the varieties of cultural experience: in Cartesian doubt, in portrait painting and the closet drama, in the private economic market and in Lockian empiricism. Personality, or what the Italian Renaissance called the *uomo singolare*, was something new and exciting in the age of Erasmus, Leonardo and Michelangelo, of the Borgias and the Medici.

In the earlier mythopoesis, the revolt of the heroic character takes place *within* the framework of tradition. The Renaissance hero does not have such ties with his community, family, state, church or God. He does not have the guiding voice of Yahweh, Moira or God, the counsel of a Chorus or the intercession of a Virgil and Beatrice. The new hero stands alone. He becomes the exploratory "journey"-man, and must seek the sanctions of belief within himself. Absolute truths and values are replaced by unlimited possibilities, the unified vision by "perspectivism." In the religious realm, this takes form in the split of the universal Catholic Church into varieties of Protestant churches.

In *The Great Chain of Being* (pp. 242 ff., 315) A. E. Lovejoy characterizes this trend as "the temporalizing of the Chain of Being." Previously, the conception of the Chain of Being rested on the principle of plenitude which precluded belief in progress or in any significant change in the world as a whole. It was based on the Solomonic dictum that there is nothing new under the sun. This principle with its reference in the past or in an eternal present broke down in the Renaissance which placed the golden age in a future consisting of endless ascending stages. The Platonic notion that the highest good lay in cessation of desire and the Dantesque vision of an eternal celestial paradise were supplanted by the principle of man's natural insatiable desires in the sensuous world. And God was interpreted as himself desiring that man should be insatiable. The new conception of God was not of a self-sufficient, timeless Absolute, but (in Lovejoy's formulation) one "whose prime attribute was generativeness, whose manifestation was to be found in the diversity of creatures and therefore in the temporal order and the manifold spectacle of nature's processes."

The new perspective was an ambiguous gift to those in the Renaissance who were sensitive to the dangers of such unlimited freedom. They welcomed the opening up of the universe, but felt bewildered by the multiple winds of doctrine; they were buoyed by the new freedom and its futuristic possibilities, but were disquieted in seeking a future which could never be present; they hailed the new science which took its reference from the cosmic scheme, but missed the older approach which centered in specifically human norms and values; they felt dignified by the stress on individual responsibility, but missed the firm guidance which had provided a steady platform in society, ethics and religion. In sum, individual freedom brought expansion and enrichment, as well as perplexity and confusion. For, as the term re-naissance indicated, the new age did not completely repudiate tradition: Rabelais' Gargantua is reared on classical models; Corneille and Racine revived ancient themes and characters; Shakespeare tried to save his kings and princes, and Goethe contrasts the idyllic life of the old couple Philemon and Baucis with Faust's "Sorge." That is, these mythmakers tried to integrate individual expression with "the great chain of being."

They pictured the emerging dislocations through the broken structure of the family—in Hamlet, Faust, Siegfried, Ahab, Mitya Karamazov, Hans Castrop and other modern figures.

THE RESIDUE OF SENSIBILITY: SHAKESPEARE'S HAMLET

The Hamlet story does not have the same ancient background which we find in earlier mythopoesis. Still, its roots reach back to the heroic age of Scandinavia, and it has a rich legendary background—Icelandic, Celtic, French, possibly Roman and Persian.[1]

Even as Hamlet appears as a strange and unique individual, we feel a deep kinship with him. Indeed, a "Hamlet-problem" and a "Hamlet-character" have become something like figures of speech. And Hamlet's mission is the same as in all mythopoesis: to rid the body politic of its diseased state. Furthermore, the play's specific motifs connect it with traditional myths. The theme of fratricide (here called "the first murder") is found in the Egyptian saga of *The Two Brothers* and in the Bible; the conflict of son and mother has its prototype in the Babylonian myth of Marduk and Tiamat; revenge on the usurping uncle in the Hindu myth of Kans-Krishna.

Shakespeare's *Hamlet* is also replete with mythic allusions. These are not a matter of decoration (as is the case with much of Renaissance literature), but are evocative of Hamlet's own situation. To Hamlet, his father was a Herculean hero with the qualities of "every god." In the closet-scene, he tells Gertrude:

> See what a grace was seated on this brow;
> Hyperion's curls, the front of Jove himself,
> An eye like Mars to threaten and command,
> A station like the herald Mercury
> New-lighted on a heaven-kissing hill;
> A combination and a form indeed,
> Where every god did seem to set his seal,
> To give the world assurance of a man.

(All quotations are from *The Tragedies of Shakespeare* [London, 1939]).

The union of Hamlet's father with an ordinary woman reenacts the mythic union of the god with a mortal woman (Zeus-Jupiter with Alcmene-Semele-Danae), giving birth to the hero-son (Hercules-Dionysus-Perseus). In Shakespeare's play, the god is also dismembered and reappears on earth to shape the destiny of the family-world.

"Remember Me"

The mythic character of *Hamlet* is established by the Ghost. He corresponds to the Greek Chthonic deity whose voice carries over into the present and the future. The Ghost's call to Hamlet, "Remember me," is the *Grundbass*-motif of the play and defines Hamlet's social and psychological burden. For the audience, the Ghost is an accepted convention; for Horatio, he may be an illusion or an evil omen. For Hamlet, he is a personal voice whose words "Remember me" echo in his mind throughout the play. The voice from the past is a portentous reality for Hamlet. He is the only one both to see and talk to the Ghost.

The Ghost is the sphinx of the play. And its function, as that of the sphinx, is to bring the hero's attention to his origins and to set his future task. In mythic vocabulary: The Ghost reaches back to Creation and forward to Re-creation, with the Quest as the necessary mediate labor toward the fulfillment of this task.

Now, the Ghost speaks an ambiguous language. In this Renaissance work, the voice of authority is no longer clear. Hamlet himself *begins* by questioning tradition. He has been to Wittenberg, Luther's university, where he may have received an intellectual framework for "protesting." Yet, Hamlet's Protestantism is dialectically limited. For, he is the son of a Catholic father who dwells in Purgatory ("Till the foul crimes done in my days of nature/Are burnt and purg'd away"). Thus, Hamlet is pressed from two sides, finds arguments for being and non-being, for acting and not acting, for self-esteem and self-depreciation. The ancestral voice has a "questionable shape," and Hamlet cannot carry out its command although it calls on him "by heaven and hell." Hamlet's over-all dilemma lies in that he can live neither with nor without this tradition. The present is gross and sensual, its mirth "heavy-headed revel." The King is a satyr, the Queen a "pernicious woman," Polonius a fish-monger, the people a "distracted multitude," the state "rotten."

Still, Hamlet will not "be bounded in a nut-shell." He is no Pyrrhic skeptic and makes a heroic effort to resolve his dilemma by thought, passion and action. The result is a pendular swing between action and inaction, between faith and doubt. He believes that there *are* objective norms of right and wrong but does not know which action corresponds to these norms. All action is in a specific direction and Hamlet's difficulty consists in *his inability to be a specialist* in an age of developing specializations. Hence, when he does act, he questions the wisdom of his decision; and when he does not act, he condemns himself for letting "all sleep." Hamlet incorporates the legacy of doubt. He doubts himself and he doubts others (unable to confide his plans even to Horatio); he doubts the "idols of the tribe," demanding adherence to the old, the "idols of the cave," inviting detachment, and the "idols of the market-place," clamoring for attention to the demands of the hour. His cosmic vision paralyzes his arm and his realistic sense prods him into action.

Such ambiguities haunt Hamlet throughout the play. He thinks that the apparition may be "an honest ghost," or that he may be a "fiend." This dialectic carries over into Hamlet's attitude towards his mother, Ophelia, even to Claudius. In sum, this Renaissance hero remains in the midway stage. He is *the first hero in mythopoesis who questions himself from the beginning, the first who fails to carry out his mission, until it no longer really matters to him.*

Act II: The Journey

Preceding the action of the play, Hamlet was presumably united in love with his family. His father had the attributes of a god, the mother of a saint, and Ophelia of a "heavenly child."[2] There follows the second stage in which the hero leaves home. Now, Hamlet is not set out as were Job, Prometheus, Oedipus and Orestes, nor deserted as was Mitya Karamazov. Yet, for Hamlet, his mother's remarriage, closely following his father's death, spells a world that is "out of joint."

When Hamlet returned from the university, he found that experience was at odds with the theory he and Horatio had learned at Wittenberg. After he has spoken with the Ghost, he tells his friend that there are more things in heaven and on earth than are dreamt of in his philosophy. His father's death estranges him from Gertrude, Ophelia, Claudius and the court. He has been expelled from Eden and must begin the tortuous journey through life's inferno.

Before Hamlet meets the Ghost, he is in relative equilibrium. His mother's remarriage shocks him into a *settled* state of melancholy. The world as a whole becomes an unweeded garden, its uses "weary, stale, flat and unprofitable." The world has rejected him, and Hamlet in turn rejects it as well as himself.

It is at this point that the Ghost appears. Hamlet feels himself "call'd," his "fate cries out," and he descends to meet the Ghost on the underground-platform, like Gilgamesh, Aeneas and Dante. Here, he undergoes the rites of initiation and is given the task of cleansing the rotten stables of the state.[3] The Ghost's command that Hamlet revenge the murder is issued at the beginning of the play, but Claudius is not killed until the end of the five-act drama. What accounts for the delay?

Ernest Jones points out that in the earlier versions, both the motive and the delay are traced to external and political factors. The murder of Feng (Claudius) is a public act, and only physical difficulties delay Amleth's revenge and triumph. In Shakespeare, not the political, but the family-situation, is in the foreground, and the external difficulties in carrying out the mission are minimized.[4]

Coleridge and the Romanticists have popularized the "inner" approach, arguing that Hamlet is too much of a speculative thinker to be a practical doer. This interpretation ascribes "Hamlet-" traits to dreamy and idling characters, such as Goethe's Werther, Jacobsen's Niels Lhynne, Ibsen's Hjalmar Ekdal, and the *nichevo* figures in Russian literature. But Shakespeare's hero is no such "Hamlet." He is a philosopher, to be sure; but he is also a soldier and a skilled fencer. Indeed, at the risk of over-statement, it can be said that *Hamlet is the most active character in the play*. Only where Claudius is involved, does Hamlet show hesitancy.

Some criticism centers Hamlet's problem in the social-political condition. For example, Smirnov's Marxist study argues that Hamlet is "caught between the corruption of the court, the vulgarity of the growing bourgeoisie, and the masses in whom he has no belief."[5]

Claudius' regime is corrupt. But, is it as corrupt as Hamlet says? The King is shown eager to make amends, and promises Hamlet the succession. His rule is no worse than that of other kings in the Tudor era. Only after Hamlet discloses his threatening designs in the playlet does Claudius move against him. Hamlet overstates the case against Claudius, as well as against Gertrude and Ophelia. And he overstates the case against himself as well. The social situation in the court is a necessary, but not a sufficient, condition for unravelling what Hamlet calls his "mystery." The analysis of *Hamlet* as the tragedy of a noble character in an ignoble society makes a sharp separation between him and his society and thereby lifts him out of his Renaissance setting. Hamlet himself says that his own "thinking" makes Denmark a prison for him, tells Rosenkrantz that "there is nothing either good or bad, but thinking makes it so." He confesses that he has "bad dreams," and is "unpregnant" of their cause.

THE PSYCHIC BURDEN

Shakespeare's *Hamlet* cannot be viewed as a Renaissance work in the same sense in which we speak of the Oedipus dramas and *The Divine Comedy* as Greek and Catholic. The problem of Oedipus and Dante is nearly identical with that of their culture. This is not the case with Hamlet. The Renaissance hero feels himself alone. There is no clear-cut voice of tradition, no existing symbols of authority with which he can identify. To know himself, Hamlet cannot engage in a social dialogue, but must try to analyze his burden by himself. This gives the play the character of *interiorization* and invites a psychoanalytic approach.

T. S. Eliot (*The Sacred Wood* [London, 1945]) observes that Hamlet's emotions are excessive without attempting to explain why they are so or why Hamlet vacillates. The most extended and brilliant exposition of this problem (suggested by Freud and somewhat developed by Otto Rank) is contained in Ernest Jones' *Hamlet and Oedipus.*

Jones argues that Hamlet's vacillation is not due to his general incapacity for action, nor to the unusual difficulty of the task, but to the fact that at heart he does not want to carry out the task. He is held back because unconsciously he identifies himself with Claudius who is the realization of his own repressed infantile wishes: sexual union with the mother and death of the father. When Claudius usurps his place, the repressed desire for the mother is stimulated. Hamlet can cover up this love by attention to Ophelia because she least reminds him of his mother. Hamlet detests Claudius, but "it is a jealous detestation of one evil-doer towards his successful fellow. . . . In reality his uncle incorporates the deepest and most buried part of his own personality, so that he cannot kill him without also killing himself." Hamlet's attitude towards Claudius is a complex projection of his attitude towards himself: disgust with his infantile wishes to take his father's place by the side of his mother, mixed with admiration for Claudius' success. The repressed energy seeks outlets in many secondary acts which wear Hamlet out. Only when the possibility of incest is removed—when his mother is dead —and Hamlet knows that he is going to die, is he free to kill Claudius. Hamlet's cosmic and social vision is disturbed by his private involvements.[6]

Although Hamlet does not actually commit incest or patricide, he is tortured by guilt-feelings from the outset

> That I, the son of a dear father murder'd,
> Prompted to my revenge by heaven and hell,
> Must like a whore unpack my heart with words.

Whether or not Hamlet does procrastinate is not as crucial as that *he himself thinks* that he is procrastinating and feels guilty. He confesses to Ophelia that he could accuse himself of such things

> that it were better my mother had not borne me . . . with more offences at my beck than I have thoughts to put them in, imagination to give them shape, or time to act them in.

And to Horatio, he speaks of his imagination which may be "as foul as Vulcan's stithy."

Hamlet's self-depreciation is his secret which cannot be accounted for by anything he has done. Indeed, the play as a whole has a tone of secrecy: It opens with a secret message, imparted to Hamlet at a secret place; when he returns, he solemnly pledges his friends to secrecy; the Ghost's appearance in the closet-scene is a secret known only to Hamlet. His over-all secret is the motive for his delay in executing the Ghost's commission, despite the fact, as Hamlet admits, that he has "cause, and will, and strength, and means" to do so.

What Hamlet does know is that he has bad dreams. The theme of bad dreams is also central in the soliloquy "To be, or not to be." Hamlet states that he is held back from suicide by "the dread of something after death." But what is the dread? Hamlet first says that it is simply the fear of the unknown ("that we know not of"). In the next lines, he twice associates death and sleep:

> . . . . .To die; to sleep,
> . . . . 'tis a consummation
> Devoutly to be wish'd, to die, to sleep;

He then proceeds to link sleep with dream—and here is "the rub."

> To sleep; perchance to dream; ay, there's the rub;
> For in that sleep of death what dreams may come,
> When we have shuffled off this mortal coil,
> Must give us pause;

Hamlet feels guilty not over something he has done, but only of what he *thought* of doing. He is the precursor of our modern characters for whom a symbolic crime, one committed in fantasy, is a real crime. The reason for this lies partly in the new historic climate.

Oedipus was able to shift part of his burden to public powers—the oracle, Apollo, "the pleasure of the gods," with whom he could identify. As he tells the Priest of Zeus at the opening of the action: "my soul mourns at once for the city, and for myself, and for thee." And, for the sake of the city, he insists on uncovering the truth, regardless of the consequences to himself. With the increase of personal freedom in the Renaissance, there came an increase of solitude and loneliness.

Aristotle declared that all men of genius are melancholy men. Isolation, or what Nietzsche called the "pathos of distance," may be a source of inspiration and is necessary for the organization of one's creative powers. Examples of such productive solitude may be seen among the Hindu sages and Christian Eremites, in figures such as Spinoza and Santayana. But, not all solitude bespeaks of genius, not where withdrawal stems from fear or guilt. In that case, one *suffers* from isolation.

Hamlet's melancholy is connected with his being apart from others and hence he has a deep need for association. In the last lines of the first act, he twice begs his friends to stand with him:

> . . . . let us go in together,
> . . . .
> Nay, come, let's go together.

His melancholy does not arise merely from a pessimistic evaluation of man and the world. He tells Guildenstern:

> What piece of work is a man! how noble in reason! how infinite in faculties!
> in form and moving how express and admirable! in action how like an angel,

in apprehension how like a god! the beauty of the world! the paragon of animals!

It is characteristic of Hamlet's broken dialectic that he goes on to say
that to him man is but the "quintessence of dust."

Hamlet's relation to Ophelia is an enigma to critics who ignore his
psychological conflict. What is the nature of this "love" that Hamlet
does not even allude to in his monologues or in his talks with Horatio?
What kind of love is it that can kill the beloved's father without a twitch
of remorse or thought of its effect on her, that (as Dover Wilson remarks) feels less distressed about her death than about the remains of
a jester dead long ago? What has Ophelia done to justify Hamlet's in-
sulting language?

From the psychoanalytic perspective, Hamlet's behavior to Ophelia
can be explained as a displacement of the prohibited love for the
mother. He transfers his affection from the one to the other, veiling the
identification by choosing a woman who "should least remind him of
his mother" (Jones). But it is a *displaced* love, and Hamlet devotes
himself but little to Ophelia. Actually, he tells her, "I never gave you
aught." What he did give was to the "idol" of his "soul," to an Ophelia
"beautified" in his projection. But because of his confusion between the
two, he treats Ophelia with the same mixture of insult, bitterness and
love which he expresses to Gertrude in the closet-scene.[7] Because Gertrude has proved sensual and deceptive, Ophelia (and all women) are
charged with "frailty." Indeed, Hamlet shows more affection for Horatio, even for Laertes than for Ophelia.[8]

The Strategy of Displacement

Ernest Jones points out that in the early version, Amleth feigns
madness to disguise his intention to revenge the murder which was a
matter of public knowledge. In Shakespeare, Claudius does not know
that Hamlet has learned of the murder. Here, the external situation does
not dictate Hamlet's simulated madness.

Hamlet's need "to put an antic disposition on" is his method of insu-
lating himself against the disturbing emotions which the Ghost's voice
set loose. Hamlet knows that he is "passion's slave" and might betray
the nature of his passion. He has as great a fear of exposing it to himself
as to others. In appearing to be aroused over Claudius' incest, he
screens his own unpermitted desire; in appearing to be concerned with
revenge for the murder, he conceals his concern over his feeling about
Gertrude. The strategy of displacement is the core of "play" in the

drama. For Hamlet, the "poet," the play *is* the thing,—the method by which he shifts attention away from his personal burden. Similarly, Hamlet substitutes preparations to carry out the action for the deed itself. A lightning verbal dialectic and rapid succession of movements are substituted for decisive steps, the play-murder and "bloody" thoughts for the murder itself.[9] Hamlet, the philosopher, the playwright, the actor, exhausts himself in continuously devising means, thereby continuously postponing the end.

Hamlet's strategy of displacement points to the coexistence of powerful forces within him which cross each other. The one calls for the murder of Claudius; the other inhibits him from carrying it out. Hamlet makes continuous preparations for both: He not only plans the killing of Claudius; he also frames these plans in a manner which prevent their success. For, as Jones points out, Hamlet's multiple devices are such as to *arouse suspicion against himself*: His antic disposition makes Polonius and Claudius wary; the playlet increases their suspicion; in the closet-scene, he nearly makes a full confession. This ambivalence appears in Hamlet's behavior as a whole: He tells Ophelia that he did and did not love her; his attitude to Gertrude bespeaks love and contempt. Even the King is not simply a Nimrod-Herod figure to Hamlet. When he sees Claudius at prayer, Hamlet reflects that only heaven knows "how his audit stands." Claudius' desire to pray shows that " 'Tis heavy with him," and that he may even be fit for "the purging of his soul."

Hamlet's strategy of displacement is further substantiated by analysis of the opening soliloquy, the platform scene, the playlet, and the closet-scene.

The Trappings of Woe

The extraordinary feature of the first soliloquy consists in what it *omits*: It contains not one word of *regret* over the death of his father. Even the clothes of mourning—Hamlet tells Gertrude—do not "denote" him truly, are "but the trappings and the suits of woe." In this soliloquy, Hamlet confines himself to condemning his mother: that she remarried, that she did so shortly after the King's death, that she married a man who is "a satyr" compared to his father, an "Hyperion." In the midst of these complaints, Hamlet reluctantly recalls the intimacy between his father and mother:

> Must I remember? why, she should hang on him,
> As if increase of appetite had grown
> By what it fed on. . . .

163

Next, he contrasts his father with *both Claudius and himself*. His mother, Hamlet complains, married his father's brother,

> . . . but no more than my father
> Than I to Hercules. . . .[10]

To be sure, Hamlet loved his father. But this love was disturbed by his mother's remarriage. The new pattern is a slightly distorted re-enactment of the young boy's oedipal conflict, stimulates this earlier hostility and partly submerges the love. As noted, Hamlet speaks of his father as god-like, likening his eye to that of "Mars, to threaten and command." And the Ghost speaks to him as a commander to his subject.[11] In the midst of calling on Hamlet to revenge him, the Ghost issues a strange and seemingly uncalled for warning:

> But, howsoever thou pursuest this act,
> Taint not thy mind, nor let thy soul contrive
> Against thy mother aught; leave her to heaven.

When the Ghost leaves, Hamlet dwells on his commandment, then interrupts this theme with the exclamation: "O most pernicious woman!" Why "pernicious," when the Ghost had only called her "my most-seeming, virtuous queen"?

Following the Ghost's departure, there takes place a remarkable change in Hamlet's mood: His melancholy is gone, and he speaks to Horatio and Marcellus in a spry, lighthearted tone, telling them that he has heard "wonderful" news, and addresses the Ghost playfully as "boy," "true-penny," and refers to him as "this fellow" and "old mole."

What is the reason for this change? Why does the news of the murder and the commandment to exact revenge lift his depression? Again, Hamlet's use of displacement offers a clue. He can now cover up the source of his personal anxiety by assuming a public mission, can put on his "antic disposition" and act out his secret burden in an acceptable form. The Ghost's command converts Hamlet's "bad dreams" into respectability by substituting a justifiable motive (a son's duty) for a guilty motive. It quickens him into life.

The Ghost's appearance is the catalyst for the subsequent action of the drama. The Voice from Purgatory *organizes* Hamlet by providing him with a mission. This vision does not express his death-wish; on the contrary, it makes for his *living, active* role. The Ghost propels Hamlet from a settled hellish melancholy towards dynamic restless activity.

However, Hamlet's high spirits do not last. While he does not revert to his earlier dejection, he begins to doubt his ability to carry through his "play." Will he be able to carry out his filial duty while

weighed down by his private burden? *Can he take over and be King?*
He, who feels himself to be no more like his father than is Claudius?
Hamlet questions his adequacy and laments the "cursed spite" which
commissions him to "set it right." The time is out of joint. But so is Hamlet. The final lines of the first act summarize the dual motif of the play:
the disjointedness and schism in the social and in the individual body.

When the Ghost leaves, Hamlet vows to "remember" only that which
the Ghost has charged him with, and to forget all those thoughts and
fantasies, associated with his father and mother, which might hinder
the execution of the assignment:

> Yea, from the table of my memory
> I'll wipe away all trivial fond records,
> All saws of books, all forms, all pressures past
> That youth and observation copied there,
> And thy commandment all alone shall live
> Within the book and volume of my brain,
> Unmix'd with baser matter: yes, by heaven!

But, for all his conscious resolve, this "baser matter" does mix with the
commandment, and gives him bad dreams.[12] Not "thought" or "reflection" as such, but memory of "pressures past" sap him of the energy
needed for resolute decision.

The Conscience of the Nephew

In "The Murder of Gonzago," Hamlet has found a ready-made play
in which a king is murdered by his brother who then marries the king's
wife. Dover Wilson has called attention to the fact that Hamlet *changes*
the play by inserting 12-16 lines of his own. It is not clear which lines
are Hamlet's. But the all-important consideration is that the playlet, as
presented, is *not* analogous to the situation as described by the Ghost.
Hamlet replaces Claudius by "one Lucianus, nephew to the king."
Dover Wilson concludes that in this substitution, Hamlet deliberately
indicates his intention to kill Claudius. The "nephew" points to Hamlet.
But who is "the king"? Is the reference to Claudius or to Hamlet's
father?[13] On either reading, Hamlet makes a central admission: that he
plans to kill Caudius, or that, concealed as the "nephew," he desired
the death of his father. In other words, the play which was to "catch the
conscience of the king," reveals instead the conscience of Hamlet, "the
nephew" who does the killing and then "gets the love of the king's wife."
The substitution is Hamlet's own poetic contribution and confession.

The scene gives other hints of Hamlet's personal involvement by the way in which he plays off Ophelia against his mother. (It is the only scene in which Hamlet confronts both women at once). When his mother asks him to sit by her, Hamlet replies that Ophelia is "metal more attractive." He lies down at Ophelia's feet and indulges in sexual word-play within his mother's hearing—"Shall I lie in your lap . . . I mean my head upon your lap . . . That's a fair thought to lie between maid's legs." To Ophelia's remark that Hamlet is "keen," he replies: "It would cost you a groaning to take off mine edge."

Confession in the Closet

Hamlet had complained bitterly that he must hold his tongue even though his heart should break. But once he stands in his mother's room, he pours forth in unrestraint. From the moment when Hamlet is told that his mother wishes to speak with him "in her closet ere you go to bed," we feel that everything else is crowded out of his mind. When Hamlet is left alone, he speaks in metaphors which suggest that he is about to enter a hellish terrain where he is to "drink hot blood" and "speak daggers":[14]

> "By and by" is easily said.
> 'Tis now the very witching time of night,
> When churchyards yawn, and hell itself breaks out
> Contagion to this world: now could I drink hot blood,
> And do such bitter business as the day
> Would quake to look on. Soft! now to my mother.
> O heart, lose not thy nature, let not ever
> The soul of Nero enter this firm bosom;
> Let me be cruel, not unnatural:
> I will speak daggers to her, but use none;[15]

In the closet-scene, he uses related metaphors:

> Let me wring your heart, for so I shall,
> If it be made of penetrable stuff,
> If damned custom have not braz'd it so,
> That it be proof and bulwark against sense.

As soon as he enters, Hamlet assumes a commanding tone: "Come, come, and sit you down; you shall not budge." It is as though he wanted to assume his father's role who had "An eye like Mars, to threaten and command. . . ." Gertrude is frightened by her son's threatening manner and when the concealed Polonius calls for help, Hamlet stabs the "rat."[16]

Hamlet is not the least disturbed by his "bloody deed," and at once reverts to his earlier tone, ordering his mother to sit down and let him "wring" her heart, hoping that despite "damned custom," it is made of "penetrable stuff." Following the Ghost's disappearance, Hamlet harps on a single theme: He begs his mother not to go to bed with Claudius:

> . . . go not to my uncle's bed;
> . . . Refrain tonight,
> And that shall lend a kind of easiness
> To the next abstinence; the next more easy.[17]

In this scene, Hamlet catches his own conscience even more than he did in the playlet. Here, his antic disposition is discarded, exposing his innermost obsession. Hamlet outdoes himself in apotheosizing the father, but does not even allude to the mission with which the Ghost has entrusted him. He seems to have completely forgotten this "memory," harping only on Claudius' unworthiness of his mother's caresses. This provides the context for the entrance of the Ghost.

Hamlet alone knows (the Queen neither sees nor hears the Ghost) the reason for his father's appearance. Before the Ghost has spoken, Hamlet anticipates him:

> Do you not come your tardy son to chide,
> That laps'd in time and passion, lets go by
> The important acting of your dread command?

The Ghost appears in his wife's closet, dressed "in his habit as he liv'd" (the first Quarto has him appear in his bedroom attire) and, in effect tells Hamlet: What are you doing in my wife's bedroom? Your business is outside with Claudius. The Ghost is the censorious voice directed against the forbidden fantasies of the son.[18] The scene is Hamlet's distorted and frantic attempt to gain the gratification of his infantile and boyhood wish, a reenactment of the meeting between the mythic Mother-Goddess and the husband-son.[19]

Act III: The Sea-Journey and Home-Coming

Harold Rosenberg suggests that Hamlet's sea-voyage to England is a turning point and crisis of the drama.[20] In speaking of it, Hamlet says to Horatio:

> Sir, in my heart there was a kind of fighting,
> That would not let me sleep. . . .

On this journey, Hamlet again faces death, escapes both execution in England and murder by the pirates, and he himself kills Rosenkrantz and Guildensterm.

When Hamlet returns from England, his first meeting is once more with death in the grave-yard scene. At this point, we notice a marked change. Hamlet has become relatively serene, no longer swerves between melancholy and spryness, between concern with himself and cosmic speculations. It has been noted that the fifth act contains no soliloquies. Hamlet's orientation has shifted towards the We and he is now ripe for social identification. As he leaps into Ophelia's grave, he names himself generically (as Oedipus does in Colonus):

> . . . . This is I,
> Hamlet the Dane.

Hamlet's last words show concern, not for himself, but for his friend Horatio, for the state and the succession. Hamlet now realizes that his personal destiny is part of a general order, that "heaven ordinant" is operative in all that happens:

> There's a divinity that shapes our ends,
> Rough-hew them how we will.

Hamlet's sensibility has gone through the Protestant quest and he appears ready for Catholic acceptance. As he handles skeletons in the grave, he becomes aware of the democracy of death.

Hamlet tells Horatio that "providence" is operative even in the fall of a sparrow, but in his own case, it was a "special" providence. And, indeed, there is more accident than necessity in his discovery of Claudius' letter, his victory over the pirates, the exchange of the swords. Where the pre-Renaissance hero could regard his fate as a function of nature or of God, Hamlet is aware that what happened to him might have been averted or modified. He has gained the deep insight which he sums up in the words "the readiness is all" (in *King Lear*, it is "Ripeness is all"). But Hamlet's "readiness" is tinged with wistful sadness. "Thou wouldst not think," he tells Horatio, "how ill all's here about my heart, but it is no matter." His readiness is not for life but for death. In this mood, Hamlet does not believe that any traveller can return from the "undiscover'd country." He has lost all zest for carrying out his task and his killing the king is more a weary gesture than an act of revenge.[21]

Homecoming presupposes a home. If there is to be a third act of re-creation, we must have a first act of creation, or in Paul Claudel's line, "To know the end, one must know the beginning." The relative absence of tradition in Hebrew and American history results in a hesitant third act in the Book of Job and in *Moby Dick*. The complete rejection of tradition in existentialism precludes its heroes from meaningful engagement and rehabilitation. In *Hamlet*, the third mythic act is as questionable as is the nature of the ghostly father.[22]

Epilogue: Fortinbras-Horatio

Fortinbras and Horatio are the Ariadne-characters who link Hamlet's entrance into and exit from the labyrinth to which he is summoned by the Ghost.

Fortinbras is mentioned at the very beginning (his threat to the state is the reason for the midnight watch), and it is he who speaks the final line of the play. Unlike Hamlet, Fortinbras can act resolutely, lacking "the pale cast of thought" and "conscience" which makes "cowards." Moral considerations do not sway him, and he has "shark'd up a list of lawless resolutes" to recover "by strong hand" the lands his father has lost. On his journey to England, Hamlet learns that Fortinbras is on his way to Poland, ready to sacrifice twenty thousand men for "a little patch of land." Yet, here is Hamlet

> That have a father kill'd, a mother stain'd,
> Excitements of my reason and my blood,
> And let all sleep. . . .

Fortinbras has also had a father killed. But he does not think "too precisely on the event," and instead of seeking revenge, adopts a practical approach, demanding return of the land taken from his father. Moreover, he readily follows the decision of his uncle, his surrogate father-king, not to make war against Denmark.

But the extremes touch. Fortinbras, too, is intent on the game, not the gain, when he sets off to win "an egg-shell," finds "quarrel in a straw when honour's at the stake." Hamlet senses their affinity when he prophesies "the election lights on Fortinbras." As Hamlet dies, Fortinbras appears and bids "the soldiers shoot" in honor of Hamlet. Once again, Fortinbras acts in the interests of a cause as such. If Hamlet is an artist of play, Fortinbras is an artist of action.

Hamlet was born on the day when his father slew King Fortinbras. Ophelia's death marks the burial of Hamlet's ambiguous love and initiates his rebirth to "readiness." The rebirth ritual closes with his death and Fortinbras' succession.

Horatio is Hamlet's other replacement. If Fortinbras is the "strong arm," Horatio is the sensitive artist-observer. Like Ahab's Ishmael he has viewed the drama, and it is to him that Hamlet finally turns and asks

> If thou didst ever hold me in thy heart,
> Absent thee from felicity awhile,
> And in this harsh world draw thy breath in pain,
> To tell my story.

Despite the eclipse of the traditional mythic temper, Shakespeare's *Hamlet* reasserts certain mythic values which are connected with the very Renaissance sensibility which condition Hamlet's hesitations.

In a passage from the second scene of the last act, Osric is sent to ask Hamlet whether he will fence with Laertes. Osric is a kind of impersonal delegate, an example of what Riesman calls the attitude of other-directedness, of mouthing that which he thinks others expect or want him to say. Thus, when Hamlet says to him that it is hot, then that it is very cold, then that it is very sultry, Osric readily agrees, as had Polonius in Act III, when Hamlet played similarly on the theme of the shape of a cloud. After Osric, the "water-fly" leaves, Hamlet sums up the emerging temper of the new "drossy age":

> He did comply with his dug before he sucked it. Thus has he—and many more of the same breed that I know the drossy age dotes on—only got the tune of the time and outward habit of encounter; a kind of yeasty collection, which carries them through and through the most fond and winnowed opinions; and do but blow them to their trial, the bubbles are out.

As against such selling of one's beliefs (or "soul"), *Hamlet* would save the remnants of two traditions: feudal honor expressed in the Ghost's command to revenge his name, and the Renaissance value of individual conscience and sensibility. This sensibility is also exhibited by other characters: Laertes confesses his "foul practice" to Hamlet; the Queen reacts to her son's reproaches with "O Hamlet, thou hast cleft my heart in twain"; even Claudius feels a "heavy burden," is "full of discord and dismay."

Of the principal characters, only two remain to carry on Hamlet's legacy: Fortinbras and Horatio. Both are vital to the plot. Yet Shakespeare preserves their honor by involving them only peripherally in the action and passion of the court drama. We accept Fortinbras, not so much for what he actually does, but mainly because Hamlet calls him "a delicate and tender prince." And we accept Horatio primarily because Hamlet has faith in him. Horatio himself is not distinguished by what he says or does. Neither Fortinbras nor Horatio is *tested* on Shakespeare's stage. Hamlet gives his "dying voice" to a man he never meets, and asks his friend to "report" his cause which he himself did not get to know "aright."

THE ART OF THE DIALECTIC PARADOX

In *Shakespeare's Use of the Arts of Language* (New York, 1947). Sister Miriam Joseph notes that Shakespeare is "especially fond of negative terms which are the contradictories of the corresponding positive terms." She cites a study by Alfred Hart which shows that words beginning with the prefix *un* amount to nearly four per cent of Shakespeare's vocabulary and that a fourth of these belong to his own coinage; that he uses synoeciosis, a composition of contraries (such as "I must be cruel, only to be kind").

The art of Shakespeare's *Hamlet* receives its unique rhythm from the use of a paradoxical dialectic which shapes the dramatic structure, situation, language and dialogue of the play. Amidst it all, we feel that Hamlet is essentially alone. For all his verbal exchanges, Hamlet has no one to talk to, and must try to understand himself by debates between the conflicting elements within himself. Hamlet speaks and acts much like Nietzsche's lonely Cosmic Dancer. This produces a language which turns and leaps, rises and ebbs, swerves between poetry and prose, set in a changing atmosphere between shadows and light.

Hamlet would approximate the Renaissance ideal of the complete man. In Ophelia's words, he possesses "the courtier's, the soldier's, the scholar's eye, tongue, sword." He can do what the others can, and do it better: he knows more about acting than the players, fences better than Laertes, can plot and counterplot with Claudius and Polonius. He would heed the Ghost's "Remember me" and also the new humanism calling for individual responsibility. In sum, Hamlet would encompass the Whole. But the new age is on the threshold of specialized labor, and, specialization is hell for Hamlet as it was for Dante. Hamlet would resolve this dilemma by absolutizing each specialty. Put differently, he would "play" with each possibility, be the political actor and the artist actor, be both Sancho and Don Quixote.

The Seasonal Ritual

The play begins and concludes with motifs which suggest the ritual of the seasonal god. It opens with the theme of winter and death, and closes with the death of Hamlet and the promise of his rebirth in the figures of Horatio-Fortinbras. The platform scene presents the seasonal ritual in a mock-form. As Hamlet waits for the Ghost, he hears in the distance the sounds of Claudius' carousal, drinking his Rhenish wines. The Ghost reveals that the new king and his spring-like marriage celebration were false assumptions. At the end of the play, the death-duel takes on the character of a similar mock-celebration ("the queen carouses to thy fortune, Hamlet"), with the hope in the succession of Fortinbras.[23]

The elements of water, fire, earth and air are interwoven with the life and destiny of the characters and appear in a state of transition. At the beginning, they hold nature and man in an icy and eery grip. The Ghost emerges from "sulphurous and tormenting flames" and summons Hamlet towards his duty on earth. At the end, the elements are loosened and dissolved: Ophelia is drowned and brought to her earthy rest, the fire of the duel is followed by the drinking of the wine, and the play ends with Horatio's prayer that "flights of angels" accompany Hamlet on his way to heaven while Fortinbras bids the soldiers "shoot."

In Hamlet, the over-all character, the elements rage as in a tempest. He begins in a sluggish state, wishing that the "solid (or sullied) flesh" would "melt." The Ghost's message instils him with the fire of revenge which unfolds itself in wild and whirling movements, in passions which would "drink hot blood," in an airy dialectic of "words." At the end, he contemplates man's earthy origin and destiny, leaps into Ophelia's grave, is wounded by the fiery poison of Laertes' sword, and is led off to the accompaniment of Horatio's heavenly invocation and the "music" of Fortinbras' soldiers.

If the opening midnight scene suggests a terrain somewhere between hell and heaven, and the ending invokes "flights of angels," the drama proper is enacted on earth.[24] This earth is weedy or "rotten." Claudius is the master of this earthly kingdom with his adviser Polonius "feeding" him maggots and carrion (the metaphors associated with his character). Gertrude is the vegetative, earthy element, fluid in her unresisting acceptance and surrender, finally "drowning" in the poisoned wine.[25] The references to Ophelia are in terms of a "sweet springflower," until she is awakened to sensuality in her mad songs. She is watery in her soft and submissive nature (Hamlet calls her a "nymph"), giving in to the slighest pressure of her father and brother. In the play as a whole, the elements appear as a human tempest. In Shakespeare's last work, the nature-elements are liberated from their distortions in the human-wordly frame and return to their native "tempest."

Shakespeare's *Hamlet* is the richest expression of English Renaissance mythopoesis. The work is the high center of Shakespeare's own dramatic art. The Hamlet-problem begins with Brutus ("poor Brutus, with himself at war") who does not belong in "the world." Neither do Macbeth, Othello and King Lear, all of whom are touched by what Friedrich Gumdolf calls "strange powers." In *The Tempest*, the problem is resolved by magic. Ferdinand is a Hamlet whose father's ghost is an unquestionable spirit, and who returns to become king. This Hamlet marries his Ophelia, undisturbed by personal discords. But the happy ending becomes possible only by being set in a fairy world in which life is "such stuff as dreams are made on." Where Claudius and Polonius appear as potent forces in Hamlet's fate, Gonzalo and Antonius are not given serious roles and are nearly irrelevant to the central action. *The Tempest* reverses the order of reality. Here, practical political strategy is illusion, and magic becomes reality; here, "the play is the thing" and the whole thing. Shakespeare has moved from the human-political tempest of Brutus-Hamlet-Macbeth-Lear-Othello to the nature-tempest of the elements for which man is an object of play. Prospero gladly abdicates in favor of worldly forces which seem to him trivial compared to the power of his poetic magic. The tragic myth of *Hamlet* is resolved in the magic fairy tale of *The Tempest*.

NOTES

1. Ernest Jones' *Hamlet and Oedipus* (New York, 1949) cites studies showing that "the Norse and Irish variants . . . are descended from the ancient Iranian legend of Kaikhosrav . . . some members of which can be traced back to the beginning of history." There were Hamlet Ballad-Cycles in Iceland and there is an allusion to Hamlet as a nature myth in the Edda. Although the story is originally a Scandinavian saga, the name of the hero, Amlothi, has no discoverable Germanic etymology. One scholar suggests that the first part of the name, Aml, means "labor without much progress," and that the whole compound may be rendered as "annoyingly mad." Cf. Sir Israel Gollancz, *The Sources of Hamlet* (London, 1926); Th. M. Parrott and H. Craig, *The Tragedy of Hamlet* (Princeton, 1936); Kemp Malone, *The Literary History of Hamlet* (Heidelberg, 1923).

2. The Ghost ascribes Claudius' success in winning over Gertrude to "witchcraft of his wits," by which he gained "the will of my most seeming-virtuous queen." We may reasonably identify the Ghost's view with Hamlet's own "prophetic voice." In any case, the mother as saint is normal for the boyhood state. In her case, as in that of Ophelia, we can surmise Hamlet's earlier view by his later extreme reaction, when the mother bcomes a prostitute, and "celestial" Ophelia fit for a "nunnery," or a house of ill fame.

3. The Ghost is the summoner or "herald" (in the third act, Hamlet refers to his father as "the herald Mercury"). Here, Hamlet reveals unhesitating courage, is ready to follow the Ghost though it "tempt" him "toward the flood," the "dreadful summit of a cliff," or draw him "into madness." The opening scene marvelously creates the mood of *foreboding* and of *transition*: The change from night to day, the irregular challenge in the change of guards, foreboding some "strange eruption." In the next scene, we hear that the funeral of Hamlet's father, followed by the Queen's remarriage produced "mirth in funeral . . . dirge in marriage . . . delight and dole," and learn of the peace-war situation created by the demands of Fortinbras. This disjointed dialectic dominates the play as a whole, its mood and metaphors, its action and philosophic expression.

4. Some critics ascribe Hamlet's delay to external factors. Since the murder was not an open act, it is argued, Hamlet must make certain that Claudius is the murderer; furthermore, he must prove publicly that it was Claudius, lest he himself be judged a murderer; finally, that Hamlet simply lacked the opportunity to kill Claudius until the end.

A. C. Bradley (*Shakespearean Tragedy* [London, 1949]), has effectively disposed of this theory. He points out: 1) Hamlet himself never refers to external difficulties. 2) Hamlet assumes that he *can* obey the Ghost. 3) Hamlet need have no fear of reprisal, as shown by the ease with which Laertes rouses the people against Claudius.

In Belleforest, Hamlet's difficulties are mainly external. Moreover, his Hamlet wants more than revenge; he seeks the crown, and to gain it, he must conquer not only Claudius, but his supporters as well. In Shapespeare, Hamlet has no such problem. He *can* be king. He has Claudius' public promise, and he is loved by the "distracted multitude."

Bradley also refutes the view that Hamlet is held back by ethical considerations. He indicates that Hamlet is not restrained by moral scruples. He stabs Polonius; he readily sends Rosenkrantz and Guildenstern to their deaths (although he is not certain of their guilt), telling Horatio that "they are not near my conscience."

On the question of Hamlet's making sure that the king is the murderer: Hamlet does not have absolute certainty, but he clearly has the strongest suspicion from the beginning. The King's reaction to the Gonzago play provides a public manifestation of guilt before the whole court.

A word on the argument that Hamlet needs to convince the court of Claudius' guilt: Hamlet, it is said, is a Renaissance man who loves life, and will not endanger it lightly. To ascribe Hamlet's central dilemma to fear of reprisal is to trivialize his character. He shows no fear in following the Ghost, in striking through the curtain to stab Polonius. Hamlet is not afraid to die. He tells Horatio:

> "Why, what should be the fear?
> I do not set my life at a pin's fee. . . ."

5. A. A. Smirnov, *Shakespeare. A Marxist Interpretation*, The Critics Group, No. 2 (New York, 1936). Similarly, Roy Walker's *The Time Is Out of Joint. A Study of Hamlet* (London, 1948) sees the play as the tragedy of a noble man, limited by a "body politic . . . poisoned at the ear, accepting fair appearances for fair reality." He holds that Hamlet is separated from his group by an impassable gulf and has "no real communication with the creatures of this world."

6. In the section on the mythic mechanism of "decomposition," Jones shows how the father-son conflict recurs in the interrelationships among Hamlet, Laertes, Polonius and Ophelia.

The psychoanalytic approach is validated only if the esthetic and the historic are considered in its context. Indeed, one could maintain that literary analysis, if it penetrates deeply enough, should come to much the same conclusion. A. C. Bradley's study is an early example. Bradley holds that the key to Hamlet's inactivity, hesitancy and procrastination lies in his "profound melancholy," where "melancholy" is used in the Elizabethan sense of nervous instability and moral sensibility. Bradley does not propose to inquire into the factors which make for Hamlet's state, saying that Shakespeare simply meant to portray "a pathological condition." Yet, in his actual analysis, Bradley is on the edges of psychoanalytic formulation. He writes of Hamlet's "unconscious self-excuses, [his] unconscious weaving of pretexts for inactivity" which he is unable to understand. He hesitatingly suggests that the kind of melancholy from which Hamlet suffers can be symptomatically expressed in paralysis or even perversion of love. He notes that the Hamlet who must hold his tongue suddenly becomes most eloquent in his mother's chamber "beside his father's marriage-bed." As to Hamlet's relation to Ophelia, Bradley says he does not understand it, but adds the suggestive footnote that "there are signs that Hamlet was haunted by the horrible idea that he had been deceived in Ophelia as he had been in his mother."

J. Dover Wilson (*What Happens in Hamlet* [London, 1935]) also speaks of Hamlet's emotional instability, notes his personal inadequacy, and that Hamlet loved Ophelia before his mother took off the rose "from the fair forehead of an innocent love." As Jones observes, Wilson is sometimes close to noting Hamlet's incestuous tendencies; but Wilson himself has argued against Jones' interpretation.

7. Jones adds that the identification may also be seen in Hamlet's killing the men (Polonius and Claudius) who stand between him and his mother.

8. Upon her death, Hamlet leaps into the grave, announcing "I lov'd Ophelia," more than forty thousand "brothers." But the love of "brothers," even of forty thousand, is not what is called for. In the primitive plot, as reconstructed by Kemp Malone, Amleth rapes his sister or foster sister, and reveals his animal sexuality.

9. Hamlet's announced intention was to use the Murder of Gonzago to catch the conscience of the king. But he becomes more interested in the effectiveness and skill of the performance, as art and drama, than in its effect on Claudius. When the King has risen, Hamlet asks Horatio whether his skill could not get him "a fellowship in a cry of players." For the most comprehensive study to date of the psychoanalytic literature on Shakespeare, see Norman H. Holland, *Psychoanalysis and Shakespeare* (New York, Toronto, London, 1964).

10. Hamlet's identification with Claudius is also indicated by the similar terms both use in condemning themselves. Hamlet calls himself "a whore" (III,2) and Claudius calls himself a harlot (III,1).

11. Hamlet addresses the Ghost first as King, then as Father; the Ghost's first words to Hamlet are "Mark me," and his last "Remember me!". Ernest Jones remarks that where hostility towards the father is repressed, it is often accompanied "by the development of the opposite sentiment, namely of an exaggerated regard and respect for him."

175

12. Bradley notes that Hamlet is so afraid that he will forget his father's command that he writes it down in black and white "to force him to remember and to believe."

13. Another ambiguity is the reference to *the duke* Gonzago whose actual murder in Vienna is supposedly imaged in Hamlet's playlet.

14. Before Hamlet goes, he temporizes, as one might before entering on a vital mission. He admonishes Guildenstern for trying to "pluck out the heart of my mystery," at the very moment when he is about to reveal his mystery to his mother. In his word-play with Polonius, Hamlet indulges in child-like transformations of objects (cloud-camel-weasel-whale). When Polonius' agrees that the cloud looks like a whale, Hamlet breaks off with the words: "Then I will come to my mother by and by." (In mythology, the whale, or its belly, represents the World Womb or the Earthly Paradise.) There follow the lullaby words "By and by" repeated three times.

15. J. Dover Wilson thinks that the "bitter business" refers to Claudius. Yet, commenting on Hamlet's very next words ("Soft! now to my mother"), he writes that Hamlet "has forgotten the King altogether."

    Hamlet's first words are spoken outside her room. He calls out "Mother, mother, mother!" as though he were warning her or himself that it is his "mother" he is about to see. At the same time, he wishes, as he later tells her, "it were not so."

16. Hamlet asks: "Is it the king," and later says that he took Polonius for his "better." But does Hamlet really believe that he has killed the king? He had just left Claudius in a mood of prayer—hardly a prelude to eavesdropping. Moreover, Hamlet heard Polonius cry out. He knows this voice well, has heard it more frequently than any other and could hardly confuse it with the king's voice.

17. Hamlet embroiders Gertrude's sexual relations with Claudius, speaking of "the rank sweat of an enseamed bed," of the king "paddling" her neck "with his damn'd fingers." It is a kind of vicarious sex-indulgence on Hamlet's part.

18. Hamlet had left his surrogate-father at prayer, on the way to "heaven," where he cannot obstruct Hamlet's "business" with his mother. But "the father" does appear, and precisely as Hamlet goes all out depreciating Claudius in favor of the dead father. Does Hamlet's reference to "A king of shreds and patches—" (at which point the Ghost enters) express an ambiguity as to which "king" he has in mind?

    Roy Walker notes that in his second appearance the Ghost does not emphasize the revenge, but calls on Hamlet to be gentle and merciful with his mother. Is Hamlet's "mind's eye" now more open to seeing that the revenge-motive could no longer be accepted as a respectable explanation for his bad dreams?

19. In the first Quarto, the Queen condemns Claudius and agrees to assist Hamlet in "what strategem soe're thou shalt devise."

    Frederic Wertham has advanced the theory that Hamlet wants to kill his

176

mother, not his father ("The Matricidal Impulse. Critique of Freud's Interpretation of Hamlet," *Journal of Criminal Psychopathology*, Vol. II, No. 4 [April, 1941]). Wertham grants that "the basis of Hamlet's hostility against his mother is his over-attachment to her," but argues that "this over-attachment to the mother need not necessarily lead to hatred against the father." He cites passages to show that Hamlet expresses no direct hatred against the father and no direct love for his mother and concludes that the analogy between Oedipus and Hamlet does not hold. Freud pointed out that in a more sophisticated era, Hamlet represses the wish fantasy, and that we discover it "only through the inhibitory effects which proceed from it."

20. In myths (as in dreams), rescue from water is connected with birth. In mythopoesis, this is approximated in Aeneas' sea-journey; Dante passes into Hell through the river Styx, into Purgatory by way of the frozen waters of Cocytus which receives all the rivers of the Inferno, and finally into Paradise after having drunk from the waters of Lethe and Eunoë. Other examples are Siegfried's Rhine-journey, Ahab's roamings in the Pacific, Aschenbach's crossing into Venice, the wandering of Thomas Mann's Joseph along the Nile and the water-journey of Grigors in Mann's *Holy Sinner*.

21. Even here, he needs to be reminded of his duty by Laertes who calls out to him: "the king, the king's to blame." In Laurence Olivier's film, Hamlet kills Claudius in the manner of a Western hero who finally gets his enemy. This mars Olivier's otherwise sensitive and consistent production.

22. Hamlet returns from England "naked" and "alone," as he writes Claudius. His rebirth into naked aloneness is followed by his death.

23. An old study (A. Zinzow, 1877) cited by Ernest Jones in *Hamlet and Oedipus*, examines *Hamlet* as a nature-myth, and modern scholarship (Gollancz) holds that the story may have borrowed from the Northern myth of the struggle between spring and winter.

24. The scheme is analogous to Goethe's *Faust* whose Prologue brings the Lord, the Angels and Mephistopheles on a common platform and whose final scene tells of Faust's Assumption.

25. It has been suggested that Gertrude is connected with the vegetation goddess Nerthus and with Groa, the Mother-Earth giant in the Orwendel myth of the Edda.

Teutonic Inwardness
Faust

OSWALD SPENGLER characterized Western culture as "Faustian" in its restless striving towards an ever-receding goal. In our own time, F. S. C. Northrop restated Spengler's designation of Western man in terms of time-metaphors, the arrow in flight and the river in motion:

> The Westerner represents time either with an arrow or as a moving river which comes out of a distant place and past which are not here and now, and which goes into an equally distant place and future which are also not here and now. (*The Meeting of East and West* [New York, 1946.])

Similarly, Wyndham Lewis argued in *Time and Western Man* that the West is pledged to the homage of time. This category is central to the Faustian folktale in which Faustus is granted a period of twenty-four years in which to indulge himself at will, after which he is to suffer hell-fire for all time. In this sense, Faustianism may be viewed as an insatiable appetite for limitless experience.

This salute to time—to Father Chronos—began with Western mythopoesis. Aeschylus' Prometheus is confident that time will deliver him from bondage; his Orestes is freed by the passage of time. The Renaissance period raised time to "a gift of God" (as Goethe puts it in *Wilhelm Meister*). This gift served individual and social expansionism, and culminated in the theories of progress by Renan, Turgot, Condorcet and Spencer. In the nineteenth century, Schopenhauer countered this trend by arguing that striving was an expression of the Satanic will. For Marx, history brought class societies with the promise of classless societies. Similarly, Melville saw both good and evil in Ahab's chase of Moby Dick and Nietzsche affirmed both the progressive transvaluations of the Superman and the theory of Eternal Recurrence. In our day, Spengler, and to a degree, Toynbee, question the equating of time with progress.

Teutonic Mythology

Teutonic mythology has three central features which are best expressed by their German terms: *Gemeinschaft* (collective solidarity), *Innerlichkeit* (inner directedness), and *Werden* (ceaseless development). They appear metaphorically in Goethe's *Faust*—his forest and cave ("Wald und Höhle") and his restless wandering.

Common to these features is German *Maasslosigkeit* or unrestraint. This temper tends to convert *Gemeinschaft* into totalitarianism, *Innerlichkeit* into isolative retreat, *Werden* into imperialist expansion for *Lebensraum*. Here, solidarity may coexist with individualism, spirituality with materialism, ceaseless striving with stasis or *Ruh*. The swing between extremes appears in another feature of Teutonic mythology: the connection between song and war. Odin or Wotan is the God of both, with war used as a sanction for song. Happiness in Valhalla consists in living as a warrior; even the goddesses, the Valkyries, are fierce and strong, rather than beautiful. And war is conceived as necessary and universal, leading to the *Götterdämmerung*, (*ragnarök*), as foretold to Odin by the "Wise Woman" in the Poetic Edda:

> Brothers shall fight and fell each other,
> And sisters' sons shall kinship stain;
> Hard is it on earth, with mighty whoredom;
> Ax-time, sword-time, shields are sundered,
> Win-time, wolf-time, ere the world falls;
> Nor ever shall men each other spare.
> (*Voluspa*, Bellows translation [New York, 1923]).

Finally, what happens to the Teutonic world is extended to the fate of the world as a whole. With the twilight of their gods, the entire universe comes to an end—a foreshadowing of Spengler's thesis that the defeat of Germany in the First World War was synonymous with the decline of the West.

Yet, this mythology also has reference to an initial and final harmony. The Edda speaks of an original Golden Age of peace which is to be reinstated following the destruction of the world, when Baldur will come back and a new green earth will arise.

Germanic Kultur-Freedom

These characteristic of Teutonic mythology are manifested in later German history. They are expressed in the rampant voluntarism of Schopenhauer's and Nietzsche's thought, in the dynamic pace of German industrialism which sought to outdistance its rivals, if necessary, by warlike means. From its semi-nomadic beginnings to the Prussian *Herrenvolk*, Germany was dominated by arrogant leaders ruling over a submissive *Gefolgschaft*.

Germany remained feudal long after other leading European countries had had their Renaissance. The German Reformation offered a chance for a break with this tradition. Goethe called it a "turning point of German history," for the age of Luther, Erasmus, Melanchthon seemed to him—as to Thomas Mann—to have held the greatest promise for establishing a humanistic German tradition. His Faust and Goetz, conceived simultaneously, are both German figures and are connected with the Protestant rebellion. Goetz is defeated in his Robin Hood adventures and Faust is condemned to hell-fire in the chapbooks. Their fate is bound up with a crucial event in German history: the Peasant Rebellion.

The Peasant Rebellion in 1529 was the first realistic German effort towards social-economic emancipation, similar to that which the French gained in 1789. Alexander von Humboldt called its failure pivotal for German history and Georg Lukacs argues in *Goethe und seine Zeit* (Bern, 1947) that the entire development of Germany was determined by this event. As a result of the Peasants' defeat, Germany continued in semi-feudalism under its Junker ideology, in contrast to the national bourgeois culture which France and England developed.

To compensate for its economic-social bondage, German thinkers developed the concept of Kultur-freedom, where the greatness of German thought was seen in its *not* having any connection with material reality. It evolved systems of "pure" metaphysics, music, mysticism and mythology from Kant's invocation of the moral law within and the starry heavens above, to Max Weber's notion of science as a vocation (*Wissenschaft als Beruf*) and Karl Mannheim's position that the intellectual viewpoint is non-partisan. This *Innerlichkeit* also makes itself felt in the absence of a realistic and critical tradition, such as the French have from Montaigne, Moliere, Diderot and Voltaire to Balzac, Flaubert, Zola, Barbusse and Aragon, or the English from Defoe to Dickens and Shaw, or the Russians from Gogol to Gorky. In place of realistic revolutions, such as the Puritan, the French and the American, the Germans produced theoretic rebellions: Kant's Copernican Revolution, Schiller's call for *Gedankenfreiheit* and for moral-esthetic education, the "Blue Flower" and "Magic Idealism" of its Romantic schools. Above all, it manifested itself in the German penchant for music—music as a specifically German affair ("eine deutsche Angelegenheit"), as it reappears in Mann's *Magic Mountain* and *Doctor Faustus*.

In practice, this airy rebellion turned into a servile bowing to *Ordnung*. Luther assailed subservience in theology, yet condemned the German peasants when they attempted to translate the theory into economic practice. Kant's Copernican Revolution went hand in hand with his appeal to the "good will" and with his submission to changing forms of authority in Prussia. The German Romantic poets readily descended from their sidereal heights to become passionate adherents of the Junker war against Napoleon, and Wagner's revolutionary conception of Siegfried was followed by his "Kaisermarsch." In our own day, most of the advocates of un-political Kultur became Hitler's professors, poets, scientists and philosophers. The whole presents the complex of spiritual freedom and political sycophancy, of arrogance and flunkeyism, or as Troeltsch formulates it, of mysticism and brutality.

To be sure, Germany's idealistic version of freedom contained an element of internationalism. But, divorced from political realities, it lent itself to becoming the tool of an universal expansionism. It allowed the translation of Siegfried into Bismarck and Hitler. In Goethe's work, this association appears in the partnership between Faust and Mephistopheles.

GOETHE'S SOCIAL AND PERSONAL BURDEN

No other mythopoeic work is so closely bound up with its author's life as *Faust* on which Goethe spent about sixty years, from his late adolescence to a few months before his death.

Biographers have generally presented Goethe as a serene "Olympian." This view has been corrected, in Barker Fairley's study and most extensively in K. R. Eissler's psychoanalytic examination of Goethe. A reading of Ludwig Lewisohn's selections from the letters, diaries and works reveals Goethe as driven and harried, from the storm and stress of his youth to the seventy-three year old man who fell violently in love with a seventeen year old girl.[1] Goethe's restlessness also expresses itself in continuous "travels": from one locality to another, from one literary and scientific effort to another, and from one love object to another.

Goethe, like Shakespeare, spanned the transition from the medieval to the bourgeois era, and like him, attempted to unite the residual value of each. For Goethe, these forces were embodied in three geographic centers—Frankfort, where he was born, Weimar, where he spent the greater part of his life and Italy, where he sought to find a symbolic home. Frankfort represented the new bourgeois civilization, Weimar the passing feudal scene, with Italy envisaged as transcending both.

Frankfort offered "life." But this life consisted primarily of commercial and banking activity. Goethe called it "a rotten hole," complaining of its bad taste, "the discrepancy between the narrowness and slow tempo of middle class existence and the wideness and swiftness" of his character. Goethe was buoyed by its energy, but repelled by its insensitivity to poetic values.

In Frankfort, Goethe met Lili Schoenemann (she came from a Catholic family of brokers) towards whom he exhibited a similar ambivalence. Goethe told Sorel towards the end of his life that he loved Lili profoundly and had never been so close to happiness as he was with her. Yet, Goethe was "not able to marry her," for she was "an alien new existence," to whom he had "nothing to say." He felt a stranger in her "carnival" circle.[2] Goethe welcomed the call to Weimar partly because it offered him the chance to escape this girl who seemed to paralyze his will.

Although Weimar was a tiny principality, Goethe preferred it because its very feudal tradition offered the artist more encouragement than he could find in the banking city of Frankfort. But he soon realized that little Weimar was another form of "the business of the world." Here, he felt himself "a poor slave," bound to the Duke in whom "again and again the child and the donkey peep out." He had fled from Frankfort to Weimar, and now had to flee from Weimar to Italy. On his return, he removed himself even more from Weimar society, as well as from "the formlessness of Germany," where "no one understands my language," where there is "nothing left but the Philistine," and injustice is the order of the day. Goethe withdrew more and more from its political and social life, stood aloof from the nationalistic fervor of the Wars of Liberation. At the age of seventy-four, he told Müller that he wished to emigrate, if only he knew where.

While Goethe felt that he had no German public to whom he could communicate his deepest feelings, the problem was complicated by the fact that he felt himself part of this very public. He realized, as he wrote Schiller, that one cannot "separate his ship from the very waves that bear it."[3] And Goethe was no revolutionary.

Parents and Lovers

Goethe's attitude towards his father and mother was roughly analogous to that towards the business town of Frankfort and the duchy of Weimar.

The father, Goethe said, gave him "stature." But it was the stature

of a stern didactic commander, a man of "iron strictness . . . unbeliev-
able consistency . . . uninterrupted determination," with whom the
son could not establish "any kind of agreeable relationship." Instead
of studying law in Strassburg, where his father had sent him, Goethe
spent his time courting Friederike Brion and writing poetry.[4]

Goethe contrasted the exactitude of his father with his mother from
whom he got his gayety and imaginativeness ("die Frohnatur" and "die
Lust zum Fabulieren"). She was nearer in years to her son than to her
husband and Goethe called her "almost a child herself." In his Supple-
ment to *Poetry and Truth* (Lewisohn, *Goethe*, I,7), Goethe wrote that
she "had not lived only for her son's sake but her son had lived for her
sake." The only girl to whom he became engaged—Lili Schoenemann—
was the one whom his mother favored. Goethe's attachment to his
mother appears to have had a secret, guilty element manifesting itself
by the strange distance he maintained towards her. More than once,
she delicately reminded her son of his rare visits—"It is now five years
since you've been here, and that is no joke." She complained to Lavater
that her son compensated her occasionally with "a magnificent letter,"
and begged Fritz von Stein to keep a diary of Goethe's doings, so that
she might know more about him, adding that if she were an actress,
she might do "the part of Hamlet's mother not ill."[5]

In his autobiography *Poetry and Truth*, Goethe frankly wrote of his
sensual relation to his sister Cornelia: ". . . she had accompanied me
through my whole conscious existence and therefore we were most
profoundly united." Together, they shared "the awakening of sensual
instincts," and Cornelia's only desire was to live "in the harmony of her
sisterly relation to me . . . it never seemed to me either natural or pleas-
ing to think of her as a wife; rather should she have been an abbess or
the head of some distinguished order." When Goethe heard that Schlosser was wooing her, he felt somewhat "dismayed," adding that "it was
only now that I confessed to myself that I was really jealous of my
sister." About the same time, the two "had drawn closer to each other
than ever." In turn, she was upset when Goethe became engaged to
Lili Schoenemann, and "begged" him, indeed "commanded" him "to
break with Lili."

Nearly all the women whom Goethe courted have some underground connection with his mother and sister. In his essay on "Goethe's
Romance with Friederike" in *Fragment of a Great Confession* (New
York, 1949), Theodor Reik points out that there is a repetitive pattern
in Goethe's relation to women: Violent falling in love, a period of torment and vacillation, followed by flight."[6] In his early poem to Friede-

rike Brion "Welcome and Departure," Goethe prophetically foreshadowed this pattern: He either ran away from those who were available—Friederike, Lili—or wooed those who were unavailable—Charlotte Buff, Charlotte von Stein, Marianne von Willemer, Ulrike von Levetzow—who were either engaged or married, too old or too young for him.[7] This is especially clear in Goethe's extraordinary love for Charlotte von Stein who was seven years older than Goethe and a mother of seven children.

Charlotte von Stein came into Goethe's life following his sister's marriage, and a poem of his would have it that long, long ago, she had been his sister or wife:

> Ach du warst in abgelebten Zeiten
> Meine Schwester oder meine Frau.

After he became attached to Charlotte, the thought of visiting his mother "doesn't even skim the surface of my mind. You have so absorbed me that I have no sensibility left for the other duties of my heart." She became, as he wrote Lavater, not only "the heir of my mother, my sister," but also "a sweetheart."

Goethe's need for Charlotte von Stein was intertwined with his need for Weimar where he met her. Weimar was the feudal-nature retreat to which Goethe fled from the bustle of Frankfort. Likewise, Goethe sought in Charlotte a curb on his stormy adolescence which had been unloosened in his relation to Friederike Brion and Charlotte Buff. She soothed the angry racing of his blood and, in her angelic arms, his breast found rest ("Tropfest Mässigung dem heissen Blute, richtetest den wilden, irren Lauf, und in deinen Engelsarmen ruhte die zerstörte Brust sich wieder auf."). He called his relationship to her "the purest, loveliest, truest that ever I had with a woman, except my sister." She became the Iphigenia who controlled the wild impulses of his Orestes. But, once again, Goethe fled. He felt the need to "wean" himself from Charlotte and wrote from Rome that the chief purpose of his Italian journey "was to cure myself of those physical and moral ills which plagued me in Germany."[8]

From now on, Goethe gave up the quest for a full union with a woman. Christiane Vulpius whom he brought into his house following his return from Italy, had worked in a flower factory and was thirteen years younger than Goethe. Christiane showed little interest in Goethe's writings, indeed, could not spell correctly. But she brought Goethe gayety and, above all, physical comfort, without making any social demands on him. This was, of course, no real marriage, even though Goethe legalized the union in 1806 (after Christiane saved his life from a threatened attack by French soldiers during the Wars of Liberation). Christiane was little more than a housekeeper and *Bettschatz*, rarely addressed him with the familiar *du*, calling him "dear, kind Privy Councillor" even after their marriage.[9]

Goethe had "an unhappy nervous fear of marriage," as Schiller put it. According to Müller's Diary (September 14, 1823), Goethe stated that love "belongs in the realm of the ideal, marriage in that of the real, and never are these two realms united with impunity." Goethe never really married, in line with the pledge which the legendary Faustus made to the devil. What he missed in life, he tried to create in symbolic forms. In another connection, he told Heinrich Luden (December 13, 1813) that he was trying to "transcend" the "wretched" German people through science and art, adding that "I have found the wings to bear me beyond these griefs."

But no degree of symbolic transformation can take the place of missed experience. A deep and tragic dichotomy remained in Goethe's life and "two souls" penetrate his symbolic world. They appear in the contrasted characters of Goetz and Werther, Prometheus and Ganymed, Prometheus and Epimetheus, Iphigenia and Orestes, Antonio and Tasso, Mephisto and Faust.[10]

THE FAUST LEGEND

E. M. Butler's *Myth of the Magus* (New York, 1948) shows that the Faustian theme belongs in the tradition of the pre-Christian magus and derives from seasonal and kingship rites. Indeed, the attempt to gain superhuman power by magic is an ancient motif, found in Persian legends, the Hebrew Kabbalah, Arabic mysticism, neo-Platonism and in St. Augustine.

In the sixteenth century German chapbooks by Spiess and Widman, Faustus is damned. His defiance of church dogma, his use of magic to gain pleasure and power are treated from the medieval perspective as unforgivable sins. When his twenty-four years are up, Faustus is dismembered and sent into Hell-Fire. Faustus' willingness to give up eternal bliss for a few years of pleasure appears as a foolish act, "a warning and example to all good Christians, so that they shall not . . . injure their souls and bodies like Doctor Faustus did."[11]

Although Faustus is damned, he represents the emerging Renaissance values of pleasure, wealth, widening experience and individual power. And Renaissance writers in the age of Don Juan, the Borgias,

185

Luther, Erasmus, Melanchthon, Leonardo and Columbus depict Faustus not merely as a pursuer of ignoble lust, but also as a proud titan with a thirst for knowledge. Paracelsus calls the devil his friend and companion, and the Lord in Goethe's *Faust* declares that Mephisto can "create as devil."[12]

This new view is apparent in Marlowe's *Doctor Faustus*, although it appeared in the era of the German chapbooks. Writing in a land where middle class values had found firmer roots than they did in Germany, the English dramatist can treat Faustus' aspirations with a greater degree of sympathy. Marlowe's hero is a tragic figure whose eternal damnation is out of proportion to his twenty-four years of sinning. The miserable weakling of the *Volksbuch* becomes a "sound magician" and "demi-god" in Marlowe's drama. He wants more than wordly pleasure; he desires boundless power and honor, to be on earth "as Jove is in the sky." The opening chorus tells of his Icarus nature and foreshadows his Icarus fate. Faustus excels

> In heavenly matters of theology;
> Till swollen with cunning and self-conceit
> His waxen wings did mount above his reach,
> And, melting, Heavens conspired his overthrow.

Marlowe is the first to *interiorize* the myth by suggesting that Faustus' good and evil angels are within himself. This is indicated in Mephistophilis' definition of Hell as the absence of Heaven:

> Why this Hell, nor am I out of it:
> Think'st thou that I who saw the face of God,
> And tasted the eternal joys of Heaven,
> Am not tormented with ten thousand Hells
> In being deprived of everlasting bliss?

This Faustus is in "hell" *before* he is delivered into its fire. As soon as he signs the pact, he begins to waver, uncertain whether honor and wealth are worth the sacrifice of heaven. At the end, his remorse amounts to a renunciation of the pact.

Although Marlowe's Faustus is damned, he emerges as the titanic scapegoat to medieval and church authority, to its denigration of experience, knowledge and beauty. Particularly beauty. In the *Volksbuch*, Helen is a devilish figure who involves Faustus in a "swinish and epicurean life." In Marlowe, love of beauty helps Faustus alleviate his despair. And Butler observes, that this "gave a tragic significance to Helen which she had not had before." Marlowe's Faustus is damned primarily because his quest is for *individual* personal gain, to be "great emperor of the world." He rejects his society completely and in turn is rejected by it.

The German dramatist Lessing is the first writer to indicate that Faust is to be saved. In his dramatic sketch, *D. Faust*, Faust is exposed to the devil precisely because of his thirst for science and knowledge, a thirst which according to the top devil, makes certain that Faust will be his.[13] But, when the hellish tribe believes that it has succeeded, their triumph is interrupted by the voice of an angel: "You have not won over humanity and science. The Godhead did not give man the most noble urge in order to render him eternally unhappy. What you saw and believed to possess was nothing more than a phantom." Lessing did not develop this theme in his sketch, but it is implicit in his life-long struggle for intellectual and social freedom, in his *Education of the Human Race* and *Nathan the Wise*.

Goethe's Mythic Thinking

George Santayana's *Three Philosophical Poets* interprets Goethe's *Faust* as the philosophy of German romanticism. It is a matter of record, however, that Goethe rejected the romantic in favor of the classic and vigorously opposed the Romanticists' esteem of the old Germanic Edda, and the Middle Ages. He found the Norse legends bizarre, rigid and gloomy, the Nibelungen fable extravagant and monstrous, the gods of Friedrich Schlegel's Vedic India formless.[14] His *Faust* draws but little on Germanic mythology, and instead incorporates multiple mythic themes, from the Oriental, the Hebrew and Graeco-Roman to the Italian and English Renaissance. Goethe traced his cultural heritage primarily to non-Germanic sources—the Greeks, the French, Shakespeare. He paid homage to Kalidasa's Sakuntala and the Persian poet Hafis, to Slavic, Lithuanian and world poetry in general. He aimed to speak "above the nations," telling Eckermann (March 15, 1829) that one should regard "the weal and woe of a neighboring people as though it were one's own."

Goethe's interests were indeed nearly universal and he leaned towards those thinkers who stressed unity and universality. He was attracted to philosophy to the extent that "it unites," to Spinoza for strengthening his belief that he "who wills the highest must will the whole."[15] Long before Fechner and Whitehead, Goethe opposed what Hocking calls "the bifurcation of nature." His "symphronistic method" aimed to find the recurrent phase, the primal phenomenon or *Urphäno-*

men; in botany, the *Urpflanze,* in the animal world, the *Urtier.* The key-words in his vocabulary are "world" and "unity." Wilhelm Meister's "pedagogic province" is dominated by the concepts of world-view, world-community, world-piety. Finally, Goethe was among the first to advocate the promotion of "World Literature."

The great Dante scholar, Karl Vossler, regards *The Divine Comedy* and *Faust* as the only instances in which a writer "grasps and draws to itself all culture and the entire world, absorbs them, recreates them lifelike in a single work of art." Yet, while Dante's epic is organically knit and the product of a few years' concentrated effort, Goethe's poem was produced over a period of some sixty years. Dante's work summarizes some thirteen centuries of Christianity; Goethe's embraces nearly all of Western culture and is perhaps the most inclusive culture myth. Goethe remarked that his story spans 3000 years of Western history, from Homer and the fall of Troy (Helena) to the Greek wars of liberation (Euphorion-Byron). It encompasses European history from the feudal era to the Revolution of 1830 and Utopian Socialism, European thought from Bruno and Spinoza to Hume's skepticism, Schopenhauer's voluntarism and Hegel's panlogism.[16]

Still, for all its universal character, *Faust* deals with a German figure and is primarily a German expression. It is invoked by German Protestants and Catholics, individualists and socialists, realists and romanticists as containing the wisest and deepest thought and the greatest art.[17]

But, *Faust* is most uniquely German in the hero's unrestraint. This German Icarus wants to fly.[18] But he has no Dedalus counseling him to stay at a moderate height and so keep close to the father. He does not know the Greek sense of limit and his rebellion takes the form of *rage* aimed at absolute knowledge, power and gratification.

Ferdinand Freiligrath's poem "Hamlet" declares that "Germany is Hamlet . . . He muses and dreams, not knowing what to do . . . That comes from too much reading in bed . . . His finest action consists in thinking. As a result, he lacks resoluteness." But, the poem might have read that "Germany is Faust." For the action in Germany's most representative work is primarily poetic and visionary. *Faust* is a poet's poem and its hero is a genius without wings.

Faust succeeds in his venture, while Hamlet fails. Yet, his is the victory of German theory. Hamlet, on the other hand, confronts a real court world; hence his failure has greater functional import than Faust's symbolic successes. Hamlet is more active in his irresolutions than Faust is in his titanic pronouncements.

FAUST I: THE INDIVIDUAL JOURNEY

> Unto God the Orient!
> Unto God the Occident!
> Northern lands and Southern lands
> Rest in the peace of His great hands.
>
> —Goethe (Lewisohn translation)

> Das Wahre war schon längst gefunden,
> Hat edle Geisterschaft verbunden:
> Das alte Wahre, fass es an!
>
> —Goethe

Dedication

The drama opens with a "Dedication," in which the poet laments that he has no public to whom he can communicate his theme:

> I bring the unknown multitude my treasures;
> Their very plaudits give my heart a pang.

Similarly, the Poet tells the Manager in the Prelude:

> Speak not to me of yonder motley masses.
> Whom but to see, puts out the fire of Song!

Goethe therefore turns to a mythic audience. The historic present recedes into the background, as the poet is seized by a yearning for the serene and solemn realm of the eternal present:

> Und mich ergreift ein längst entwöhntes Sehnen
> Nach jenem stillen, ernsten Geisterreich . . .
> Was ich besitze, seh' ich wie im Weiten,
> Und was verschwand, wird mir zu Wirklichkeiten.[19]

The living Faust who had become a legend in the sixteenth century is to be transformed into a myth.

Act I: Creation—Illusion and Reality

"Prelude on the Stage" and "Prologue in Heaven" are the two gates of the Faustian world, within which the drama of man is enacted. Both the stage, representing the realm of illusion, and Heaven, standing for the world of Reality, create. The first is interested in a theatrical product—the Manager (the Lord of the theatrical world) wants a play that will attract a paying public; the Lord of Heaven aims at creation of the whole man. And the Manager's Poet and Jester have their correspondence in Faust and Mephisto.[20]

The stately lines chanted by the archangel Raphael, with which "Prologue in Heaven" opens, bring Goethe's favorite sun-metaphor, sounding the motif of a harmonious and ordered world.

> Die Sonne tönt nach alter Weise
> In Brudersphären Wettgesang,
> Und ihre vorgeschriebene Reise
> Vollendet sie mit Donnergang . . .
> Die unbegreiflich hohen Werke
> Sind herrlich wie am ersten Tag.

Gabriel's song then introduces the imagery of the earth, the night and the raging sea, and the third, Archangel Michael, views these polar forces as interconnected parts of creation.

Birth-Stirrings

Faust comprises variations on the theme of creation and birth. Goethe's poetic-philosophical drama unfolds a titanic effort to give birth to a culture hero. The effort is "German" in its recourse to magic and romantic vision. All births fail: Gretchen drowns her child; Helen is a symbolic mother and her offspring is a "song" which fades into the air; Homunculus is a mechanical artifice which sinks into the ocean. Faust's final project to create virgin land, with the ocean as the mother-source, is a Utopian vision.

The celebrated soliloquy with which the drama proper begins breathes a feverish restlessness. It expresses Germany's *Sturm und Drang*, Goethe's own Promethean rebelliousness and desire to taste every possible experience:

> Und was der ganzen Menschheit zugeteilt ist,
> Will ich in meinem innern Selbst geniessen . . .

But insatiableness spells unfulfillment, and Faust cannot be satisfied with what he has. Here, as in the Hegelian dialectic, continuous transcendence lacks a logical scheme for its own determination. The anxiety of which Sorge makes Faust aware at the end is due to the nature of his passion which can never be requited. "All business," Goethe wrote Schiller (July 5, 1802),

> resembles marriage. You imagine you've done a great thing when one's copulation is accomplished, and it's exactly then that hell breaks loose . . . everything effectual must be regarded not as an end but as a beginning.

Shakespeare's Hamlet sees his task as limited to revenging his father's murder, and he is constantly beset with doubts as to his mission.

The German hero wants nothing less than to wrest the innermost secret of the world ("was die Welt im Innersten zusammenhält"), yet is not bothered by any doubts or scruples. Hamlet never forgets his father's admonition "Remember me," even though he appears in "questionable shape." Faust, on the other hand, would repudiate his parental tradition completely, declaring that it offers "nothing." The four medieval faculties to which he had devoted his life, amount only to an abstract unity, to a theory with which one can neither live alone nor with others.

Faust's opening soliloquy is a rejection of his heritage and an attempt of the German hero to emerge from the medieval womb. But the German scene did not offer the normal conditions for birth and Faust must turn to magic: "Drum hab' ich mich der Magie ergeben." Yet, the magical powers which Faust invokes are aspects of the very ancestral guidance he would spurn. The Macrocosm holds out a serene vision of an unchangeable substance. But, where Dante finds peace in such a vision, Goethe's Renaissance hero sees in it only a grand "pageant," an abstract universal which he can "contemplate," but not affect. Faust next turns to the magical sign of the Earth-Spirit which is a concrete universal, manifesting itself in dynamic living forms, suggesting the nature-spirit of Renaissance activism. It defines itself as

> A fluctuant wave,
> A shuttle free,
> Birth and the Grave,
> An eternal sea,
> A weaving, flowing
> Life, all-glowing . . .[21]

The appearance of the Earth-Spirit imbues Faust with "strength and heart to meet the world." But the German hero has only an intellectual grasp of its living unity and he is told by the Earth-Spirit that he measures up only to that spirit which he is able to "understand" (Germany had had no real Renaissance). He who had "expanded" himself to be its peer now realizes that he is but an infant (*Wurm*). Like an infant, he had been eager to "seize" the "breasts" of nature:

> Wo fass' ich dich, unendliche Natur?
> Euch Brüste, wo? Ihr Quellen alles Lebens, . . .
> Ihr quellt, ihr tränkt, und schmacht' ich so vergebens?

That Faust is not ready for creative activity is further seen in Wagner, his intellectual product. Wagner is an arrested Faust who still believes that human problems can be solved in the study and laboratory, that one can grasp the substance of things by examining their genesis and development. Historically, Wagner embodies the dried up form of German Humanism and Enlightenment, expressed in rhetoric and pedantic scholarship. He is the sexless product of his master's pure knowledge. Yet, he is loyal to Faust and tempers Faust's despair over the unattainableness of the absolute. Like Mephisto, he tends to debunk Faust's romantic strivings.

Death and Resurrection

Although the Earth-Spirit denies Faust's claim to be his peer, the German hero would still prove that he is god-like through an act of suicide. This final step is not accompanied by despair, but by "godlike rapture."[22]

As Faust lifts the cup of poison to his lips, the chimes of Easter bells and the song of angels break in. They tell of Christ's resurrection, reminding him of one who became God, not by the "heroism" of suicide, but by the passion of love. The Easter bells also bring memories of youth and of spring festivals, celebrating the eternal rebirth of man and nature. These multiple associations move Faust to tears, draw the cup away from his lips, and win him back to life—"Die Träne quillt, die Erde hat mich wieder":

> And Memory holds me now, with childish feeling,
> Back from the last, the solemn way.
> Sound on, ye hymns of Heaven, so sweet and mild!
> My tears gush forth; the Earth takes back her child![23]

Faust's tears are the first sign of a break in his arrogant self-sufficiency and prepares us for the next scene ("Before the City Gate"), where he comes down from his Gothic tower to mingle with the townspeople and the peasant-folk, who are also celebrating their day of resurrection—Easter Sunday. Where Dante begins with experience in Hell and ends with contemplation in Heaven, the Renaissance man begins with the contemplative life and descends to the valley of experience.

For a moment, Faust feels that among the folk, he can dare be a human being. But he soon realizes that a wide gap separates him from their gossipy and self-satisfied life. At this point, Faust speaks the famous lines of the "two souls" struggling within him:

> Two souls, alas! reside within my breast,
> And each withdraws from, and repels, its brother.
> One with tenacious organs holds in love
> And clinging lust the world in its embraces;

192

Jonah, by Albert Pinkham Ryder (ca 1890)
(National Collection of Fine Arts, Smithsonian Institution)

Don Quixote Crossing the Mountain, by Honoré Daumier
(The Bettmann Archives)

The other strongly sweeps, this dust above,
Into the high ancestral spaces.

Faust attempts to bridge or at least to narrow this gap by his pact with Mephistopheles.

Mephistopheles: The Pleasure Principle

Also muss die Feuerquelle
Sich im Abgrund erst entzünden,
Und die Niederfahrt zur Hölle
Soll die Himmelfahrt verkünden.

We know that what first attracted Goethe to the legend was the condition that Faust may not marry. To gain power and pleasure, he has to renounce unity and harmony, and this renunciation constitutes the pact with the devil.

Goethe's Mephistopheles is no Dantean Lucifer from whom "all streams of sorrow roll," does not hold the terror of Milton's Satan or of Marlowe's Mephistophilis. Indeed, he has few physical marks of the traditional devil. He appears in various forms—poodle, traveling scholar, squire, professor—and answers to various names—snake, animal, strange son of chaos, spirit of contradiction. He defines himself as the spirit who denies, as sin and destruction, as part of the primal Darkness or "Mother Night." The most novel feature of Goethe's devil is *his human and creative nature.* The Lord talks to him in a friendly tone and the author pictures him as quite likeable. Indeed, aside from Gretchen, he is the most human, if all-too-human, figure in the drama. His productive function is indicated by the Lord when he states that he has deliberately made the devil man's companion to counteract man's tendency towards lethargy. The devil, he says, rouses, excites, and thereby "must create," as devil. Mephisto too admits that he works the Good, even as he wills the Bad.

Goethe himself suggested that Mephisto's positive function emanates from his elemental nature. In *Poetry and Truth* (Book 8), he calls Mephisto the representative of all that "which we recognize as the form of matter, what we picture as heavy, firm and dark." In the drama, he is the earthy volcanic cobold who brings Faust in contact with sensuous life and fans his passion. Faust recognizes this earthy-fiery aspect when he calls Mephisto a mock-product of filth and fire ("Spottgeburt von Dreck und Feuer").[24]

In a highly suggestive essay, Hermann Reich has called attention to the relation between Mephistopheles and the demonic nature spirits connected with fertility rites, tracing his connection with the ancient followers of Dionysus, the satyrs and sileni. The sign of their nature power is the immense phallus (the only suggestion of this in *Faust* is Mephisto's "indecent" gesture in "The Witches' Kitchen" and in "Forest and Cave") which again points to their fertilizing nature.[25]

Faust calls Mephisto the son of chaos. Here, Faust touches on the devil's work as the Trickster who would dissolve order by abolishing all lines of demarcation, including the boundary of sex. And when Mephisto names himself "the Spirit that denies," he is referring to his denial of abiding principles and the worth of creative effort—in mythic language—Creation and the Quest. He tells the Lord that man uses reason only as a screen to become "far beastlier than any beast."

From one perspective, *Mephisto is also the spirit who affirms.* To begin with, he affirms his dark underground sources in "Mother Night," or chaos, which was "once All," calling himself an expert on "The Under-World" (Act I, Part II). And he affirms sexual indulgence in its disguised "incognito" forms. As a relative of the snake, Mephisto belongs to the species of mankind's first seducers. In the role of Merry-Andrew ("Prelude on the Stage"), he urges the Poet to use his gifts "As in a love-adventure," and following the pact, he advises Faust:

> Take hold, then! let reflection rest,
> And plunge into the world with zest!
> I say to thee, a speculative wight
> Is like a beast on moorlands lean,
> That round and round some fiend misleads to evil plight,
> While all about lie pastures fresh and green.

He stimulates the sensuality of the student, rouses Faust's animal desires in "The Witches' Kitchen," leads him to Gretchen, and through the wild, dissolute Walpurgis-Night, where Faust sees Lillith, Adam's first wife, who lures young men with her beautiful hair.

Mephisto's confidence that he can call forth Faust's erotic desires rests on the fact that Faust had repressed them, minimizing "earthly meat and drink," guided solely by reason and "gray" theory. Thomas Mann's *Doctor Faustus* shows that such denial of the senses exposes one all the more to them, shows that the German *Denker und Dichter* have yielded to the material and bestial precisely because they had long restricted themselves to living in a *Luftreich des Traumes.* Faust acknowledges to Mephisto:

> I have myself inflated too high;
> My proper place is thy estate.

Faust's philosophical, juridical and theological rationalizations had not taken care of his deepest desires. And, when he finds no gratification in the four faculties, nor in his vision of the forbidding Macrocosm and the Earth-Spirit, Faust turns to Mephisto. The modern devil is a product of the repression enforced by the Nordic-Christian world.[26]

In the Faust legend, the devil is sent by Satan, whereas in Goethe's drama, as in the Book of Job, he is assigned by the Lord. But only in *Faust*, does *the hero himself invite the devil and suggest the terms of the pact*. In "Walpurgis-Night," Faust states that the devil may help him find the answer to the human riddle:

> They seek the Evil One in wild confusion:
> Many enigmas there might find solution.

Faust's readiness for the devil's temptations also stems from his appetite for infinite experience.[27] In sum, *Mephisto represents Faust's secret wishes.* (The devil's secretive office is indicated by his traveling "incognito," his proficiency in spying, overhearing and "prompting.")

Now, the distinctive character of Goethe's devil consists in that his creative effect is connected with his role as tempter. When the Lord states that man errs as long as he strives, he implies that if man is to find the right way, he must err, that is, yield to temptation.[28] The Lord agrees with Mephisto that the idealistic, ascetic Faust we meet at the beginning is "confused," but promises that he will ultimately gain "clarity." And the Lord chooses Mephisto as the means by which this is to be accomplished. Goethe's devil is the corrective of Faust's aspirations to be a superman. Moreover, the Mephistophelian temptations offer Faust a genuine choice, one based on a *knowledge of* alternatives, which can thus lend his choice a moral character. In this sense, Goethe's devil becomes an instrument of Faust's salvation.[29]

Pact and Wager

Mephisto's diabolical substance consists in the excess of his sensuous correction. On the one hand, Faust is to eat dust and like it; on the other hand, he is to leap restlessly from one object to another:

> That, to his hot, insatiate sense,
> The dream of drink shall mock, but never lave him . . .
> Refreshment shall his lips in vain implore.

Mephisto nearly succeeds. In "Forest and Cavern," Faust cries out:

> Thus in desire I hasten to enjoyment,
> And in enjoyment pine to feel desire.[30]

In the legend, the devil promises to be Faust's servant on earth, if he can possess Faust's soul after death. However, Goethe's Renaissance hero is not concerned with the beyond, but with the joys and sorrows of earthly life:

> Aus dieser Erde quillen meine Freuden,
> Und diese Sonne scheinet meine Leiden;

and he demands that Mephisto lead him "through the wildest life":

> Let us the sensual deeps explore,
> To quench the fervors of glowing passion!

At the same time, *he vows*—and this is the heart of the wager—*that he will never succumb to the pleasure principle*. Should he yield to it, then and only then would Faust lose his "soul," that is, become a slave of the devil. This Faustian wager is summed up in the crucial lines spoken by Faust (misleadingly translated by Bayard Taylor):

> Wie ich beharre, bin ich Knecht,
> Ob dein, was frag' ich, or wessen.

Here, loss of soul is equated with stagnation and inertia, seen as states of human enslavement. This point is made earlier in metaphorical language:

> When on an idler's bed I stretch myself in quiet,
> There let, at once, my record end!
> Canst thou with lying flattery rule me,
> Let that day be the last for me! . . .
> When thus I hail the Moment flying:
> "Ah, still delay—thou art so fair!"
> Then bind me in thy bonds undying,
> My final ruin then declare!

In this wager, Faust pledges himself to the perpetual quest, to critical questioning, persuaded that man's creative forces can lead towards "highest life" (Act I, Part II). Mephisto had wagered that if the Lord allowed him to fan Faust's sensuousness, he could get him to "eat dust."[31] And what Faust wagers is that the enjoyment of "the moment" would never gain dominance over him, reminding Mephisto that it "is not of joy we're talking." For Faust, the soul connotes activity grounded in basic principles. And, he would lose his soul either if he became satisfied with a life of ease or with pointless moving from one activity to another.[32]

Act II: The Journey

Like Don Quixote, Hamlet and other Renaissance heroes, Faust has no guide and no attachment to the folk, family or church. He, too, goes forth on a journey without a plan. To his question "Then how shall we begin?" Mephisto replies: We'll just go ahead ("Wir gehen eben fort."). Faust's journey is unconfined, limited primarily by his poetic will, in search of adventures with the arch-adventurer, Mephistopheles.

In the middle of his life's journey, Faust realizes that he had not lived. His bond with the devil is a desperate attempt to experience a "re-nascence." However, the historic basis for such rejuvenation was absent in Goethe's Germany whose Renaissance was an esthetic-literary awakening, stimulated by the study of classical culture. To regain his youth, Faust has recourse to a magic potion prepared by Mephisto's Witch. But the potion produces only a mock-rebirth—it only brings *his wish* for youthful living to the surface.[33]

Gretchen

The Gretchen scenes are an outgrowth of Goethe's deep personal experience and are the most realistic and effective executions in the drama. Goethe assigns Gretchen the role of providing Faust with an Ariadne-thread in his labyrinthine passage. Gretchen is at first a harlot figure to Faust who demands that Mephisto get him the girl he saw on the street. Next, he sees in her the Madonna who moves him to prayer in the "hallowed shrine" of her room. He then hears her speak of performing the duties of a mother to her little sister. At the end of the drama, she intercedes for Faust before the Mother of God and leads him towards Heaven. Gretchen is at once the object of Faust's major temptation and the instrument of his redemption.

Thomas Mann calls Gretchen a German folk-song.[34] She strikes us at first as the prototype of a German *Natur-Kind*—good, wholesome, genuine, spontaneous. But love transforms this simple girl into a rebel, like Faust. As a Catholic, living in a Protestant Germany, she too would leave the "Gothic" prison of her narrow "den." If Faust is hemmed in by his scholastic heritage, Gretchen is imprisoned by the German tradition that woman's world is limited to the three K's: *Küche, Kinder, Kirche*. As a woman, she faces more severe condemnation than Faust does and becomes a homeless fugitive:

> Meine Ruh' ist hin,
> Mein Herz ist schwer;

Ich finde sie nimmer
Und nimmermehr.

Gretchen knows that she is leaping into the abyss, but her love is "demonic", that is, anti-pragmatic, and she surrenders to it unhesitatingly:

Mein Busen drängt
Sich nach ihm hin.
Ach dürft' ich fassen
Und halten ihn,

Und küssen ihn,
So wie ich wollt',
An seinen Küssen
Vergehen sollt'![35]

The love of Dante's Francesca is limited to sensuous passion; Ophelia's love for Hamlet is passive and pitiful, that of Racine's Phèdre is veiled and furtive. Gretchen's love goes out for Faust's whole person. Even as the world is about to crumble and bury her, Gretchen still affirms her love which was good and sweet:

Doch—alles, was dazu mich trieb,
Gott! war so gut! ach, war so lieb!

Dante makes a sharp division between the carnal passion of Paolo and Francesca and the spiritual love of Dante and Beatrice. Croce points out that although Dante has deep compassion for the fate of the lovers, the Catholic poet never questions the necessity for their being in hell. Goethe, on the other hand, likens Gretchen to the Virgin Mother who knows her agony. The drama closes with her exaltation, as she leads Faust towards Heaven in the train of the Mater Dolorosa.

Faust develops a deep love for Gretchen, yet never considers marrying her. Goethe only hints at the social barrier in characterizing the German Walpurgis-Night as "monarchic," exhibiting "bourgeois limitation, moral confusion, superstitious belief."[36] It imprisons Gretchen in her den and later in the dungeon. Faust sees her on Walpurgis-Night as

She falters on, her way scarce knowing,
As if with fettered feet that stay her going.

In contrast to Faust, Gretchen would gladly accept a permanent union with Faust. Her affirmation of such a "moment" is expressed in the tender lyrical lines she speaks to Faust in the dungeon:

O weile!
Weil' ich doch so gern, wo du weilest.

But for the German "doctor," Gretchen is only a passing "moment" on his way to new conquests.

FAUST II: THE SOCIAL QUEST

In the first part of the drama, Faust yields to the Teutonic temptations of *Innerlichkeit* and *Werden* to the degree of *Maasslosigkeit*, resorting to magic and necromancy. In his unrestrained self-indulgence, Faust commits symbolic parricide: He declares that his ancestral tradition is "nothing," derogates his father, and is instrumental in the death of Gretchen, her child, brother and mother. At the end of Part I, Faust leaves Gretchen in the dungeon. However, Goethe indicates that his hero is redeemable. For Faust is not a Don Juan adventurer, but feels remorse, calls himself a "monster without aim or rest," wishing that he had "ne'er been born."

In the second part, Faust enters the supra-individual world in which he becomes aware of social powers and their pressures on the individual. He comes to realize what he had sensed earlier when he said that when one thinks that he is doing the pushing, one is actually being pushed.

Prologue on Earth

The opening scene of Part II (it contains some of the most lyrical and philosophical lines of the drama) is a kind of Prologue in an Earthly Paradise. Lying in a pleasant valley, a restless Faust, presumably troubled over Gretchen's fate, is vainly seeking sleep. A chorus of Nature-Spirits, led by Ariel, attempt to compose him. Like Dante, Faust is to drink from Lethe and Eunoë to forget the bad dreams of his past, regain his youthful hope, and be restored "to the holy light." The Chorus sings of the eternal recurrence of spring and calls on Faust to "Trust the new, the rising Day." Faust awakens refreshed and pledges to strive for "highest life." In Part II, Faust's spring-like awakening is followed by his "summer"—marriage to Helena, his "harvest"—the project that is to produce free land for a free people. The drama ends with Faust's "winter"—his death, with a promise of his redemption.

In Part I, Faust expressed the wish to travel with the sun. In the opening scene of the second part, he attempts to look at the sun, but blinded by its rays, he turns his eyes earthwards. He is now content with looking at the refraction of the sun-rays, the colors of the rainbow formed by the spray from the mountain-falls.[37] He transposes the meaning of this phenomenon into the idea that man can experience only the symbolic manifestations of life: "Am farbigen Abglanz haben wir das Leben,"—an insight which is also voiced in the final verse of the drama:

Alles Vergängliche	All things transitory
Ist nur ein Gleichnis.	But as symbols are sent

It has been said that in Part II Mephisto recedes into the background. It is true that Goethe's devil is here less prominent as a character, but this is so only because *the terrain as a whole is more Mephistophelian.* If, in Part I, the devil's temptations appear in the form of individual aggrandizement where the self would swallow the world, in Part II the temptation lies in the self allowing itself to be swallowed by currents of the world.

In Part I, the social forces behind Gretchen's tragedy are veiled. By the time Goethe wrote the second part, he had gotten to know the court of Weimar and the shadowy figures of "Walpurgis-Night" are clearly recognizable as the disintegrating feudal order. In the court-scenes, it attempts to create the illusion of active life by pomp and pageantry by mummery and masquerade, with Mephisto, the devilish jester, as master of its ceremonies.[38]

The Mothers

One of the ironies of the drama is that the court-world of shallow amusements leads to the most basic quest—Faust's descent to The Mothers. The young emperor wants to see Helena and Paris, "The model forms of Man and Woman." Since Mephisto, the Northern devil, has no contact with the "old heathen race," Faust is entrusted with the mission to produce them by seeking out The Mothers.

Upon hearing this word, Faust is "terrified." His dread is similar to Dante's as he is about to undertake his journey into the hellish chasms. Homunculus, who later descends to the ocean-mother—speaks of the terminal nature of this ordeal:

> Who to the Mothers found his way
> Has nothing more to undergo.

Even Mephisto is moved to eloquent earnestness in mentioning The Mothers:

> Unwilling, I reveal a loftier mystery.—
> In solitude are throned the Goddesses,
> No Space around them, Place and Time still less;

> Only to speak of them embarrasses.
> They are THE MOTHERS!

To Faust's question "Where is the way," Mephisto replies:

> No way!—To the Unreachable,
> Ne'er to be trodden! A way to the Unbeseechable,
> Never to be besought! Art thou prepared?
> There are no locks, no latches to be lifted;
> Through endless solitudes shalt thou be drifted.

Faust will have to "delve in the deepest depths,"

> Naught shalt thou see in endless Void afar,—
> Not hear thy footstep fall, nor meet
> A stable spot to rest thy feet.

In *The King and the Corpse*, Heinrich Zimmer calls The Mothers "that domain (which) has been for milleniums the holy goal of all the questing heroes," from Gilgamesh onwards. The journey is nearly always accompanied by dread in mythology and mythopoesis, and no other scene in *Faust* has the same mystery, terror and promise. Faust's journey to The Mothers is an attempt by the mythic hero to wrest the secret of nature by retracing his way to the origins of creation.[39]

In Part I, Faust is nearly damned for his destructive invasion of Gretchen's life. In Part II, Faust repeats the act with The Mothers, *but this time, his action is symbolic.* And, as in the case of Sophocles' Oedipus, Faust's symbolic reenactment brings him "heavenly gain," first Helena and at the end the Mater Dolorosa.[40]

Faust succeeds in bringing up the images of Helena and Paris, and in a spectral play "The Rape of Helena," he would use the key to rescue Helena for himself:

> What! Rape? Am I for nothing here? To stead me,
> Is not this key still shining in my hand?
> I'll rescue her, and make her doubly mine.
> Ye Mothers! Mothers! crown this wild endeavor!
> Who knows her once must hold her, and forever!

In this attempt, Faust is as violently impatient as when he challenged the Earth-Spirit. He is not ready for this task either, and is knocked unconscious by an explosion.[41]

Homunculus and the Classical Mother

While Faust lies unconscious in his study, his former student Wagner, who has since become a famous scholar, is busy trying to make a

201

human being. His method of creation does not entail a descent to The Mothers, nor any sexual contact, but only a mixture of chemical elements.[42] The resulting synthesis, Homunculus, lives in a sealed glass-vial. Born with a mature mind, he knows at once that Faust is dreaming of Leda and the swan and wants to reenact Zeus' union with Helena's mother. He advises that Faust be taken to the Classical Walpurgis-Night where the spirits of classicism are gathered to celebrate their Hellenic legends. Faust must come in contact with the naturalistic spirit of Greece if he is to regain consciousness. Homunculus himself must make the same journey, but for the opposite reason—this cerebral product must acquire a body to become human. As he nears Galatea's chariot, longing for her beauty expands his light-body so that his glass-vial breaks and Homunculus sinks into the amorphous ocean to begin his gradual, organic development towards the human.[43]

Faust's wanderings through the classical terrain in quest of Helena are connected with Goethe's Italian travels. Italy, the home of humanistic art, was to Goethe a welcome alternative to the feudal-burgher commercialism of his homeland.[44] Faust's journey takes him from the archaic period to Hellenism where beauty is incorporated in the human figure of Helena.[45]

In classical and medieval mythology, Helena is a temptress and the Faust legend makes her an object for pleasure only. In Goethe, she becomes a wife and a mother. Faust's wedding with Helena is meant to symbolize the union of Northern unrestraint with Southern calm, the Gothic quest for the boundless and the infinite with the Grecian sense for the limited and finite, Germanic dynamism with Apollonian equilibrium.[46]

Ironically enough, this union results in combining only the extremes of Graeco-German culture. On the one hand, Faust and Helena disappear from the action and, watched over by Mephisto-Phorkyas, enjoy a bliss "Arcadian and free," that comes close to lying on "an idler's bed." On the other hand, their son Euphorion exhibits only his father's Germanic *Maasslosigkeit* and none of his mother's Hellenic *sophrosyne*:[47]

> I must clamber ever higher,
> Ever further must I see . . .
> Dream ye the peaceful day?
> Dream, then, who may!
> War! is the countersign:
> Victory—word divine!

However, Euphorion ("the lightly borne") is a *German* Hermes and Icarus, a "genius" without wings. Like Homunculus, he is the artificial product of German theory. Whereas Homunculus takes the downward journey to the ocean to become human, Euphorion takes the "German" way upwards: He throws himself into the air, leaving his garments and lyre on the ground, and calls out to Helena:

> Leave me here, in the gloomy Void,
> Mother, not thus alone!

Helena heeds his call, embraces Faust, saying to him that an "old word" becomes true: "That Bliss and Beauty ne'er enduringly unite."[48]

Before Phorkyas reverts to the form of the German devil, he advises Faust to preserve the garment and veil which Helena left in his hands:

> Hold fast what now alone remains to thee!
> The garment let not go! . . .
> It is no more the Goddess thou hast lost,
> But godlike is it. For thy use employ
> The grand and priceless gift, and soar aloft!
> 'Twill bear thee swift from all things mean and low
> To ether high, so long thou canst endure.

The point Goethe is making is that the usable heritage of Greece cannot lie in its historical material, no longer available, but in its mythic residue. It alone can save him "from all things mean and low," that is, from being engulfed by the pressures of the historic present. The value of the Greek way is not in its what, but in its how.

Now, Faust returns to his Northern "high mountains." To be productive, Faust must work with his native material and on his native ground. Faust's esthetic experience prepares him for his first moral act.

The Mighty Plan

While Faust was being transported home, his eye was drawn to the ocean:

> There endless waves hold sway, in strength erected
> And then withdrawn,—and nothing is effected.

The spectacle of this unfruitful effort roused "excited passion of the blood," and gives rise to Faust's "mighty plan" to create land by forcing the waters to recede.

Faust's plan to fertilize the "watery waste" and gain virgin land is a continuation of his effort to be a God-man. He would repeat the act of

Genesis and create a world out of watery chaos. Yet, a significant change has taken place. In the beginning, Faust sought first causes by invoking the Macrocosm and the Earth-Spirit. This absolutism is modified in the opening scene of Part II where he expresses the thought that man must be content with their symbolic reflection. Now, Faust takes a further step: In planning to set limits to and make use of the oceanic waters, *Faust turns from the substantive to the functional.* He is no longer concerned with first and final causes: "I ask not, Whence? and ask not, Why? . . .", satisfied that "Nature in herself her being founded." Where the rainbow was a spectacle used for philosophic reflection, Faust's new vision calls for work, for making natural power socially productive. It is Faust who suggests this task and in this sense, he moves towards *self-determination.*

The new scheme is announced to Mephisto on the "High Mountain." This setting and Faust's declaration that the new-won land would give him power and property ("Herrschaft gewinn' ich, Eigentum!") recall the temptation which Satan dangled before Christ on the High Mountain—power over the earthly kingdom. Christ rejected the temptation, even though he was assured that such power could bring universal peace and freedom. Faust yields to the temptation and it involves him in war. To receive title to the under-water land, Faust must help the Emperor in a battle against his rival.[49]

While Mephisto's sober realism serves to correct Faust's romantic idealism, his practical orientation knows no substance, but only process. In the social sphere, he stands for the fetichism of things and of money, believes that Gretchen can be bought with jewels, that the tottering feudal regime can be saved with paper money. His values are property, power and exploitation with which he tempts the Emperor. As the "foreman" of Faust's project to win land back from the sea, he would convert Faust's ideal of a free people on a free soil into the trinity of "War, Trade and Piracy," aiming at surplus accumulation:

> We sailed away with vessels twain,
> With twenty come to port again.

For this modern devil, a man is evaluated not by what he is, but by what he has:

> If I've six stallions in my stall,
> Are not their forces also lent me?
> I speed along, completest man of all,
> As though my legs were four-and-twenty.

and might makes right:

You have the Power, and thus the Right.
You count the *What*, and not the *How*.

Faust-Mephisto points to the polarity in German history: Idealistic theory and *Real-Politik*.[50] At the end of the drama, Faust is dead and Mephistopheles remains to "implement" Faust's idea. In German history, this implementation became Bismarck and Hitler.

Act III: Homecoming

Lass den Anfang mit dem Ende
Sich in Eins zusammenziehn.

The last act of *Faust*, completed shortly before Goethe's death, is the poet's testament, the precipitate of his long and rich life. The language is resonant, lapidary, with runic undertones. And the characters—Philemon and Baucis, the Wanderer, Lynceus, the Four Grey Women, the Angels and the Mater Dolorosa—derive from Classical and Christian mythology.

We have reached the last stage of the hero's journey. And, it is precisely now that Goethe expresses his reservations over Faust's "progress" by having recourse to overtly mythic themes. Part I had shown that Faust's titanic way wrecked Gretchen and her family. In Part II, Faust's social project entails a social sacrifice. Goethe dramatizes his reservation by drawing a contrast between his hero and Philemon.

In Ovid's *Metamorphosis*, Philemon and his wife Baucis save Zeus and Mercury from shipwreck. The sole reward they ask is that, at their death, they be converted into trees near their temple so that they might never be parted. In Goethe's drama, we see them living contentedly on their little hill, their only wish to end life in their old home, praying to the "old God" in their chapel.

In the opening scene, the old couple tell the Wanderer (Goethe's composite figure for Zeus and Mercury) of Faust's aspiration to become master over the ocean, complaining that his venture is claiming human lives:

Nightly rose the sounds of sorrow,
Human victims there must bleed.

Faust has become the leader of a vast colonizing enterprise which uses "serfs," and he has ordered Mephistopheles, his "Overseer," to use *any* means to accomplish the task:

However possible,
Collect a crowd of men with vigor,

205

> Spur by indulgence, praise, or rigor,—
> Reward, allure, conscript, compel!

Still, Faust is not satisfied and in addition demands that Philemon and Baucis surrender their little hut and chapel. Baucis tells the Wanderer:

> Since he lords it as our neighbor,
> We to him must subject be.

Philemon had engaged in a task, similar to Faust's, when he rescued the Wanderer from shipwreck. But, in contrast to Faust, who employs technical-devilish devices, Philemon labored alone, using only his hands, and solely in the interest of another.

To be sure, Faust offers to compensate the old couple with a strip of the land which he is winning back from the sea. But Baucis warns her husband that this new ground rests on quicksand:

> Trust not the watery foundation!
> Keep upon the hill thy stand!

They are self-sufficient, do not want any of Faust's "modern improvements." He, on the other hand, despite (or because of) his spectacular acquisitions, is dissatisfied.

Faust's explanation why he needs their small holding is that the linden trees and hut spoil his desire for world-possession ("Verderben mir den Weltbesitz"):

> No sorer plague can us attack,
> Than rich to be and something lack!

Faust feels that, without the lindens, his grand estate is not "pure." He would use them to recuperate from his feverish activities ("Und wünscht' ich dort mich zu erholen. . . ."), would erect a scaffold on the hill from where he can view the whole:

> Till for my gaze a look be won
> O'er everything that I have done.

It would seem then that Faust needs the quiet rhythm of their agrarian life to offset the hustle and bustle of his technological activities. In his "Night-Song," Goethe wrote of the "sweet peace" which the Wanderer yearns for:

> Ach, ich bin des Treibens müde!
> Was soll all der Schmerz und Lust?
> Süsser Friede,
> Komm, ach komm in meine Brust![51]

But, it is the tragic dilemma of the Faustian way that to gain peace, it must use terror. Philemon and Baucis refuse the exchange, (the old pair is shown to be "unprogressive" and unproductive—they have no children), their home goes up in flames and they are burned to death. The conservative principle is purged by the "revolutionary" process and the Moloch of industrialism steamrollers over the agrarian idyll. As Faustian titanism had destroyed Gretchen's peace, so now it uproots ancient values, what Goethe called "das alte Wahre."

> What erstwhile the eye enchanted
> With the centuries is gone.

Sorge

At this point, Sorge enters Faust's preconscious. (Bayard Taylor renders Sorge as Care. In the context of Faust's dilemma at this point, the word suggests anxiety or worry.)

Previously, Faust had not questioned the limitations of activity as such. To be sure, Goethe recognized that industrialization made the violence inherent in continuous technological innovations inevitable. He also knew the blood sacrifice they entailed, knew that its fire could be used to destroy, as it consumes Philemon and Baucis in the drama.

Immediately following the death of Philemon and Baucis, four grey women enter Faust's palace. Three of them—Want, Debt[52] and Need—leave almost at once, but the fourth, Sorge stays. An eerie, mystic colloquy takes place between Sorge and Faust. In the setting of a timeless "Midnight," she asks Faust whether he has ever known Sorge. Faust replies:

> I only through the world have flown:
> Each appetite I seized as by the hair;
> What not sufficed me, forth I let it fare,
> And what escaped me, I let go.
> I've only craved, accomplished my delight,
> Then wished a second time, and thus with might
> Stormed through my life . . .
> In marching onwards, bliss and torment find,
> Though, every moment, with unsated mind.

The overt import of Faust's reply is to deny that he has ever known anxiety or worry, that he found "bliss" as well as "torment" in his "incessant rolling." Sorge retorts that his kind of life spells perpetual postponement of joy:

Whom I once possess, shall never
Find the world worth his endeavor: . . .
Perfect in external senses,
Inwardly his darkness dense is; . . .
Luck and Ill become caprices;
Still he starves in all increases;
Be it happiness or sorrow,
He postpones it till the morrow;
To the Future only cleaveth:
Nothing, therefore, he achieveth.

From a broader perspective, Sorge is the concomitant of the Western apotheosis of time and progress, particularly of Germanic *Werden*. The breathless pursuit of an ever-receding tomorrow makes for an "unsated mind."[53] While Faust had gotten to realize the limitation of a contemplative life, he has remained insensitive to the limitation of restless activity. Hence Sorge can say to him:

Throughout their whole existence men are blind;
So, Faust, be thou like them at last.

Sorge's blinding of Faust is the peripety of the drama. As the blinded Faust steps out of his palace, he hears a clattering of spades and is happy in the belief that the sound is made by laborers digging moats for his project. Actually, Lemures (spectres of the night) are digging his grave. (The original plays on the words *Graben*, moat and *Grab*, grave). In Goethe's own time, "progress" brought the era of Metternich which is digging the grave of Faust's social idealism. Only by blinding Faust to this historical terror can Goethe have Faust "see" his Utopian plan. He would save its idea in a Platonic heaven, with the hope that it might be enacted in a more favorable historic moment.

The Utopian Vision

Lasst alle Völker unter gleichem Himmel
Sich gleicher Gabe wohlgemut erfreun.

According to Greek legends, Tiresias' prophetic power was greater when he became blind. Similarly, Sophocles' Oedipus began to understand his past after he put out his eyes and Thomas Mann's Joseph recognized his self-centredness when thrown into the dark pit by his brothers.

Goethe's blind hero repeats this pattern with deeper Germanic *Innerlichkeit*. As the night presses around him, Faust feels that a bright light shines within him:

Assyrian Sun God Pursuing the Demon of Chaos
(The British Museum)

The Enigma of a Day by Giorgio De Chirico (1914)
(Private Collection, New Canaan, Conn.)

> Die Nacht scheint tiefer tief hereinzudringen,
> Allein im Innern leuchtet helles Licht . . .

With this inner light, he visualizes a social Utopia:[54]

> And such a throng I fain would see,—
> Stand on free soil among a people free!
> Then dared I hail the Moment fleeing:
> "Ah, still delay—thou art so fair!"
> The traces cannot, of mine earthly being,
> In aeons perish,—they are there!—
> In proud fore-feeling of such lofty bliss,
> I now enjoy the highest Moment,—this!

With this hope for the promised land, Faust dies.
Mephisto now claims that in uttering the words

> Then I hail the Moment fleeting:,

Faust has accepted the immediate present and has therefore lost the
wager. However, examined in the context of Faust's pronouncement
*the words salute a continuous task in which the "Moment" is forever
renewed*. His free soil is "not secure," and must ceaselessly be fought
for. Ultimate wisdom ("der Weisheit letzter Schluss"), Faust states, is
the realization that

> He only earns his freedom and existence,
> Who daily conquers them anew.

Mephisto had vowed that Faust would eat dust and like it ("Staub soll
er fressen, und mit Lust"). Faust was made to eat dust, but he did *not*
like it. That he did not yield to the pleasure principle is admitted by
Mephisto himself in the line he speaks following Faust's death: "No joy
could sate him, and suffice no bliss." Faust withstood the devil's temptation to lie down on an idler's bed, and the angels proclaim that Faust
can be redeemed because he labored "eternally:"

> The noble Spirit now is free,
> And saved from evil scheming:
> Who'er aspires unweariedly
> Is not beyond redeeming.

According to Eckermann, Goethe saw the key to the poem in the last
two lines which make Faust's activism the ground for his salvation.
Thus, Goethe's hero is presumably saved by "The Act" which Faust
had declared to be at "the beginning." The act is indeed a key-term in
the German Renaissance—in Lessing's *Laocoon, The Hamburg Drama-*

turgy and *Nathan the Wise*, in Kant's *Critique of Practical Reason* and in Schiller's *William Tell*.

Now, this line of interpretation loses sight of the fact that the devil's temptation lies not only in man accepting a stagnant existence but also in his *directionless activity*. So the question of Faust's redemption hinges on whether Faust avoided the other threat as well. And, the point I would make is that *Faust is not saved by the act alone*.

Examination of Goethe's work makes it clear that he did not absolutize striving as such. One of Goethe's *Maxims and Reflections* states that "unconditioned activity, whatever it might be, makes for bankruptcy in the end." Goethe reflected with bitterness on his own activistic life which he likened to that of Sisyphus: "At bottom," he told Eckermann, "I have had nothing but trouble and toil. . . . Eternally I rolled a stone up the mountain; eternally it had to be done anew."[55] And Faust's activity comes close to having been "unconditioned." Also, when we consider his indifferent attitude towards Gretchen's mother, his own child and his behavior towards Philemon and Baucis, we are hardly prepared for his pronounced social idealism. Even as Faust speaks of freeing "many millions," he remains something of a charismatic leader, thinks of the project as *his* idea ("One mind suffices for a thousand hands"), and as assuring *his* immortality.[56] Indeed, some Faust criticism (Wilhelm Böhm, Reinhold Schneider) condemns Faust as an incorrigible and unscrupulous criminal who has made "history in the last hundred years" (Schneider). In Karl Viëtor's formulation, Faust remains

> one of the modern titans of will who knows only one need, one law: the own hybrid Ego. The cultures of the East do not know the Superman, and classical culture did not know him. . . . What the Greeks regarded as a cardinal crime and called hybris . . . that is for the modern European the real possibility to fulfill oneself and at the same time to further humanity. . . . What the colonizer Faust does to the patriarchal pair, Philemon and Baucis, that has always and everywhere happened, where the 'pioneering-spirit' of the European has come in contact with the so-called primitive peoples. When Goethe wrote these scenes, he stood under the impact made by the newest phase of the conquest by the white people of the North American continent. He admired this as a gigantic feat, but he also knew what blood-letting accompanied it. (*Goethe, the Poet* [Cambridge, 1949])

To the extent, then, that the would-be superman continues his unconditioned activity, the devil "wins" his wager." Yet, as Goethe remarked to Schubarth (November 3, 1820), Mephisto "may win the wager only by half." For, in Part II, Faust begins to reconcile himself to human limitation, realizes that the basis of creation and the conditions for self-development lie outside of himself: Act I shows these conditions in society, Act II ("Classical Walpurgis-Night") in the phenomenology of the race, Act III in Hellenic culture, Act IV in the forces of nature, Act V in the Mother of God. At the end, he would subordinate personal aggrandizement to a supra-individual goal, would stand *"among"* a free people. That is, Faust is redeemable to the extent that he renounces his super-human quest, and develops from an adventurer to a culture-hero.[57]

Goethe at once feared and hailed the Faustian man. His march brought Metternich and imperialism as well as Beethoven and Utopian Socialism. The German idea of social freedom was primarily "theory," and remains such in *Faust*. Goethe, who battled against German romanticism is forced to reintroduce it in his drama.[58] Faust admits to Sorge that he was unable to do without black magic:

> If I could banish Magic's fell creations,
> And totally unlearn the incantations,—
> Stood I, O Nature! Man, alone in thee,
> Then were it worth one's while a man to be.

But the scientific-natural means to bring about social and human freedom were unavailable in Goethe's Germany and his Faust must cling to Mephisto. The last act was written in the period of Metternich which Goethe characterized as barbarous, a time in which "confused doctrine [is] leading to confused action" (To Eckermann and von Humboldt). In his drama, the devil becomes the "Overseer" of Faust's venture. Historically, the Mephistos were digging a grave for the Fausts and Goethe blinds his hero so that he might "see" the possibilities in the future.[59]

As in Shakespeare, "inner-directedness" is brought into focus precisely at the time when it is threatened to be overrun by "other-directedness." Amidst the Wars of Liberation, Goethe wrote (to Knebel, November 24, 1813) that his task was

> to preserve, to create order and to lay the foundations in contradiction to the age . . . to preserve the sacred fire, which the coming generations will need so sorely, were it only beneath the ashes. . . .

In *Faust*, Goethe would rescue this imperishable kernel in German idealism itself. In "Forest and Cavern," Mephisto satirizes Faust for living in caves like an owl, adding ironically: "The Doctor's in thy body still." Faust replies that his isolated life is the fount of a blessed vitality:

> What fresh and vital forces, canst thou guess,
> Spring from my commerce with the wilderness?

> But, if thou hadst the power of guessing,
> Thou wouldst be devil enough to grudge my soul the blessing.

Goethe would save this German "idea," save it supra-historically or mythically.

Matriarchal Grace

Faust never mentions his mother, yet it is to mothers that he turns in his greatest need. He feverishly demands "the breasts of nature," is drawn to the earthy mother-figure of Gretchen and descends to the Earth-Mothers. The poem begins with a patriarchal God of justice and ends with maternal figures dispensing grace, with the final lines of the poem honoring the Eternal-Feminine:

> Das Ewig-Weibliche
> Zieht uns hinan.

That man cannot be saved by the act alone is suggested by the Lord himself when he declares in the "Prologue in Heaven" that man errs as long as he strives. Put another way: Man must err because any act entails means, and means are in their very nature imperfect. Hence, man cannot be saved by his works, but only by grace. On June 6, 1831, while Goethe was putting the finishing touches on *Faust*, he told Eckermann: "We are not saved through our own efforts but through the addition of Divine Grace." The poet makes this also explicit in the drama. Following the lines

> Whoe'er aspires unweariedly
> Is not beyond redeeming,

the angels add:

> And if he feels the grace of Love
> That from on high is given,
> The Blessed Hosts, that wait above,
> Shall welcome him to Heaven!

Faust had declared that in the beginning was The Act, but learns that in the beginning was Love.

The drama begins with an individual personal God and ends with collective guides. Faust's Ascension is prepared by the group of Blessed Boys (they can free Faust from his bodily remains because having died at birth, they have no trace of "earthly" ways), by the angels who declare: Him *we* can redeem,[60] and by the Chorus of Women Penitents. The final plea is made by Gretchen and Doctor Marianus.[61]

Epilogue

In the last summer of his life, Goethe composed "The Song of Lynceus" which he inserted in the Fifth Act of *Faust*. In the Dead of Night, Lynceus the Warder, who has a sharp and over-all view of both "the Distant" and "the Near," sings on the watch-tower of the Palace. He begins by affirming the human journey, "Whatever it might be":

Zum Sehen geboren,	For seeing intended,
Zum Schauen bestellt,	Employed for my sight,
Dem Turme geschworen,	The tower's my dwelling,
Gefällt mir die Welt.	The world my delight.
Ich blick' in die Ferne,	I gaze on the Distant,
Ich seh' in der Näh'	I look on the Near,—
Den Mond und die Sterne,	The moon and the planets,
Den Wald und das Reh.	The forest and deer.
So seh' ich in allen	So see I in all things
Die ewige Zier,	The grace without end,
Und wie mir's gefallen,	And even as they please me,
Gefall' ich auch mir.	Myself I commend.
Ihr glücklichen Augen,	Thou fortunate Vision,
Was je ihr gesehn,	Of all thou wast 'ware,
Es sei, wie es wolle,	Whatever it might be,
Es war doch so schön!	Yet still it was fair!

This mood is abruptly disturbed by a dissonant note, as Lynceus witnesses the horror which befalls Philemon and Baucis. The song of harmony is jarred by the blood sacrifice which issues "from some darksome world below!" Goethe himself found no harmony in his life. What he called the Demoniacal forever prevented resolution between thought and action, the self and society, providence and chance.

The Catholic setting of Faust's Heaven has led some critics to argue that Goethe saves Faust by repudiating his paganism and the Protestant nature of his personality. But this ignores Goethe's own statement to Eckermann that he used this device to give pictorial, sensuous form to Faust's Ascension. It is a matter of record that Goethe rejected ascetic religions, calling himself "a non-Christian" and "an old pagan."[62] Faust's social vision is an earthly paradise and the Mater Gloriosa, as Rickert points out, appears not as the Virgin of Immaculate Conception, but as the guardian of love between man and woman. More telling is the marked non-Catholic note which permeates the scenes themselves. Faust's Heaven is not a divinely ordered Dantean Paradise.[63] Its "Mountain-Gorges, Forest, Rock, Desert," ravines and foaming waves have more the character of a hellish terrain, and its ascending "higher

213

spheres" do not culminate in rest and peace. Pater Ecstaticus hovers in "endless ecstatic fire," suffers boiling breast pains, invites "arrows ... lances ... bludgeons ... lightnings" to pierce and shatter him, and for Father Profundus, love is heralded in the phenomenon of rocks heaving and swaying in savage roaring.

Goethe denied Kant's radical evil and the unknowability of "das Ding an sich." But, his hope was *optative*. Faust states that *if* he could see a free people on free soil, then he *might* hail that moment ("Zum Augenblicke dürft' ich sagen. . . ."). And he is shown not as reaching, but only as being led *towards* Heaven, with "das Ewig-Weibliche" remaining unreachable. These "Protestant" notes are the basis for the Epilogue in the Faustian mythopoesis.[64] *Faust* is called a tragedy and the hero dies before his task is completed. Like Moses, Oedipus, Virgil, and Don Quixote, Faust can see, but not enter the Promised Land. Still, Faust's personal tragedy contributes towards the draining of the social swamps and he becomes a kind of scapegoat for humanity.[65] In this way, Goethe's *Faust* transcends its Teutonic roots, linking itself into the great chain of mythopoesis.

NOTES

1. In his storm and stress period, Goethe spoke of "constant inner conflict and rebellion," of "sudden gusts of temper and ... self-will." He speaks of his "inner restlessness," leaving him "no repose anywhere." (Letters of December 23, 1774, October, 1777, December 9, 1777. These and subsequent quotations from Goethe's letters, diaries, memoirs etc. are taken from Ludwig Lewisohn's *Goethe. The Story of a Man* [2 vols.; New York, 1949].

    Cf. Barker Fairley, *A Study of Goethe* (London, 1947); K. R. Eissler, *Goethe: A Psychoanalytic Study*, 1775-1786 (2 vols.; Detroit, 1963).

2. Letters of November 28, 1771, August 11, 1781, March 5, 1830, February 13, 1775, April 10, 1776.

3. Letters, Diaries etc. of August 7, 1799, November 21, 1782, October, 7, 1777, May 12, 1782, March 3, 1784, March 10, 1781, March 12, 1828, January 16, 1818, December 31, 1808, December 23, 1797.

4. In *Faust*, the father is called a *dunkler Ehrenmann*. Taylor translates the words to mean "a sombre, brooding brain," but they also suggest a man of ambiguous honor.

5. Letters of May 3, 1802, August 20, 1781, September 9, 1784.

6. Reik believes that Goethe was largely abstinent until about the forties, and that he probably suffered from psychic impotence until his Italian journey when he was cured by a "nature-" girl, Faustina.

7. Goethe was attracted to mother figures, such as Charlotte von Stein, as well as to young girl figures, such as Christiane Vulpius and Ulrike von Levetzow. The mother was his secret, and one of the most secret scenes in *Faust* is the

hero's descent to *The Mothers*. In the poem, all the mother-figures are killed off: Gretchen's mother, Gretchen and Baucis; Helena vanishes, after she gives birth.

8. After Goethe fled from Charlotte, he asked her to let his mother share in all he wrote her. Later, Charlotte expressed the wish that Goethe were "a child" to her. In time, the relationship levelled off to a respectful friendship and Charlotte reverted to addressing Goethe as "dearest Councillor." See Letters of June 11, 1784, October 28, 1784, December 13, 1812, September 20, 1780, March 10, 1782, May 24, 1776, January 15, 1776, May 12, 1776, January 25, 1788.

9. The recurrent motif in Goethe's letters to Christiane is his request that she be a good housekeeper: "Keep the house nicely in order. . . . Be a good domestic treasure . . . prepare yourself to become a dear little cook. . . . I look forward with pleasure to our well-ordered house." See Letter of July 15, 1795. Following his break with Charlotte and his union with Christiane, Goethe was able to accept his mother—he now invited her to live with him.

10. See Appendix IV.

11. These words of an English folk-book by P. F. are quoted in E. M. Butler's *The Fortunes of Faust* (Cambridge, 1952). This work discusses the treatments of the Faust theme from the Spiess version to Thomas Mann's *Doctor Faustus*. It should be noted that in the Catholic tradition, black magicians, such as Cyprian, Theophilus, Pope Sylvester II are not damned, but receive grace.

12. Even the medieval devil is part of God's world and his power is controlled by the deity. St. Augustine admits the existence of *good* magic. Cf. *Civitas Dei,* XII, 4.

13. Faust meets with seven spirits each of whom claims to be the quickest spirit of Hell. Faust accepts only the claim of the seventh devil who is "no more and no less quick than is the transition from good and evil." Lessing suggests here the ambivalent nature of the devilish, a notion developed by Goethe and Thomas Mann.

14. Fritz Strich's *Goethe und die Weltliteratur* (Bern, 1946) points out that Goethe expressed his antipathy against the Hindu gods precisely in his *West-Östlicher Divan* which calls for a union of East and West. Goethe's strong sense for historic-genetic development made the metaphysical absolute of Eastern thought distasteful to him. See *Recollections of Riemer*, August 28, 1808; Letters, etc. of October 22, 1826, to Jacobi, 1801, 1786, to Eckermann, January 31, 1827.

15. See my essay "Goethe and the Philosophic Quest," *The Germanic Review* (New York), III, No. 3 (July, 1933).

16. Its wide range is expressed in the most varied poetic forms, from the folk-song, the doggerel, free rhythms and blanc verse to the Alexandrine, Greek metres and Dantesque triple rhymes.

17. Yet, outside of Germany, *Faust* has found less appreciation than any other literary classic. Thus far, it has proved itself intractable to translation into English. Except for Shelley (who confined himself to a few short scenes), none of the many versions has recaptured its lyric-philosophic rhythms.

18. There are numerous allusions to flying: Lines 1074, 1091, 6984, 7034 ff., 9897, 10041.

19. The translations are by Bayard Taylor, available in the Modern Library edition. I quote the original to give the English reader a sense of Goethe's lyrical rhythms.

20. The organic connection between the two scenes has generally been missed. In particular, "Prelude on the Stage" is regarded as irrelevant and is omitted from some translations. Even though Goethe worked on *Faust* in various stages of his life, its final version has structure and dramatic sequence, as I will try try to show in passing.

21. Goethe likened the Earth-Spirit to Jupiter. In *Faust, Erd-Geist* is both masculine and feminine (he defines himself in terms of earth and water metaphors— tides, wave, storm, sea). Faust is lacking in the harmonious interaction of these principles. He speaks later of his "Two souls," the one clinging with crude passion to the earthy, the other lifting itself from the dust "into the high ancestral spaces."

22. The celebration of "free death" (*Freitod*) is a recurrent motif in the Germanic tradition, beginning with the *Götterdämmerung* in the old Edda. Other examples are the ecstatic letters of Heinrich von Kleist written before his suicide and the "Liebestod" duet of Wagner's Tristan and Isolde. The most recent instance was the glee with which the Nazis greeted the news that Hitler, Goebbels and Goering cheated the Allies by their self-inflicted deaths.

23. Faust's attempted suicide sums up the social mood of Goethe's time. Where the French middle class prepared for social and political revolution, the weak German bourgeoisie indulged in philosophic-esthetic revolutions or in suicidal attitudes.

    A note on the psychological import of Faust's attempted suicide: The death wish may express frustrated love for an object with whom the suicide hopes to "unite" through his act. Prior to the suicide scene, Faust yearns for "the breasts of life," and in the scene expresses the hope that death may show him the way to the "high seas."

24. Following a suggestion by G. W. Groddeck (*The World of Man* [London, 1934]), Mephisto may be considered the anal-phallic principle in the drama: He is lord of the vermin and of fire; in Auerbach's Cellar, he calls the flame "friendly element," and in The Witches' Kitchen, he is master of the witches who "fart and stink" and who watch over the flaming cauldron. Mephisto's anal function is manifested in his connection with money and gold: It is he who brings the Emperor "money" that lies "buried in the earth," and Mammon glows on his Walpurgis-Night. (In Milton's *Paradise Lost*, Mammon builds a palace for Satan in which the cells are crossed by veins of fluid fire.) Mephisto appears as Avarice in the scene "Spacious Hall"; provides the gold-casket by which Faust is to gain Gretchen's favors; Mephisto's companions in the "Classical Walpurgis-Night" are griffins, ants, arimaspians which (according to Herodotus) are connected with gold.

216

25. In the court-scenes (Act I, Part II), the medieval chancellor rejects Mephisto as a nature-spirit. Here, Mephisto appears in the company of satyrs, silenes and the Great Pan. In "The Classical Walpurgis-Night," his primary contact is with nymphs, lamiae and phallic cobolds. Mephistopheles also claims kinship with the snake-family. In *Myths and Symbols in Indian Art and Civilization* (New York, 1946), Heinrich Zimmer states that the representation of serpent genii occurs "in association with a variety of other divine patrons of fertility, prosperity, and are earthly health."

26. Faust invokes Mephisto partly by recourse to Christian symbols. The devil's medieval-Nordic sources are made explicit by Homunculus (Act II, Part II):

    ". . . Thou, from the North,
    And of the age of mist brought forth,
    In knighthood's and witchcraft's murky den."

    Mephisto feels at home in the German Walpurgis-Night, but not in the Classical Walpurgis-Night.

27. Faust's desire to emulate the sun has erotic undertones. He would enter the sun's "portals of fulfillment" ("the sun" is feminine in German), which open up in wings (*"flügeloffen"*). Similarly, in the suicide scene, he hopes that the poison in the long-necked bottle will lead him out to the "high sea," enable him to "pierce" the ether, tear open the "gates." He will be able to show that "male" dignity (*Manneswürde*) does not tremble before that "dark cave" by forcing that passageway (*Durchgang*) around whose narrow mouth are the flames of all the fires of Hell. By the opening Part II, Faust is reconciled to the fact that he lacks the power to enter the "portals of fulfillment," and he renounces "the flood of flame" which issues from it.

28. This is also Mephisto's judgment! He tells Homunculus in Part II: "Unless thou errest, thou wilt ne'er have sense."

29. The irony is that Mephisto's function is *to serve* without the hope that he will succeed in his mission. He tells Faust that despite his eternal destructive work, there ever circulates new, fresh blood. In serving without asking or expecting any reward, the devil is akin to the artist and saint. At the close of the drama, Mephistopheles likens himself to Job:

    "How is't with me—Like Job, the boils have cleft me
    From head to foot, so that myself I shun;"

    Moreover, he cannot even appeal to God, as Job could:

    "But unto whom shall I appeal for justice?
    Who would secure to me my well-earned right?"

    In this light, Mephisto is the sacrifice to Faust's development.

30. These lines indicate that, contrary to general interpretation, "Forest and Cavern" does not show that Goethe achieved complete serenity during his Italian journey.

31. The *Paralipomena to Faust* makes clear that Mephisto is after more than Faust's flesh and blood ("Allein die Seel' ist unsre rechte Speise").

32. To the extent that Goethe's stress is on action and limitless development, his

conception of the soul has Western character. The Eastern notion is expressed in Tolstoy's *Anna Karenina* where Levin says that "living for one's soul" consists in spiritual equilibrium—a conception more attuned to the agrarian East.

33. The theme of the male climacteric is also present in the middle-aged figures of Dante, Don Quixote, Ibsen's Rubek and Thomas Mann's Gustav Aschenbach. Goethe himself sought repeated "cures" in Carlsbad and also by courting young girls.

34. In the dungeon scene, Goethe sounds folk-motifs of the step-mother: Gretchen sings a plaintive song of the mother who has put her to death and of the father who has eaten her. Gretchen's mother behaves in a stepmotherly way—leaves the chores of the household and the upbringing of her other daughter to Gretchen. In this context, Faust becomes "the father" who "eats" her in that the older man becomes the indirect cause for her pitiable end.

35. This Faustian rebel has her Mephisto in the wordly and cynical Marthe whom Mephisto calls fit "To ply the pimp and gypsy trade." She encourages and guides Gretchen towards fulfilment of her secret wishes for the casket and for Faust.

36. "Aufsätze zur Literatur," March or April 1827.

37. In this connection, it is relevant to note that Goethe wrote a book on the theory of *color*, not of light.

38. Neither Shakespeare in *The Tempest* nor Goethe in *Faust II* can summon up enough poetic enthusiasm to depict this social system with artistic effectiveness. As noted, while Goethe was attracted by the glamour of Weimar, he was depressed by its pettiness and historic anachronism. In the drama, as in Weimar, poetry (the Boy Charioteer) is entertainment, dependent on the state (Plutus), as Goethe was dependent on the good will of the duke.

39. The scene is charged with phallic-vaginal imagery: Mephisto gives Faust a "key" which he calls "That little thing." After he has taken hold of the key, it "grows" (*waechst*) in his hand. With it, Faust is to "mount" gradually to "happiness" ("Gelassen steigst du, dich erhebt das Glück"). The key leads Faust "Through realms of terror, wastes and waves," and brings him to "a blazing tripod" in whose glow and "immense mist" Faust will find The Mothers residing in "the utterly deepest bottom." However, he will not be able to open the realm of The Mothers with the key, but only "scent" the "true place." If his mission is to succeed, Faust must bring the tripod back. Theodor Reik calls attention to the sexual symbolism in the line (spoken by Mephisto): "Descend, then! I could also say: Ascend!" See also chapters 7 and 8 of Reik's *The Secret Self* (New York, 1952).

40. Goethe's conception of The Mothers well illustrates his manner of concretizing universal concepts. In *Goethe's Faust* (Tübingen, 1932), Heinrich Rickert effectively refutes the theory that The Mothers represent Platonic Ideas. The Mothers do not have the Reality of Plato's Ideas, but are shadowy, schematic forms. The Platonic way of deriving universals by the method of abstraction is opposed to Goethe's *gegenständliches Denken* which would present concepts

by concrete objectification. Thus, Goethe would replace Newton's mathematical theory of light by a theory of color (*das trübe Mittel*). And, when Schiller called Goethe's *Urpflanze* an "idea" he retorted that he can "see" his idea. Goethe's *Pandora* comes closest to expressing a Platonic universal. Yet, as Ernst Cassirer has shown, even this figure descends and particularizes itself. Goethe had nothing to say about the Absolute "in the theoretic sense." He argued for a philosophy which presented its concepts phenomenologically.

41. Faust's attempted short-cut to get Helena corresponds to the German effort to acquire a Renaissance through study of Hellenic art and culture. But Hellenism could not be acquired in feudal Weimar as it could not in the Emperor's court.

42. Even here, two people cooperate—Wagner and Mephisto. The latter is only an interested, if sensuous witness, but his female aspect becomes evident when he later appears as Helena's female attendant. Proteus calls Homunculus "a genuine virgin's-son."

43. No sooner is Homunculus born than he is eager to act. Goethe personifies in him the mechanistic and the romantic expressions of German theoretic activism. Both are formulae which can "live" only within a hermetically sealed system. Referring to himself, Homunculus says that "What's artificial, needs restricted space." Goethe's preference for the evolutionary process over revolutionary German *Schrecklichkeit* is shown in Homunculus' following the advice of Thales, the "Neptunist," who is contrasted with Anaxagoras, the "Volcanist."

44. Goethe called the Italian journey his "great leap. . . . If I perish, I perish! Without this experience, I was of no use any more." (Letters of December 13, 1786, January 20, 1787.) This journey takes on a "German" character in that Goethe confessed to Karl August that his longing for Italy assumed "the form of a sickness." (Letter of November 3, 1786.)

45. Goethe planned—but never wrote—a scene in which Faust propitiates Persephone to give up Helena. This would have been in the mythic tradition in which the hero wins the bridal bed by descending to the underworld.

46. Goethe invents the following plot: On her return from Troy, Helena has been sent ahead by her husband Menelaus to prepare a sacrifice. Mephisto-Phorkyas tells her that Menelaus intends *her* to be the sacrifice and suggests that Faust, a medieval knight in Pelepponesia, can save her. The entire episode is poetically flat. Not only does Faust win Helena by a ruse, but the marriage is contrived and gone through without the slightest manifestation of affection on either side. Its form is a "literal" ritual: Faust teaches the Greek woman to speak in German rhymes!

47. Euphorion is an allegorical figure (foreshadowed by the Boy Charioteer in Act I), representing Romantic poetry and action. Goethe had Byron in mind—his "unsatisfied temperament and his war-like tendency." Euphorion suggests two aspects of German nineteenth century Romanticism: its musical estheticism and its call for political freedom in the Wars of Liberation. Yet, whereas Byron

intended to fight for Greek independence, the younger German Romanticists supported the German princes against Napoleon and his democratic code.

48. Goethe attempted to bridge such Kantian *Kultur*-division between the beautiful and the useful, but could see only the possibility of a *symbolic* union, such as he projects here. While Gretchen was created out of Goethe's deepest personal experience, Helena is a culture-vision and esthetic compensation for Faust's loss of Gretchen.

49. Mephisto's paper-money scheme for solving the Emperor's economic problems brought false prosperity. A rival emperor, aided by papal power, challenges the legitimate ruler. The scene echoes the Wars of the Holy Alliance against Napoleon in which the German poets and thinkers also sought "liberation" by supporting the authoritative powers. Goethe's critical attitude towards such wars of liberation appears in his picture of the frivolous Emperor and of the Mephistophelian bullies who are used to win the battle. A more direct satire on the "Holy" Alliance is presented through the Archbishop who demands "Tithes, levies, tax,—the total income of the land,/Forever." He also demands the estate which Faust has not yet wrested from the ocean! Only if the Emperor will grant all this, can he be forgiven for having made a "covenant with Satan." The Archbishop's insistence on a "formal document" is similar to Mephisto's formal request that Faust sign his pact with a drop of his blood.

50. Mephisto's violent methods express his volcanic nature. His creation legend in Act V suggests an analogy between geologic, social and political revolution.

Goethe planned a scene ("Disputationsaktus"), presenting a debate between Faust, arguing for idealism, and Mephisto, upholding realism. Goethe may have decided to omit this scene, realizing that the drama as a whole consists of such debate.

51. Goethe told Eckermann: "Had I refrained from public business and lived in greater solitariness, I would have been happier and more productive," and wrote to Zelter (June 6, 1825): ". . . what everyone strives after are wealth and speed. Even educated people rival each other and try to surpass each other in order to establish railroads . . . and all kinds of facilities for communication."

52. Bayard Taylor translates the word *Schuld* as Guilt. However, *Schuld* also means Debt, and that it is used in this sense here becomes clear when this grey woman says that she has no place in a rich man's house.

53. Sorge makes her entry following Faust's destructive action against the old couple. She appears to him as darkness and mist and is Faust's dim recognition of his Mephistophelian involvements. The connection between Sorge and conscience is developed in H. Jaeger's penetrating essay "The Problem of Faust's Salvation" (*Goethe Bicentennial Studies* [Bloomington 1950]). Jaeger cites Goethe's paralipomena to the Midnight scene in which Sorge tells Faust: "Grad im Befehlen wird die Sorge gross." He argues further that Faust's love is one of the conditions for his salvation, referring to his love for Gretchen, and his "unselfish" and "self-surrendering" love for Helena. However, Faust's love for Gretchen is not great enough for him to consider marrying her or giving

any thought to their child. Nor does Faust surrender to Helena—she is placed at his disposal through Mephisto's trickery.

Jaeger also contends that Faust's guilt-feeling at the end is due to "self-deception, not . . . lust for unlimited power," and that Sorge makes him conscious of this and thereby *frees* him of his guilt. As to this point, we should note that, unlike other mythic heroes, *Faust never repents.* He curses Mephisto's "impatient" deed which results in the death of the old couple, and he gives their land to the robbers. But that is all. Following the scene with Sorge, Faust orders that Mephisto "Reward, allure, conscript, compel" to assure the success of his project. Faust's subsequent humanistic pronouncement is a *salto mortale.*

54. The idea is also suggested in the *Weltbund* of *Wilhelm Meister's Travels.* Goethe thought that America, which has no "useless memories," might realize this vision.

55. Goethe did affirm, what he called, "pure activity," by which he meant action which mediates between experience and an idea. On this point, see Georg Simmel's *Goethe* (Leipzig, 1923), pp. 136 ff.

56. The only indication in the drama of Faust's identification with the people appears in "Before the City Gate," where he says that among the common folk, he dare be a human being. In his letter from Goslar to Charlotte von Stein (December 4, 1777), Goethe writes of having "again fallen in love with that class of people which is called the lower class, but which may be the highest in God's sight. It seems to combine all virtues—a limitation of desire, contentment in frugality, straight thinking, loyalty, delight in merely tolerable possessions, harmlessness, long-suffering, steadfastness. . . ." To be sure, Goethe's emphasis here is on the ability of the lower classes to accept their limited life.

57. Lunacharsky's drama *Faust and the City* develops this theme. One of Goethe's *Maxims and Reflections* states: "All that which frees our spirit without giving us self-control, is ruinous." Elsewhere, the insight is summed up in the celebrated line: "In der Beschränkung zeigt sich erst der Meister." In Goethe's *Pandora*, written during the Napoleonic wars, Prometheus is no longer the absolute rebel of Goethe's storm and stress poem. He limits himself to the sphere of the attainable and has learned *to put out the fire.* On this, see Arnold Bergstraesser's *Goethe's Image of Man and Society* (Chicago, 1949), chapter 9.

58. The utopian nature of Faust's idea also appears in the fact that his projected commonwealth is agrarian, "a land like Paradise." Faust ignores the circumstance that the basis for his project is technics.

59. In the *Recollections of Henrich Luden* (December 13, 1813), wherein Goethe speaks of the German people as "wretched," and of his attempt "in every way to transcend them," he adds: "The only thing that can console me is the faith in Germany's future."

60. "Den können wir erlösen." The point is lost in Taylor's translation: "Is not beyond redeeming."

61. Marianus is the "father" who asks the mother that the son be allowed to ap-

proach her, pleading that Faust's breast, now purified from its earthly element, is filled with serious and tender emotions of holy love.

62. Goethe also regarded miraculous revelation a blasphemy against God, and wrote: "I cling more or less to the teachings of Lucretius and confine myself and all my hopes to this life." (Letters of January 11, 1808, August 9, 1782, February 2, 1789.) The historical Faust was a Protestant and one of Goethe's *Maxims and Reflections* calls for constant "protesting." He expressed strong aversion against the German Romanticists who became converts to Catholicism. Ecclesiastical history was to him "a union of error and brute force" and the doctrine of Christ's Divinity "had always tended to promote despotism" (Müller's Diary, October 20, 1823). After completing the scene of Faust's Assumption, Goethe turned to the fourth Act which ends with a sharp satire of the Archbishop.

63. Goethe's judgment of Dante was unusually harsh, calling the Inferno "loathsome," Purgatory "ambiguous," Paradise "boring." Dante's greatness, he said (1821) was "disagreeable," often "detestable."

64. The divine, Goethe told Eckermann, consists not in the motionless and finished, but in that which develops and is transmuted. Goethe's final category is no finished absolute, but what he calls *Steigerung*, connoting a process of intensification. He confessed to Kanzler von Müller that he would not know what to do with heavenly joy, if it did not offer him new problems. The play, according to the Manager in "Prelude on the Stage," is to move "From Heaven, across the World, to Hell!" and Goethe's notes indicate that the drama was to end with an epilogue.

65. Georg Lukacs sees here an analogy to the argument in Hegel's Phenomenology that the progress of the species is accomplished by the "List der Vernunft," which exacts the sacrifice of the individual.

The Quest for an American Myth
Moby Dick

AMERICA'S HISTORY has not provided the conditions which are necessary for the development of a rooted mythic tradition. Henry James
complained that America had no state, no personal loyalty, no museums
and no political society. And, in our own day, George Santayana found
America still raw and juvenile.

The lack of tradition is partly based on the circumstances that *Amer-
can history begins with an act of secession* from its "Old World" parent-
age. Where Hamlet and Faust are haunted by the ghosts of their past,
the American mythic hero is more concerned with the future.[1] Some
Europeans have envied us for this. America, Goethe sang, is better off
than the old continent—it has no decayed castles and no burdening
heritage. Similarly Heine:

> This is America!
> This is the new world! . . .
> This is no graveyard of Romance; . . .
> Of fossilized wigs and symbols
> Of stale and musty Tradition!

(Louis Untermeyer, *Heinrich Heine: Paradox and Poet*. Vol. II: *The Poems*
[New York, 1937], p. 338)

To be sure, we did find the Indians; but they became a curious movie
vestige. The Negro brought with him a native tradition, but we have
used his "service" more than his "spirituals." And, while the Negro is
being emancipated, he is also being "freed" from his mythic heritage.

Yet, despite our relatively short history, we still cling to an indigenous lore. We have our legends of the Indians, of pioneers and gold-
seekers, our Kit Carsons, Paul Bunyans and Mike Finns. And, due to
the accelerated changes in American life under the pressure of rapid

technological development, the era of the Indian, of the adventurous pioneer, and the daring Western Robin Hood seems to belong to an ancient past.

The myth imbedded in these pictures of earliest American life is that of a land offering a surfeit of opportunities, "a golden land," as it has been known to countless immigrants. The myth of America is that of a new, open, expanding world where "the sky is the limit," and *anybody* can go from rags to riches.[2] This success story is supplemented by the idea (portrayed in the earlier Chaplin pictures) that here the little man can maneuver amidst the big and powerful, and even outwit them. In place of fixed ancestral norms, we have the open future of limitless possibilities. The traditional myth of Creation becomes the Quest for the newest and latest.[3] This characteristic American temper is embodied in two of our major intellectual movements: transcendentalism and pragmatic operationalism.

Our legendary figures are "outdoor" heroes, wandering like Paul Bunyan and Davy Crockett through woods and forests, like Mike Finn and Huck Finn down the rivers, with Captain Ahab and Wolf Larsen in the Pacific, with Walt Whitman throughout our continent. They are American in their direct, empirical approach and in the practical nature of their pursuits — gold, whales or seals. These symbolic journeys draw on the feverish migrations in our earlier history. The task faced by our pioneers was not to re-create a Golden Age, not to redeem an old heritage, but to create a new community by gaining control of forest, land and river.

The ebb and flow of migratory living did not allow the hardening of a traditional core or the formation of a steady mythic reference. Instead, they encouraged unlimited play of "free enterprise," of an independence and adventurism, unchecked by feudal memories.

But there were those who saw a threat in this unrestricted freedom, individualism and futurism. And, indeed, they contained the basis for a Nietzschean "I will, therefore I am," leading to the ethics of the sea- and land-wolves. For the Puritans and for Jonathan Edwards, the myth of expansionism appears ambiguous, if not evil. By the time of Theodore Dreiser, William Faulkner and Robinson Jeffers, it has lost most of its legitimacy. The success story of Dreiser's "Titan" becomes suspect and the efforts of the little man to hit it rich provide the foundation for an "American Tragedy." The magic short cut to the happy ending receives more acid treatment in Faulkner and Jeffers. Among our contemporary writers, the myth of expectancy appears frozen (O'Neill's *The Iceman Cometh*), cornered (Tennessee Williams' *Streetcar Named*

Desire), dead (Arthur Miller's *Death of a Salesman*), and self-destructive (Clifford Odets' *The Big Knife*).

However, the celebration of rugged, self-reliant individualism was tempered by the enormous task of exploring a new world. The pioneer had to lean on the "good neighbor policy." Moreover, America is the expression of a *common* effort. Many races, religions and customs found themselves on one boat. The individualism of the American hero is modified by his fraternal affiliations—with the good neighbor, buddy and friend. Fraternity and Freedom are the American replacements for European Paternity and Order.

But what constitutes the core of this fraternity? Who is the "American?" Is it Melville's New Englander who yearns for the South Seas? Is it Mark Twain's Southerner with his chivalry and slave-plantations or his Huck and Jim who strike out for freedom? Is it the Western rancher? Is it the Indian, Negro and foreigner? Is it Dreiser's Quaker, Willa Cather's Bishop, Mike Gold's Jew? Is America the "melting pot" of its multiple elements?

Herman Melville stands at the watershed moment of a historic cycle. In his time, American was still tied to its European parent. But it is also the hour of Emerson's American Scholar and of America's growing economic independence and dynamism. And Melville is among those who question the ethic of expansionism. His *Moby Dick* at once continues the American Myth of unlimited possibilities and expresses disenchantment with it. Herein, Melville meets with Goethe whose Faust likewise at once affirms and questions the myth of modern expansionism.

The need for a native myth begins to be voiced as America develops towards economic and cultural autonomy. Emerson's Journal speaks of our need for "a theory of interpretation or Mythology." Alcott, Margaret Fuller and the Brook Farm Utopians sought to live it. In our own time, Thomas Wolfe called it the quest for a father. Wolfe became a "Far Wanderer" seeking the equivalent of a home and paternity. Faulkner and Hemingway labored to find replacement values, as did writers such as John Steinbeck, Benjamin Appel, and Alfred Kreymborg. The earliest and possibly the most passionate expression of the American quest for its common sources and resources is Melville's *Moby Dick*.[4] In American literature, Ahab stands closest to the classic, mythic prototypes of Job, Prometheus, Hamlet, and Faust. Melville is the first outstanding American writer to express the need for an American myth of creation.

In the past, *Moby Dick* has not been viewed as characteristically

American. Its labored symbolism and metaphysics seemed nearer to the European than to the American manner. Recent years have brought an unprecedented Melville interest. His vogue coincides with that of Franz Kafka and the existentialists. Both Melville and Kafka present the antagonist as a baffling "secret"—the feeling many have today that we are confronted by an ineffable, elusive opponent. Both are modern in making science an instrument in the quest. Still their heroes are almost at the complete mercy of ubiquitous and apparently indestructible forces.

The Borrowed Myth

In Melville's earlier conception, *Moby Dick* was to be simply an adventure story of a whaling expedition, and it can still be enjoyed as such. But the final version is clearly more than that. Melville interlaces the narrative with mythic, moral, social, metaphysical and allegorical allusions.

However, many of these are borrowed. The language of *Moby Dick* is an amorphous mixture of Biblical, Elizabethan and tough American speech; its form has elements of the epic, dramatic and lyric. These ingredients remain uncoordinated, as uncoordinated as is the Pequod crew and the congregation in Father Mapple's chapel. Melville attempts to give Ahab's quest an Oriental, Greek and Biblical geneology. The glory of whaling is shown to have a rich mythic ancestry in Perseus, St. George, Hercules, Jonah, and Vishnoo.

The Biblical analogies predominate: Elijah, the warning prophet, Jonah in Father Mapple's sermon, Captain Bildad whose "utilitarian character" suggests the Bildad from the Book of Job. Ishmael recalls the son of Abraham and Agar who was driven from home by Sarah's jealousy, became an "orphan," a wanderer and rover. It is he who, at the close of the novel, quotes the words from Job: "I only am escaped alone to tell thee."[5] Ahab bears the name of the Hebrew king who, misled by false prophets, worshipped Baal, thereby provoking the Lord more than any other of the Israelite kings. When tested by Elijah and challenged to invoke a fire under Baal's altar, King Ahab failed. He was then thrown to the dogs who licked his blood.

Moby Dick is the myth of what the novel calls an "unfathered birth."[6] The novel begins and ends with Ishmael, "another orphan." Miraculously saved from the grave of the sea, he may have learned "the secret of our paternity."[7]

The Savage Elements

"Long exile from Christendom and civilization," we read in *Moby Dick*, "inevitably restores a man to that condition in which God placed him, i.e. what is called savagery. Your true whale-hunter is as much a savage as an Iroquois. I myself am a savage."

Melville's most persuasive references are to primitive and elemental powers. Having but an indirect kinship with the old legends, the American mythmaker invokes the earliest and most common memory of all, that of man and the universe in their primordial state.

On this level, the world seems to be governed by magical forces. The novel begins with animistic fantasies suggested by the Spouter Inn and by Elijah's warning. They are consistently associated with the Pequod and the White Squid. There is a magic about Ahab's personality, his strange power over the crew, and about the White Whale. Melville draws analogies between the chase of Moby Dick and the Western legends of the Jet-Black Stallion, the White Deer and the Big Bear of Arkansas.

The characters in *Moby Dick* are in a societal stage roughly approximating what Morgan called "savagery." Here, man is almost completely dependent on the elements which assume anthropomorphic character and divine power. Water and sea, fire, storm and lightning, air, wind and mist are leading "characters" in Melville's drama, are addressed, challenged or propitiated. As in the primitive myth and in Wagner's Siegfried cycle, the elements are sexualized and appear as parental and familial powers. The sun is spoken of as a king, the sea as a man, the air as bride, the fire as father.

Water and fire, or their interaction in storm, are in the foreground. The sea is the all-encompassing terrain of the story. For the crew on the Pequod, it is the "earth" on which they live and to which they return. It appears as an "underground-" reservoir, unplumbed, unknown, and unlimited, suggestive of an archetypal unconscious. Here, we are told, "millions of mixed shades and shadows, drowned dreams, somnambulisms, reveries; all that we call lives and souls, lie dreaming, dreaming still; tossing like slumberers in their beds."

Water (along with the other elements) has an ambivalent character of birth or rebirth (nourishment) and of death (drowning). For Starbuck, the sea induces a soothing, contemplative mood. Even Ahab is not immune to this peaceful aspect of the Pacific. In "The Symphony," he yields for a moment to the spell of the gentle day and drops a tear into the sea. But the stormy sea is also demonic, swallowing and devouring its victim.[8]

Addressing the fire, Ahab declares: "Thy right worship is defiance." Fire is most ominous when, combined with air and water, it produces thunder and lightning. Ahab's meeting with the White Whale is foreshadowed by a storm in which the waters are churned and the air is rented by fiery darts.

AHAB: THE MAIMED SATANIC HERO

Ahab was condemned by his own mother. In naming him "Ahab," she assigned him the fate of the king who was killed and whose blood was licked by dogs. Before his voyage on the Pequod, Ahab loses a leg to the White Whale.[9] We are also told of an event which suggests a kind of self-castration: Ahab was found unconscious in the street "by some unknown, and seemingly inexplicable, unimaginable casualty, his ivory limb having been so violently displaced that it had stake-wise smitten, and all but pierced his groin." Ahab stands before his crew "with a crucifixion in his face; in all the nameless regal overbearing dignity of some mighty woe." The Christ analogy is also suggested by Ahab's subsequent withdrawal, as a man apart, and his later return. However, he returns, in Satanic hatred, not in Christian love.

In forging the harpoon for the "white fiend," Ahab enacts the ritual of the bond with the devil. The ceremony is performed in a state of near-delirium, Ahab drawing "the baptismal blood" from the three pagan harpooners, howling "Ego no baptizo te in nomine patris, sed in nomine diaboli." Ahab's ritual is a pact with the Evil one, and an expression of his death wish.[10]

Ahab is the Satanic hero growing out of the Protestant tradition, and belongs to the lineage of Iago, Hagen and the Norse Loki. He spurns mediators and guides, would be his own Virgil, Beatrice and St. Bernard. In his "fixed and fearless, forward dedication," Ahab's revolt takes on a diabolic character which would destroy everything, including himself. Ahab is Satan, as *the maimed hero.*

Ahab's Satanism follows the old form: the attempt to be more than a man. And the price is the same: Thou must not love. And not to love means to be consumed by restlessness, doomed to ceaseless wandering. Goethe's Protestant Faust can be redeemed in that, at the end, he desires to be a man among men, and enjoys the futuristic vision of a free people on free soil. Ahab is closer to the guilty wanderers, to Cain, to the Flying Dutchman and the Wandering Jew. Like Cain, his crime is against fellow crew brethren; like the Wandering Jew, he repudiates the God in man.

Ahab is the focus for most of Melville's mythic parallels. He is Job who demands to know why he has been mutilated, calling on his adversary to appear and confront him; but he is a Job who does not submit to the Lord. He is Prometheus who challenges his enemy, but without Prometheus' tool and love for mankind. He is Oedipus attempting to bring his sources to light; but he is one who does not attain the redemption of Oedipus in Colonus. He is Don Quixote in his rigid consistency, without the Don's lovable humanity. He is the Flying Dutchman, determined to chase his object "round the world." He calls himself "Shem," referring to the son who uncovered his father's nakedness. Finally, in the end, he is Homunculus who descends into the waters to acquire a body.

The Pequod is a kind of Noah's Ark, harboring elements from the savage and civilized world. Its hero would catch the great Fish Leviathan, but unlike the Messiah, his intent is not to divide it among the faithful. He is not a preserver, but a destroyer of his group. The devil's price is exacted to its fullest on the social level as well. It appears in Ahab's relation to the crew.[11] Ahab is the ruler over his social universe. All must submit to his will and do his bidding to the point of jeopardizing their collective existence. But what is the legitimacy of Ahab's rule? What is the cause in which they are sacrificed?

In the classical myth, the "cause" has a public, all-human reference —to bring peace to Thebes and Athens, to build the city of Rome, to revive the Golden Age of Chivalry, to rid the state of Denmark of its rottenness, to build a Faustian free city. To be sure, in all instances, a personal need is interwoven with the public task; but in the end, the individual need is a function of the public good.

The exclusive stake in the chase of *Moby Dick* is the righting of a *personal wrong* suffered by Ahab. It is Ahab's leg which the White Whale bit off. It is his and only his person which was violated. To the crew, whaling is a practical business, a form of employment. They have no special interest in Moby Dick. Yet, Ahab succeeds in persuading the crew that his objective is identical with their own. They are somehow hypnotized by their leader's demon and they act as if they were all a collective Ahab. The transformation is achieved by something akin to black magic.

Ahab succeeds in imposing his "sultanism" because at this stage of American development, there is as yet no cohesive social grouping. The crew belongs in the category of "Loose-Fish," which Melville defines as "fair game for anybody who can soonest catch it."[12] It is unable to act jointly in its common interests. They are the raw, eclectic form of the American lower depths towards the middle of the nineteenth century. Artistically, Melville shows this by making them all (with the exception of Queequeg) more or less stereotypes. Hence, Ahab can silence their rebellious murmurings, can melt their will down to the point where it serves his purpose.

Ahab's relation to the crew is the hero pitted *against* his community. He curses the "mortal inter-debtedness" of man and frets that he, who would be "a sovereign being in nature," must depend on the carpenter for a bone to stand on. In Schopenhauer, the wilful ego merges with the nothingness of Nirvana, what Freud later called the deathwish. In both, the individual is at the end "socialized" in a cosmic unity. Modern existentialism—which claims Melville as one of its forerunners—contains a variant of this dialectic. Its individual would also be "as free as air." It begins with "nothing," and by a series of "leaps," reaches death or shipwreck. Similarly Ahab. His commanding voice ends in helpless voicelessness and his dictatorial ego is communalized in the womb of the sea.[13]

Transposed into American social history, Ahab foreshadows the way of the Robber Barons.[14] If Ahab stands for an unbridled individualism, the crew stands for a loose, unorganized fraternity. In the novel, the will of the one and the willessness of the other produce their common catastrophe.

The Psychic Burden

Moby Dick also contains Melville's secret psychological burden. The author repeatedly states that the White Whale is a secret which remains hidden to him. Hamlet freely admits that he has "bad dreams," condemns and depreciates himself for his hesitancy in avenging his father's murder. Ahab has "nightmares" but they do not paralyze his will for revenge. Although his eye is "troubled," he remains arrogant and defiant.

Now, the novel suggests that it was Ahab's own "thoughts" which produced the vulture that "feeds upon the heart forever" ("The Chart"). Following this clue, it would appear that Ahab *invites* punishment to relieve deep-seated guilt-feelings.

The novel tells us almost nothing about Ahab's past, as though that too must remain a secret. But, early in the story, we learn that Ahab married when he was past fifty, and that he has a son. Towards the end of the novel, Ahab tells Starbuck in a confessional moment, that the very day after his marriage, he sailed for Cape Horn, "leaving but one dent in my marriage pillow." A "mild, mild wind, and a mild looking sky" wring the admission from Ahab that he half suspects why he has exposed himself to "forty years of privation and peril, and storm-time! forty years on the pitiless sea!" There follows his reference to "that young girl-wife" whom he wedded late in life and left the succeeding day. "Aye, I widowed that poor girl when I married her," he tells Starbuck. The next sentences return to the theme of his frenzied life:

> And then, the madness, the frenzy, the boiling blood and the smoking brow, with which, for a thousand lowerings old Ahab has furiously, foamingly chased his prey—more a demon than a man!—aye, aye! what a forty years' fool—fool—old fool, has old Ahab been! Why this strife of the chase? why weary, and palsy the arm at the oar, and the iron, and the lance? how the richer or better is Ahab now?

This passage indicates an association in Ahab's mind between his having left "but one dent" in his marriage pillow and the "frenzy" with which he chased his prey—"furiously, foamingly . . . more a demon than a man."

Is there a connection between the "troubled" look in Ahab's eye and his marriage late in life to a "young girl-wife"? Was Ahab's mutilation by the White Whale but an intensification of an already existing feeling of personal inadequacy? Is Ahab's pursuit of whales an attempt to prove himself? To prove himself *master at sea* to cover up his not being *master on land*? Would his conquest of Moby Dick give him the illusion that he can be a man, just as his ivory leg makes him feel that he possesses a sound limb?

Homoeroticism and Isolation

Attention has been called to Melville's fixation on his mother. The theme of incest which breaks out openly in *Pierre*, remains underground in *Moby Dick*. However, the homoerotic motif which is connected with it, is pervasive in the novel.

A striking feature of the book is the almost complete absence of reference to sex, even though the crew is composed of rough primitive men who spend months at sea. The men allow themselves but dreamy erotic snatches when, in "Midnight, Forecastle," they dance and sing together. And only when the Pequod, bound for the waters of the White Whale crosses the Bachelor returning home with its jubilant crew dancing with their Polynesian brides, do we have mention of sex-joy. The "love-" element in *Moby Dick* is confined to the world of men.

A revealing passage in the chapter "A Squeeze of the Hand" describes the way in which the lumps of the sperm are converted into fluid. The process entails "squeezing":

It was our business to squeeze these lumps back into fluid. A sweet and unc-
tuous duty! No wonder that in old times sperm was such a favourite cosmetic.
Such a clearer! such a sweetener; such a softener; such a delicious mollifier!
After having my hands in it for only a few minutes, my fingers felt like eels,
and began, as it were, to serpentine and spiralize.

As Ishmael continues to squeeze, he is filled with a strange sort of
good will, almost a kind of "insanity," an "affectionate, friendly, loving
feeling," especially when he finds himself

unwittingly squeezing my co-laborers' hands in it, mistaking their hands for
the gentle globules. Such an abounding, affectionate, friendly, loving feeling
did this avocation beget; that at last I was continually squeezing their hands,
and looking up into their eyes sentimentally; as much as to say. . . . Come;
let us squeeze hands all round; nay, let us squeeze ourselves into each other;
let us squeeze ourselves universally into the very milk and sperm of kindness. . . . In thoughts of the visions of the night, I saw long rows of angels in
paradise, each with his hands in a jar of spermaceti.[15]

A more overt homoerotic note is manifested in the relationship between Ishmael and Queequeg. On the morning of the night in which
they sleep together at the Spouter Inn, Ishmael finds Queequeg's arm
thrown over him in a most loving manner—"you had almost thought I
had been his wife." And, by the savage's side slept the tomohawk, "as
if it were a hatchet-faced baby."[16]

Ahab, who was socially "inaccessible," and whose concern is only
with himself, embodies the most extreme form of the Narcissus-motif
which is sounded at the beginning of the novel. The crew, too, are what
Melville calls "Isolatoes." As Ishmael enters the chapel he finds

a small scattered congregation of sailors and sailors' wives and widows. . . .
Each silent worshipper seemed purposely sitting apart from the other, as if
each silent grief were insular and incommunicable . . . silent islands of men
and women . . . each *Isolato* living on a separate continent of his own.

There is isolation in Ahab's lonely monologues, in Pip's mad self-
absorption and, at the close, in the isolated rescue of Ishmael.

THE WHITE WHALE: THE PARENTAL
SEX-MYSTERY

It was suggested that Ahab's pursuit of whales is a mask for covering
and relieving his private burden. Yet, Ahab is also a representative
figure, and we must ask ourselves not only what Moby Dick means to
Ahab, the "old" man, but also to Ahab, as an American mythic hero.

The White Whale is an individualized animal, who has earned his name "Moby Dick." At the same time, the story endows this whale with magical powers, and even with a degree of sanctity. Here, Melville's Moby Dick assumes some of the characteristics which are associated with the Rhine Gold, the Golden Fleece and the Holy Grail.[17]

Moby Dick is called a "god," indestructible, eternally elusive and "unknowable." His brow reveals no distinct features, no face, nothing but a forehead, "pleated with riddles." Watching him in his elements, he seemed heavenly: "Not Jove, not that great majesty Supreme! did surpass the glorified White Whale as he so divinely swam."

Melville-criticism has popularized the notion that to Ahab the White Whale is the personification of Evil. This view is supported only by what Ahab says about Moby Dick. The problem becomes more complex when we analyze Ahab's *attitude* and *behavior* towards the Whale.

Ahab fears Moby Dick. But he is also hypnotized by him. He is both repelled by the White Whale and drawn to him. The reader is expressly told that Moby Dick is a "magnet" to Ahab. It is Ahab, not Moby Dick, who is the pursuer. On the third day of the chase, Moby Dick is seen swimming away from the ship, pursuing his own straight path in the sea. At this point, Starbuck pleads with the Captain: "Oh! Ahab, not too late is it, even now, the third day, to desist. See! Moby Dick seeks thee not. It is thou, thou, that madly seekest him!"

Moby Dick is a "secret" to Melville and to Ahab precisely in that he is *not* an unambigous incarnation of evil. Describing the Whale as he is about to plunge into the deep, Melville remarks that if one is in the Dantean mood, "the devils will occur to you; if in that of Isaiah, the archangels." Even on the third day of the chase, in the very midst of the Whale's ferocious attacks, we read that Moby Dick then seemed possessed "by all the angels that fell from heaven."

The awe with which Melville surrounds Moby Dick is connected with the hero's attempt to plumb the origins of his being. *Moby Dick* is replete with parental references and with allusions to the sex-act. One of the more revealing chapters is "The Gilder."

Towards the close of this chapter, Melville-Ahab asks despairingly:

> Where is the foundling's father hidden? Our souls are like those orphans whose unwedded mothers die in bearing them: the secret of our paternity lies in their grave, and we must there to learn it.

This passage is preceded by references to the sea as a field of "long-drawn virgin vales." The ship is compared to horses who show only their "erected ears, while their hidden bodies widely wade through the amazing verdure." "The Symphony" speaks of the sun as "a royal czar and king . . . giving this gentle air to this bold and rolling sea; even as bride to groom," and of "the loving alarms, with which the poor bride gave the bosom away."

Sex-allusions are particularly crowded in the descriptions of the White Whale. They point to Moby Dick as a male-female, father-mother figure.

Male-Female Dialectic

The chapter on "The Tail" is crowded with phallic and coitus-imagery. It is a hymn to the vast power of the tail:

> The broad palms of his tail are flirted high into the air! then smiting the surface, the thunderous concussion resounds for miles. You would think a great gun had been discharged; and if you noticed the light wreath of vapor from the spiracle at his other extremity, you would think that that was the smoke from the touch-hole.

When he is about

> to plunge into the deeps, his entire flukes . . . are tossed erect in the air, and so remain vibrating a moment, till they downward shoot out of view. Excepting the sublime *breach*—somewhere else to be described—this peaking of the whale's flukes is perhaps the grandest sight to be seen in all animated nature.

The gigantic organ seems to emerge

> out of bottomless profundities. . . . spasmodically snatching at the highest heaven. So in dreams have I seen majestic Satan thrusting forth his tormented colossal claw from the flame Baltic of Hell.[18]

As Moby Dick appears,

> his whole marbleized body formed a high arch, like Virginia's Natural Bridge, and warningly waving his bannered flukes in the air, he reveals himself as the grand god.[19]

Moby Dick is not only a god-king-father figure. The male is joined to the female. We get an allusion to Aphrodite, as the White Whale emerges from the waters, like "some plumed and glittering god uprising from the sea." And, we have more direct indication of Moby Dick's bisexuality in the metaphors Melville uses to describe the whale. The head is said to be both a "battering ram" and "a dead blind wall," enveloped by a boneless toughness. It has "the rare virtue of thick walls," and "the rare virtue of interior spaciousness." The tail possesses terrifying power; yet, the immense flukes sweep "with a certain slow softness" the surface of "the masculine sea," and the tail moves with "maidenly gentleness" and "delicacy." On the first day of the chase, Moby Dick appears with a tall shattered pole projecting from his back. The sight recalls to Melville the myth of Jupiter carrying Europa:

> . . . the white bull Jupiter swimming away with ravished Europa clinging to his graceful horns; his lovely leering eyes sideways intent upon the maid; with smooth bewitching fleetness, rippling straight for the nuptial bower in Crete.

The White Whale is the disguised form of the hermaphroditical mystery.[20] Ahab invades the "man-like sea," challenging it to give up its primal secret. His attitude is a mixture of defiance and fear, of hatred and love. In "The Candles," Ahab addresses the lightning as "my fiery father." Even as he owns that the father is "omnipotent," and "an incommunicable riddle," he would dispute his "speechless place-less power" and "unconditional, unintegral mastery." Yet, amidst this Promethean harangue, Ahab confesses that his deeper desire is to "worship," to "burn" and to be "welded" with him. A suppliant note steals into Ahab's defiance, a womanly submissive tone, as he speaks of "the queenly personality" in himself which demands "her royal rights." He would rather not make war, and he pleads: "Come in thy lowest form of love, and I will kneel and kiss thee."

A still deeper secret envelops the "foundling sire:" the Mother. Ahab cries out: "My sweet mother, I know not. Oh, cruel! what hast thou done with her? There lies my puzzle." Wagner's Siegfried also wonders what his mother was like. Siegfried, in his fearless "innocence," finds a surrogate mother in Brunhilde. Ahab, in his unacknowledged guilt finds one in final "attachment" to Moby Dick.[21]

Did Melville become somewhat aware of this? In a letter to Hawthorne, he stated that he had written a "wicked book," and now felt "spotless as the lamb." Moby Dick is followed by Pierre in which the parents' attitude stands in the way of Pierre's becoming a mature man.[22] And Billy Budd readily accepts the death-judgment of Captain Vere, his father-figure. Billy Budd is primarily "body" as Ahab is primarily "spirit." Billy has the innocent physical power, Ahab the guilty fiery passion with which they dominate and kill. Both revert to speechless infancy. Ahab returns to it with desperate defiance, Billy in serene passivity.

From the psychoanalytic perspective, Moby Dick and Pierre present the interlocking pattern of the oedipal and incest drives. In Moby Dick the oedipal predominates (modified by Ahab first "getting" his woman, abandoning her and his son later). And here, the oedipal is linked to the homosexual—Ahab's attitude towards the father-element in the White Whale is also a wooing. Ahab would cover up this impermissible desire and projects it on to the Whale, insisting that it is Moby Dick who pursues him—a paranoid manuever, characteristic in latent homosexuality. In *Pierre*, incest (distributed between mother and sister) and matricide predominate. And again, these impulses are used to mask the homosexual drive. But the artistic thinness of *Pierre* is an esthetic confession that this defense has failed.

However, we need to bear in mind that Melville's works are *novels*, not psychological tracts, and that his sexual symbolism is an aspect of his aesthetic symbolism. His art gives us the *resistance* against the primitive urges. In all-over terms, his work contains various levels of attempted integration of the ego with the id.

The Quest for Creation

The passages cited indicate that the White Whale stands for the feared and desired object harboring the secret of the sexes and of parental creation. It is a fearful thing, Melville tells us, "to have one's hands among the unspeakable foundations, ribs, and very pelvis of the world." Ahab's journey represents a maximum effort to face and solve the riddle. But this hero is maimed, and his very efforts expose his impotence: His leg had been torn off; on the first day of the chase, the whale's jaw comes within inches of his head, and Ahab falls flat-faced on the water; on the second day, his ivory stump is snapped; on the third day, he is strangled. Crippled Ahab lacks the power to penetrate Moby Dick's "thick walls." The hunter feels "impotent" before this prey: "The severest pointed harpoon, the sharpest lance darted by the strongest human arm, impotently rebounds from it." The wall remains "impregnable," and Ahab never reaches its most "buoyant thing within." Melville draws an analogy between the fate awaiting him who would conquer Moby Dick and that which befell "the weakling youth" who desired to lift "the dread goddess' veil at Sais."

Despite these terrors, Ahab does hurl his spear at the White Whale. As Ahab sees Moby Dick successfully breaching the thick walls of the Pequod, he makes his final supreme effort "to give up the spear." The gesture is performed in an orgiastic frenzy and exaltation, Ahab feeling "like a billow that's all one crested comb." At the end he is "united" at last to the whale by his line. The umbilical cord is retied, and Ahab sinks like an infant, "voicelessly" into the ocean by the side of the mystery he has been unable to fathom.

The novel calls the whale "king of creation" and "the incarnation of Vishnu." What Brahma, Moira and God were to earlier mythmakers, that Moby Dick is to Ahab. Ahab's voyage is the American journey to bring its birth to light.[23]

Whiteness: Demonic Ambiguity

Melville attaches special importance to his chapter on "The Whiteness of the Whale," remarking that he must try to explain what it was to Ishmael, "else all these chapters might be naught."

Traditionally, he notes, the color white represented the white man's "mastership over every dusky tribe." In *Typee* and *Oomoo*, Melville had questioned the idea of white superiority. *Moby Dick* goes beyond the social towards the legendary and mythic.

The apparent intent is to explain why the whiteness of the whale "appalled" Ishmael, filling him with a "vague, nameless horror." Melville cites examples of white objects which instill terror: The white bear and white shark, the albatross, the white steed of the prairies in the Indian tradition, the whiteness of ghosts, and of the shroud.

Yet, Melville begins the chapter by enumerating examples which have benign, even reverent associations. Whiteness stands for virginal bridal purity and the benignity of old age. He speaks of white as the sign of divine spotlessness and power, as "the very veil of the Christian deity."

What emerges from the dual set of illustrations is not the malign character of whiteness but its *ambiguity*. Like Melville's "Whiteness," Moby Dick is a mixture of good and evil, the angelic and the satanic, which may appear to human understanding as indifference.[24] All this makes life seem like a High Comedy and death as "only sly, goodnatured hits . . . bestowed by the unseen and unaccountable old joker."[25]

The Reflexive Metaphor

Ahab is the leader without or against the group. The crew is a community lacking in social cohesion. The two extremes meet in a reflexive arc.

The reflexive is the leading metaphor of the story. The geometric sign is the circle:

> There is no steady unretracing progress in this life; we do not advance through fixed gradations. . . . But once gone through, we trace the round again.

Whales are marvels. Yet, like all marvels, they are

> mere repetitions of the ages; so that for the millionth time we say amen with Solomon—Verily there is nothing new under the sun.

Melville pays tribute to the idea of metempsychosis:

> Oh! Pythagoras . . . I sailed with thee along the Peruvian coast last voyage —and foolish as I am, taught thee, a green simple boy, how to slice a rope.

Ahab's journey is called a "round the world voyage," which takes one back "to the very point whence we started." Ahab sees himself as "the image of the rounder globe, which like a magician's glass, to each and every man in turn but mirrors his own mysterious self." Here, Ahab has a fleeting recognition that his journey is a circular narcissistic quest.[26] Childlike, he challenges the elements, dashes the quadrant to the deck, sails against the wind. Childlike, he sinks into the deep.

The elemental nature of Melville's writing makes itself felt in those passages in which his imagination draws on his personal experiences at sea. Here, his prose swells and undulates in lyrical wave-rhythms. But the art of the book is uneven. Passages vibrating with genuine passion are broken up by vague, mystico-religious dissertations and expressionistic monologues. *Moby Dick* is primarily the story of the self obsessed with itself. The book is largely a drawn out soliloquy. This gives Melville's prose an "ejaculatory" character to use Matthiessen's term.[27] Only in the last chapters, does the novel approach a high level of drama.

Epilogue

Ishmael is the only member of the crew who completes the journey and returns home. Ishmael is Ahab's Horatio, left to "tell" his story. He represents the principle of maximum consciousness and interdependence in the novel, bridging the religious and cultural distance between himself and the rest. As the spectator of the drama, he has "full sight of the ensuing scene." As the narrator, he is the esthetic mediator among the various perspectives in the book. The Journey is his ritual of initiation from which he learns—what Ahab does not—the price exacted for dictatorial wilfulness, as well as for automatic obedience.

Yet, Ishmael does not earn heroic stature. As a character in the novel, he is colorless, almost anonymous. Ishmael is the only one who has no relationship to Ahab, nor does he communicate his thoughts and feelings to anyone on the ship. Ishmael has been likened to the Greek Chorus. But, unlike the Greek Chorus, he does not take part in or suffer from the action (except at the end). His knowledge of the whole issues in a kind of cosmic sympathy approaching an ironic indifference, an indifference akin to that of the Carpenter. Ishmael does not show Starbuck's human receptiveness to Ahab's agony; he does not possess the quality of spontaneous sharing and self-sacrifice of Queequeg.[28]

Ishmael is saved, not by his works, but by miracle and grace: the miracle of Queequeg's "coffin" floating by his side and the gracious action of the Rachel's captain. Ahab, obsessed by his private grievance, had refused to help the Captain find his son. The Captain reverses Ahab's temper, "adopting" the Pequod's orphan as a replacement for his own son. Following the three-day chase and his descent into the watery pit, Ishmael is saved.[29]

Through the character of Ahab, Melville gives us both the threat and the promise in the American quest. Ahab is more intent on conquest than on comradeship. In *Moby Dick* the Quest is restricted to its egocentric or demonic quality and is not transmuted into a communal blessing. Ahab's *hybris* is closer to religious sin than to mythic error or crime. He lacks the communal bond which rehabilitates the hero in mythopoesis. While Ahab's ruthless egotism is not for material gain and ownership, his "irresistible dictatorship" foreshadows the individual enterprise which Jack London pictures in *The Sea Wolf*.[30]

Still, *Moby Dick* is not altogether lacking in a social ethos. To be sure, the crew is not an Athenian chorus, not the noble citizen of the Roman state, not even Hamlet's "distracted multitude," but is "chiefly made up of mongrel renegades and castaways, and cannibals." Yet, Melville writes in praise of the "democratic God" who selects champions "from the kingly commons," who gave power to "the swart convict Bunyan," to "the pampered arm of old Cervantes," and who picked up Andrew Jackson "from the pebbles." He would celebrate "that democratic dignity which, on all hands, radiates without end from God." Ahab himself is a "democratic" hero, one who does not possess "the dignity of kings and robes." But Melville's paean is first of all to Ahab's mates, the "Knights and Squires," to the harpooners, to the arm "that wields a pick or drives a spoke." They all belong to the "same ancient Catholic Church . . . the great and everlasting First Congregation." Melville translates the transcendental democracy of Emerson and the idyllic internationalism of Thoreau into a communal idea.

In a sense, it is the crew which compose the tragic note in *Moby Dick*. They are placed in a situation with which they cannot cope; yet, they face it with courage. The crew accepts Ahab, sensing his "humanities." Their acceptance is an element of grace which contributes towards his redemption. Starbuck suffers with Ahab in "The Symphony." All witness his human relationship to little Pip. They see suffering written on his face, as he stood there "in all the nameless regal overbearing dignity of some mighty woe." In such moments, the Satanic hero almost becomes the sacrificial scapegoat.

In this phase, Ahab has affinity to the figure of the Fisher King, connected with the legend of the Holy Grail. As developed by Jessie L. Weston's *From Ritual to Romance*, the Fisher King is incapacitated by the effects of a wound and becomes known as the Maimed King. In the Grail Legend, the wound of the King is a punishment for his sinful passion towards a pagan princess, and the nature of the wound suggests injury to the reproductive energy. The Fisher King, who is either in middle life or an aged man, is healed by his successor, a youthful figure.

Ahab would be at once the middle-aged Fisher King and the young hero who saves him, would be both Satan and the Messiah.[31] He fights the colossus although he knows he will be defeated, and emerges with the dignity of the tragic which arises from his very flaw. This flaw and the redemption are foreshadowed in "The Sermon" which states the two main motifs of the book.

The text of Father Mapple's sermon is "And God had prepared a great fish to swallow up Jonah." Jonah's sin lay "in his wilful disobedience of the command of God." Now, Jonah finally makes his confession and accepts his punishment as just, and the sermon declares him to be "a model of repentance." However, Father Mapple poses the dilemma which comes with the Judaic-Christian, and specifically, the Protestant epoch: "if we obey God, we must disobey ourselves." And his sermon is partly in praise of being true to one's "own inexorable self." He concludes: "Delight is to God, a far, far upward and inward delight—who against the proud gods and commodores of this earth, ever stands forth his inexorable self."

To this self, Ahab has been true, and to that extent, he is a tragic and redeemable figure.[32] Like Job, he insists on maintaining his own ways before God. However, in the end, Ahab reverses Job, as well as the Greek and Christian mythic heroes.[33] Only in his relation to Pip, and when he urges Starbuck to stay on the boat and be saved, does Ahab reveal a measure of social sympathy.

Melville's *Moby Dick* is the first major American mythopoeic work which sounds the motifs of Creation and Quest. Its distinctive American quality lies in its uncertain attitude towards Creation. Dante and the mythmakers before him accepted Creation as their natural and communal heritage, and were concerned with its how, not its what or why. Even Hamlet feels himself bound to origins, although his father appears in "such a questionable shape," and at the close, he gives his dying voice to a new king. The American mythic hero is still in search of his creative sources and in doubt as to the possibility of their transformation and succession.[34]

The American Renaissance, as Matthiessen's study shows, was not a re-birth, but America's first maturity. Melville's *Moby Dick* shares some of the features of the other Renaissance myths, has some of the breadth, sense of varied experience and expansiveness of Hamlet, Faust and Siegfried. But its hero does not reach the tertiary phase of reintegration because he questions or cannot find his primary sources. *Moby Dick* comes at the point when industrialism begins its forward movement. Ahab and Ishmael leave the solid land, where men are "nailed to benches." But on the ocean, Ahab continues the way of the landsmen, driving others and himself towards conquest. Yet, he knows that his way is circular and, in this sense, *Moby Dick* questions a "progress" which does not know its original base and therefore has no conception of its destiny.

Still, *Moby Dick* carries the insight that if America is to know its destiny, it must recollect and transmute its creative beginnings. In figures such as Paul Bunyan we have a hero who combines Ahab and the crew, the exceptional and the democratic, perseverance and kindness. Paul Bunyan moves mountains, tames rivers, slays beasts, all in the interests of his loggers. America began as an interracial grouping with the desire to be free. Technics and automation threaten to reduce our unity to streamlined conformity, compensated by a capricious freedom. Theodore Dreiser's *The Bulwark* warns that the American tradition of brotherly linkage ("religion") was being supplanted by a religion of gadgets and of a gambling freedom. Yet, Melville saw great promise in the harmonious interplay between fraternity and freedom which constitute America's unique original values. He thought that Americans were "the peculiar, chosen people—the Israel of our time; we bear the ark of the liberties of the world."[35]

NOTES

1. The philosophy of John Dewey is the systematized expression of this temper. See the section "Philosophy of the Possible: John Dewey" in my *No Voice Is Wholly Lost*, pp. 43-56.

2. In Franz Kafka's *Amerika*, for example, Karl Rossman leaves Europe to find

employment in the free nature-theatre of Oklahoma. Here, *everybody* is welcome and no one is asked about his qualifications.

3. One thinks of our New Year celebrations with their unreserved impiety towards the old and their unbounded expectancy of the new year. Twelve months later, we treat the new as hopelessly old.

4. References throughout this chapter are to the Modern Library edition (New York, 1926).

5. An indirect reference to the Book of Job is Melville's correlation between the White Whale and the Leviathan of whom Job's Lord says:

> "None is so fierce that dare stir him up
> . . . he is a king over all the children of pride."

6. Whaling is compared to "that Egyptian mother, who bore off-springs themselves pregnant from her womb."

7. All mythic heroes are "orphans" in the sense that they are set out. It is a particular characteristic of Renaissance mythopoesis in which the hero repudiates his heritage (Hamlet, Faust, Siegfried).

8. In mythology, the earth-mother destroys her son Adonis, after giving birth to him. The effigy of the dead god Adonis is not buried, but thrown into the water —a part of the fertility ritual. Cf. Jessie L. Weston's *From Ritual to Romance* (New York, 1941), p. 48.

9. We are reminded of Oedipus whose club-foot is due to his parents having set him out, of Hephaesthus who was lamed by being hurled down from a height by the Goddess Hera, of the Scandinavian Smith-God Wieland who was lamed by a woman. In Greek mythology, laming and emasculation were equivalents.

10. The whole suggests the analogy to initiation ceremonies in primitive hunting communities. The White Whale is the totem of the tribe and the basis of its cohesion. Ahab is "the novice" who is tested by the amputation of his leg. He undergoes a further period of probation by living among men on the Pequod ("the Men's House" in the primitive rite). The supreme test is his quest of the White Whale.

11. I am indebted here to suggestions made by Benjamin Appel.

12. In "Fast-Fish and Loose-Fish," Melville carries the social analogy further: "What was America in 1492 but a Loose-Fish, in which Columbus struck the Spanish standard by way of waifing it for his royal master and mistress? What was Poland to the Czar? What Greece to the Turk? What India to England? What at last will Mexico be to the United States? All Loose-Fish. What are the Rights of Man and the Liberties of the World but Loose-Fish?"

13. The fate which overtakes Ahab is similar to that of the hunter Actaeon who invades the privacy of the virgin goddess Diana, of Pentheus who sought to view the secret ritual of his mother Agave, of Oedipus who is blinded by recognition of his incestuous life. When, at the end, Ahab beholds Moby Dick, about to pierce the hull of the Pequod, he staggers, smites his forehead, and cries out: "I grow blind; hands! stretch out before me that I may yet grope my way. Is 't night?"

14. All officers of whaling ships were Americans. Ahab is the captain ruling over a motley colonial group. We know of Melville's stand against exploitation of the colored people, against slavery and economic imperialism.

15. Ahab's ivory leg is referred to as his "man," and Ahab calls the carpenter who fashions it "man-maker." The carpenter thinks that in the ivory leg, Ahab has "a stick of whale's bone-jaw for a wife."

There are indications of Melville's attraction for male strength and power in *Oomoo* and *Typee*. *Billy Budd* is dedicated to Jack Chase, the handsome sailor under whom Melville worked in the Pacific.

16. The theme of love between a white man and a colored outcast also appears in Fenimore Cooper's *Leatherstocking Tales* and is prominent in Mark Twain's *Huckleberry Finn*. I came across an unpublished manuscript in which the term "Ishmael Complex" is suggested, to designate such relationships, and which the authors think is characteristic of the American scene. Here, homoeroticism is not overt, but has the character of juvenile innocence. It is acted out in social isolation, on the high seas, rivers, or in forests, remote from conventional mores. The colored character acts as the parent to the white man. In Mark Twain's novel, Jim reenacts the role of Queequeg. He is the mother of Huck (in his gentle, tender and sensual care of the boy) as well as a father (tall, strong).

17. In many mystery cults, the fish is a holy food, and the myth often identifies him with the primal Creator, connected with the God Vishnu, the Goddess Astarte and others. Cf. Jessie L. Weston, *From Ritual to Romance*, pp. 119 ff.

18. In "The Cassock," Melville describes the huge male organ of the whale. The passage would invoke an attitude of Biblical piety towards this "Grandissimus." It follows the chapter, "A Squeeze of the Hand."

19. The White Whale is the "herald" of Ahab's adventure. Like Hamlet's father, he announces himself in "midnight-spouts."

20. In discussing the tail, Melville refers to the hermaphroditical Italian paintings of the Son of God.

21. For the mythic imports of the Whale's Belly, see Joseph Campbell's *The Hero with a Thousand Faces* (New York, 1949), pp. 90 ff. Ahab is *jealous* of anyone who might first sight or touch Moby Dick.

22. Melville's mother apparently had little love for him, was cold and hard. The imagery used in describing the mother's face in *Pierre* ("too familiar, yet inexplicable") is similar to that used for Moby Dick. Melville's work knows no gracious figures, such as Beatrice, Dulcinea, Gretchen or Grushenka.

23. William E. Sedgwick hinted at this when he wrote that the White Whale "stands for the inscrutable mystery of creation" (*Herman Melville* [New York, 1962]).

24. Moby Dick gained the name "white" from the "milky-way wake of creamy foam" which he leaves as he glides through the sea. Melville's seminal metaphors further suggest the erotic element in Ahab's quest.

25. This unintegrated dialectic is also suggested by the fact that each of the whale's eyes focuses on a different object. Ahab's own vision is "one-eyed" and

makes for his fixed and distant relation to the others. In Moby Dick, the two eyes do not meet. This dual perspective first appears in Don Quixote-Sancho Panza. There, the two eyes are "harmonized" by remaining parallel to each other. They come in conflict in Hamlet's and Faust's two souls.

26. The biologic image is cannibalism—the cannibalism of the sea, with sharks snapping at each other's disembowelments. Ahab calls himself "old cannibal me." In his *The Great Mother* (New York, 1955), Erich Neumann examines the uroboros, "the circular snake biting its tail," as the symbol of the original situation, the "Great Round," in which male and female, consciousness and unconsciousness, are intermingled, a totality of the united primordial parents.

27. Melville writes that the subject makes him "expand to its bulk." In his effort to do it justice, his "arms" tire, and he calls out: "Friends, hold my arms."

28. Queequeg, the "soothing savage" in a "wolfish world," is "the mother" who delivers both Tashtego and Ishmael into life. But he is primarily a fairy-tale figure in comparison with the rest.

29. The number three occurs in other contexts: Ahab married three voyages prior to setting out on his hunt for the White Whale; there are three mates and three harpooners. As in other mythopoeic works, the number three suggests ambivalent values: The White Whale is God-Devil; the Pequod is at once the Ship of the Dead and "the mother" of the boat in which Ishmael is saved.

30. In F. O. Matthiessen's formulation (*American Renaissance* [New York, 1941]). Ahab anticipates much of America's development:

> "The strong-willed individuals who seized the land and gutted the forests and built the railroads were no longer troubled with Ahab's obsessive sense of evil, since theology had receded. . . . They tended to be . . . as blind to everything but their one pursuit, as unmoved by fear or sympathy, as confident in assuming an identification of their wills with immutable plan or manifest destiny, as liable to regard other men as merely arms and legs for the fulfilment of their purposes . . . [Melville] also provided an ominous glimpse of what was to result when the Emersonian will to virtue became in less innocent natures the will to power and conquest."

Jack London's Wolf Larsen approximates the combined features of Ahab and Moby Dick. He is fascinating and terrifying, unites intellect with "savage instincts." Like Ahab, Larsen is only outwardly formidable. Actually, he is a very sick man, goes blind, and dies in a helpless state. In Larsen's own terminology, he moves from a living "to do" towards a deathly "to be," an existence without movement.

31. W. H. Auden, "The Christian Tragic Hero," *The New York Times Book Review* (December 16, 1945). Miss Weston notes that in Christian art and tradition, "the Lance or Spear, as an instrument of the Passion, is found in conjunction with the Cross, nails, sponge, and Crown of Thorns." We find this conjunction in Ahab's spear and his mark of crucifixion which is "completed" as he gives up the spear and is strangled.

MOBY DICK

32. For this reason, I cannot go along with Matthiessen who holds that Ahab suffers, but remains damned. But Auden overstates the case in calling Ahab a "saint" who wills one thing for which he gives up everything.

33. Fedallah is not Ahab's evil spirit, as some maintain. His death only intensifies Ahab's demoniac drive. More is made of Fedallah than the story itself justifies. Melville's *intention* was to make Fedallah's speechless impersonality the Eastern counterpart to Ahab's Western rhetorical and wilful individualism. But this is not executed. Fedallah remains a "shadow" as a literary character as well.

34. Melville "tacks on" a hopeful portent: The sky-hawk is nailed to the Pequod by Tashtego's hammer. The bird goes down with the ship which, "like Satan would not sink to hell till she had dragged a living part of heaven with her, and helmeted herself with it." Joseph Campbell's *The Hero With A Thousand Faces* notes that in many myths, the birds rescue the hero from the Whale by pecking open the side of the Whale's belly.

35. See Appendix V for note on Mark Twain and Walt Whitman.

The Pan-Slavic Image of the Earth Mother

The Brothers Karamazov

OF THE MYTHOPOEIC WORKS considered in this study, only the Russian does not stem from a patriarchate civilization.[1] The core of the Pan-Slavic myth is connected with the matriarchy, and the most cherished values are presented in terms of the Mother image: The country is Mother Russia, the church Mother Church, Kiev, is regarded as "the mother of Russian Cities." In contrast to the Western Father, the Russian Mother stands for mercy and equality, and her image merges with that of the fertile Earth. For Maria Timofevna in Dostoyevsky's *The Possessed*, "the Mother of God is the great Mother Earth, and she offers great joy to man." And F. Fedotov writes:

> In Mother Earth, converge the most secret . . . religious feeling of the folk. . . . The source of all fertilizing powers, the nourishing breast of nature, and their own last resting place. The very epithet of the earth in the folk-songs, "Mother Earth, the Hermit," known also in Iranian mythology, alludes to the womb rather than to the face of the Earth. It means not beauty but fertility is the supreme virtue of the earth . . . Earth is the Russian "Eternal Womanhood," not the celestial image of it; mother, not virgin; fertile, not pure: and black, for the best Russian soil is black.
>
> (*The Russian Religious Mind*, pp. 12, 13)

Fedotov further indicates that there is no Russian parallel to Athena or other virgin goddess, and that the Slavic myth lacks the erotic features found in the Oriental-Greek accounts of marriages between Earth and Heaven. (There is no Russian word for "sexy" in the Anglo-American usage, although, of course, there is a word for sexual in the anatomical sense.) Demeter, the fruit-bearing goddess, not Aphrodite, is in the center of the Russian pantheon.[2]

246

The social analogue of the earthy Mother-Goddess is the common folk. Salvation—this is the theme of many Russian writers—lies in return to the people who are conceived as the all-nourishing source of the nation. From the people, writes Dostoyevsky, "everything will come to us: our thoughts and our images." And, just as in Russian legends, the earth does not have the character of "blood and soil" nationalism, so the people are thought of as all-human rather than as exclusively Russian,—an idea which may be connected with the fact that Russia comprises a vast variety of ethnic groups.

Here is the context for the emphasis on *sobornost*, the principle of communality, which permeates the mythology and legends of the Slavs.[3]

Bylini and Skazky

The *Bylini* and *Skazky* (ballads and folktales) of early Russian literature likewise express the Slavic values of communality. *The Slavic myth has no God of war and its literature has no hero cult.* Like the American Paul Bunyan, the hero in the Russian ballads and folktales uses his super-human strength in the interests of the people. Mikúla Selyáninovich, along with Ilyá Múrom (the chief and most popular figure in the ballad cycles) champion the poor and widows, defend the peasants and their native soil. The emphasis is on strength which stems from the earth (Ilyá can use his strength because the earth *can* bear it) and from the mothers, who are represented as wise and practical.

Many of these features are combined in the legend dealing with Igor's campaign. The tale is based on the struggle of the Russian princes against the nomads of the southern steppes, and relates Prince Igor's imprisonment and his escape. A characteristic note is the defensive nature of Igor's campaign and his obvious dislike of bloodshed. As is the case in early Slavic mythology, the most striking imagery is the identification of man with nature and the anthropomorphic function of the elements: the sun bars the way, the grass droops in pity, the tree bows down in grief, the night groans. Similarly, the Russian people and folk singers are spoken of as descended directly from nature-gods: They are the grandchildren of Dazhbog, the god of prosperity, of Volos, the god of cattle, of Stribog, the god of winds.[4] Igor's escape is effected by the three laments of his wife, addressed to Wind, the River and the Sun. Written when Kievan culture was in decline, the poem invokes the older values of Slavic unity.[5]

This temper took historic form in the *mir* which approximated a type of primitive communism despite its patriarchal structure.[6]

The Earthy Mother Church

Russia adopted Byzantine Christianity without its Hellenic culture. And the earthy element in Slavic mythology was akin to Greek orthodoxy which put stress on man's opportunity on earth. Discussing the character of religious Byzantism, Fedotov points out that whereas Western Christology adopted Pope Leo's distinction between the divine and the human, Byzantism taught with Cyril of Alexandria that Christ was God in human flesh:

> In this sacramental religion, the Deity ceases to be transcendent. It takes its abode in the temple. The Church becomes "heaven on earth," according to classical Orthodox saying. The Divinity is accessible through matter, that of sacraments and sacred objects: it can be not only seen, but even smelled, tasted, kissed. . . . Practically the whole of Byzantine religion could have been built without the historical Christ of the Gospels, upon a simple myth of the heavenly saviour similar to Hellenistic saviour myths. . . . The Eastern pathos is: heaven on earth, God's presence here in His temple in His mysteries, icons, relics, in sacred matter. . . . The dome of the Byzantine temple is large and round, a living symbol of heaven descending upon earth.[7]

And Maynard remarks that perhaps Dostoyevsky thought of this when he said that he belonged to a people capable of making a religion of materialism.

The earthiness of the church is an aspect of its democratic motherliness. God, says Dostoyevsky's Prince Myshkin, finds gladness in man's gladness, like a mother who sees her baby smile. In *The Brothers Karamazov*, the Orthodox Church is "a tender, loving mother." While the Grand Inquisitor prophesies that "we shall triumph and shall be Caesars," Father Paissy declares:

> The Church is not to be transformed into the State. That is Rome and its dream. That is the third temptation of the devil. On the contrary, the State is transformed into the Church.[8]

While the official church was despotic, the Russian monk, nearly as poor as the peasants among whom he worked, leaned towards a kind of primitive socialism, represented by "underground" movements, such as the Khlysty. The chapter on "The Russian Monk" in *The Brothers Karamazov* is a panegyric on one of its orders, projected in the figure of Father Zossima. Why, asks this Elder

> should not my servant be like my own kindred? . . . Even now this can be done, but it will lead to the grand unity of men in the future, when a man will not seek servants for himself, or desire to turn his fellow creatures into

servants as he does now, but on the contrary, will long with his whole heart to be the servant of all, as the Gospel teaches.

On such grounds, Berdyaev thinks that socialism "is deeply rooted in the Russian nature," for which man is a higher principle than property. While Berdyaev opposed communism, he argued that it must be transcended, not destroyed:

> Communism is the Russian destiny. . . . The Russian Revolution awakened and unfettered the enormous powers of the Russian people. The Soviet constitution of the year 1936 has established the best legislation on property in the world; personal property is recognized, but in a form which does not allow of exploitation.[9]

These primitive components stem from Russia's retarded development. Its geographical remoteness from the West, the long, devastating invasions of the Mongols, did not allow the rise of a strong, independent middle class, precluded a Renaissance, Reformation or revolutions, such as the American and the French. (The emancipation of the serfs in 1861 only burdened the impoverished peasantry by forcing redemption payments upon them). In sum, Russian undervelopment did not favor Western notions of free enterprise, of social, political and intellectual emancipation. In Berdyaev's words—Russia has never been bourgeois and its mentality was averse towards taking a "middle" position. By the time of Dostoyevsky, the ancient matriarchate and its strong family tie had given way to a tyrannical patriarchate.[10] Apart from the *mir*, the only equality which the Russian people knew in the Tsarist era was that of equal oppression and exploitation by the princes, the large landowners and the church. This situation produced the *nichevo* attitude—passive acceptance and resignation—or wild explosions, expressed in sporadic "Dionysian" acts of nihilism. Berdyaev speaks of this when he quotes a Pole during the Soviet Revolution as saying that "Dionysus is abroad in the Russian land."[11]

The Slavophiles And The Intellegentsia

Peter and Catherine the Great attempted to westernize Russia. This trend was opposed by the Slavophiles in the nineteenth century who, Herzen said, loved Russia as a Mother. They idealized the plain folk or the *narod* and saw in the very backwardness of the peasant commune the basis for a *Russian* socialism.[12] The Westerners drew their adherents from the ranks of repentant nobles and theoretic social revolutionaries. This Russian "intellegentsia"—Turgenev, calls them Don Quixotes and Hamlets—had roots neither in the established Tsarist rule nor in the oppressed masses. They were what the Russians call "superfluous people," men and women who had no function in their society and spent their energy in passionate discussion.[13] The social radicals among them felt that Russia was threatened by both Western and Russian exploitation. In its desperate and futile attack on both the Slavophiles and the Russian regime, the Intellegentsia approached an anarchist mood of what Toynbee terms "pure futurism."

Yet, the two opposing groups were at one in that both opposed the existing state. They decried the emptiness and ugliness of middle class commercialism, repudiated the bourgeois conception of private property and hoped that Russia would escape the evils of capitalism.[14]

Dostoyevsky transcended both camps. He was severely critical of Western freedom and extolled Russia.[15] Yet, as his speech on Pushkin makes clear, what he meant by being "truly national" is the ability of the Russian to identify with and to understand other peoples. To a Russian, he stated, Europe is also dear, precisely because it is Russia's vocation to realize all-human unity: "Our future lies in universality, not won by violence, but from the strength derived from our great ideal —the reuniting of all mankind." Russia's mission is "to lead the common interests of entire humanity." To be a Russian is to have

> the gift of world-wide sympathy . . . means being a brother to all men . . . to be a true Russian means nothing but to reconcile European contradictions within oneself, to give European longings an outlet in the all-uniting Russian soul, to receive all into this soul of brotherly love, and so, perhaps, to say the last word of universal harmony, and of the understanding and peace among all peoples according to the Evangelical law of Christ.[16]

DOSTOYEVSKY'S ODE TO LIFE

"The most important thing in life," says Hippolyte, the doomed consumptive in *The Idiot*, is "life and nothing else." And, amidst his torturous ordeal, the heart of Mitya Karamazov beats to the rhythm of Schiller's "Ode to Joy."

The life which Dostoyevsky and his characters celebrate is wild, uninhibited or anti-bourgeois. His Underground Man disputes the theory that man's interests, "include only prosperity, riches, freedom, tranquillity," and holds that there may indeed be

> some supreme interest of interests . . . for which man . . . is ready to contravene every law, and to lose sight alike of common sense, honour, prosperity, and ease.

Man may wilfully choose what is foolish, and

such folly may also be the best thing in the world for him, even though it work him harm. . . . This is because it is possible for his folly to preserve to him, under all circumstances, the chief, the most valuable, of all his possessions—namely, his personality, his individuality.[17]

Dostoyevsky's own life is characterized by such underground tremors. During his adolescence, Dostoyevsky lost his mother and father within the space of two years. The father was a stern patriarch, and Dostoyevsky later told his wife Anna that when he would dream of his father or brother Michael, he knew that a misfortune was about to descend upon him.

In his essay "Dostoevsky and Parricide" (*Collected Papers,* V), Freud passes over Dostoyevsky's mother and gives central place to the murder of his father. If we assume that Dostoyevsky secretly wished this murder, then we are tempted, Freud writes, "to see in that event the severest trauma and to regard Dostoyevsky's reaction to it as the turning point of his neurosis," as having released his epileptic seizures. Prior to the murder, Dostoyevsky suffered from a groundless melancholy, accompanied by a feeling that he was going to die on the spot. Freud sees this melancholy as a self-inflicted punishment: "One has wished another person dead, and now one *is* this other person and is dead oneself . . . the attack . . . is thus a self-punishment for a death-wish against a hated father." And when the fantasy became reality, the attacks assumed an epileptic character.

In letters to Strakhov and Soloviev, Dostoyevsky expressed himself freely about his epileptic fits. According to Myshkin's account in *The Idiot*, the fit was preceded by supreme rapture and ecstasy, so sweet "that one is ready to exchange ten years of life or even life itself for the bliss of these few seconds." Then came the "fall" which brought extreme depression, accompanied by the feeling "of being a criminal" who has committed some unknown awful deed. The account suggests the analogy between the epileptic and sexual discharge. Freud calls attention to the fact that physicians once described copulation as a little epilepsy.

Dostoyevsky's characters also seem fearful of sexual consummation. Mitya Karamazov solemnly asserts that his Grusha is holy and that he had never been her lover. Dostoyevsky's own life was ruled by sexual irregularities. To begin with, there was the prolonged abstinence of his youth and the enforced continence during the four years of his Siberian imprisonment. Moreover, we have indications of pedophelia, hinted in "Starvrogin's Confessions," and in Dostoyevsky's talk with Turgenev.[18]

In his book, Marc Slonim treats the three women in Dostoyevsky's life as approximating the triad of mother-mistress-child. Maria, his first wife, was the mother of a seven year old son. Like Dostoyevsky's own mother, she was consumptive and her solicitude for Dostoyevsky had a maternal character.[19] Although Maria was bed-ridden in the latter part of her life, Dostoyevsky felt that his bonds to her were unbreakable. A year after her death, he wrote to Wrangel that she "was the most honest, the most noble and magnanimous woman of all those whom I have known in all my life." If Maria was a mother figure, Polina was the harlot. Twenty years his junior, Dostoyevsky thought of her primarily as a sex object, although she apparently never surrendered to him.

In Anna, his second wife, Dostoyevsky found a woman who combined the child, mother and mistress. Anna was his adoring youthful secretary, completely submissive and concerned only with making him physically comfortable. Above all, she accepted the abnormal expressions of his eroticism. With her, he could do as he wished. As Slonim puts it:

> He may have felt embarrassed with others but with her everything was permissible. . . . With her he could play the husband, the lover, the father, the child. . . . Her role was a liberating and cathartic one; therefore she released him of his burden of guilt, and he ceased to feel like a sinner or a voluptuary. (*Three Loves of Dostoyevsky*, p. 241)

She also accepted his gambling mania. Relieved of shame in this area as well, Dostoyevsky was soon able to give up gambling and perhaps also his masturbatory practice. Of all his women, she alone does not appear in a recognizable form in his writings. Perhaps he had no need to create her symbolically since she fulfilled him in reality.

However, only in his last years did Dostoyevsky enjoy relative contentment. His life as a whole was filled with, what Gide calls, a "perfect mania for assuming burdens": His first marriage was to a consumptive widow whose son he adopted and cared for; later, he undertook to support his brother Michael and, after his brother's death, his family. Aside from his compulsive gambling, the most telling example appears in Dostoyevsky's attitude towards his Siberian imprisonment.

According to Simmons, there is evidence that the Petrashevsky circle to which Dostoyevsky belonged did not confine itself to reading and discussing the Utopian socialists, and that Dostoyevsky was among those in the group who planned even violent action to overthrow the despotic Tsarist regime. Yet, Dostoyevsky was accused only of having associated with the group and its reading of Belinsky's famous letter to

Gogol in which the critic attacked Gogol's apology for the social conditions in Russia. For this "crime," Dostoyevsky and others were sentenced to be shot. At the very last moment, the Tsar theatrically commuted the sentence to imprisonment and Dostoyevsky was sent out into the Siberian winter in an open sledge, weighed down by ten-pound chains. In prison, he suffered from terrible cold in the winter and from stifling heat in the summer. Yet—Dostoyevsky calmly accepted this disproportionate punishment: "I do not complain," he wrote, "this is my cross and I have deserved it." And, far from feeling resentment, he added that he "venerates" the Tsar, who is "infinitely generous and kind."

Freud believes that Dostoyevsky accepted punishment from the Tsar (whom Russians called the Little Father) "as a substitute for the punishment he deserved for his sin against his real father." From this viewpoint he could regard the commutation of the sentence by the all-powerful authority as an act of grace.[20] Freud further sees in Dostoyevsky's gambling mania—he gambled until he lost everything—"another method of self-punishment" which he connects with his long-buried compulsion to masturbate, that his burden of guilt took shape "as a burden of debt."

These dramatic events made for a feeling that precipitate disasters were impending, that there was a disparity between cause and effect. And this feeling carries over into Dostoyevsky's art. Its structure, form and organization are loose, chance predominates and anything seems possible. His characters are unpredictable, leap in emotional extremes from one abyss to another. They have no organic development and seem fully grown from the start. Their creator too could find no middle course. His death, as well as his life, was explosive. Dostoyevsky died by bursting a blood vessel.

THE BROTHERS KARAMAZOV

Dostoyevsky was deeply affected by a Claude Lorraine painting which he renamed "The Golden Age." In *The Possessed*, this age is called the first act of mythology:

> Here was mankind's earthly paradise, gods descended from heaven and united with mortals, here occurred the first scenes of mythology. Here lived beautiful men and women! They rose, they went to sleep, happy and innocent; the groves rang with their merry songs, the great overflow of unspent energies poured itself into love and simple-hearted joys. . . . The most im-

probable of all visions, to which mankind throughout its existence has given its best energies, for which it has sacrificed everything, for which it has pined and been tormented, for which its prophets were crucified and killed, without which nations will not desire to live, and without which they cannot even die! (Modern Library edition, p. 715)

But Dostoyevsky recognized that his Russia was not an earthy paradise, but an inferno, where "money-lenders and devourers of the commune were rising up . . . I've seen in the factories children of nine years old, frail, rickety, bent and already depraved."[21] *The Brothers Karamazov* echoes such social criticism through Rakitin and Zossima, through Ivan's stories of tortured children and Mitya's dream in the court-room. At the trial, the attorney receives the most "irrepressible and almost frantic applause" by at least "a good half" of the audience, including "persons of high position," when he declares that the Mityas are a product of the Russian social situation, of the unreasonable acts of their fathers.

In Dostoyevsky's era, memory of the Pan-Slavic Earth Mother was fading. At this point, two outstanding writers attempted to re-create her mythic values in symbolic form: Tolstoy counterposed the "motherly" Pierre, Platon Karatayev, Levin and the Russian peasant to the Western and Eastern Napoleons; Dostoyevsky countered Sonia, Myshkin, Marie, Zossima and Alyosha to the would-be Caesars, the Raskolnikovs, Stavrogins and Grand Inquisitors. In *The Brothers Karamazov*, Dostoyevsky's summary and terminal novel, we have the most dramatic mythopoeic expression of Pan-Slavism in its historic nineteenth century dress: In Zossima and Alyosha, it presents holy Mother Russia; in Ivan and Smerdyakov its modern rationalistic and "epileptic" forms; in Mitya, Russia "*as she is* . . . our mother Russia, the very scent and sound of her . . . a marvellous mingling of good and evil." The Karamazov family as a whole is the *selva oscura* of the Russian inferno, a distortion of the ancient Slavic "Big Family."

Act I: Adam

The Father (Dostoyevsky gives him his own name, Fyodor), is the "Adam" of the Karamazov family. A prominent feature is his Adam's apple:

I have mentioned already that he looked bloated. . . . Besides the long fleshy bags under his little, always insolent, suspicious, and ironical eyes; besides the multitude of deep wrinkles in his little fat face, the Adam's apple hung below his sharp chin like a great, fleshy goitre, which gave him a peculiar, repulsive, sensual appearance; add to that a long rapacious mouth with full

lips, between which could be seen little stumps of black decayed teeth. He
slobbered every time he began to speak.

Fyodor used his energies to look after his "wordly affairs" and after
nothing else. In the words of the prosecuting attorney at the trial,

his vitality was excessive. He saw nothing in life but sensual pleasure, and he
brought his children up to be the same. He had no feelings for his duties as
a father. He was an example of everything that is opposed to civic duty, of
the most complete and malignant individualism.

Yet, Fyodor's "primitive . . . and . . . unbridled" zest for life is also
fertile.[22]

Even as Dostoyevsky depicts Fyodor as the devouring parent, he
also suggests hidden creative elements in him. To begin with, he is said
to be "of noble birth." Alyosha thinks that his father is "not ill-na-
tured, but distorted," and the author points to the environmental pressures which drove Fyodor to play the buffoon. Fyodor himself explains
it as "revenge for my youth, for all the humiliation I endured," says
that his buffoonery has the object "of amusing people and making myself agreeable."

That Fyodor's nature is not exhausted by his sensualism is obliquely
shown by the women he married. The outstanding characteristics of
his first wife, Adelaida, were her beauty and proud independence, of
his second wife, Sofya, her meekness and innocence (this greedy man
married her although she came to him penniless). The first became
the mother of the rebellious Mitya, the other gave birth to the Christ-
like Alyosha and the Judas-like Ivan.

Now, according to rumor, Fyodor had another son, Smerdyakov,
whose mother is Lizaveta, described as a "dwarfish creature," with
"a look of blank idiocy," more of an earth-animal than a woman:

Her coarse, almost black hair curled like lamb's wool. . . . It was always
crusted with mud, and had leaves, bits of stick, and shavings clinging to it,
as she always slept on the ground and in the dirt . . . She could hardly speak,
and only from time to time uttered an inarticulate grunt.

Yet, to Fyodor, her very sub-earthy appearance lent her a certain pi-
quancy and he is quoted as having said that it was by no means impossible to look upon her as a woman. Shortly afterwards, she is found
in Fyodor's garden bathhouse, having given birth to Smerdyakov.

In his choice of the three women, Fyodor did not exhibit sensuality,
but a desire for beauty and rebelliousness, for saintliness and innocence, and even an appreciation of the amorphously earthy.[23] We
should also note that the author shows Fyodor to be somewhat cul-

tured (he quotes Diderot), critical of social evils in the Russian church (living "at other people's expense"). He is said to have moments of "spiritual terror," is troubled over the question as to whether there is a God and whether there is immortality.

Every one of Fyodor's sons partakes of his sensualism and drunken rebelliousness. They are all intoxicated: Alyosha with God, Ivan with theory, Mitya and Smerdyakov with justice. They are all "Karamazovs," —Alyosha too calls himself one. And, to be a Karamazov, Alyosha says, is to war against father and brother:

> My brothers are destroying themselves, my father, too. And they are destroy-
> ing others with them. It's the primitive force of the Karamazovs, as Father
> Paissy said the other day, a crude, unbridled, earthly force. Does the spirit
> of God move above that force? Even that I don't know. I only know that I
> too, am a Karamazov. . . . And perhaps I don't even believe in God.

This primitive restlessness breaks through Alyosha's religious and Ivan's rationalistic censor. In Smerdyakov, it expresses itself first in "orgiastic" fits, and later in murder. In Mitya, the pleasure principle is wild and inchoate.

Act II: The Four-Fold Quest

If Fyodor may be regarded as the principle of Creation in the story, his four sons approximate the four-fold Quest taking form in rebellion against the father who exploits the Russian mother and her sons: Smerdyakov explodes in the underground, Mitya rages with every nerve in his body, Ivan rebels with cold dialectic, and Alyosha with religious fervor.[24]

Ivan

Ivan's problem is perhaps closest to the author's, in that his Western-ism, grafted on to his Russian character, was Dostoyevsky's own most troublesome problem. He is the deepest secret of the book and some of the most secret chapters—the poem about the Grand Inquisitor, the interviews with Smerdyakov and with the Devil—deal with Ivan.[25]

Ivan is the most alienated of the four brothers. His "Euclidian" mind keeps him from a "living life," and he is unable to express or to accept love. He has contempt for his father and for Smerdyakov, hates Mitya, and even Alyosha appears to him as a "fanatic." Yet, he is unable to find rest in his negativism, not so much because he has a Hamlet-like sensi-bility, but because he too is a Karamazov. In his confessional scene with Alyosha in "Pro and Contra," Ivan tells Alyosha that he too has a "frantic . . . thirst for life . . . that thirst for life regardless of everything," and "in spite of logic." He adds that even if he did not believe in life and lost faith in the order of things, he would still want to taste of the cup and not turn away till he had drained it.

> I have a longing for life . . . I love the sticky leaves as they open in spring. I love the blue sky . . . without knowing why. . . . It's not a matter of intellect or logic, it's loving with one's inside, with one's stomach.

Ivan's Westernism is only loosely attached to his Karamazovism. In contrast to Miusov and Rakitin (the Western liberals), Ivan uses reason to find grounds for proving contradictions. He argues "Pro and Contra," for and against the domination by the church over the state, for and against freedom and security. And, precisely because he would give exclusive priority to his rational motives, Ivan is helpless in coping with his underground forces. He expects that Mitya will kill his father, that "one reptile will devour another," and that he himself was ready to bring this about. But his unconscious wish is that Smerdyakov commit the act. At a decisive stage in the plot, Smerdyakov hints that by leaving, Ivan would be granting him permission to kill Fyodor. Ivan means to tell Smerdyakov that he is a miserable idiot. But, "to his profound astonishment, he heard himself say, 'Is my father still asleep, or has he waked?' He asked the question softly and meekly, to his own surprise. . . ." In the end, Ivan's airy rationalism undermines his reason and drives him to the ultimate antinomy of madness.

Ivan's Russian character, his deep skepticism over reason and logic, are exposed in his colloquy with Alyosha in "Pro and Contra." Ivan begins his confession "as stupidly as I could on purpose." When Alyosha asks him why he did this, Ivan answers:

> To begin with, for the sake of being Russian. . . . And secondly, the stupider one is, the closer one is to reality. The stupider one is, the clearer one is. Stupidity is brief and artless, while intelligence wriggles and hides itself. Intelligence is a knave, but stupidity is honest and straightforward.

On the philosophical level, Ivan raises here the "eternal question" about the dilemma between freedom and happiness. But this question arises out of his personal dilemma. Ivan has just broken off with Katya, despite the fact that they love each other. This is his private "Pro and Contra." Ivan wants to celebrate his "freedom" from Katya and he tells Alyosha that his heart is now light. Actually, his heart is heavy, and he has a great need to speak with Alyosha. His Western logic cannot cope with the irrational situation in which two people have decided to part despite the fact that they love each other. And, in this scene, the anti-Euclidian aspect of Ivan breaks through: He speaks in soft, pleading tones of his need for faith. His cold exterior opens up to expose his wounds, and he tells Alyosha that perhaps he wishes to be "healed" by him. The problem he poses—the theologic-metaphysical antinomy between freedom and happiness, between innocence and suffering—is an extrapolation of his personal burden: He is free from Katya, yet unhappy; he has done no wrong, yet suffers.

Ivan begins by confessing his Karamazovism. He would drain the cup at least until he is thirty, and then dash it to the ground. While he does not allow himself Fyodor's dissipations, Ivan's "Everything is lawful," sanctions his father's unbridled sensualism. In this sense, we can understand Fyodor calling Ivan "the dearest of my flesh," and Smerdyakov's saying: "If there is one of the sons that is like Fyodor Pavlovitch in character, it is Ivan Fyodorovitch."

Ivan's Jobian Poem

The Book of Job was one of Dostoyevsky's favorite poems. While Ivan himself does not mention the Book, it is the Jobian question of why the innocent suffer that preoccupies him here.

Ivan narrows the problem to the sufferings of children. He refers to accounts of children tortured or torn to pieces before their mothers' eyes for some trifling act. He proceeds to the theologic-metaphysical implications and sums up by his poem of the Grand Inquisitor.

Like Job, Ivan cannot accept the argument that children suffer because of their parent's sins. Nor is he consoled by the promise that otherworldly happiness will compensate for their suffering. Ivan wants justice "here on earth." This "rationalist" is at bottom "a believer," as he tells his brother. But, he says, "there are the children." Why should these innocent ones too "furnish material to enrich the soil for the harmony of the future?" If such harmony is at the expense of a child's suffering, then "From love for humanity I don't want it." Ivan grants the existence of God, that is, of an order incomprehensible to man, yet he cannot accept his world. He admits that this is rebellion, and that one cannot live in rebellion, adding somewhat pathetically, "and I want to live."

The heart of Ivan's argument is reached in his poem of the Grand Inquisitor. He, who would appear as a cold logician, finds it necessary to clinch his point by recourse to analogy, metaphor and dramatic fiction. His "Poem" is a closet drama which takes place during the Inquisition in the sixteenth century, in which a Spanish cardinal confronts the Christ of the Gospels who has come down to earth. The Grand Inquisitor has him seized and imprisoned. The next night, the cardinal appears in the cell and there takes place a "dialogue" in which Christ remains silent throughout.

The cardinal begins by stating that Christ has come "to hinder us" and that he will be burned at the stake "as the worst of heretics." He harangues Christ for having refused the three temptations — turning stones into bread, accepting earthly domination, and assuming authoritative power — and having exalted freedom instead. Yet, while nothing is more seductive for man than his freedom of conscience, "nothing is a greater cause of suffering." Freedom entails choice, and most men are weak, and having to make a choice brings confusion and suffering into their lives. Freedom makes them rebellious, but they are "impotent rebels," hence the lot of mankind has become "unrest, confusion and unhappiness." What the many desire above all is bread and "some one to worship, some one to keep his conscience, and some means of uniting all in one unanimous and harmonious ant-heap."

The Inquisitor recognizes that there is an even more powerful appeal to man than bread, namely his conscience. He admits that

> if some one else gains possession of his conscience—oh! then he will cast away Thy bread and follow after him who has ensnared his conscience. In that Thou wast right. For the secret of man's being is not only to live but to have something to live for.

But he insists that Christ's mistake lay in making men's freedom greater than ever instead of taking it away from them. Christ rejected the miracle and called for faith and love given freely. The Church has "corrected" Christ's work and founded it upon miracle, mystery and authority. In this way, the Inquisitor proclaims

> we shall triumph and shall be Caesars, and then we shall plan the universal happiness of man. . . . The most painful secrets of their conscience, all, all they will bring to us, and we shall have an answer for all. And they will be glad to believe our answer, for it will save them from the great anxiety and terrible agony they endure at present in making a free decision for themselves.

Now, Ivan and Alyosha agree that the secret of the Inquisitor is that he "does not believe in God" in that he does not believe in man. (This is the basis for Dostoyevsky's saying that the West has lost Christianity through "the error of Catholicism".) The Inquisitor is the Western father-authority who would keep his son in perpetual childish dependence.

Yet, the scene is more than an intellectual-theologic disquisition. It is a drama. To be sure, Christ remains silent, although challenged by the cardinal to "speak" and to "be angry." Still, there is a kind of speech in the listener's soft, mild eyes and demeanor. Indeed, the Inquisitor changes his tone and argument *as though he were being answered.* Furthermore, the cardinal voices his own reservations on his position in admitting that man's secret "is not only to live but to have something to live for." He is uneasy in his position and would show that what the church has done stems from its *love of man.* It has imposed mystery, miracle and authority because otherwise man, faced with a terrible choice, would have been unhappy. Indeed, this same love of man has led the church's leading representatives to take the burden of freedom upon themselves, "lovingly lightening their burden, and permitting their weak nature even sin with our sanction. . . ." Thus, there is a conflict within the cardinal owing to the co-existence of Christ's gospel of freedom and the church's assumption of authority. And Christ recognizes the anguish of the cardinal when he approaches him at the end, and softly kisses his bloodless aged lips. "That was all his answer," Ivan adds.[26] The kiss is given in the spirit in which Zossima bowed down before Mitya, and it is reenacted when Alyosha kisses Ivan at the close of his story. Here, Alyosha acknowledges the agony within Ivan, the conflict between his rationalistic "everything is lawful" and his Russian concept that all human life is sacred. Ivan cannot argue himself into killing Fyodor. He can act only unconsciously, through Smerdyakov.

Father Zossima

In the chapter on "The Russian Monk" which follows Ivan's Poem, Dostoyevsky would counter the Western Caesaristic Father, in the form of the temporal Catholic Church, with the Eastern Mother Goddess, as embodied in the teachings of the *Russian monk* and the institution of the elders.

The Inquisitor argues that if people are to be happy, they must be led to accept mystery, miracle and authority. In contrast, Father Zossima would shun mysteries, specifically the mystery that hell-fire is material, and underplays miracles (denying Fyodor's story about the saint who carried his head in his hands). Above all, his stand is a repudiation of the cardinal's central thesis that people are weak and vile and cannot be allowed freedom of choice. Father Zossima teaches, on the other hand, that he who believes in God will believe in God's people. And, where the cardinal held that salvation rests in the ruling church, Zossima states: "The salvation of Russia comes from the people. And the Russian monk has always been on the side of the people," getting his image of Christ, not from the organized church, but "fair and undefiled . . . from the times of the Fathers of old, the Apostles and the martyrs."

Here is the basis of the monk's Russian "socialism" which opposes the new individuality and freedom of the West which result, not in fullness of life and self-realization, but in self-destruction and complete solitude. Western freedom, Zossima teaches, leads men to "distort their own nature."

Zossima's theology is based not on law but on what he calls, "active love." And, he applies it in a way which has startling analogies to modern psychological therapy. He calls hell "the suffering of being unable to love." And, in speaking of self-deception, he admonishes Fyodor:

> Above all, don't lie to yourself. The man who lies to himself and listens to his own lie . . . loses all respect for himself and for others. And having no respect he ceases to love, and . . . gives way to passions and coarse pleasures. . . . The man who lies to himself can be more easily offended than any one.

Similarly to Madame Hohlakov:

> Above all, avoid falsehood, every kind of falsehood, especially falseness to yourself. . . . What seems to be bad within you will grow purer from the very fact of your observing it within yourself. . . . Love in dreams is greedy for immediate action, rapidly performed in the sight of all. . . . But active love is labour and fortitude.

Zossima speaks of the earthliness of the monk's religion, its exultant celebration of life. He relates how his dying brother begged his mother not to cry, for "life is paradise."

Zossima's social critique and his notion of freedom nearly justify rebellion. But, he shrinks from violence and hopes that "salvation will come from the people, from their faith and meekness." This attitude becomes focally relevant to his role in Mitya's ordeal. Zossima can only bow down to but not help Mitya. And, Dostoyevsky obliquely exposes Zossima's impotence here by removing him early in the story, before Mitya's problem becomes acute. In this way, the author spares himself the embarrassment of revealing the Elder's helplessness in Mitya's trial.

Dostoyevsky's complex view of Zossima is also manifested in the style and structure of the section "The Russian Monk." Dostoyevsky spent more time and labor on this section than on any other, planning to make it the "culminating point of the novel," the answer to Ivan's Inquisitor. "For its sake," he wrote to Liubimov, "the whole novel is being written." Yet, only the account of Zossima's sinful youth and the pages on his brother are executed with artistic power. The rest, dealing with Zossima's teachings, is in the form of a lawyer's brief. Dostoyevsky himself felt that he had not succeeded in his attempted refutation of Ivan's stand.[27] The artist invokes more fervor in picturing the skepticism of Ivan, the passion of Mitya, even the nihilistic act of Smerdyakov. Such esthetic consideration tells us more about Dostoyevsky's position than his forensic statements.[28]

Alyosha: "The Man of God."

The determining force in Alyosha's life is the memory of his mother and the treatment she received from his father. Although Alyosha lost his mother in his fourth year, he remembered her all his life. He recalled one particular fragment in which his mother prayed for him to the Mother of God:

> one still summer evening, an open window, the slanting rays of the setting sun (that he recalled most vividly of all); in a corner of the room the holy image, before it a lighted lamp, and on her knees before the image his mother, sobbing hysterically with cries and moans, snatching him up in both arms, squeezing him close till it hurt, and praying for him to the Mother of God, holding him out in both arms to the image as though to put him under the Mother's protection. . . . And suddenly a nurse runs in and snatches him from her in terror. That was the picture! and Alyosha remembered his mother's face at that minute. He used to say that it was frenzied but beautiful as he remembered.

And one might say that Alyosha dedicates himself *to redeem the life of his mother.* He carries forward not only her meekness, passivity and submission, but also something of her "crazy" character, as when he shakes in hysterical paroxism of weeping when Fyodor mentions his mother.

Dostoyevsky tells us that Alyosha's love had to be "active," that he had to help the one he loved. Now, "to do so he must know what he was aiming at; he must know for certain what was best for each." But Alyosha's love could not discern a clear way through the distortions of his day. Not only did this "early lover of humanity" not know "for certain what was best for each," but the very character of his religious outlook to accept everything "without the least condemnation," precluded his acting on the basis of a choice. Hence, Alyosha's absolute acceptance meets with Ivan's absolute skepticism (the two brothers are the only ones who have the same father and mother). To Ivan, all is lawful, to Alyosha, all is lovable; that is, in both cases, all is "acceptable,"—for Ivan in the light of pure reason, for Alyosha in the eyes of a loving God. The pragmatic consequences are that *neither can act* on the basis of a clear-cut resolution—Ivan cannot because for him every pro has its contra; Alyosha cannot because for him every contra has its pro. Hence, Ivan can only talk and argue; Alyosha can only feel and weep. Both can be only passive, suffering spectators. Although the author expressly refers to Alyosha as "the young hero I love so much," he cannot be a heroic character in the plot because accepting everything, *he cannot be the guide* they all look to. Towards the end of the novel, Mitya needs Alyosha's consent before he will agree with Ivan's plan for his escape; but Alyosha is unable to lend his active support. While the others are busy planning for Mitya's rescue, Alyosha devotes himself to the boys and to Ilusha's funeral.

Alyosha is at most Dostoyevsky's "future hero," as he calls him in another place. In the planned sequel, Alyosha was to marry Lisa (his moral opposite) and "sin his way to Jesus." But, in *The Brothers Karamazov*, he does not sin, is as sexless as Prince Myshkin. In his Foreword to the novel, Dostoyevsky admits that he did not succeed in molding Alyosha to heroic proportions:

> . . . although I call Alyosha my hero, I myself know that he is by no means a great man, and hence I foresee such unavoidable questions as these: "What is so remarkable about your Alyosha Fyodorovitch that you have chosen him as your hero? What has he accomplished?" . . . For me he is remarkable, but I doubt strongly whether I shall succeed in proving this to the reader. The fact is, if you please, that he is a protagonist, but a protagonist vague and undefined.

Dostoyevsky draws Alyosha with less literary power, pours less of his artistic blood into him than he does in the case of his criminal brothers. And this has esthetic "justice." For, Alyosha does little to affect the central problem. He is a hero only in Tolstoy's sense—in being non-heroic. Alyosha, and Father Zossima are the novel's moral censors. But neither can or do help Mitya. Zossima is removed from the story before the trial opens and Alyosha is on the sidelines during Mitya's ordeal.

In his essay on Dostoyevsky, Freud sees the patricidal guilt distributed among Mitya, Ivan and Smerdyakov, but exempts "the contrasted figure of Alyosha." However, it may be said that Alyosha is both one of the four "elements" and one of the four "causes" in the Karamazov murder, perhaps even the "final" cause. To begin with, Alyosha confesses to being a Karamazov, full of low desires. He admits to Lisa that there is some truth in her saying that "every one loves having killed his father." Alyosha had been strongly admonished by Father Zossima to keep an eye on Mitya, having in mind the latter's threat to kill his father. But Alyosha "forgets" this and instead busies himself with the boys.

A crucial psychological motif for Alyosha's feeling of guilt appears in the fact that, like Father Zossima, Alyosha *invites punishment and begs forgiveness*. Now, unlike Father Zossima, Alyosha is not shown to have sinned. Does he feel guilty only because of his impotence in relation to the problem of the Karamazovs?

Alyosha's actions following the death of Father Zossima suggest clues of more latent guilt-feelings.

When Father Zossima dies, Alyosha expected, in his naive faith, that the elder's body would not decompose. But, when the smell of decay becomes evident, Alyosha is shaken to the core. He talks, like Ivan, about rejecting God's world, and readily accepts Rakitin's invitation to visit Grushenka. In a perceptive essay, Dr. Mark Kanzer sees in Alyosha's encounter with this temptress the psychological pivot of the novel. With the death of the father-figure, Alyosha's repressed erotic drives erupt and he goes to Grushenka who is a mother-sister figure to him. At this point, Grushenka's former lover appears and Alyosha returns to the bier of Father Zossima. This "critical moment" in Alyosha's life is followed by a dream-like scene in which Alyosha beholds Christ reenacting the first of his miracles—the conversion of water into wine.[29] There follows the passage in which Alyosha embraces, kisses and wets the earth, "vowed passionately to love it, to love it for ever and ever." Gazing on the coffin of the elder, Alyosha "longed to forgive every one and for everything, and to beg forgiveness. . . ."

Still, Alyosha's personality has a productive function. He is the steady, ever-present listener, a liquid vessel in which passions tend to be softened. He is a catalyst, not only for the rage, but also for the love latent in the others.

Smerdyakov: The Underground

Smerdyakov is the Russian Underground Man whose surface calm hides a diabolic abyss. If Fyodor embodies the pleasure principle that leads to its own destruction, Smerdyakov embodies the principle of destruction itself, receiving its sanction from Ivan's conceptual dialectic.[30] His resentment is stored up in his mental underground:

> A physiognomist, studying his face would have said that there was no thought in it, no reflection, but only a sort of contemplation.

The author compares him to a painting by Kramskoy in which a peasant stands lost in thought:

> Yet he is not thinking; he is "contemplating" . . . if he were asked what he had been thinking about, he would remember nothing. Yet probably he has hidden within himself, the impression which had dominated him during the period of contemplation. Those impressions are dear to him and no doubt he hoards them imperceptibly, and unconsciously.

Fyodor refers to him as "a Balaam's ass . . . that thinks and thinks, and the devil knows where he gets to."

Dostoyevsky endows Smerdyakov's mother with mysterious subearthy features. His account of her delivery suggests that it had a supranatural character—in her pregnant condition, Lisaveta climbed a high fence to reach Fyodor's bath-house where she gave birth. In Grigory's words, she comes "from the devil's son and a holy innocent," and so is a "child of God," and the author remarks that she is regarded as an "idiot," which means, one "specially dear to God."

In Smerdyakov's own mind, he is "descended from a filthy beggar" with no father. (He is the only character in the novel who has no surname and is called by the nickname given to his mother—a kind of fatherless son of the Russian earth-mother).

Smerdyakov is the Slavic Alberich with a fierce resentment against his father-authorities who despise him and, like Alberich, he steals the gold. To Ivan, he is "raw material for revolution. . . . His kind will come first, and better ones after." He is the harbinger of the revolutionary underground which was to explode in Russian history.

Dostoyevsky assigned his personal epileptic burden to Myshkin, one of his noble characters, and to Smerdyakov, one of his base characters. In Dostoyevsky's dialectic, the two are interrelated: their idiocy has a malevolent and a cathartic function. Dostoyevsky suggests this aspect in Smerdyakov by assigning him—along with Mitya—the stages of the Rankian hero: A "difficult" conception and delivery, abandonment (in a "stable"), rescue by a servant (Grigory), and subsequent revenge for his humiliation.

Smerdyakov is not simply "a parody of Ivan," as Simmons calls him. While he lets himself be guided by Ivan, Smerdyakov has personal grounds for hating Fyodor and, at the end, he rejects Ivan. In the course of his three interviews with his brother, Smerdyakov's former awe of Ivan is turned to contempt. He discovers that his "God almighty" was unsure of himself and refused to take responsibility for his maxim that "everything was lawful." He now defies Ivan to kill him: "You won't dare to do anything, you who used to be so bold."

Commenting on Smerdyakov's face, Dostoyevsky writes that a man, such as he

> may suddenly, after hoarding impressions for many years, abandon everything and go off to Jerusalem on a pilgrimage for his soul's salvation, or perhaps he will suddenly set fire to his native village, or perhaps do both.

After the murder, Smerdyakov undergoes a remarkable change. He, who was said not to have "the Russian faith at all," attempts to find consolation by reading The Sayings of the Holy Father Isaac the Syrian. (It should be mentioned that Smerdyakov developed epilepsy after he expressed doubt over God, for which Grigory slapped him violently.) And, he who had been thought to have bourgeois ambitions, refuses to take Fyodor's money. In the end, he repudiates Ivan, unable to live by his brother's values after all. To be sure, he does not confess and clear Mitya, and his suicide is an act of despair, not of penance. Yet, it is an indirect confession of his share in the guilt and his self-destruction is a distorted self-sacrifice.

The Devil

Smerdyakov is the Mephistopheles of the book, and, like Goethe's devil, has "some kind of compact, some secret" with Ivan, the would-be man-God. He, too, is the "Overseer," helps to implement the thoughts and desires of his Russian Faust.

The devil appears to Ivan at about the hour when Smerdyakov hangs himself. His death deprives Ivan of "the raw material" for his theory and he is now left with "pure reason" which involves him in antinomies. The bodily, irrational element which he attempted to deny rises to the surface of his mind and he can now recognize the devil in himself.

Ivan's devil lacks the terrifying aspect of the classical or medieval adversary. He is reduced to a poor relation who would give all "simply to be transformed into the soul of a merchant's wife. . . ." This devil is a vulgar accommodator, "ready to assume any amiable expression as occasion might arise," a bureaucrat for whom hell is mechanical routine. He is the modern devil, tempting men with commercialism and "adaptation." This form of evil also appears in Raskolnikov's vision of microbes threatening to destroy man and in the mechanistic socialism of *The Possessed*. Such denial of God, the devil tells Ivan, can destroy mankind.

Ivan is unable to exorcize the devil because he is an aspect of his own self. He admits to the devil:

> You are the incarnation of myself, but only of one side of me . . . of my thoughts and feelings, but only the nastiest and stupidest of them.

The appearance of the devil is Ivan's partial awareness of the unconscious role which Smerdyakov played in his life, the ideas which came to Ivan "when he was asleep" and did not "want to believe."[31]

Dostoyevsky gives even his devil a "Russian" character by having him repudiate his destructive function. Although he is predestined "to deny," Ivan's devil is "not at all inclined to negation," and to evil. He calls himself "perhaps the one man in all creation who loves the truth and genuinely desires good," would use his critical powers to make men disbelieve in him and thereby sow "a tiny grain of faith." Likewise, the Ivans are "secretly longing" to save their souls. At the end, it is Ivan who makes the most persistent efforts to rescue Mitya, would even sacrifice himself for his brother. Neither he nor Raskolnikov have the persuasion that justice is the interest of the stronger. In Alyosha's words, Ivan's illness is "the anguish of . . . an earnest conscience," in which God and the devil were battling and where "God, in whom he disbelieved, and His truth were gaining mastery over his heart, which still refused to submit."

Katya: The Incest Figure in the Brothers Karamazov

Dostoyevsky criticism has accepted Grushenka as the incest figure in the novel, since Mitya publicly competes with his father for her favors. However, Mitya's major dilemma centers, not in Grushenka, but in Katya who, as this section will show, is the deeper of Mitya's incest burdens.

Freud names *The Brothers Karamazov*, *Hamlet* and *Oedipus Rex* three literary masterpieces, dealing with patricide, motivated by sexual rivalry.[32] Now, *The Brothers Karamazov* is a later, more complex form of the oedipal situation. In Sophocles, Oedipus actually commits patricide and incest. Shakespeare's modern, sophisticated scene, as we have noted, presents more tangled relations.

In Dostoyevsky, the pattern is still more intricate. We have three father figures: Fyodor, Grigory (who brings up Mitya and Smerdyakov) and Father Zossima; three or four sons: Mitya, Ivan, Alyosha and Smerdyakov, who divide the patricidal guilt. Grushenka is the manifest object of Mitya's desire. The hidden and latent incest-figure is Katya.

Katya is the source of Mitya's obsessive feeling of his "debt" to her. His inability to return the money he took from her is the chief ground of his emotional disturbance. This is the reason, Mitya says, "why I fought in the tavern, that is why I attacked my father." Here, Mitya associates his patricidal impulse with his "debt" to Katya. What tortures him when he is arrested is not the false charge that he murdered his father, nor so much the thought that he killed Grigory, but "the damned consciousness" that he had not repaid Katya and had become "a downright thief." (In passing, we might note that Mitya recalls that as a boy he stole some kopecks from his mother which he returned "three days later.") Why does Mitya feel that this is "the most shameful act of my whole life," that his very *"life"* depends on his returning the 3000 rubles to Katya?

Dostoyevsky gives Katya features which are similar to those he assigns to Mitya's mother, Adelaida. Both belong to fairly rich and distinguished families and become heiresses. Both possess an imperious beauty and are described as strong, vigorous and intelligent. Mitya's mother was "a hot-tempered, bold, dark-browed, impatient woman," and according to rumor used to beat her husband. She left Fyodor, running away with a divinity student. Katya strikes Mitya as proud, reckless, defiant, self-willed. She too defies convention: She comes to Mitya alone, impulsively offers to become his wife.

From the outset, Katya appears to Mitya as a kind of goddess. At the meeting in Father Zossima's cell, he is particularly outraged by his father's aspersions of Katya's good and honorable name for whom Mitya feels "such reverence that I dare not take her name in vain." And just as the question is raised how Adelaida could have married "such a worthless puny weakling" as Fyodor, so Mitya cannot understand that Katya should choose "a bug" like himself.

Mitya comes to Katya's attention by his wild exploits which set the whole town talking. He felt that this made him "a hero." But, he complains, Katya "didn't seem to feel it." When she first saw him, she "scarcely looked at me, and compressed her lips scornfully." Thereupon, Mitya plans revenge on Katya by humiliating her. The opportunity comes when Katya, desperately trying to save her father from dishonor, gets word from Mitya that he will give her the money if she comes to him alone, Mitya promising "to keep the secret religiously."

When Katya came to him, Mitya's first thought "was a—Karamazov one," to treat this "beauty" as a prostitute. But, she also appeared to him beautiful "in another way . . . because she was noble . . . in all the grandeur of her generosity and sacrifice for her father." In contrast, Mitya thought of himself as a little animal, "a bug . . . a venomous spider." His feelings towards her comprised a mixture of hatred and love. His hatred for Katya, he tells Alyosha, was such as he never felt for any other woman. But, it is the kind "which is only a hair's-breath from love, the maddest love."

Katya's visit roused a powerful sexual desire in Mitya. He was so excited by the "venomous thought" of possessing her that he nearly swooned "with suspense." Although Mitya gained mastery over his demon, his deep guilt begins at this point. It is as though by offering herself to him, Katya divined his hidden wish to enter into an impermissible relation with her. But Mitya curbed his desire, gave Katya the money (we should bear in mind that it is the money left him by his mother). After she left, Mitya drew his sword, nearly stabbing himself—"why, I don't know," he adds. Mitya's ability to control his Karamazov sensualism in this scene is a major test of his manhood and *foreshadows that he will resist the other temptation, that of killing his father.* He was held back from taking Katya by—perhaps also despite —the thought that she was ready to surrender herself for the sake of her father.

However, soon afterwards, Mitya yielded to another enticement. He took the 3000 rubles which Katya asked him to post and spent half of the sum on his mistress-figure, Grushenka (repeating his father's act in which Fyodor attempted to keep the dowry of Mitya's mother). At about the same time, he agreed to Katya's proposal or demand that they become engaged. (How this comes about, Dostoyevsky-Mitya does not make clear.)[33] For some unexplained reason, Mitya sends his brother Ivan to her who thereupon falls in love with Katya. This "one stupid thing," he says later to Alyosha, "may be the saving of us all now."[34]

Katya as the Possessive Mother

The identification of Katya with Mitya's mother lies above all in their attempt to dominate their men. Katya's authoritative character is suggested first by her outward appearance. Alyosha is struck "by the imperiousness, proud ease, and self-confidence of the haughty girl." Her love for Mitya is that of a commanding or pitying mother for a wayward son. She would be Mitya's "God," as she says:

> Let him feel ashamed of himself, let him be ashamed of other people's know-
> ing (that he had not returned the money he owed her), but not of my know-
> ing. He can tell God everything without shame. . . . I want to save him for
> ever. Let him forget me as his betrothed.

The Pan-Slavic Mother Goddess is worshipped for her fruit-bearing
and yielding qualities, not for her beauty. She is generally identified
with the good Russian earth and its earthy peasant folk. Katya, with
her aristocratic pride, stern virtue and possessiveness is a distortion of
this Eastern Mother Goddess. She cannot produce because she cannot
yield.[35]

Katya offers to sacrifice herself for Mitya. But she would *impose*
her sacrifice on him, *would be his Mother-Saviour by command*.[36]
Mitya senses that her love for him is "more like revenge." It is the
threat of the mother engulfing the son by her all-possessive love.

Mitya keeps speaking of his "debt" to Katya and of his "disgrace,"
referring to the fact that he had squandered 1500 of Katya's 3000
rubles on a spree with Grushenka. Mitya makes desperate efforts to
free himself from the "debt" to his "God"-mother. This, although Katya
herself does not press him for the money, indeed, acts as if she did not
care what he did with it. Furthermore, Mitya *could* get the money:
Alyosha offers him 2000 rubles and says that Ivan would give him another 1000. Moreover, he could borrow from Grusha. But no! Mitya is
obsessed with the feeling that *he can pay his "debt" to Katya only by
giving her the money which he has inherited from his mother and
which his father is withholding from him*. (Mitya's attempts to get the
money from Samsonov, Lyagavy, Madame Hohlakov are a wild goose
chase which invites failure.) And he wants no more than 3000 rubles,
although by his reckoning, his mother left him 28,000 rubles. If his
father would give him 3000 rubles, Mitya tells Alyosha, he would draw
his soul "out of hell:"

> Let him give me back only three out of the twenty-eight thousand. . . . For
> that three thousand—I give you my solemn word—I'll make an end of every-
> thing, and he shall hear nothing more of me. For the last time, I give him the
> chance to be a father.[37]

Grushenka: The Hetaira-Magdalene

From this perspective, Grushenka is the lesser of Mitya's burdens.
The conflict with his father over her is open and somewhat literal.[38]
Mitya is ready to accept all his rivals, except Fyodor. It is of some sig-
nificance that Mitya's attitude towards Grushenka is a transference of
Katya's towards him. As Katya was willing to accept any conditions if
Mitya would agree to be her husband, so he declares:

I'll be her (Grusha's) husband if she deigns to have me, and when lovers come, I'll go into the next room. I'll clean her friends' goloshes, blow up their samovar, run their errands.

However, Mitya does not want to force his love on Grusha. And, it is his hope that she may be the means by which he can free himself from Katya. Her soft, voluptuous, noiseless movements contrast with Katya's bold and vigorous step, her simple "childlike good nature" with Katya's complex ironic consciousness.

Mitya speaks of Grusha's "infernal curves." Yet, the story does not have a single erotic scene between them. Even at his "wedding" with Grusha at Mokroe, Mitya does not go beyond kissing his beloved. Dostoyesvky himself remarks that Grusha is Russian in that her beauty is only of the moment. Russian literature, as Berdyaev notes, does not know the erotic motifs of the West. It has no stories comparable to Tristan and Isolde or Romeo and Juliet. The attraction of Russian women (as of the Russian Mother Goddess) lies not in their seductiveness but in their earthy productivity.

Mitya's meeting with Grushenka at Mokroe is the poem of *The Brothers Karamazov*, the lovers' Dionysian song to life. For the first and only time, the two are united, at one with "the people," the Russian peasants, over whom they reign as King and Queen. It is their Eden where all is love, kindness, forgiveness and generosity. To the rhythm of children's songs, Mitya and his bride themselves act like children. Everything—down to the language and mood—is simple, elemental and earthy. Here, all are equal (except for the "foreigners," the Poles, who leave before the high point of the revel is reached).

But it is a Karamazov-Eden, and the celebration takes on the character of a delirious orgy. Mokroe is the scene of Mitya's and Grushenka's "wedding." It takes place at about the same time when the father is murdered and after Mitya thought he may have killed his surrogate-father Grigory. At this point, "society" steps in and arrests Mitya.

Like many of Dostoyevsky's women, Grushenka turns from the hetaira to the Madonna. Her transformation begins during Alyosha's visit when his kindness acts as a catalyst freeing her for a generous, overflowing love of the "soul," becoming "more loving than we," as Alyosha puts it. The change takes on a stable form after Mitya's arrest. Now, there were

signs of a spiritual transformation in her, and a steadfast, fine and humble determination that nothing could shake. . . . There was scarcely a trace of her former frivolity.

Through Grusha's love, Mitya declares, he has "become a man himself."

Mitya's Need of the Two Women

Although Mitya states that Grusha has made "a man" of him, it appears that she does not completely fulfill his needs. *She accepts Mitya as he is.* But Mitya also needs the censorious conscience, especially since his father lacks this quality altogether. Fyodor is a Satyr-figure, embodies an amorphous, chaotic sensualism intent solely on the pursuit of pleasure. And Mitya has only a distant relation to Father Zossima, Alyosha and Ivan, the religious and rational super-egos in the novel.

This may explain why Mitya cannot and does not want to free himself from Katya, why he kneels and prays "to Katya's image" in Grusha's presence. When she produces the letter which virtually condemns him, Mitya cries out:

> We've hated each other for many things, Katya, but I swear, I swear I loved you even while I hated you, and you didn't love me![39]

When, at the trial, Katya tells of her visit to Mitya and her bow to him, Mitya sobs: "Katya, why have you ruined me? . . . Now, I am condemned!" Does her recital reactivate his incestuous desire for her? Does her attempt to save him again put him in her "debt?"[40]

Even as Mitya turns towards Grushenka, he remains bound to Katya. Following the trial, he seems concerned only about seeing Katya. Alyosha tells her:

> He needs you particularly just now . . . he keeps asking for you. . . . He realizes that he has injured you beyond reckoning. . . . He said, if she refuses to come, I shall be unhappy all my life.

When Katya appears in the doorway of his prison cell,

> a scared look came into his face. He turned pale, but a timid, pleading smile appeared on his lips at once, and with an irresistible impulse he held out both hands to Katya.

And now, the two confess their mutual tie. Katya tells him:

> Love is over, Mitya! but the past is painfully dear to me. . . . I shall love you for ever, and you will love me; do you know that? Do you hear? Love me, love me all your life! she cried, with a quiver almost of menace in her voice.

Mitya replies: "I shall love you . . . all my life! So it will be, so it will always be. . . ." He pleads with her that she forgive him for having wanted to humiliate her, for his desire to have "the proud aristocratic girl" appear as "the hetaira." His plea is granted in Katya's final resigna-

272

tion, in her words to the rival Grushenka: "Forgive me. . . . Don't be anxious, I'll save him for you."

Dostoyevsky-Mitya divide the mother-figure into Katya and Grushenka. Mitya moves from attachment to the commanding goddess-mother to the yielding mistress-mother. In the end, he needs both: "the proud aristocratic girl and the 'hetaira.'" Grusha can only follow, but not guide. He needs both, moreover, for the mixture of elements in each. Grusha is submissive. Yet, in the scene with Katya, Mitya recognizes in her "the queen of all she-devils." Katya is defiant, haughty and domineering. Yet, Alyosha notes that her face can beam "with spontaneous good-natured kindliness, and direct warm-hearted sincerity." In the end, the two women-figures tend to merge.

Mitya almost marries Katya and nearly kills Fyodor. Like Hamlet, he wrestles with the demon driving him to violate the primary taboos. Mitya, too, shows no hesitation to "act"; except where it concerns Katya and Fyodor. His promise lies in a gradual awareness of the nature of his "debt" and guilt, awareness that his involvement with Katya was injurious to her and himself.[41]

Act III: Mitya—"Our Mother Russia"

While his brothers seem to stand for 'Europeanism' and 'the principles of the people,' he seems to represent Russia *as she is*. Oh, not all Russia, not all! God preserve us, if it were! Yet, here we have her, our mother Russia, the very scent and sound of her. Oh, he is spontaneous, he is a marvellous mingling of good and evil, he is a lover of culture and Schiller, yet brawls in taverns and plucks out the beards of his boon companions.

This characterization by the prosecutor at the trial points to Mitya as embodying the central problem of Russia. The plot of the novel has its pivot in his dilemma, and we are told that his trial has all Russia excited.

Mitya incorporates the most inclusive traits of the Karamazov character, combining the elements of the others: his father's primitive lust, Ivan's culture, Smerdyakov's resentment, and Alyosha's conscience (his "guardian angel" which holds him back from killing Fyodor). Yet, basic in Mitya's Karamazovism is his zest for life, his feeling that "There's no living without joy." Where Ivan's pro-contra logic paralyzes his action and passion, where Alyosha's all-embracing acceptance bars him from an active choice, and where Smerdyakov's passion can discharge itself only in his fits, Mitya dares live out his intoxication with life in a sensuous "Russian" manner. If one wants to become a man (Mitya quotes from Schiller's *Eleusinian Festival*):

273

> He must turn and cling forever
> To his ancient Mother Earth.

Mitya's earthiness is a promise that his passion may become productive.

In his talk with the Mysterious Visitor, Zossima makes the point that the real revolution must be psychological, must involve the heart of man. Mitya expresses a similar idea in discussing the problem of God's existence with Rakitin. He is greatly upset by Rakitin's theory that one is not to be blamed for murdering his father, that it all has to do with having been corrupted by the environment. But Mitya argues that if a man's actions are a resultant of social forces, then there is no standard for human conduct, man has no clear moral choice, and this means that God does not exist. It is this which worries Mitya:

> It's God that's worrying me. That's the only thing that's worrying me. What if He doesn't exist? What if Rakitin's right—that it's an idea made up by men? Then, if He doesn't exist, man is the chief of the earth, of the universe. Magnificent! Only how is he going to be good without God? . . . For whom is man going to love then? . . . Rakitin says . . . "You'd better think about the extension of civic rights, or of even keeping down the price of meat. You will show your love for humanity more simply and directly by that, than by philosophy." I answered him, "Well, but you, without a God, are more likely to raise the price of meat, if it suits you, and make a rouble on every kopeck." He lost his temper.

To Mitya, Rakitin's social-biologic determinism entails a denial of first principles. Its relativism opens the way for an egocentric morality which precludes a meaningful human quest. To believe in God means to believe in man and his strivings, means the integration of individual freedom within the framework of a universally valid morality. Mitya passionately rejects Rakitin's mechanical order in which he is but a product of a biologic and social system. This imbues him with the feeling that a "new man" has risen in him, and he can now exclaim that *he exists*:

> And I seem to have such strength in me now, that I think I could stand anything, any suffering, only to be able to say and to repeat to myself every moment, "I exist." In thousand of agonies—I exist. I'm tormented on the rack —but I exist!

In this exultant feeling, Mitya is freer in prison than the "other-directed" characters in contemporary literature.[42]

Mitya's conception of freedom avoids becoming a mystic individualism due to his societal impulse. When Ivan discusses the sufferings of children, he is raising primarily a metaphysical-theologic problem. But, for Mitya, suffering is a concrete social phenomenon and he translates it into the suffering of the exploited Russian mother and her child. During the preliminary investigation, Mitya falls asleep and dreams:

> He was driving somewhere in the steppes . . . and a peasant was driving him in a cart with a pair of horses, through snow and sleet.

He sees the land desolate, the peasant women and their little children thin and wan. Mitya doesn't understand why they are so dark from misery and in his dream cries out: "Why don't they feed the babe?":

> And he felt that, though his questions were unreasonable and senseless, yet he wanted to ask just that, and he had to ask it just in that way. And he felt that a passion of pity, such as he had never known before, was rising in his heart, that he wanted to cry, that he wanted to do something for them all, so that the babe should weep no more, so that the dark-faced, dried-up mother should not weep, that no one should shed tears again from that moment, and he wanted to do it at once, at once, regardless of all obstacles, with all the recklessness of the Karamazovs.

Later, he tells Alyosha that it's "for the babe" that he is going to prison:

> Because we are all responsible for all. For all the "babes," for there are big children as well as little children. All are "babes." I go for all, because some-one must go for all. I didn't kill father, but I've got to go. I accept it.

Here, Mitya moves from concern with himself to concern for others. He would step out of the Russian *troika* to save its big and little children from poverty and suffering, would rid the state of its social disease.

Mitya's development approximates the stages of the Rankian hero: His family claims to have an ancient and noble lineage; his conception may be said to have been difficult in that his mother "seems to have been the only woman who made no particular appeal" to his father's senses. When Mitya was three years old, he was abandoned by both his mother and father, later by parent-surrogates, and rescued by Grigory, the faithful servant. He then returns to challenge his father on the heritage his mother left him and on the woman for whom they compete. However, unlike Smerdyakov, he has a "guardian angel" who keeps him from murdering his father and he gradually develops into a kind of culture hero, thirsting for "reformation and renewal." Although he is condemned for an act which he did not commit, he accepts his ordeal for the sake of man, for the sake of "all the 'babes'."

Mitya is the hero of the book because he *learns* most from his trial. And he learns most because, more than the others, he descends to and goes through the Satanic depths. Where Ivan would meet the human situation by dialectic, Smerdyakov by the brute act, Alyosha by faith and submission, Mitya grapples with it by *Praxis*.[43] He experiences something of a catharsis by *emotionally living through* the Russian inferno and Purgatory. Mitya alone is not emasculated by his father-authorities and is the living hope that the Pan-Slavic values of communality and individual freedom might be re-created.

Epilogue: The Boys

The Brothers Karamazov ends with an account of the meeting between Alyosha and the boys. Here, the problem of the Karamazovs reappears on another level, with Kolya and Ilusha as possible future heroes. Mark Twain also saw the hope for America in her youth, the embodiment of America's native values of freedom and equality. Kolya exhibits the self-laceration and reckless daring of the Karamazovs, the passion of Mitya, the intellectualism of Ivan; he has his Smerdyakov (in the errand boy to whom he suggests killing the goose) and, at the end, reveals something of Alyosha's forgiving nature.

Yet, the boys are not intended to represent a repetition of the Karamazovs, for Ilusha reverses the trend. He loves his father who, in turn, is ready to sacrifice himself for his son. In reconciling Ilusha and Kolya, Alyosha would save the Russian Boys from Rakitin's Western materialistic "socialism," save them for the Slavic principle of *sobornost*. In his speech by the stone of Ilusha's grave, Alyosha calls on the twelve boys gathered there to "be generous and brave like Ilusha, clever, brave and generous like Kolya . . . as modest, as clever and sweet as Kartashov." He emphasizes the importance of good childhood memories:

> there is nothing higher and stronger and more wholesome and good for life in the future than some good memory, especially a memory of childhood, of home. People talk to you a great deal about education, but some good, sacred memory, preserved from childhood, is perhaps the best education.

However, in Dostoyevsky's Russia, children were abandoned or outraged. Following his dream of a happy age, Stavrogin notices a tiny red spider and sees Matrojosha, the little girl he violated,—sunken, fevrish, her undeveloped body threatening him helplessly with her little fists. The final two chapters of *The Brothers Karamazov* likewise point to Dostoyevsky's reservations about the possibility of a human paradise. The first depicts the continuation of Mitya's plight; the second pictures the helpless little fists of the boys, helpless even in the case of Ilusha. For Ilusha is only a prayer on the part of Dostoyevsky—his dead body miraculously does *not* decompose.

Dostoyevsky saw no clear way for the resolution of the Russian trial. He transformed his criminals into saints with apocalyptic suddenness and Dionysian unrestraint precisely because the "natural" way was not available in his Russia. The country was ruled by an oppressive patriarchy and the Russian earth-mother was supplanted by a willful protectress. Dostoyevsky's Katya, along with Tolstoy's Anna Karenina, are analogous to the power-driven women, such as Strindberg's Laura and O'Neill's Lavinia. Hence, Dostoyevsky's heroes remain wildly rebellious. Raskolnikov continues to be a "dissenter" in Siberia—in his notes, the author has him planning a new crime—, and Mitya tells Alosha at the end: "I am not ready! I am not able to resign myself!"

Viewed as a whole, Dostoyevsky's work pictures the tension between the old Eastern myth of communal equality and the Western quest for individualism and freedom. The tension is expressed in the convulsive form of Dostoyevsky's novels, the precipitateness of the action, the wild swinging between extremes. Dostoyevsky finished none of his major novels and his characters never "finish" anything; when they reach the stage of betrothal, they run away from the altar, as Stefan Zweig observes. They plunge into the lowest depths in quest of the whole or of God. But this deity is never envisioned as in Job or Dante. Dostoyevsky's characters have no guide, act without "reason" in a bottomless underground in which the "first cause" remains unknown.

Yet, the widespread notion that Dostoyevsky found a value in suffering as such is misleading. He distinguished between characters, such as Father Ferapont and Lise for whom asceticism and torture are final values and those who suffer for an idea—the Zossimas and Mityas, the Raskolnikovs and Shatovs. Raskolnikov tells Sonya:

> They say it is necessary for me to suffer! What's the object of these senseless sufferings? Shall I know any better what they are for, when I am crushed by hardships and idiocy, and weak as an old man after twenty years' penal servitude?

Dostoyevsky did think that his hosanna had to come "through the great furnace of doubt," and that to transform the world, we must first "go through the period of isolation," as the mysterious visitor tells Father Zossima. Still despite its agonizing process, we feel the affirmative mood in Dostoyevsky's work because his people embrace the sensuousness of life. The Russia of his day was losing the memory of ancient Slavic values. *The Brothers Karamazov* would re-create their symbolic import and thus save them for all time.

NOTES

1. Russia's historic origins are obscure, since the records are oral. The patriarchal family developed later, as the Slavs moved north and the work of clearing woods, etc. fell to the men. Evidence pointing to the matriarchate as the earliest form can be found in M. Kovalevsky, *Modern Customs and Ancient Laws of Russia* (London, 1891), and in E. Elnett, *Historic Origin and Social Development of Family Life in Russia* (New York, 1926).

    The subsequent discussion draws on N. A. Berdyaev's *The Russian Idea* (New York, 1948), F. Fedotov's *The Russian Religious Mind* (2 vols.; Cambridge, Mass., 1946-1966), and Sir John Maynard's *Russia in Flux* (London, 1946). For related discussion, see L. Niederle, *Manuel de l'antiquité Slave* (2 vols.; Paris, 1923-26), F. Dvornik, *The Slavs: Their Early History and Civilization* (Boston, 1956), Adolph Stender-Petersen, *Russian Studies* (Copenhagen, 1956). Petersen emphasizes that Russia's pagan religion was that of "of the tillers of the soil." He refers to the concept in Russian folklore of "Mother moist earth" (*Mat' syra zeml'a*). Yet, he holds that the pre-historic Russian community was "essentially patriarchal."

2. Cf. V. Ivanov's *Freedom and the Tragic Life* (London, 1952). In the absence of a good *pater familias*, Dostoyevsky saw the Russian woman as "our only great hope, one of the pledges of our revival." ("The Pushkin Speech" in *The Diary of a Writer* [New York, 1954], pp. 959-1010.)

3. This "choric" mentality (Berdyaev's term) appears in the use of generic names: Strangers are addressed as "Mother," "Father," "Brother," "Uncle," etc.

4. See B. D. Grekov, *The Culture of Kiev Rūs* (Moscow, 1947) and N. K. Gudzy, *History of Early Russian Literature* (New York, 1949).

5. In his *Russian Folklore* (New York, 1950), Y. M. Sokolov notes the role of folklore and legend in Gorky's life, quoting from Gorky's essay on literature:

    ". . . by far the deepest and most vivid, the most artistically fashioned types of heroes are created by folklore, by the oral creations of the working people. . . . The better we come to know the past, the more easily, the more deeply and joyfully we shall understand the great significance of the present which we are creating."

    Sokolov's study also shows that Soviet ballads invoke ancient figures, such as Ilya Murom, Stepan Razin, leader of the peasants who revolted in the seventeenth century. See also T. V. Popova, *The Russian Folk Song* (Moscow, 1946).

6. In this old Slavic community, rights in land (although not the land itself) were held in common. According to B. H. Sumner (*A Short History of Russia* [New York, 1949]), the *mir* organized periodic redistribution of land "in accordance with either working strength . . . or the number of 'eaters' in the family," with the village meeting making all decisions with regard to cultivation of the land. Prior to the introduction of money-economy, there was economic equality among the members. Summing up, Maynard states that the *mir* was "an agent of equalization; and equality made a stronger appeal than freedom."

The *mir* persisted even after Peter the Great and his followers consolidated feudalism and was used by the centralized state as a convenient means for collecting taxes from the whole community.

The spirit of the *mir* penetrated pre-modern Russian life which was organized into "big families," or clans which encompassed several generations and included adopted children: "Each member of the household was not an individual but merely a component part of a collective individuality — the family to which he belonged." Even in its patriarchal stage, the clan was "monarchical in its form but democratic in its substance," with the Common Council at the head of all. The whole spelled "a sort of family communism." Cf. E. Elnett, *Origin and Social Development of Family Life*, pp. 4 ff. To Fedotov, the Russian nation "could once be thought of as an immense *gens* or *rod*, of whom the Tsar was the father." Where the Greek Eleusian mysteries promised immortality to the individual soul, primitive Russian paganism considered the individual only as a transient moment in the eternal life of the *rod*. *Russian Religious Mind*, pp. 16, 19. See also G. T. Robinson, *Rural Russia under the Old Regime* (New York, 1949).

7. *Russian Religious Mind*, pp. 33, 35, 55 ff. Aside from the "black" clergy which practiced celibacy, orthodox theology does not feature original sin and atonement. In Maynard's formulation, this prepared the way for the Communist "vision of the Kingdom of God *upon earth*," with communism stressing the service of Man. On the differences between Orthodoxy and Dostoyevsky's religious concepts, see N. Gorodetzky, *The Humiliated Christ in Modern Russian Thought* (London, 1938).

8. Translations are by Constance Garnett, the Modern Library Giant edition of *The Brothers Karamazov*.

    As the official church became subservient to Tsarism, religion "became increasingly divorced from the organized panoply of the Orthodox Church." (Cf. B. H. Sumner, *Short History of Russia*, p. 164.) Yet, we should note democratic features: a collective synod, instead of a Pope, and the teaching that the Son is not separated from the Father and the Holy Ghost. Furthermore, the Bible was brought closer to the masses in that the liturgy came from Slavic Bulgaria and the common people were able to pray in an idiom near to their own. It should also be noted that the saints of old Russia were laymen. Fedotov stresses the social mindedness and the pagan-Christian symbiosis in their faith, in contrast to Byzantine self-mortification. See his Introduction to *A Treasury of Russian Spirituality* (London, 1950).

9. *The Russian Idea*, pp. 250 ff.

10. In early Russian history, woman was an economic-social partner of the man and the *Bylini* picture her as bold, strong and dauntless. While she often chooses and captures the groom, she is also a symbol of love and peace. With the development of the patriarchate and under the influence of Byzantine Christianity, the values of virginity, asceticism and passivity come to the fore. In the nineteenth century, the revolt against woman being treated as a chattel

expressed itself in George Sandism where the woman cried out for freedom, giving up the responsibility of educating her children.

11. Here is the context for Dostoyevsky's sympathy with the criminal. Father Zossima in *The Brothers Karamazov* is especially devoted to the greatest sinners.

12. To be sure, some, such as Khomiakov, thought that a form of monarchy was necessary to fulfill the Russian mission. They apotheosized the national past including the pre-Petrine social system. Here, they were at one with nineteenth century German Romanticism. However, they were opposed to both Catholicism which Khomiakov called "an unnatural tyranny" and to Protestantism which he called "an unprincipled revolt."

13. Turgenev's recollection of Belinsky is apropos: In the course of a heated debate, someone suggested that they eat. To this, Belinsky exclaimed: "We have not yet decided the question of the existence of God and you want to eat!"

14. This opposition was also manifested in the populist, terrorist and Marxist movements of the time. See Hans Kohn, *The Mind of Modern Russia* (New Brunswick, N. J., 1955), A. Yarmolinsky, *Road to Revolution* (London, 1957).

15. See Dostoyevsky's attack on the West in *Winter Notes of Summer Impressions* (New York, 1955). Dostoyevsky was particularly outraged by child labor in the West, and thought that its freedom was only for those who had the means and power to satisfy it. Western Europe, he wrote, lives on "the personal principle, the principle of separateness, intense self-preservation, selfish labor, self-determination of one's ego." Quoted in A. Yarmolinsky's *Dostoyevsky. A Study of his Ideology* (New York, 1921), p. 28. See also Ernest J. Simmons, *Dostoyevsky* (New York, 1940), pp. 289, 331-332. Even Turgenev who lived much of his life in the West was critical of Westernism. In his biography of Turgenev, Yarmolinsky refers to one of his tirades: "The Latins were *hommes de la loi*, in whose veins ran the milk of the Roman she-wolf, sticklers for the conventions, conformers to a code, martyrs to an artificial sense of honor. The Russians, on the contrary, were *hommes de l'humanite*, possessed of a warmer social consciousness, irreverent toward man-made rules, rooting for fundamentals, unafraid of the crude, the bare, the simple."

16. In his speech, Dostoyevsky idealized Pushkin as the incarnation of the common Russian folk. Indeed, Pushkin is regarded by many as the most typical Russian figure of the rootless "wanderer" who is to be redeemed by the Russian woman. On the Pushkin cult, see Marc Slonim, *The Epic of Russian Literature* (New York, 1950).

17. Dostoyevsky, *Letters from the Underworld*, trans., C. J. Hogarth (London and New York, 1913), pp. 27, 34.

18. Marc Slonim (*Three Loves of Dostoyevsky* [New York, Toronto, 1955]), suggests that his pedophelia may go back to the relationship with his younger sisters who were the only females he knew up to the age of sixteen. The two women Dostoyevsky loved most passionately, Polina and Anna, were some twenty years younger than he.

19. Dostoyevsky's sexual difficulties with Anna are dramatically indicated when on the bridal night, he suffered an epileptic attack. We should also note his strange attitude towards her former lover Vergunov. Following his marriage to

Anna, Vergunov became "dearer than a brother" to him and, despite his own
financial straits, Dostoyevsky borrowed money to help him. There may be a
connection here with his feeling towards his own brother Michael. While waiting to be executed, Dostoyevsky wrote him: "I thought of you, brother, and of
yours; and at the last moment you alone were in my thoughts, and then I realized how much I loved you, beloved brother!" And from Siberia: "I dream of
you every night." He asked Baron Wrangel to write what his brother thinks
of him, adding: "He used to love me passionately. . . . Has his feeling towards
me grown cold?"

For a portrait of Dostoyevsky as revealed in his letters, see Jessie Coulson,
Dostoyevsky. A Self-Portrait (London, 1962).

20. In a letter (to S. D. Janofsky in 1872), Dostoyevsky wrote that he was "*sick
in mind* (I realize it now) *before my journey to Siberia,* where I was cured."
Freud argues that if this refers to his seizures, then that "would merely sub-
stantiate the view that his sezures were his punishment. He did not need them
any longer when he was being punished in another way." Dostoyevsky writes
from Siberia that he "had some epileptic fits." Cited in André Gide, *Dostoyevsky* (Norfolk, Connecticut, 1923), pp. 35, 62.

21. Quoted by Sir John Maynard, *Russia in Flux*, p. 96.

22. Mitya calls him Silenus and he is also referred to as Aesop. In his essay "Dreams
and Myth" (*Clinical Papers,* Vol. II [New York, 1955]), Karl Abraham quotes
from old Indian myths where the drink of the gods is considered equivalent
to semen and to Creation (the birth of Dionysus, the God of wine, shows the
same identification between drink and creation). He notes that wine is often
used as a symbol of procreation or fertilization.

23. In the case of Lizaveta, Fyodor exhibits something akin to "grace": Had he
not acted out his buffoonery, Lizaveta might never have gotten to know moth-
erhood.

24. They may also be seen as approximating the four elements: the sub-soil in
Smerdyakov, fire in Mitya, air-water in Ivan-Alyosha.

25. Ivan loosens Alyosha's faith in the divine order of things, and provides the
logic for Smerdyakov's murder of the father.

26. According to the Inquisitor, the Western Church has reversed the Christ who
rejected the devil's three temptations.

27. Cf. Simmons, *Dostoyevsky*, pp. 376, 377.

28. Dostoyevsky's position towards political radicalism is ambiguous, especially
after his Siberian imprisonment. But, there is no ambiguity about Dostoyevsky's affirmation of rebellion as a *psychological* attitude. Simmons' comment
is here relevant: "The more he strives to make Verkhovenski (*The Possessed*)
the symbol of a hated doctrine, the more the character divests itself of the stuff
of reality." He is "merely a caricature of a revolutionist."

29. Mark Kanzer: "The Vision of Father Zossima" (*American Imago,* VIII, No. 4
[1951]). Dr. Kanzer notes first that Fyodor and Zossima meet their ends on
successive nights. He also points out that Alyosha's released impulses in the
scene with Grushenka are predominantly oral—craving for food and drink. He
next beholds Christ converting water into wine, "as though to say that food

may be obtained from the body of the father as well as the mother." And, as Alyosha clutches and kisses the earth, we find symbols of "bisexual gratification." The disgust aroused in Alyosha by the odor of the monk's corpse "is familiar to analysts as a defense against the desire of oral incorporation." Furthermore, "we find little difficulty in recognizing, in Alyosha's swoon, his falling to the ground, his writhing and his ecstasy, phenomena of epilepsy; his ambilavent religiosity, suppressed criminal impulses and hallucinatory experiences represent familiar psychic concomitants."

30. In his relation to Ivan, Smerdyakov is the submissive "female" partner, waiting for a "sign" from "the God Almighty." Smerdyakov is fond of cooking and fastidious in his dress. When Fyodor suggests getting him a wife, Smerdyakov becomes pale with anger. His epileptic discharge seems to be his sole sexual expression. After Fyodor learns of Smerdyakov's epilepsy, he begins to show some kindness towards him. Does Fyodor sense in Smerdyakov's fits a kinship to his own distorted sexuality?

31. Ivan's persistent questioning of the devil and of Smerdyakov (in his three interviews with each) is an ironic uncovering of his own function in the murder of his father, analogous to Oedipus' persistant questioning of the Herdsmen and of Tiresias. There is an analogy between Ivan's attitude towards Smerdyakov and the Grand Inquisitor's towards the people: Both have erected a rationalistic scheme to circumscribe the thoughts of others. The difference is that, for Dostoyevsky, Western Caesarism is a foreign drop of blood in the Russian Ivan. Where the cardinal wants the masses to remain subservient, Ivan unconsciously wants Smerdyakov to rebel.

32. Mitya, in particular can be likened to Oedipus and Hamlet. He too is more intent on uncovering the truth than is anyone else. In doing so, he likewise arouses suspicion against himself and contributes most to his condemnation. Father Zossima's kneeling before Mitya (seen by a member of his order as the elder's sensing that Mitya is contemplating the murder of his father) is a kind of warning, such as the oracle gives Sophocles' Oedipus. Mitya's celebration with Grushenka at Mokroe (it is their "wedding") takes place after his near-attempt to kill his father and after he thought he had killed his surrogate-father Grigory.

33. Dostoyevsky offers but scanty material for Katya's motivation. He does suggest some identification between Katya's father and Mitya. Both were lieutenants, are in disgrace and "gamble" away their honor and that of the family. Katya conceives her role to be that of saving both, first her father and later Mitya. Is her offering herself to Mitya a form of revenge, an acting out of a masochistic sexual fantasy?

34. A related "strategy" occurs in Thomas Mann's *Doctor Faustus* where Leverkühn sends a friend to woo Marie, whereupon the friend and Marie fall in love with each other.

35. Katya would also impose her will on Grushenka. She invites the rival to her house and would have her be "an angel" who will give up Mitya because that

is best for him. Alyosha feels that Katya has fastened on Mitya because "a character like Katerina Ivanovna's must dominate, and she could dominate some one like Dmitry, and never a man like Ivan."

36. In this sense, there is something to the point made in Komarowitsch's *Die Urgestalt der Brüder Karamasoff* (München, 1928) that Katya's love demands the same unlimited subservience as the Grand Inquisitor's. Komarowitsch refers to Dostoyevsky's comment in his Notebooks: "Katya: Rome, unique objet de mon ressentiment." The line is taken from Corneille's *Horace* and is spoken by a heroine who curses her native land. Incidentally, Grusha calls Katya "mother" (in a derogatory sense). Garnett regrettably translates the Russian word *matj* as "my girl."

37. The number three is a leading "motif" in *The Brothers Karamazov* as it is in other mythopoesis. In Dostoyevsky's novel, it also has a diabolic sign (the violence of the three brothers, the abandonment of Mitya when he was three years old, the 3000 rubles, the three blows with which Smerdyakov kills Fyodor, Ivan's three interviews with Smerdyakov and the devil's three visits with Ivan) and its resurrectory sign (Mitya's three ordeals, his arrest on the third day of his struggle to save himself).

38. As Fyodor would buy Grusha with 3000 rubles, so Mitya offers the Pole 3000 rubles if he would release her. Grusha herself is at first attracted to or binds herself to father-figures: Samsonov, the Pole and Fyodor, whom she does not discourage at first.

39. Mitya himself is not aware of his complex involvement with Katya. She is, indeed, the great "secret" of his life and of the novel. She comes to Mitya secretly, asks him to send off the 3000 rubles secretly; Mitya would keep the fact secret that he spent half of her money on Grushenka. Above all, the nature of his "debt" to Katya is Mitya's "great secret" and "disgrace."

40. Earlier Mitya declared that what he wants is "to have done with her and with father!" It seems to Mitya that he could be freed from Fyodor if his father returned the heritage his mother left him. Would Mitya be getting his "mother" back from father in this way and thus be liberated from the temptation to kill him? And would he be released from the "debt" to the surrogate mother by giving her his own mother's money?

41. For a note on Freud's Analysis of a Katya Figure in Zweig's Story, see Appendix VI.

42. The point of Dostoyevsky's long account of the trial seems to be this: Both lawyers argue "pro and contra," like Ivan, both missing Mitya's "angel." Their primary interest is not Mitya, or "the babe," but to get votes from the public.

43. In his notes on *Crime and Punishment* ("Idea of the Novel"), Dostoyevsky wrote: ". . . life's calling and consciousness (i.e., the immediately-felt in body and spirit, i.e., in the whole vital process) is acquired by experience *pro* and *contra* which must be felt in the process of living." (Quoted by Simmons, *Dostoyevsky*, p. 150.)

The Marxist Homage
to Creative Labor
Pelle the Conqueror

THE MOST PROMINENT argument in Marx's theory has an oppositional character. It would unmask metaphysical, religious and other absolutes as maneuvers by which ruling groups have veiled their ideologies. To reverse this strategy, Marx placed emphasis on change and historical process, on class-truths and class-values.

Marx did not face the problem of how his own system transcended such historical limits and escaped being another type of ideology. Yet, an examination of his work, especially his earlier writings, reveals that Marxism does contain certain universal categories, centering in the idea of man and of human labor. To be radical, Marx declared, means to go to the roots of things, and the root of things, he added, is man. This thought has implications for the place of history in man's development.

Marx regarded history as "a nightmare on the brain of the living." Yet, commenting on the seizure of power by Louis Bonaparte, Marx wrote that every revolution was accompanied by the "conjuring up of the dead." He realized that man does not make history by himself, but "in circumstances directly found, given and transmitted from the past." Here, Marx referred to those elements in history which persist as lasting values. This idea is specifically applied to art and culture.

Contrary to some interpretations, Marx and Engels did not identify culture with its passing social basis. Engels acknowledged in *Anti Dühring* that seminal thoughts arose in class societies. He stated that the broad outlines of the dialectic method were discovered by the early Greek physicists, were analyzed by Aristotle, and that Descartes, Spinoza, Diderot, Rousseau and Hegel were its brilliant exponents. Marx had high praise for Shakespeare, Goethe, Hegel, Balzac, and particularly for Greek art and mythology. In his *The Critique of Political Economy* Marx notes that Greek art and mythology could not exist under modern technological conditions. Jupiter, he notes, could do nothing against the lightning rod and Hermes against the Crédit mobilier. But, Marx continues:

> the difficulty does not consist in understanding that Greek art and the epic are bound up with the well known forms of social development. The difficulty consists in understanding that they still continue to give us artistic pleasure, and in a certain sense preserve the value of a standard and an unattainable example.

Greece, he writes, is the most beautiful example of the childhood of human society, and possesses "an eternal charm." He likens them to children "who have the wisdom of old age," adding: "Many of the ancient peoples belong to this category. The Greeks were normal children."[1]

In the Marxist system proper, the mythic category is labor which it regards as "an eternal necessity imposed by nature itself," one that is independent of all forms of society.

In his discussion of Russian folklore, Sokolov traces the Marxist position on the interrelationship of work, rhythm and speech to Karl Bücher's *Arbeit und Rhythmus* (Leipzig, 1924). According to Bücher, the decisive factor in the rise and development of art was the rhythm of work which evoked the rhythm of bodily movement, melody and speech: "The sounds of speech . . . were, originally, an imitation of sounds, and reproduced the sounds of work and of rhythmicized emotional exclamations." In time, culture and language lost their direct connection with the laboring process; yet the origins of poetic creation still are evident "in so far as rhythm and melody play an important part in it; and in oral reproduction, where gesture and movement are also factors."[2]

Marxian anthropology centers in Engels' notion that labor is

> the primary basic condition for all human existence, and this to such an extent that, in a sense, we have to say that labour created man himself.

Similarly, according to Marx,

> labour is a necesary condition for the existence of the human race, and one that is independent of all forms of society; it is an eternal necessity imposed by nature itself, without which there can be no material exchanges between man and nature, and therefore no life.

The point is also made by Gorky:

> For the main hero of our books we must take labour, that is, the human be-
> ing organized by the labour process . . . the human being who in turn orga-
> nizes labour to be easier and more productive, elevating it to the degree of
> art. We must learn to think of labour as creative effort.[3]

Labor is Marx's universal constant and its process is the lever for the
changes and developments in man's biological nature. And, since labor
entails cooperation, it converts the animal herd into human society. By
virtue of the laborer's close and sensuous handling of materials, he has
the most direct relation to the material aspect of reality. Beyond this,
he molds and forms the raw material, that is, gives it an individual form.
Herein, the laborer is something of a creative artist who develops his
own "slumbering powers:"

> By thus acting on the external world and changing it, he at the same time
> changes his own nature. He develops his slumbering powers and compels
> them to act in obedience to his sway. . . . We presuppose labour in a form
> that stamps it as exclusively human. . . . What distinguishes the worst archi-
> tect from the best of bees is this, that the architect raises his structure in
> imagination before he erects it in reality.[4]

Viewed in terms of the structure of the myth, the first act in the
Marxist drama is the stage of primitive communism. But, it is primarily
concerned with Act Two in which private ownership and exploitation
have produced alienation in which man is estranged from his tool, his
work, his fellowmen, and finally from himself as a whole human being.
Class divisions and divisions of labor make the worker

> a cripple, a monster, by forcing him to develop some highly specialized dex-
> terity at the cost of a world of productive impulses and faculties . . . the in-
> dividual himself is split up, is transformed into the automatic motor of some
> partial operation. Thus is realized the foolish fable of Menenius Agrippa,
> which depicted a human being as nothing more than a fragment of his own
> body.

Even where the worker does not suffer economic servitude, he is still a
slave. For, in being used as a tool, he is determined by his external nature. The implication of Marx's argument in "The Fetichism of Commodities" in *Capital* is that the mystique of exchange value, particularly
money, converts qualities into quantities and man into a profit-pro-
ducing commodity. A man's value now consists not in what he is, but
in what he has, not in what he gives, but in what he acquires.

Although man is conditioned by his history, he can still become its
master and make it his own. Marx and Engels rejected the notion that
man is at the mercy of natural, divine or historical powers:

> History does nothing. . . . It is rather man—real living man—who acts, pos-
> sesses and fights in everything. It is by no means "History" which uses man
> as a means to carry out its ends as if it were a person apart; rather History
> is nothing but the activity of man in pursuit of his ends.[5]

The means for this transformation lie in social consciousness. The Spinozistic axiom "Man thinks" is transposed by way of the Hegelian logic into the social realm and becomes a philosophy of conscious activity leading to liberation from "external purposiveness." Control over economic and social determinants spells human freedom. The ultimate aim is not only economic, social and political emancipation. Freedom, for Marx, lies "beyond the sphere of purely material production," and begins with "that development of human power which is its own end."[6]

The working class is the lever for human freedom because it becomes conscious of the fact that class divisions dehumanize not only the oppressed but also the oppressor: "The owning class and the proletariat represent the same human self-alienation. . . . The former possesses through it the *illusion* of human existence." In *True Humanism*, Jacques Maritain pays tribute to Marx's moral indictment of capitalism. Marx, he says,

> had a profound intuition, an intuition which is to my eyes the great lightning
> flash of truth which traverses all his work, of the conditions of heteronomy
> and loss of freedom produced in the capitalist world by wage-slavery, and
> of the dehumanization with which the possessing classes and the proletariat
> alike are simultaneously stricken. (pp. 38, 39)

The working class aims not only for the abolition of the capitalist order, but of itself as a dictatorship, realizing that it can be redeemed only "through the redemption of the whole of humanity." Philosophy, Marx wrote, "cannot realize itself without abolishing the proletariat; the proletariat cannot abolish itself without realizing philosophy." In these formulations, Marx attempted to fuse class and classless values, the particular and the universal, existence and essence.

Is the classless society Marxism's third and final act? Does the revolutionary dialectic cease to function under communism? Will modern specialization which, as Marx charged, transformed the worker into an "automatic motor" no longer present the same threat? Will tragedy be eliminated when economic-social conflicts no longer exist?

Marx and Engels did not seem to rule out the need for stages beyond socialism. In *Ludwig Feuerbach* (New York, 1934), Engels stated that each historic stage must be succeeded by a higher form which, in turn, will also decay. And Maxim Gorky even paid tribute to the perennial revolutionary temper, saying that the task is to go beyond the existing to "the desirable, the potential," adding that thus:

> We arrive at that romanticism which is the basis of all myths and which is of great value because it favors the birth of a revolutionary attitude towards reality, i.e. of an attitude that wants to change the world. (*Literature and Life* [London, 1946], p. 138.)

There remains the wide realm of natural necessity, of decay and death, disappointments and frustrations which cannot be eliminated by "practically changing the world." Indeed, when man can no longer attribute human suffering to avoidable social maladjustments, then tragedy emerges pure and absolute.

PELLE AS MYTHIC HERO

The idea of the hero implies an exceptional status differentiating him from the mass. Yet, all our culture heroes are "democratic" in that their quest is in the interests of the others. All mythopoeic heroes from Prometheus, Oedipus and Aeneas to Hamlet, Faust and Mitya Karamazov rebel against a diseased state and would revitalize their society. Yet, with the exceptions of Don Quixote, Ahab and Huck Finn, they come from the upper social strata.

Martin Andersen Nexö's *Pelle the Conqueror* (New York, 1913) is the first major epic in which the hero arises from the ranks of labor. At the same time, the work pictures him as representing the universally human. Pelle is drawn neither as a pitiful victim nor as an invincible superman, neither as a class-angled automaton nor as a free existentialist, but as the bearer of human values which are worthy of being redeemed.

The novel interweaves Pelle's development with the history of labor—his childhood and adolescence with feudalism and the guild system, his early manhood with capitalism, his marriage and family life with the establishment of a socialist cooperative. Beneath the personal and the historic run mythic motifs: Pelle is the dangerous child who rebels against his rotten state and engages in a journey to find the answer to the problem of the social disease.[7] In his quest, Pelle becomes a sacrifice, with the promise that his idea will be carried forward by others. But in this myth of labor, evil authority is balanced by good authority, embodied in father Lasse and Marie. And Pelle's disciples, Dreyer and Morton, are not mere followers, but re-creators of his social idea.

Pelle's Boyhood is his Eden-state. He is at one with the world of nature and of man, drawing nourishment and strength from the earth and the sea which offer comfort and stability. To be sure, this Eden is set in nineteenth century Denmark, still governed by the vestiges of feudalism. Yet, the book is a joyous affirmation of life, of nature and man:

> It was so good to be here. . . . Every sound was like a mother's caress, and everything was a familiar toy, with which a bright world could be built. . . . Pelle's childhood had been happy by virtue of everything: it had been a song mingled with weeping. Weeping falls into tones as well as joy, and heard from a distance it becomes a song. And as Pelle gazed down upon his childhood's world, they were only pleasant memories that gleamed toward him through the bright air. . . . He had seen enough of hardship and misfortune, but had come well out of everything: nothing had harmed him. With a child's voracity he had found nourishment in it all; and now he stood here, healthy and strong—equipped with the Prophets, the Judges, the Apostles, the Ten Commandments and one hundred and twenty hymns! and turned an open, perspiring victor's brow toward the world.

The memory of this world remains the leading reference of the epic which is dominated by the seasonal metaphor. At the end, Pelle returns to the land, bringing with him knowledge of the social barriers which disturb this world and of the tragic surd in the human situation itself.[8]

NOTES

1. Quoted by Y. M. Sokolov in his *Russian Folklore*, pp. 30-31.
2. H. Werner, *Die Ursprünge der Lyrik* (München, 1924), cited in Sokolov, *Russian Folklore*.
3. See Engels, "Dialectics and Nature" in *Marx-Engels Archiv*, II (New York, 1940); Marx, *Capital*, Vol. I; (New York, 1929); Maxim Gorky, "New People" in *Soviet Literature*, VI (1949), 119.
4. *Capital*, section on "The Labour Process or the Production of Use-Values and the Capitalistic Character of Manufacture."
5. Engels, "Dialectics and Nature," p. 165.
6. This concept brings Marxism near to the classical tradition of Plato, Aristotle, Spinoza and Hegel. What differentiates Marxism from these thinkers is its stress on the social means for bringing this goal about. See Vernon Venable's *Human Nature: The Marxian View* (New York, 1945).
7. There are suggestions of parricide in Pelle's neglect of father Lasse and the little mother Marie.
8. For a detailed discussion of the novel, see the chapter, "Pelle the Conqueror" in my *Three Ways of Modern Man* (New York, 1937. Reprinted by Kraus Reprint Corporation, New York, 1969).

The French Myth of the
Living Social Chain
André Gide's *Theseus*

FRENCH LITERATURE has not produced a mythopoeic hero comparable to the Greek Prometheus, the Roman Aeneas and the Italian Dante, the Spanish Don Quixote, the German Faust or the American Ahab. Its classical stature consists less in outstanding single works by individual authors than in collective products of schools and academies. The myth of the hero is not treated with the solemnity which the Teutonic tradition accords Faust and Siegfried, but—where the theme of the exceptional personality is projected, as in Gargantua—is approached in a comic mood. Aided by a fortunate historical development which allowed for early consolidation of the nation and its language, French literature has been molded by the values of tradition and continuity. The hero is not so much a prophet and savior as part of a communal chain. In short, the myth of the hero becomes *the myth of the living social chain.* However, this attachment to tradition has not resulted in idolatry of the existing society. As Romain Rolland indicated in *Jean Christophe*, it has been constantly quickened by sensitiveness to innovation and revolution. Society does not become identical with the state or nation. *L'État* never attains eulogistic overtones. Society, as a mythic category, is both French and universal.

The work of Racine is the nearest French approximation of classic mythopoesis. However, Racine labored under an extraordinary historic burden. French seventeenth century society was true neither to French nor to human tradition. It was not in continuity with the rich medieval residue of French literature, but broke sharply with it. And its Palace society encouraged only a formal and narrow identification. The Phèdre of the court-dramatist is held down by an imprisoning *raison* and *gloire* of an hierarchial order, and her *amour* can express itself only in underground revolt.[1] In Corneille and Racine, the Salon takes on the mythic form of a devouring parent. Both dramatists (Corneille quite indirectly) picture the false myth of the court suppressing the human myth of *coeur*. In accepting their fathers' values, Corneille's sons and daughters gain *honneur*, but surrender their individual will and human desires. Racine's characters react in near-primitive Bacchic revolt against the polished sterility of their society.

This critique became a major note in French literature from Molière to Voltaire, from Balzac to Zola, from Barbusse and Aragon to Sartre and the existentialists. It reaches its most organized and sustained form in André Gide.

The Secessionist Myth

The myth, as we have noted, rests on and finally reaches out towards a harmonious state. The secession of the hero is but a transitional moment in its total dialectic. From this angle, Gide appears to be at the other pole of the mythic perspective. His work has always seemed to be at war with all that which strains towards collective integration and the visionary projection of syntheses. However, his latest story on the myth of Theseus should correct this estimate of Gide. That a man of his dissident temper should come to affirm the myth is a striking testimony to its persistence. It is a further instance of the recurring phenomenon that mature and responsible artists experience an irresistible pull towards mythopoesis.

Gide's concern with the myth is not new.[2] But in his earlier work where he dealt with the myths of Narcissus, Philoctetus, Prometheus, and later with Oedipus and Persephone, the focus is largely on its narcissistic elements.[3] The hero is "the bastard," glad that he resembles no one but himself, and his heroism consists in carrying out the unmotivated "gratuitous" act. In this phase, Gide questions not only organized society, but the organized self as well.

This emphasis lent Gide's work the character of a secessionist Protestantism. The very titles of his works—"Counterfeiters," "Immoralist" —sounded this note. His central characters are the unattached and the illegitimate who defy convention either by indulgence (*The Immoralist*) or by asceticism (*Strait is the Gate*). Gide himself stated that the raison d'être of the artist is "to be at odds with the world," and that his own function is "to disturb." In *Le Prométhée*, man is defined as "the animal capable of the gratuitous act." Critique tends to become identi-

cal with morality. Individual non-conformity, such as practised by Nathanaël, takes on divine character ("Nathanaël" means "gift of God").
In *Les Nourritures terrestres*, he is told to adopt the motto: "Ne de-
meure jamais," for "nothing is more dangerous to you than your family,
your room, and your own past." He is urged: "Throw away my book,"
for (as we hear in another work, *Un Esprit non prévenu*) "nothing is
more inhibiting than disciples." Here, Gide approaches Nietzsche, the
Nietzsche whose Zarathustra asks his followers to leave him. "It is all
alone," Alissa tells Jerome in *Strait is the Gate*, "that each of us must go
to God."

In this oppositional mood, Gide's characters may be said to have
made a pact with the devil, a pact which does not allow final grace. Indeed, *L'Immoraliste* identifies art with *nouveauté* and with *vice*.
The *Journal* (1916) transforms Descartes' *cogito ergo sum* into *cogito
ergo Satanas*. The Evil One has been invited and is believed in as a positive, enterprising principle.

Gide carried this temper into his style. His writing took the form of a
soliloquy (*L'Immoraliste* was conceived as a monologue) or as an internal debate (the *Journal*). *The Counterfeiters*, Gide's "only novel,"
would violate its traditional "fictional" form. It would include "everything," infringing on the esthetic requirement of selection; it would destroy the idea of illusion by introducing the author as one of the characters. In his zeal for "truth", Gide went so far as to aim at non-metaphoric
writing (*Les Nourritures terrestres*).

Gide's life itself exhibits this apartness. His opposition to conformity
(which Gide sometimes identified with "the bourgeois," not as a class,
but as a level of thought) is carried forward in his later criticism of the
Soviet Union. It is continued during the Second World War. When the
Allies entered Tunis, Gide was asked to speak about the liberation of the
city from the Fascists. But Gide refused. "I fail to see," he notes in *Imaginary Interviews*, "what 'declaration' I could make which, if it remained
sincere, would not be of a nature to offend all parties."

Such individual intransigence brought Gide close to Nietzschean
transvaluations, if not to existentialist freedom, and furthest removed
from the mythic attitude which begins and ends with a "yes".

The Negation of Negativism

What militated against Gide's criticism becoming mere protest was
his deep sense of moral and social responsibility. One of his favorite
books was the Bible (particularly the New Testament),[4] and one of his

recurrent themes has been social injustice (particularly in *Travels in the Congo*). Gide's rebelliousness has been in the Latin-Mediterranean tradition—realistic and social opposition. Gide realized that one cannot live in Cartesian doubt, that a society cannot function solely on the basis of individual morality. Sisyphus, the existentialist hero, is not an example of fortitude to Gide, but an instance of a sorry effort. *Se depasser* becomes one of his favorite terms.

Gide's critical dialectic is applied to criticism itself. The hero of *L'Immoraliste* realizes at the end that freedom must have an object. Bernard's rebelliousness in *The Counterfeiters* incites him "to rebel against his very rebellion." Above all, the novel distinguishes between genuine and "counterfeit" secessionism. Real freedom does not lie in the unscrupulous licentiousness of Passevent or Lady Griffith, not in the nihilism of Strouvilhou which leads to Vincent's madness, to the masturbatory dissipation and suicide of Boris. Such "freedom" is transcended in Olivier and Bernard. Boris' suicide is the traumatic event which shocks Olivier into rejecting Passeventism. Bernard rebels only against a counterfeit society, and in the end, he *returns* to his home. In his awareness that negation was but an interim phase which must be passed through and beyond towards affirmation, Gide must be distinguished from his nihilistic following.

THE LIVING CHAIN: THE MYTH OF THESEUS

In *Imaginary Interviews* (New York, 1944), Gide makes an important concession to tradition. He calls it "a living chain" and the basis for culture. For culture, he notes, "implied a continuity, and therefore it called for disciples, imitators, and followers to make a living chain: in other words, a tradition." This pull towards unity and affirmation makes itself felt throughout Gide's work. The *Journal* expresses sadness over the prevalent tragic need to hate. To be sure, critique is essential if we are not to be enchained by fossilized tradition, by the dead past and the dead myth. Yet, the self cannot operate responsibly without a communal reference and art cannot create an enduring hero, that is a myth, without it. Already Gide's *Oedipus* (1931) thinks not of defiance and thrills, but is set on the adventure of liberating men from the dead past. And the work ends on a humanistic note. But it is in *Theseus* that we find this note fully developed and sustained. "What happens, in the case of the hero," we read here,

is this: his mark endures. Poetry and the arts reanimate it and it becomes an enduring symbol. That is how it is that Orion the hunter is riding still, across Elysian fields of asphodel. That is how Tantalus' throat is parched to all eternity, and how Sisyphus still rolls upward towards an unattainable summit the heavy and ever-rebounding weight of care which tormented him in the days when he was King of Corinth.[5]

Theseus makes it possible for us to view Gide's work as a whole. The theme had occupied the author for some three decades. It is not so much a reversal of Gide's earlier persuasions as their incorporation within a broader compass. It joins Gide's former anti-bourgeois esthetics with a communal ethic, the earlier fear of organization with the affirmation of the need for the Ariadne-thread linking beginnings and ends.

The style and mood of this story indicate the shift. Where Gide's work had been largely stern and unsmiling, *Theseus* is carried along by ease and relaxedness. It has a rhythm of play and a mood of high comedy. The multiple perspectivism of *The Counterfeiters* has given way to a focal mythic center. The new character begins as a Narcissus and an Absalom, but ends as an Oedipus, Aeneas and Faust, becoming the founding father of a people's city.

The mythic theme of identification and re-creation is stated in the opening sentence. Theseus says that he wanted to tell the story of his life "as a lesson for my son Hippolytus." Now Hippolytus is no more, but Theseus will tell it "all the same," as a lesson for us, his symbolic sons. The opening also speaks of a *good* heritage. Theseus' father Aegeus was "one of the best." Here, Gide affirms the living residue of mythic Creation which serves as a nodal reference in the labors of *re-creation*. From his father (Aegeus or Poseidon), Theseus also got his inconstancy and unsettledness of temper, that is, the urgency of the Quest. Finally, he learned from him to go beyond this state, "to rebel against myself." To this, "I owe all that I have achieved."

The body of the story deals with the second act of the mythic process: the Quest through apostasy, adventure and conquest.

Theseus begins his story with a playful reference to his half-conscious act of patricide. Theseus "forgot" to run up the white sails, the sign that was to announce to his father that he was returning alive and in triumph. This caused the father's death. It was not really forgetfulness for, as Theseus admits, "Aegeus was in my way," particularly since he formed "the exasperating idea that a second meridian of (marital) enjoyment was his for the asking—thus blocking my career. . . ." This act is necessary in the hero's battle with "the gods," if he is "to purge the earth once and for all of a host of tyrants, bandits and monsters." This impious attitude becomes an interim way of life for the young hero. He despises comfort, idleness, ease, crying out, "What have I to do with safety." He would break free, drawn to what lies ahead, never allowing the past to involve or detain him. Carrying out the pact with the devil, he will not love or marry, but enjoy an adventurous life.

His supreme adventure is with the Minotaur who was annually devouring seven young men and seven young girls from Attica. The Minotaur is the "herald," the summoner to the test. He initiates the ritual of the Journey, a journey by water and through the labyrinth, the passage through which the hero is to gain the maturity of manhood. At the end of the journey Theseus, the "savage," is socialized, marries and founds a city.

To vanquish the monster, Theseus needs the help of others. Assistance comes from Ariadne, Minos' older daughter, who provides him with the thread which leads him out of the labyrinthine maze in which the monster lives. This thread becomes the symbol of the binding chain between beginnings and endings, Creation and Re-creation. This thread, Theseus is told, "will be your link with the past. Go back to it. Go back to yourself. For nothing can begin from nothing, and it is from your past, and from what you are at this moment that what you are going to be must spring." The real difficulty in conquering the monster, he hears, is "to preserve unbroken, to the last inch of thread, the will to come back."

Ariadne and her thread are one of his guides. The other is Dedalus, his father-mentor, who explains to Theseus the nature of the labyrinth he built to house the Minotaur. This labyrinth points to a dual danger: the danger of sloth and the danger of pointless activity: "I thought that the best way of containing a prisoner in the labyrinth", Dedalus tells Theseus,

> was to make it of such a kind, not that he couldn't get out (try to grasp my meaning here) but that he wouldn't want to get out. I therefore assembled in this one place the means to satisfy every kind of appetite . . . The prime necessity was to fine down the visitor's will power to the point of extinction.

Dedalus burned plants in the stoves which distributed heavy gases, inducing

> a delicious intoxication, rich in flattering delusions, and provoke the mind, filled as this is with voluptuous mirages, to a certain pointless activity: "pointless," I say, because it has merely an imaginary outcome, in visions and speculations without order, logic or substance. The effect of these gases is not the same for all of those who breathe them; each is led on by the complexities implicit in his own mind to lose himself, if I may put it, in a labyrinth of his own devising.

The most surprising thing about these perfumes is that

> when one has inhaled them for a certain time, they are already indispensable.
> . . . And that, above all, is what keeps one inside the labyrinth.

In this adventure, Theseus experiences the demonic threat in which the hero is "possessed" by a "numinous dread" (R. Otto's term in *The Idea of the Holy* [London, 1950]), menacing him at once from without and from within. They are the threats to Aeneas in Dido's Carthage, to Dante in the dark woods, to Faust in Helen's Arcadian idyll, to Siegfried on Brunhilde's mountain top, to Mann's Joseph in Egypt. The threat lies in the two-fold temptation to deny Creation and the Quest, to invite the slavery of stagnation and the slavery of "pointless activity."

In Dedalus' admonition that Theseus may not linger in the labyrinth nor in the embrace of Ariadne, we recognize the characteristic stress of the Gide we have known. This stress is not discarded but transformed.[6] Having slain the monster, Theseus is now ready to assume the responsibility of organization: "Where I had sought to conquer, I now sought to rule . . . there is a time for conquest, a time for cleansing the earth of its monsters, and then a time for husbandry and the harvesting of well-cherished land." Only now is he fit for "great things," things "beside which these exploits will seem, in the future, to have been the amusements of a child." He is ready to marry and to found the city of Athens.

"This was not easy." Theseus finds an inherited mass of petty townships continuously quarreling for dominance. His father thought he could assure his own authority by perpetuating these quarrels. And, although he was "one of the best" fathers, Theseus finds another way. He traces the source of most evils to "the general inequality of wealth and the desire to increase one's own fortune." He sets about to do away with these social divisions by abolishing the unreal supremacy of wealth, but maintaining the supremacy derived from personal merit, "an aristocracy not of wealth, but of intellect." Thanks to Theseus, the Athenians thus came to deserve "the fine name of 'people'." And herein, he adds, "lies my fame."

The mythic epilogue is, of course, peculiarly suited to Gide's temperament. In *Theseus*, we meet it first in a comic view of the myth itself. Theseus calls some of the exploits which legend ascribes to him "imaginary," and admits that he even improved upon some of them, so as not to encourage irreverence. It appears especially in the final section where Oedipus is brought in as a contrasting mythic hero. Here, Gide's Oedipus accepts suffering as a means of redeeming man from his natively sinful taint. Where Oedipus failed in all which he undertook, Theseus succeeded. Yet, Theseus himself feels that, in comparison with Oedipus, his own triumph seems "merely human—inferior, I might say." However, Theseus' fate has not been an unmitigated triumph. He loses his wife Phedra and his son Hippolytus. He now admits that he feels lonely and that he is old.

Still, Theseus is content. He has played out his mythic role, fulfilled his destiny to build the city which is dearer to him "even than my wife and son." He is happy to think that "after me, and thanks to me, men will recognize themselves as being happier, better and more free." The story closes with this note: "I have worked always for the good of those who are to come. I have lived." The thought in the last lines is new. Yet, it has its precedent in the earlier Gide. The *Journal* speaks of a constant need for reconciliation, for marrying Heaven and Hell, à la Blake, for reconciling individualism and communism. Gide once expressed gratitude to Edmund Gosse for discerning under the new France the old France that has always been. His *Theseus* is at once a "remembrance" of his Huguenot-Catholic origins and beyond that a reaffirmation of his belief that man strives towards the good. In *Theseus*, the Gidean debate between dissidence and affirmation has moved from a split Protestant dialectic towards the fullness of mythic dramatism.

Still, the epilogue carries over into Gide's Theseus. His final years are in a sense more tragic than Oedipus' who is at least left with his two daughters. Theseus has lost his one son Hippolytus and, at the end, is all alone. Theseus states that Athens "has been dearer to me even than my wife and son." This may be the attitude of a God or demi-God. But Theseus is wholly human and his loneliness is the tragedy of *la condition humaine*.

NOTES

1. See M. Turnell, *The Classical Moment* (New York, 1949).
2. In 1919, Gide published *Considérations sur la mythologie grecque. Fragments du Traité des Dioscures*, in which he briefly discusses Greek mythic heroes (including Theseus) as exhibiting "un fatalité psychologique."
3. *Le Traité du Narcisse* (1891), *Philoctète* (1899), *Le Prométhée mal enchaîné* (1899), *Oedipe* (1931), *Perséphone* (1934).
4. Characteristically, Gide interprets the Gospels in the manner of St. Paul, as emancipating men from false divinities. He finds the Gospel "more emancipated . . . more concerned about individual value" than Nietzsche did, and (with Dostoyevsky) sees them as standing in contrast to organized religion, especially Roman Catholicism.
5. Gide, *Two Legends: Oedipus, Theseus* (New York, 1950). All subsequent references are to this edition.
6. In this sense, Theseus' social act is prepared by his earlier role.

Contemporary Myth of the
Impersonal Antagonist
Franz Kafka

THE WESTERN MYTH of Franz Kafka meets with the Eastern of Fyodor Dostoyevsky in the threat posed by modern coordination, conformity and the steamroller of the anonymous machine. Dostoyevsky's Underground Man does not want to become "the keyboard of a piano"; Kafka's characters do not want to be condemned by faceless committees. Dostoyevsky saw hope in countering Western technological collectivism by the sensuousness of Slavic impersonality, rooted in an agrarian people and its memory of the fertile, earthy Mother-Goddess. By the time of Kafka, man had come to be dominated by an impersonal, sexless Moloch, by the invisible and intangible dictatorship of trusts and documents. Yahweh, Moira and God had become anonymous secretaries.

The Hebrew Job, the Greek Prometheus and Oedipus, the Catholic Dante are never in doubt as to the authority behind their "arrest." The doubts begin with Hamlet and become "organized" in Kafka to the point where his figures have lost nearly all the passion with which earlier characters confront their accusers. That is, they too take on the quality of their antagonist, become shadowy epiphenomena.

Kafka's work centers in depicting the nature of the Quest for the illusive Lord and the illusive Devil. The High Court of *The Trial*, the Authorities of *The Castle* remain invisible and unreachable.

The theme of the impersonal enemy runs through much of modern literature. The individual is shown confronting communal ghosts, is diverted from basic quests by a busy-ness civilization which operates by intermediaries, delegates and by pushing buttons, driven and ridden by things.

The single-mindedness with which Kafka concentrated on presenting impersonality as the quality of our time has found a startling reception. His cult began during his own lifetime, before any of his major works had been published. In the forties, the Kafka-vogue took on something of a legendary character. W. H. Auden declared in 1941 that Kafka "bears the same kind of relation to our age that Dante, Shakespeare and Goethe bore to theirs." He has been hailed as one of our profoundest religious thinkers, on a level with Pascal, Kierkegaard and Karl Barth.

Kafka has also been called the most extraordinary *artist* of our day. Now, art is distinguished from religion in that its "insights" are not abstract propositions but are embodied in concrete, individual characters and situations. Given the specific nature of Kafka's task—to present de-individualized, de-personalized forces—he could "succeed" only by creating ill-defined, ghostly characters and scenes. From here follow the necessary limitations of Kafka's art. His work consists of spare modifications of a single theme: all of his characters are in search of Justice, Truth or Goodness, and all of them much in the same way. We read again and again that modern existence obstructs the human quest by a maze of hierarchies. This makes for a slender esthetic compass, severely limits its flexibility and manifoldness. In a sense, Kafka's theme is exhausted after the first chapters; thereafter, we get variations of the initial motif. There is no dramatic development of plot or character and little suspense. Edwin Muir, perhaps the staunchest admirer of Kafka's style, implicitly admits this limitation. He states that Kafka was concerned with religious *truth*. He was not concerned with religious *characters*, as were Dostoyevsky, Tolstoy, Undset or Claudel. In Zola, "evil" is embodied through Chaval, in Tolstoy through Anatol; in Shakespeare through Iago and Goneril; in Goethe through Mephisto. Herman Melville, also concerned with the elusiveness of the quest, finally *shows* us Moby Dick.

Absence of sensuousness also characterizes the non-dramatic character of Kafka's work. His novels are lacking in genuine dramatic conflict, and for this reason, there is no catharsis. The feeling of dread and anxiety is rarely lifted, and at the close the reader is still in the grip of the modern furies. It is not a question of an "unhappy ending." The great classical heritage is mainly that of tragedy; and the modern novel, from *Madame Bovary* and *The Possessed* to *Buddenbrooks* and *The American Tragedy*, also ends on a tragic note. But we are purged of pity and fear partly because the enemy appears in dramatic-sensuous form and can therefore be *met*. And defeat at its hands is rendered noble because it has been met. No such freedom issues from Kafka. His passionless dialectic does not resolve tension.

To be sure, these limitations of Kafka's art also contain its value. Its very restricted nucleus gives it compactness. While the First and Final Causes remain a secret in Kafka, he does suggest the regions which border on original and ultimate mysteries.

JOSEPH K'S MYTHIC CRIME

In *The Trial* (New York, 1937), Joseph K. is arrested and "tried" for a crime which is never stated by the authorities.[1] Yet, the novel suggests that Joseph K. is guilty. As in the case of Job, his crime is not in the nature of an overt act. It consists in his having been content with leading a routine life, according to the accepted conventions. In this sense, his arrest (as that of Job) constitutes his awakening to the fact that he had not lived. Although he states that he "cannot recall the slightest offence that might be charged against me," he admits that he is "by no means very surprised" at his arrest. It expels him from a false Eden towards a questioning of the values he had automatically accepted.

Now, it is characteristic of Kafka's dialectic that his figures seek their way through the labyrinth with the guidance of the very "court-" authorities which hem them in. This approach is reenforced by the priest's legend of the doorkeeper who stands on guard before the Law. The doorkeeper tells the man who begs for admittance that he cannot admit him "at the moment," but adds that if the man is strongly tempted, he might try "to get in without my permission." But the man continues to sit before the door "waiting for days and years" until he is nearly ready to die. At this point, the doorkeeper tells him: "No one but you could gain admittance through this door, since this door was intended only for you." The implication is that had the man not been a simpleton (suggested by the German *Mann vom Lande*), and had insisted on entering, he could have done so.

Franz Kafka had less ground for faith in his tradition than earlier mythmakers in theirs. Yet, he possessed enough faith to seek *Logos* within the Law, to discern the potential heroic qualities in his characters. Joseph in *The Trial* is not only a routinized bank official; he is also something of Joseph the Dreamer in his "insatiable" quest. His arrest catapults him towards something approximating rebirth:

> He felt as if he were seasick. He felt he was on a ship rolling in heavy seas. It was as if waters were dashing against the wooden walls, as if the roaring of breaking waves came from the end of the passage, as if the passage itself pitched and rolled and the waiting clients on either side rose and fell with it . . . Could his body possibly be meditating a revolution and preparing to spring something new on him, since he had borne with the old state of affairs so effortlessly?

300

In *The Castle*, Kafka moves towards the third act of his mythic drama, turns towards the people of the village, in the feeling that he was fighting "not only for himself, but clearly for other powers as well which he did not know." Such promise of salvation by alignment with selected "others" is faintly suggested in Joseph K's vision at the end of *The Trial*:

> His glance fell on the top storey of the house adjoining the quarry. With a flicker as of a light going up, the casements of a window there suddenly flew open; a human figure, faint and insubstantial at that distance and that height, leaned abruptly far forward and stretched both arms still farther. Who was it? A friend? A good man? Someone who sympathized? Someone who wanted to help? Was it one person only? Or were they all there?[2]

Kafka realized that the self needs to go beyond itself to find the full expression of its individuality. He did not penetrate far enough to distinguish between necessary and avoidable social-individual evil, to see the broader and deeper bearing of temporal pressures on *la condition humaine*. Nor did Kafka have enough of the hope which lies in converting submerged experience into consciousness—he was unable to communicate the identity of the enemy. Perhaps the enemy was too deeply submerged in him to become "known," and it was not possible for him to find the perspective and distance necessary for esthetic embodiment.[3]

NOTES

1. A comic-tragic form of this type of trial appears in Bert Andrews' story of "Mr. Blank" (*Washington Witch Hunt* [New York, 1938]). Mr. Blank was dismissed from the Department of State, without being informed of the charges against him. The committee before which he appeared would neither put nor answer any questions, but asked him to say anything he pleased which he believed relevant: "You might think back over your own career and perhaps in your own mind delve into some of the factors that have gone into your career which you think might have been subject to question." A distinction is made between "loyalty" as "a conscious proposition" and "security risk" which "might be conscious or unconscious." The situation is analogous to psychoanalytic procedure where the patient is asked to "talk" and thus discover his hidden guilt.

2. In Kafka's work, it is primarily the female figures who offer help without asking for any reward. Nearly all come from "the underground," especially Pepi in *The Castle*.

3. For fuller discussion of Kafka's work, see the chapter in my book, *No Voice is Wholly Lost*. See also my essay "The Vogue of Franz Kafka" in *Franz Kafka Miscellany* (2d ed; New York, 1946).

The Existentialist Myth
The Value of Homelessness
The Myth of Sisyphus and *The Flies*

IN SOME ANALYSES, existentialism is viewed as an expression of the historic dilemmas confronting man in the aftermath of the Second World War. To be sure, these have been the catalysts for the movement, have provided its mood and accent. Yet, existentialism is based on old principles with a renowned philosophical ancestry, reaching back to the "either-or" of Kierkegaard, the voluntarism of Nietzsche, the phenomenology of Husserl, up to the "anxiety" and "anguish" of Heidegger and the irresolvable antinomies of Karl Jaspers.

The supra-historical import of existentialism appears more directly in its reference to the myth. Camus, at one time closely related to the movement, wrote of the Sisyphus myth and Sartre has treated the Orestes myth in *The Flies*. Now, the differentiating character of the existentialist approach is that it is concerned exclusively with the second act of the mythic drama, that is, with the revolt of the individual. Its primary motive is to affirm the individual's unconditioned freedom from "systems," "essences," and any type of organized control, and to accept the resulting homelessness and anguish as final. It does not explore the question of the sources and bases out of which this homelessness arises. The individual is not born—he is "thrown" into existence. He has no parents and produces no offspring. For this reason, existentialism cannot and does not ask the question of rehabilitation. Existentialism does refer to "temporality" and the future. It even speaks of the past and of tradition. But this past is "freely" created, not discovered as an objective existence. Where the classic myth relates the ego's rebellion to the common ground of things, existentialism would relate it to the groundlessness of things, to "Nothing." It begins with "Nothing" and its goal, at least with some, is the nothingness of death.

SISYPHUS

The characteristic mythic hero of existentialism is not Prometheus, created by his mother Terra, and finally coming to terms with Father Zeus, but Sisyphus. Not Prometheus who would free mankind both *from* fear of nature and man as well as *for* control of physical and human nature, but Sisyphus, forever condemned to roll a rock to the top of a mountain, with the rock always falling back of its own weight. It is Sisyphus who absorbs the interest of Albert Camus at the moment when he descends to the plain "towards the torment the conclusion of which he will not know."[1] For this is "the hour of consciousness!" In these moments, Sisyphus transcends his destiny. Although powerless, he "knows that the entire extent of his clairvoyance which constitutes his torment contains at the same time his victory." In this moment, Sisyphus sees that his destiny belongs to him; the very succession of unconnected actions which is his destiny, has been created by him, "unified under the gaze of his memory, and soon broken off by his death." His is the superior loyalty "which denies the gods and lifts the rocks." And Camus imagines that in all this, Sisyphus experiences a silent joy. Sisyphus is happy in his useless labor, his labor of indifference, happy because it is *his* uselessness and *his* indifference, happy because he continues, even in his punishment, to rebel against the system. It is he, not someone else, who is being tormented; it is he, not some other, who continues to roll the rock up the mountain.

In its abstract formulation, existentialism may well be philosophically untenable. Spinozists, Kantians, Hegelians and Marxists, critics from Guido de Ruggiero to Günther Anders have attacked its notions of undetermined freedom and causeless action. They question the claim that a non-objective attitude can have an objective value, that you can derive a morality from non-moral action, and quote Marx's characterization of Stirner, (the "proud possessor of no possessions") as applicable to existentialism.

However, it is doubtful whether the heart of the doctrine is reached by this approach. Nor does its meaning necessarily emerge from the affiliations of the existentialists. In point of fact, various groups, from Catholics to atheists claim that their platforms derive from existentialism. Its art work, on the other hand, presents its philosophy in sensuous, dramatistic form. It can tell us what is meant by personality, freedom, involvement, action, and anguish, since it presents characters in concrete relations and inter-participation. Art is also the most favorable context for revealing the element of irony or self-criticism. Sartre's *The Flies*,[2] his most effective art work, deals most directly with a myth, that of Orestes.

THE MYTH OF ORESTES

The scene is Argos whose people (with the exception of Electra) have been enchained by a propaganda technique of fear and guilt. They fear the ghosts of the past and feel guilty in keeping silent about the murder of Agamemnon. The dead are used to rule the living. The people have been reduced to a cringing attitude of submission, are slaves to "the good old piety of yore, rooted in terror." The religious and secular "systems" of Zeus-Aegisthus have brought "the flies" to plague the city. Its people have indeed become "flies" themselves, humming and buzzing about without human communication. When Orestes appears with his tutor, they try to speak to someone. But no one opens the door or listens to them. Their very fear and guilt are officially regulated. Their piety is to dead mummery. The Greek Chorus has been converted to the people as a mob-swarm.

Orestes has come to restore to the people "their sense of human dignity." As a result of the liberal education given him by his tutor, he has become "free as air," free from prejudice and superstition. He has "no ties, no religion, and no calling . . . no home, no roots." However, this homelessness has created a void within him, and he wishes he could acquire the people's memories, their hopes and fears. He admits to his sister Electra that "of all the ghosts haunting this town today, none is ghostlier than I." And he confesses: "I want to be a man who belongs to some place, a man among comrades." Undecided as to whether he should stay and avenge his father, he calls on Zeus to point a way. Now Zeus, like Aegisthus, has but one passion, the passion for ritual and order. His sign counsels Orestes to live at peace. This at once makes for Orestes' resolution to do the very opposite—not to take orders from gods or men, but to follow his own path. He gives up his "aery lightness," and would take over the people's crime and remorse by killing Aegisthus and Clytemnestra. By thus "stealing" the burden of guilt from the people, he means to liberate them to act freely.

The play was purportedly written as an attack on the Nazi system and Vichy collaboration. Yet, it is more an indictment of the people than of the system which forged their chains. In fact, Zeus, Aegisthus, and Clytemnestra have some stature or evoke sympathy. Aegisthus has kept order, but at the sacrifice of hope, love, even of lust. "No man in Argos is sadder than I," he tells Clytemnestra. Nor is he unscrupulous: he does not resist Orestes and opposes Zeus's urgings to throw him into a dungeon. Clytemnestra is a resigned, almost pitiful figure, bearing "the heaviest load of guilt." Zeus is actually depicted as having dignity. He is a French Wotan without the Wagnerian metaphysical pretensions. He accepts his defeat gracefully with fore-knowledge that it had to come.

The most dramatic repudiation of Orestes' freedom is objectified in Electra. She begins in a challenging, though ineffective, fearlessness *before* the arrival of Orestes but after she is exposed to Orestes's teaching and behavior, Electra renounces his form of freedom. Although she loves her brother and offers the closest and most direct subject for Orestes's persuasions, she decides to stay behind with Zeus to be saved "from my brother, from myself." She is frightened by Orestes who shows no regret over having killed his mother. Electra is the warmest and most human character in the drama. It is she who offers the most telling critique of Orestes' freedom from all ties when she asks: "Can you undo what has been done? Something has happened and we are no longer free to blot it out." She is converted by Orestes—*in reverse*. Orestes helps no one, not the people whom he despises, not his sister whom he loves. He only helps himself to anguish.

Even as Orestes would reject biological and social determinants, he actually *does commit* himself, and does react to existing authorities. His acts are not causeless, as are those of Dostoyevsky's Kiriloff. "Man is nothing but what he makes of himself," writes Sartre. Orestes does not "make himself," but re-acts to Zeus in *precise reverse*. The sole act that might be said to have "nothing" as a motivation is the murder of his mother. In Aeschylus, and even in O'Neill, some attempt is made to explain matricide. There is none in Sartre's play. Orestes kills his mother for no "reason." Even his sister's pressure is absent—Sartre's Electra rather urges: "She can do us no more harm," now that Aegisthus is dead. Orestes himself thinks that his act is right. But this "knowledge" is his own mystery. He makes no attempt to *make* it known to others or even to himself. The sole basis for Orestes' murder is the traditional plot of the legend. That is, in this "free" existentialist act, Sartre's hero acts like an unfree man, enslaved by the mere ritual of the old myth.

305

At the end, Orestes leaves. He does not know or care where he is going. With Wagner's Siegfried, he might say: "In der Ferne bin ich heim." He has rejected his origins (he has no "memories"), rejected the authorities of Zeus, Aegisthus, and his mother. For the people he has only contempt. With no base to start from, he has no lever to propel himself. His "free" act consists of the cold, mechanical, and unmotivated murder of his mother.

Now, Orestes presumably kills for the sake of the people. That is, Sartre would reintroduce the social motif into existentialism. But the play depicts the people in a manner which does not make them worthy of being saved. They show no change in attitude which might be a basis for their future self-liberation. On the contrary, Orestes' treatment of them only tends to de-dignify them even more. His freedom-act remains a gesture.[3]

In Aeschylus' version, Orestes violates the tradition of tribal guilt enacted by the Erinyes. But the turning-point of the Oresteia is the *transformation* of the malign Erinyes into the benign Eumenides, not their elimination. The old harbors elements which make possible its assimilation with the new, under the aegis of a rising Athenian democracy. Athena herself employs "social" means in her recourse to an Athenian jury, in her use of reason and persuasion on the Erinyes. And Orestes, who begins with matricide, ends by accepting and being accepted by the surrogate mother, Athena.

The situation in Goethe's *Iphigenia in Tauris,* as in the Euripides version, is that, following the murder of Clytemnestra, Iphigenia has found refuge with King Thoas in Tauris. The king first appears as primitive authority intent on exacting tribal vengeance on all Greeks who enter his land. Orestes is in a related state and would oppose Thoas by stealth and force. But he and Iphigenia tame their demon, and in the end Thoas is persuaded by both, as Aeschylus's Erinyes are persuaded by Athena. To be sure, in Goethe's play, there is no chorus, no jury of Athenian citizens to contribute to the redemption. Goethe is writing in eighteenth century Germany, when the people's voice is largely subdued, and when the inner, ethical approach of the individual alone appears representative.

Thus, in Aeschylus and Goethe, the hero defies an old tradition, but chooses an alternative high tradition. In Sartre, there appears to be no room for any tradition, no room for persuasion, reason, or ethics to banish the Furies. His Orestes would carry the burden by himself without reference to God, society, or family.

A more related approach to Sartre's Orestes appears in O'Neill's

Mourning Becomes Electra. Electra (Lavinia) is the central pivot. (Orestes is a weak, sickly figure.) Her form of freedom is acted out in satanic defiance and in a will to power. In pursuit of this power, O'Neill's characters defy their origins. But this does not free them, and his Electra remains in the grip of the Furies. In his earlier and later work (*The Hairy Ape* and *Days without End*), the dramatist suggests the need for communal reference. But in *Mourning Becomes Electra*, the self is freed only to be forever alone with itself, at home only in blank and black despair.

Temporal Involvements

The variations of the Orestes myth in Aeschylus, Goethe, and O'Neill are bound up with their varying historic and cultural demands. Existentialism too has received its accent in response to particular historic pressures.

Existentialism would annul the category of mediation. Its protest is against *mediators,* (the machine, documents, organization) which strip the person of his singularity and of his human warmth, dissolving him in a gray anonymity. Yet this protest against the reduction of the individual to the role of an intermediary is itself the expression of a midway position. It is the voice of those resisting a situation where they hover somewhere *between* upper and lower powers, are not *themselves,* but are manipulated to serve either group.

This midway status may be said to have received its impetus with the Renaissance and the rise of the middle classes. But the themes of homelessness and solitude are peculiarly relevant to the German bourgeoisie. Its late rise and retarded development long placed it at the mercy of the Junker strata, and later in fear of the proletariat. Existentialism is primarily a *German* import. Elements of it are to be found in Goethe's Faust, who would emancipate himself completely, first from his Gothic heritage, and later from the old pair, Philemon and Baucis. Yet in the end, Faust joins a social and religious communality. Wagner's Siegfried, on the other hand, would be born out of nothing. He does not know his father or mother, kills his surrogate parent Mime, bypasses Wotan, and falls victim to society, "the court" of Gunther, finally to end in "nothing," the pyre of the *Götterdämmerung.* He is not born *from* but *against* society (Fricka), free of tradition and of fear, existing in pure opposition to existing tables of value. And, as Sartre's Zeus cannot prevent the birth of the free man, so Wagner's Wotan is helpless against Siegfried.[4]

This note is continued by Nietzsche who warred simultaneously against German metaphysics and Wagner's aristocratic pretensions, and against "the many, all too many." In Nietzsche too, we find "leaps" and transcendence, which make for the restless and nervous pace of the Superman. Nietzsche could still attempt to limit freedom by the determinism in his theory of eternal recurrence. Kierkegaard countered the world of "clearance sales" by a leap of faith, and Strindberg approximated a similar leap in his last years. Ibsen launches his heroic men on their free path. But dramatically he shows that the Brands and Peer Gynts are in need of grace to be redeemed, that the Stockmanns cannot help the people by remaining their "enemy."

Twentieth-century Germany could be more "heroically" desperate. It sought consolation in Spengler's proud *Untergang*, in expressionistic freedoms, and in Heidegger's dignification of *Sorge*. As Günther Anders points out,[5] Heidegger's return from the First World War was a homecoming to no home. There arose the insistence "to be there," to be "themselves" (the basic existentialist vocabulary). He had faced "Death" and "Nothing" in the war and now wanted "to be" and to be "himself," to exist—not in general and for others—but to himself. In Anders' formulation, this expressed the bourgeois despair, the despair of those who are the victims of the abused bourgeois freedoms, who have never had real opportunities for freedom, but have lived for the objectives of more powerful groups. This also fitted in with the ideology of the Third Reich on the analogy of the German self coming to itself after being robbed by the "world" and the Versailles "system." In reality, this freedom is a desperate affirmation of boundedness.[6]

Sartre tells us that his studies in Heidegger immediately after Hitler's accession to power led to his theory of existentialism. This German product grew in the soil of the Vichy era among those who felt themselves caught midway between foreign and native systems both of which denied their individual existence. But this German phenomenon has been a drop of foreign blood in the French body. Irrationality, free individualism, metaphysical concern with "nothing," all this is indigenous to the historic curve of the German bourgeoisie. The roots of modern France lie in Cartesian rationalism, the critical tradition of Montaigne, the realism of its literature, in its sense of tradition, its concentration around "schools" and "academies," and finally, in the *reality* of its revolutionary tradition from 1789, 1830, 1848, 1871 to the self-liberation of Paris.

There are indeed some differentiations between Sartre and Heidegger. The latter supported the Nazis—half-heartedly; Sartre was a staunch supporter of the Resistance movement. We find a deviation in theory as well. Sartre recognizes that "individualism is impossible without collective responsibility," that "man must use his free will to establish a working basis for living collectively without destroying the dignity of the individual."[7] To be responsible for oneself means to be responsible for all men. This is the principle of "inter-subjectivity" which holds that "the man who becomes aware of himself through the *cogito* also perceives all others, and he perceives them as the condition of his own existence."[8] While Sartre denies that there is a universal human nature, he speaks of a universal human condition, the necessity to exist in the world with others, the duty of involving oneself in the problems of the day.[9]

However these qualifications remain sketchy and are not worked through towards linking freedom with tradition. Sartre says that primary reality is "being-in-the-world." Kenneth E. Douglas well points out that Sartre "forgets his hyphens and dwells exclusively on the conflict between man, with his inescapable freedom, and the external world which is in-itself but not for-itself."[10]

Are exisistentialists aware of the insufficiency in their individual stress? They argue that freedom spells anguish. Does anguish arise from their sensing that "collective responsibility" is not met by the individual free act? That the gratuitous act by the isolated individual is not effective in a world of private and public corporate powers? Have not the existentialists generalized existence so that it has itself become an essence, albeit a particularized essence?

The insufficiency of exclusive centering in the second act is dramatically illustrated in Sartre's account of the student who came to him for advice. The young man faced the choice of joining the Resistance movement or staying at home with his mother. Sartre told him that this must be his own choice. The young man then decided to stay with his mother; and Sartre adds that, in deciding to come to him, the young man had already made his choice. He had wanted to stay with his mother and knew that Sartre would not make any decision for him. This story presents an astoundingly naive attitude toward the problem of human choice. It assumes that what a person thinks he wants, on the basis of his immediate knowledge about himself, is equivalent to what he might want if he learned more about his motivation. Might not an analysis of an individual's choice reveal that his motives are based on an immediate desire which is contrary to his broader and long-range interests? In that existentialism discourages such analysis, it tends to encourage a freedom in terms of compulsive wish-fulfillments. Perhaps Ruggiero has this in mind when he charges that Existentialism corrupts the youth.

Still, the movement has a salutary function. It is a wholesome warning against the dead and false myth, against a sexless, mechanical collectivism. Writing about America, Sartre notes that there

> the myth of liberty co-exists with a dictatorship of public opinion; the myth of economic liberalism with monster corporations which embrace a continent, which finally belong to no one . . . 100 million Americans who try to satisfy their need for the marvellous by reading the incredible adventures of Superman or Mandrake the Magician.[11]

The cathartic value of the movement is to rouse the individual against surrender and submission to impersonality by placing in the center of its thought the idea that man continuously transcends himself.[12] In a time when the individual feels that he is a powerless thing, the existentialist's insistence that man is "nothing else but what he makes of himself" can contribute to a true human condition.

NOTES

1. Albert Camus, *The Myth of Sisyphus and Other Essays* (New York, 1957).
2. Jean-Paul Sartre, *No Exit and Three Other Plays* (New York, 1946). Subsequent references are to this edition.
3. Translated into forensic existentialist terminology, the people of Argos have "being" (*Dasein*), whereas Orestes is true "existence." The first are finite, temporal, and guilty; the latter is an emergent transcendence out of being. But existentialism does not make clear *how* emergence transpires. The antithesis between the two catetories (Orestes and the people) is drawn so sharply that it is difficult to see how existence can "emerge" from being. Ruggiero's comment on this point is relevant: "Existence springs like a fungus from the flat ground of the *Dasein*, or better, to twist a metaphor wrongly used by existentialists against idealism, emerges like Baron Münchhausen pulling himself by the hair out . . . with the strength of his own arm. . . . To make of existence the protagonist of becoming means to exchange the effect with the cause." *Existentialism* (London, 1947), pp. 48-49.
4. For elaboration of O'Neill's position and of the factors in German development discussed below, see chapters on O'Neill, Nietzsche, and Spengler in my *No Voice Is Wholly Lost*.
5. "Nihilismus und Existenz," *Neue Rundschau* (October, 1946). Hamlet has been wrongly interpreted as an existentialist character. His problem arises precisely from the circumstance that he *cannot* justify—morally or socially—complete severance from the Ghost, his mother, and even Claudius. Hamlet goes to Wittenberg and later to England, but each time returns to the court. The situation in the Scandinavian countries, placed in a non-heroic position in relation to European industrial development, is more relevant, as indicated by the problems in Kierkegaard, Strindberg, and Ibsen.

6. Karl Jaspers' doctrine of final "shipwreck" is a version of Heidegger's "Death." He also inveighs against the *unity* of opposites. But he is more aware of the dialectic relation between opposites. This moves him away from the camp of existentialism.

7. Interview with Dorothy Norman, *The New York Post* (April 9, 1946).

8. *Existentialism*, New York, 1947.

9. "We Write for Our Time," *The Virginia Quarterly Review*, XIII (Spring, 1947).

10. "The Nature of Sartre's Existentialism," *The Virginia Quarterly Review*, XIII (Spring, 1947).

11. Quoted in *The New York Times* (February 2, 1947).

12. Sartre, in his social stand, and Jaspers in his philosophy veer away from such extreme individualism. To Jaspers, philosophy is "a faith in communication," and an individual "cannot become human by himself."

Threat and Promise in
Germanic Insulation
The Magic Mountain and *Doctor Faustus*

THOMAS MANN introduces his *Doctor Faustus* by quoting from the second Canto of Dante's *Inferno*. In preparation for the terrifying and warlike journey he is about to undertake, Dante invokes the Muse and high Genius to help him in the task of giving expression to the true nobility of Memory.

For Mann, memory of tradition is preeminently incorporated and lived by the folk. In *The Beloved Returns*, (New York, 1940), Mann gives us Goethe's musings on its nature-wisdom:

> Ah, the folk! the folk-nature, part of nature, itself, elemental, earthy, pagan, full of folk- and nature-wisdom, fruitful soil of the unconscious, nourishing vale of renewed youth! How good to mingle with them at their immemorial feasts, fontanalia and maypole games. (p. 284)

But Mann warns that myth may mean the destruction of life when memory of tradition deteriorates into idolatry or is used to bolster a national *Blut und Boden* ideology.[1]

Awareness of man's mythic role constitutes for Mann "the lived myth," and choice of the *high* norms of a tradition signifies "the birth of the Ego out of his mythical collective." In a letter to Carl Kerenyi, Mann states that psychology is "the means by which the myth can be wrested from the Fascist obscurantists and be made into a function of the human. This connection seems to me to represent the world of the future." In the Joseph story, "the myth has been taken out of Fascist hands and humanized down to the last recess of language,—if posterity finds anything remarkable about it, it will be this." Mann regarded his work as having a mythic function and he himself went into exile, calling on Germany to recollect its human tradition to counteract the destructive tradition of Nazism.

The Germany with which Thomas Mann has always identified himself is that associated with Dürer, Bach, Luther and Goethe, that is, the period of Germany's first awakening to a national consciousness with a universal cultural mission. Mann's birthplace, Luebeck, exhibited some of these traits: Head of the Hanseatic League and a "free city" from the 12th century on, it retained the character of a bourgeois cultural tradition, relatively free of the Junker and industrial barons who dominated German history.

The work of Thomas Mann deals with four mythic levels: the Germanic in *Buddenbrooks* and *Death in Venice*, the European in *The Magic Mountain*, the international in the Joseph story and the Fascist transformation of primitive Teutonism in *Doctor Faustus*. In each, Mann counterposes the human to the inhuman myth. In the first, German memory of *Gemeinschaft*,—in the form of a philosophic and musical pantheism—is to correct Prussianism; in the second, the Latin-Mediterranean concept of "civilization" is to correct the German Kultur-cult; in the third, monster nationalism is to be counteracted by a human internationalism, based on the Judaic-Hellenic-Christian tradition; finally, the motif of musical "howling" in *Doctor Faustus* is seen as a possible "breakthrough" beyond the howling of Fascism.

Yet, these corrections are themselves affected by the very intractable situations in which they arise. The result is ambiguity or, to use Mann's favorite term, "irony."[2]

DER ZAUBERBERG

In his Foreword to *The Magic Mountain*, Thomas Mann tells us that the story of Hans Castorp has "something of the legend about it," that it "belongs to the long ago," and "comes out of the depth of the past."

Hans Castorp as Mythic Hero

Hans Castorp's "hermetic" seven years on the enchanted mountain hints at the association of his story with legends in which a character leaves the world for some forest-island-or mountain-retreat. Writing of Merlin's enchanted forest, Henrich Zimmer notes in *The King and the Corpse* that the forest

> has always been a place of initiation, for there the demonic presences, the ancestral spirits, and the forces of nature reveal themselves. . . . It holds

313

> . . . secrets, terrors, which threaten the protected life of the ordered world of common day. (p. 182)

All lose their way in it except the chosen one who leaves it a changed man.

The author calls Castorp a "mediocre hero," quickly adding that he is such "in an entirely honorable sense." Castorp's apparent mediocrity is conditioned by the age in which he lives which induces "a certain laming of the personality":

> A man lives not only his personal life, as an individual, but also, consciously or unconsciously, the life of his epoch and his contemporaries. . . . Now, if the life about him, if his own time seem, however outwardly stimulating, to be at bottom . . . hopeless, viewless, helpless, opposing only a hollow silence to all the questions man puts, consciously or unconsciously, yet somehow puts, as to the final, absolute, and abstract meaning in all his efforts and activities; then, in such a case, a certain laming of the personality is bound to occur, the more inevitably, the more upright the character in question.[3]

Here, then, is the "honorable" aspect of Castorp's character: finding the deficiencies of his epoch "prejudicial to his own moral well-being," he unconsciously rejects the ruling symbols of a commercialized world where "one is rich—or else one isn't," as he later says to Settembrini. Castorp's revolt takes on the German, Romantic form of passive resistance. The unconscious nature of Castorp's rebellion appears in his anemic state which prevents him from going ahead with his engineering studies and sends him up to the Berghof sanatorium for a period of seven years.

Journey In The Labyrinth

Early in the story, Settembrini characterizes Castorp's arrival on the mountain as a descent into the inferno. Hell on the Berghof consists in time appearing to stand still. Now, Castorp's "flatland" was another form of hell. When Castorp has acquired sufficient "distance," he readily accepts Settembrini's designation of this world as both "phlegmatic and energetic,"—phlegmatic with respect to human values and energetic about business and pleasure. And, on this plane, the "round" mountain is the replica of the "flat" land. Castorp's mountain harbors the classical temptations faced by the mythic hero—the alternatives of insensibility and of directionless motion. Castorp has rejected "the tyranny of time," only to fall victim to the tyranny of timeless apathy, has rejected one labyrinth only to fall into another. The "utopia" of the Olympian mountain is the "ideology" of the commercial market rushing towards the First World War. Yet, even as the mountain is the counterpart of the valley, its symbolic life contains an element of transcendence through which Castorp's insulated existence saves his mythic role.

Castorp's mountain with its sharp and clear air is a twentieth century Olympus. It suggests a Platonic Republic, composed of the artisan (Castorp), the soldier (Joachim) and the philosopher (Settembrini and Naphta). But here, the Socratic truth is split into two ideologies which contradict each other. Castorp's philosophic guides are ambiguous "talkers," and the "Earthly Paradise" towards which Settembrini leads Castorp is as suspect as the City of God which the Augustinian Naphta would reveal to Castrop.

Settembrini: the Brother Guide

Ludovico Settembrini is Castorp's Virgilian guide through the shades of the enchanted mountain, instructing him in the Latin precepts of political and social virtue—a theme which the German un-political *Kultur-Mensch* has ignored. Settembrini is the Mediterranean critic of German musical romanticism as well as of all authoritarianisms. He is the herald of secession, opposes all traditional absolutes, championing the endless continuity of the quest. He urges change, work, action, and freedom without basing them on firm principles. Settembrini urges Castorp to go back to the world of work. But Castorp is only "half-listening," for Settembrini does not meet his reservations about this "cruel and ruthless" world where values consist of money and possessions. Indeed, Settembrini's guidance is ambiguous. This spokesman for Protestantism comes from Catholic Italy, the critic of bourgeois life maintains bourgeois forms, the social internationalist supports the nationalistic war of 1914. He who prompts Castorp to leave the Berghof for a life of action himself can only talk. Settembrini admits that he is "rather ill," that is, he too is "honorable," and cannot live in the world of "progress." On the first night on the mountain, Castorp dreams of Settembrini, calling him "a brother":

> he was unexpectedly vouchsafed a signal insight into the true nature of time;
> it proved to be nothing more or less than a "silent sister," a mercury column
> without degrees, to be used by those who wanted to cheat.

On Walpurgis-Night, Castorp thanks Settembrini for lecturing him about freedom and progress, individualism and work, thanks him at the very moment when he is about to dismiss this champion of Western values and approach the Eastern Mother. The thanks are deserved: the very logic of Settembrini's negative liberalism, which offers Castorp no replacements, only serve to lead Castorp *away* from his disciplined

world of labor. In this ironic way, Settembrini "frees" Castorp for indulging himself in the licenses and licentiousness of the Witches' Kitch-
en on Walpurgis-Night.[4]

Clavdia: The Mountain-Mother

The Mountain is Castorp's womb in which he finds protection, security, comfort. Its "invisible government" makes no demands, offers a
surfeit of food and induces sleep. On Walpurgis-Night, Castorp, takes
leave of his Virgilian guide to be enveloped by the mother-mistress in
"Eden." Regressed to a child-like state, "blind," (his eyes closed,)
"speechless," ("parler sans parler," in a language which is neutral to
both), Hans Castorp kneels before Clavdia Chauchat, "swaying and
quivering," begging for admission and recognition. Later that night, in
a scene "wordless to our ears," engulfed in bliss,

> his twitching lips had stammered and babbled, in his own and foreign
> tongues, for the most part without his volition, the maddest things: pleas,
> prayers, proposals, frantic projects, to which all consent was denied.

Settembrini had issued warnings, had referred to Clavdia as Adam's
first wife, Lillith, "a night-tripping fairy, ... dangerous to young men especially." But on this night, Castorp has become a *ragazzo*, who cannot hear his mentor's foreign admonitions not to jeopardize his Western
individualism.

In her careless *nichevo* manner, Clavdia is old Russia, in its ambiguous "French" form. In Castorp's associations, the ambiguity extends
to her sex, reminding him of his schoolmate, the boy Hippe. The hours
he spends in her room on Walpurgis-Night only produce a "spiritual"
x-ray picture of the upper part of her body. Castorp's union with Clavdia, like Faust's with Helena, is in the nature of union with a shade.

Leo Naphta: The Distorted Christ

As an ironic guide, Settembrini also leads Castorp to his adversary,
Leo Naphta. Where Settembrini views history as continuous progress
by reason and individual freedom, Naphta teaches the values of Christian communality and sees history as split into dual warring forces. If
Clavdia *lives* the decline of the West, Naphta *argues* the decline
of Settembrini's "capitalistic world-republic." On the historical plane,
he represents the variety of authoritarian systems, from Catholicism to
Fascism and Communism which exert a special appeal to our 20th century Hans Castorps.

Naphta too is an ambiguous "talker," is sick and belongs on the mountain-sanatarium. His ambiguity arises from the fact that his precepts stem from a private burden. He was "set out" in the pogroms suffered by his family, with his father "nailed crucifix-wise on the door of his burning home." Later, Leo rebelled against the rabbi, his surrogate father, and was once again cast out. This event took place "precisely at the time when Rahel Naphta (his mother) lay dying."

At this point, Leo turned to Marx and then to Hegel. The latter (whom he called a "Catholic thinker") becomes the bridge to his Catholicism and Jesuitism. In joining the church, Naphta forgave, indeed, identified himself with those whose warped Christianity had been the instrument of his father's murder. Is this identification with his family's crucifiers the source of his deep guilt feeling, guilt over disloyalty to his personal father? Are his implacable dualism and his doctrine of "The Terror" an attempt to reach the very bottom of the Satanic abyss, to find and wrestle with the archdevil, seeking an absolute explanation for pain and suffering? So deep and exposed were Naphta's personal wounds that he was in desperate need of a physical home. And, since Marxism offered only a conceptual framework, a rational, socio-economic explanation for the pogroms, Naphta found it necessary to move within the "walls" of the Catholic-Jesuit enclosure. However, his reading of Marx led him to a revolutionary interpretation of Catholicism for which he saw a theological basis in St. Augustine. The world-proletariat, he declares, is

> today asserting the ideals of the *Civitas Dei* in opposition to the discredited and decadent standards of the capitalistic bourgeoisie. . . . The proletariat has taken up the task of Gregory the Great. . . . Its task is to . . . win back at length to freedom from law and from distinction of classes, to (man's) original status as child of God.

But Naphta's communistic Catholicism has a Fascist mode. He adopted not only the Augustinian castigation of the state and the Catholic critique of bourgeois commercialism, but also the Manichean heresy, of viewing the struggle between God and the devil as an eternal process which calls for the never-ending "Terror." But all this is also mainly "talk." He cannot practice what he preaches, develops his own "moist spot," rendering him unfit to apply his teachings in the practical realm. At the end, he turns the terror against himself. He did not want to be saved, but in his despair only hoped that his personal sacrifice might be the means of mankind's salvation.[5] In these distorted acts, Naphta reveals the "honorable" element by which Mann would save him as well.

317

Mynheer Pieter Peeperkorn: The Dionysian Corn-King

The most impressive character on the mountain, the only one who *is* a character, and who most visibly incorporates mythic traits is Mynheer Pieter Peeperkorn. With his mask-like face, he is a "persona," whose kingly features and majestic personality make him the father-guide of the mountain-community. In Mann's allusions, Peeperkorn becomes Jupiter (the eagle), Silenus (his royal drunkenness), Saturn-Pan (his celebrations and his homage to the nature water-fall). His name, Mynheer Peeperkorn, suggests the Corn-King whose arrival ushers in an apparent spring-like revival on the mountain. In his brief stay, he undergoes the ritual of the seasonal god, his spring and summer quickly turning to his fall and winter, with a faint promise that his death is not final, but that he only "went away."

Peeperkorn's role is that of the Dionysian god of wine and rapture on the Apollonian mountain. As in the case of Euripides' *The Bacchae*, his primitive force rouses the phlegmatic Western community towards a short-lived *Rausch*. He replaces Castorp's father-brother-authorities (Settembrini-Naphta, Behrens-Krokowski) and makes him his "son," who thereupon renounces his desire for the mother.

Yet, beneath Peeperkorn's pagan enjoyment of the "gifts of life," beneath "the heathen priest," one detects "the man of sorrows," whose talk consists of signs and portents. The evening repast takes on the character of a Last Supper at which Peeperkorn, surrounded by his twelve disciples, speaks of Gethsemane and the Last Judgment. The mixture of the pagan and the Christian is also evident at the water-fall, where "Peter" stands by "the rocks," and gives his "absolute" signs:

> They saw his head sink sideways, the broken bitterness of the lips, they saw the man of sorrows in his guise. But then quite suddenly flashed the dimple, the sybaritic roguishness, the garment snatched up dancewise, the ritual impropriety of the heathen priest.

Jesus' last request on earth was for something to drink. Peeperkorn's final gesture is to empty his beaker of wine in three gulps.[6] The scene at the waterfall combines Grecian *sparagmos* and Christian crucifixion. Where Naphta lives for the idea, Peeperkorn lives for passion. The extremes meet: Both commit suicide.

Peeperkorn is a sick Dionysus surrounded by a sick chorus. This corn-god is a watery figure, "prepotent," if not impotent, his "bread" turned to liquid which gives him a feverish fire. Outwardly dynamic and flourishing, he is inwardly static and tainted. Historically, Peeperkorn embodies the decline of the West. Yet, he too, is honorable in that he voluntarily abdicates his absolutism and is not a party to the Thunderbolt of 1914.

Return to the Folk

At the end of the novel, Hans Castorp returns to the world he had left behind. But his seven years' sojourn on the mountain has developed the "mediocre" into something of a mythic hero. From Settembrini he has learned the value of individual freedom and the need to join politics to poetry; from Naphta, the communal idea based on primary categories; from Peeperkorn, the "holy claims" of life. When Castorp returns, he does not join the "phlegmatic and energetic," but his "comrades," in his belief that they are fighting for love and peace. On the battlefield, he does not sing "Deutschland, Deutschland über alles," but Schubert's "Lindenbaum."[7] The *Lied* sums up Hans Castorp's *geniale Weg*, which leads to reconciliation with his folk.

Castorp's journey takes him through the several acts of the mythic drama. The first act is his nostalgic memory of his grandfather's "timelessness," the pre-technical, pre-bourgeois world which is later idealized in the first part of his dream in "Snow." The novel itself begins with the second act. The "orphan" leaves the flatland where he had lived a repressed existence, ascends the mountain-top in quest of another form of "timelessness," of a "free" life, similar to that sought by Joyce's Dedalus, Kafka's Joseph K, and other modern characters. Here, he would peer into the forbidden mysteries of the Mountain-Mother. These urges are partially held in check by the spokesman for Western patriarchal tradition, Ludovico Settembrini. For this "crime," Castorp is nearly "lost to life." But at the end, he returns "home", in an attempt to resolve the conflict of ideologies, not by philosophical dialectic, but by *Praxis*.

But only Castorp has changed. His society is fighting, not for Schubert's *Lied*, but for the firms of Tunder and Wilms which Castorp's "body" had rejected seven years before. At the end, our hero appears to be back in another Walpurgis-Night and Inferno, as he stumbles blindly in the murky chaos of the "shadow-land," with its "nude, branchless trunks of trees," in the "bemired woods," hearing "groans and shrieks" in the "fiery filth."

In his failure to recognize the historic reality, Castorp is as blind as Goethe's Faust was to the fact that his grave was being dug.[8] Yet, both Faust and Castorp are blind only in the manner of the man in Plato's cave who had gone forth to the sunny realm of the eternal Ideas and, on his return, is unable to distinguish between "the shadow" and "the substance." To be sure, from the historic platform, Castorp's "prospects are poor." Yet, as Joachim, Peeperkorn and Naphta are redeemed by their "honorable," supra-historical import, so hope remains for Castorp. For, he has not yielded to the pressures of his partisan guides, has witnessed the contradictions and disintegration of the authorities in their temporal guise: The Army (Joachim), the State (Peeperkorn), the various forms of authoritarianisms (Naphta). Castorp has rejected them and has returned to the authority of the Earth-Mother to participate in the agony of his people. Indeed, a Christ-motif is introduced when we see his bearded figure, "wet and glowing," singing "loving words" on his Golgotha-way. On the mountain, Castorp paid reverence to the sick and the *moribundi*, that is, he *invited* suffering, and following his purgatory, he came to the false paradise of Walpurgis-Night. At the end, the author allows a faint hope that "out of this extremity of fever. . . . Love one day shall mount."

This hope depends on the extent to which the Castorps recollect the high tradition inscribed in his "Christening Basin," and beyond it, the vision of the harmonious state he "remembered" in his dream in the snow. Castorp forsakes the realm of technics and rhetoric to "take stock" among the elements. In this dream, Hans Castorp reverses Walpurgis-Night. Then, he was nearly emasculated by the devouring mountain-mother. Here, he is saved from castration in the icy snow by his "anonymous and communal" dream which links him with the high points of his heritage: the promise of a polity in which work and play, life and art, the plastic and the musical coexist in harmony. To be sure, this harmony is only a wish and it is disturbed by the reality of the blood sacrifice which Hans *der Träumer* would rather not face. Still, the promise is there, imbedded in the deep recesses of Castorp's memory, and in the *Lied* which he "unconsciously" sings on the battlefield.[9]

Thomas Mann's work as a whole pictures the dissolution of the bourgeois world: In *Buddenbrooks*, through the decline of the family, in *Death in Venice*, through the decline of the artist in a pestilential city, in *The Magic Mountain*, through the war-convulsion of a continent, extended to nearly the entire world in *Doctor Faustus*. And the way in which Mann's sensitive artist-figures would escape the bourgeois world is by retreat to a *Kultur*-realm. *The Magic Mountain*, in particular, reverses the quest which began with Don Quixote, Hamlet and Faust. Where they leave their seclusion for a life of experience, Castorp leaves the world of experience for his insulated mountain.

Mann's subsequent work envisages two ways of transcending the bourgeois sphere. In the Joseph story, it leads upwards towards one human world. Here, Mann wrote, we leave the modern bourgeois sphere far behind to "pierce deep, deep into the human," in search "for man's essence, his origin, his goal." The pressures of Fascism forced Mann to seek another road, the way "downwards," in the hope that in the elemental, man find his common humanity.

The Magic Mountain ended on a hesitant and questioning tone. Castorp had moved from static insulation to dynamic, devouring "communication." His song of peace and love became a cacophony of music and strife, reestablishing the ancient Teutonic myth in which Wotan is at once God of war and music. The ambiguity of this union becomes deeper and more tragic in Thomas Mann's last major work, *Doctor Faustus*.

DOCTOR FAUSTUS:
THE MYTH OF BREAKTHROUGH

In his penetrating discussion of *Doctor Faustus*, Fritz Kaufmann connects the theme of isolation with Protestant freedom of the individual.[10] The German hero, in particular, would make solitude his home, and one is reminded of Nietzsche's "Oh Einsamkeit, du meine Heimat, Einsamkeit!" Goethe's Faust still attempted to break through his isolation by the social act. At the turn of our century, the artist passively distances himself from the insensitive world. Mann's Gustav Aschenbach would shun life and pay heed to artistic form. But the consequence is only that he falls victim to a life of formless disorder. In such phenomena, Thomas Mann saw Germany's pact with the devil, the "secret union of the German spirit with the Demonic." This pact appears, above all, in German music which he called "a demonic realm," a "Christian art with a negative prefix . . . such musicality of soul is paid for dearly in another sphere,—the political, the sphere of human companionship."[11]

Settembrini once urged that Castrop and his country will have to choose between East and West. And when Castorp maintains a stubborn silence, Settembrini movingly exclaims that one suspects Germany may break her silence with some deed. His surmise foreshadows Castorp's act at the end of his seven-year silence and sums up the pendular swing of the German hero between seclusion and expansion, between cultural autarchy and political coordination, between the *Lied* and *Schrecklichkeit*. Thus, Gustav Aschenbach moved from Prussian discipline to dissolute abandonment, Castorp from enchanted insulation to bewitched war-coordination, and Potiphar's wife from the chaste nun to the raving bitch. The same passage is taken by Adrian Leverkühn in *Doctor Faustus*.

Leverkühn's birthplace, Kaisersaschern, has somehow maintained the spirit of the older burgher life. But as Leverkühn experiences the Germany that is proceeding towards Hitler, he seals himself off to work on his musical compositions. But the "howling" which he would leave behind reenters his art and his music becomes an accompaniment of the wars in the world and of Nazi coordination.

Adrian's atonal technique replaces the diatonic system by an absolute order which does away with the central tone, is carried out in "total indifference to harmony and melody." Here, everything is mathematically organized and coordinated, with all twelve tones of the chromatic scale treated as equals. In Fritz Kaufmann's formulation, even the dissonant is put in uniform. (Earlier, Adrian had sought such absolute order in mathematics and theology). The compositions of Leverkühn, the *Tonsetzer*, are the tone for that steely *Gleichschaltung* which is being carried through in his social world. At the same time, his music is homeless, a breakdown of harmony and rhythm, with no fixed tone to which the music returns. This is the import of Mann's detailed analysis of Leverkühn's compositions: he would translate its technical forms into verbal meaning to show that music is not pure, but has realistic implications, that it may be "politically suspect," as Settembrini once said to Castorp.

Leverkühn's descent to the Bavarian valley repeats Castorp's ascent to the Swiss mountain. He maintains an even greater distance, distance from family, women, friends, people. The price for insisting on *noli me tangere* is that which the devil has demanded in the earliest forms of the Faust myth: "Thou maist not love."[12] One extreme is met by another: In the episode where Leverkühn insists on the love of the prostitute Esmeralda, the pure seeks the impure, the most solitary, the most promiscuous, the most individual, the most anonymous.[13] Adrian makes other attempts at "breakthrough," but they also take on a distorted form: his devotion to the friend has homoerotic overtones; his wooing of the woman is done from a distance and in a manner which invites betrayal by the friend.[14] In sum, insulation from human love results in Esmeralda love, lust of the brain in lust of the body, demonic spirituality in diabolic animality, romantic genius in romantic madness. In Adrian's German world, it manifests itself in autarchic nationalism attempting world domination by bestial methods.

Return to the Congregation

In his life, Adrian (like Faust) harmed or killed the people with whom he came in contact. At the close, he makes a final desperate effort to "communicate" in person and by the word to his "brethren and sisters." He confesses that his intoxication was born not of human warmth and love but of devilish cold and heat. It is Adrian's recognition-scene in which he becomes partially reconciled with his group. Here lie elements of hope in this stark, dreary and sombre story, the hope which comes from putting hopelessness into words. In his composition "Dr. Fausti Wehe-klag," the words stand above the choral and orchestral movements and "the final despair achieves a voice." The lament has no other consolation than "what lies in voicing it, in simply giving sorrow words." It is an echo of the consolation which Goethe's Tasso finds.

Hope is also embodied in Echo. The boy belongs to the mythic chain of the Heavenly Child, aspects of which were suggested in Mann's Hanno, Tadzio, young Joseph and Benjamin. As Fritz Kaufmann points out, Echo combines the features of the Christ-child (his prayers) and of a pagan Ariel who, at the end, returns to the elements. He dies for Adrian, helping him find the way to his congregation. In the final scene, Adrian himself appears as a pagan-Christian figure: Surrounded by a little troop of women, he speaks in a prophetic, anachronistic language of how one should *not* live. This sermon on hopelessness and his death are his sacrifice in the hope that the others might live.

Mythic Redemption

In the Joseph story, written during the ascendancy of Nazism, Thomas Mann said that he took the step from "the bourgeois and individual to the mythical and typical," and created a poem of world citizenship. In it, he looked back to the productive roots of the Western myth, and created a hero who combined sensitivity with health, art with politics. Likewise, he would redeem Adrian Leverkühn's music. And, it is characteristic of Mann's dialectic that the redemption arises out of the very material which produced the distortions. Hope resides in music which, by its very nature, is the language of international communication, above all, in Adrian's recognition that music can become this vehicle if it finds its way back to the people. In *The Magic Mountain*, this note is sounded in the *Volkslied* with its motif of communal love and peace which breaks through the fiendish cacophony of "The Thunderbolt." And, at the end of the secular hell in "Dr. Fausti Wehe-glag," the high G of a cello vibrates as an "echo" in the night:

> For listen to the end, listen with me: one group of instruments after another retires, and what remains, as the work fades on the air, is the high G of a cello, the last word, the last fainting sound, slowly dying in a pianissimo-fermata. Then nothing more: silence and night. But that tone which vibrates in the silence, which is no longer there, to which only the spirit hearkens, and which was the voice of mourning, is so no more. It changes its meaning; it abides as a light in the night.[15]

Like Goethe, Thomas Mann would redeem the living mythic values within the German *Innerlichkeit, Gemeinschaft* and *Maasslosigkeit,* which he sees in Bach's chorales and polyphony, Beethoven's chorus "Alle Menschen werden Brüder," in Faust's vision of a free people on a free soil. But this idea can be revitalized only if corrected by the European-Mediterranean tradition of society, an integration suggested in the unity of Hanno and Kai (*Buddenbrooks*), of Tadzio, Jaschu and Aschenbach (*Death in Venice*), of Castorp and his comrades. Together, they contain the promise in the union between Western freedom of the personality with Eastern equality and fraternity.

Thomas Mann once was fond of referring to Germany as "das Land der Mitte," as a country seeking balance and harmony. In *Germany and the Germans,* he stated that "wicked Germany is merely good Germany gone astray, good Germany in misfortune, in guilt and ruin." As in the case of Goethe, Mann's treatment of the Germanic myth is at once a warning against its diabolism and a tribute to its genius.

NOTES

1. Mann's entire work is oriented towards the mythic, the Joseph cycle and *Doctor Faustus* specifically treating mythic heroes and *The Beloved Returns* viewing Goethe as a mythic prototype of the genius. Mann has also devoted considerable critical discussion to the myth problem, especially in "Freud and the Future," "Goethe's Faust," "Richard Wagner and the Ring," "Voyage with Don Quixote" (all in *Essays of Three Decades* [New York, 1947]), *Pariser Rechenschaft* (Berlin, 1926), pp. 60 ff., *Nietzsche's Philosophy in the Light of Contemporary Events* (Washington, 1947), *The Theme of the Joseph Novels* (Washington, 1942), *Germany and the Germans* (Address delivered before the Library of Congress, May 29, 1941), and in his correspondence with Carl Kerenyi, (Carl Kerenyi, *Romandichtung und Mythologie. Ein Briefwechsel mit Thomas Mann,* Rhein Verlag [Zürich, 1945]).

2. I am restricting myself here to an analysis of *The Magic Mountain* and *Doctor Faustus.* The myth of Joseph is treated in my studies, *Thomas Mann's Joseph*

Story. An Interpretation (New York, 1938) and *No Voice is Wholly Lost.*

3. *The Magic Mountain* (New York, 1938). All subsequent references are to this edition.

4. Settembrini approximates the role of Faust's Mephistopheles: Both are critics of German idealism; for both, action is an absolute value. Following Settembrini's lecture on Western freedom, Castorp feels encouraged to approach Clavdia!

5. The inadequacy of Settembrini and Naphta as guides also appears in their apparent sexlessness, with Settembrini managing mild flirtations. Behrens also sublimates the loss of his wife by practicing medicine on the spot where she died and by his amateur paintings. Settembrini refers to him as Minos and Rhadamanthus. Minos is the judge in Dante's Second Circle of Hell who scrutinizes each sin, and "sees what place Hell holds for it fittest stall"; Rhadamanthus is the Judge in Virgil's Hell bringing to light crimes done in life which the perpetrator vainly thought were hidden (*Aeneid*, Book VI).

6. The number three is constantly associated with Peeperkorn. We should also note Mann's use of the number seven, representing a psychic-biologic cycle. Cf. the chapter on *The Magic Mountain* in my *Three Ways of Modern Man*, and the section on "The Seven Myth" in J. M. Robertson's *Christianity and Mythology* (London, 1936). For the sexual connotations of threefoldness and fourfoldness, see C. G. Jung and C. Kerenyi: *Essays on a Science of Mythology*, pp. 20 ff.

7. The linden tree belongs to the tradition of the German village, town and castle. Here, the elders held their counsels, the community gathered to hear sermons. In Goethe's *Faust*, the peasants gather under it ("Before the City Gate") and the home of Philemon and Baucis is identified by the old lindens.

8. Mann deliberately creates situations which are analogous to Goethe's *Faust*, at times employing actual quotations out of the poem. Both begin by turning against their tradition, and both end with war, and the theme of love and peace. Clavdia is Gretchen become dissolute in the twentieth century.

9. As Castorp's Walpurgis-Night corresponds to Faust's Witches' Kitchen and his German Walpurgis-Night, so the first part of his dream in snow approximates Faust's Classical Walpurgis-Night. In Goethe, Faust seeks Helena in a dreamlike state; in Mann, Castorp dreams of the harmony of classical culture. Faust's quest for Helena is followed by war and the Philemon-Baucis sacrifice; in the second part of his dream, Castorp sees the blood sacrifice foreshadowing the war which breaks out at the end of the novel.

10. "Dr. Fausti Weheklag," *Archiv fur Philosophie*, 3/1. See also the chapter on Doctor Faustus in Fritz Kaufmann's *Thomas Mann* (Boston, 1957).

11. *Germany and the Germans*, pp. 5, 6.

12. Mann's novel follows the Faust version of 1587, at times employing its precise wording, such as the formulation of the pact and Faustus' final speech. See my essay, "The Devil of Many Faces," *12th Street*, The New School for Social Research (Summer, 1949).

13. Adrian's Esmeralda episode corresponds to Faust's "Witches' Kitchen," where he hopes to be rejuvenated.

14. The woman has the features of his mother and the child Echo (the son of his sister), becomes his child by symbolic incest.

15. *Doctor Faustus* (New York, 1948). In his essay *Freud and the Future*, Mann speaks of Nietzsche's understanding of disease "as an instrument of knowledge." Nietzsche "well knew what he owed to his morbid state, and on every page he seems to instruct us that there is no deeper knowledge without experience of disease, and that all heightened healthiness must be achieved by the route of illness." Mann's description of Adrian's disease bears striking similarity to his account of Dostoyevsky's epilepsy (*The Short Novels of Dostoevsky with an Introduction by Thomas Mann* [New York, 1945]). He writes that Dostoyevsky's epilepsy entailed "the incomparable sense of rapture . . . and the state of horrible depression . . . that follows it." It was also similar to Nietsche's disease: "A typical symptom of paralysis, presumably due to hyperenia of the affected cerebral parts. . . . Before it clouds its victim's mind and kills him, the disease grants him illusory (in the sense of sane normality) experiences of power and sovereign facility, of enlightenment and blissful inspiration." In his address on *Nietzsche's Philosophy in the Light of Contemporary Events*, Mann speaks of "the susceptibility of the saint to sin," and notes that Nietzsche's illness "was intertwined and connected with his genius, that the latter unfolded with it."

Conclusion

AT THIS HISTORIC MOMENT, mythopoesis leads a precarious existence. The effort to communicate across national and cultural boundaries, to sound the theme of the human condition is in danger of being lamed by a thermonuclear Golem which our age has fashioned. With the discovery and application of nuclear fission, Robert Oppenheimer once declared, physicists had come to know "sin."[1] This sin carries the seeds for generating hosts of "Doctor Strangeloves" in the Pentagons of the world, foreboding a Spenglerian "Untergang" for all life everywhere. The spectre of the Damocles Bomb gives one the feeling that the notion of permanence, of a meaningful human journey and destiny is irrelevant. Some retreat into existential apartness or, like Nietzsche, see homelessness as a home. Some settle by paying homage to the faceless computer and pragmatic operationalism. Others embrace the Methistophelian moment or, like Arnold Toynbee, somehow place hope in a miraculous "Transformation." (See Appendix VII.)

In the nineteenth century, Karl Marx had argued that industrial capitalism gives primacy to the fetishism of commodities and Emerson complained that "things ride mankind." In our century, Franz Kafka symbolized and allegorized the *human* inefficiency of mechanical "efficiency."

Kafka wrote before automation developed the hydrogen and neutron bomb. The bomb introduced a new Moloch of archaic nature, perhaps unknowable and uncontrollable, threatening a Nirvana of universal death. Individual or even collective responsibility for such a cosmic Armageddon is reduced to insignificance: It needs but one finger pressing a button thousands of miles away.

The incalculable power of this monster has not only caught us up in a mechanical reflex reaction, but has also brought an uncanny fascination for the sudden, violent death which is its promise—the terrifying theme in the film *Doctor Strangelove*.

Current preoccupation with Thanatos has its counterpart in the obsession with an explosive "Eros", set to a "rock and roll" pace—a contemporary version of the Bacchantes. This tendency to "live it up" alternates with and results in a "living it down." The contemporary Eros assumes a Thanatos dress or, one could say that the Thanatos drive takes the form of a frenzied narcissistic Eros.[2]

In the arts, this situation has brought forth what Ihab Hassan calls "The Literature of Silence."[3] We have the vogue of Zen which, as one of its spokesmen puts it, offers a philosophy without words. Norman O. Brown's recent book calls language "the fall," and silence "the mother tongue."[4] For Marshall McLuhan, the logical step after electric computers which need no words would be to bypass language.

The difficulty in achieving desired communication has also given rise to "self-expression," now being practiced by some of our distinguished literary critics. In much of our art and literature, this "self" skips over traditional syntax and grammar, comes close to pre-verbal expression of private "oceanic" feelings. In many of our novels and dramas, we have the non-or anti-hero in a state of psychological paralysis. We are presented, not with individualized characters, but with anonymous figures who, like "Dumbwaiters," passively await being acted upon. In plays, such as those of Harold Pinter, Jean Genet, Eugene Ionesco Samuel Beckett and Edward Albee, dramatic dialogue is replaced by spasmodic utterances, jerky pronouncements and "profound" pauses. Plot consists of unrelated scenes and "the absurd" is raised to a first principle.

In classical literature, in Shakespeare and even in Chekhov, silence does have a communicative function, and sometimes "speaks" with awesome effect. One thinks of the lapidary words, spoken by Hamlet at the end: "The rest is silence," of Christ's dramatically eloquent silence in Ivan's Poem of The Grand Inquisitor, of Mynheer Peeperkorn's unheard "speech" by the roaring waterfall which holds those about him spell-bound.

Now, literature which has some artistic form, always says "yes." And, the contemporary voices of silence or of Dionysiac rage are also crying out *for* something— for the restoration of what makes man human. Even as its vocabulary is reminiscent of primitive mythology, it is saying, as does the little man in *Rhinoceros*: I refuse to capitulate. This literature is a protest against our Babylonic chaos and computerized happy ending, and it is saying that when the canons roar, we can make ourselves heard only by whispering or stammering.

Indeed, there are creative impulses here even when they take the form of Beatniks and Hippies and of psychedelic art. What they are saying is that the creatively new can come only if we bypass or break through the miasma of our institutionalized processes. They are saying, with Peer Gynt, that we must go "round" the Behemoths of the Establishment. They are saying that, if we are not to be ensnared by the chimera of a linear progress or be sucked in by the whirlpool of circular motion, we must go "underground." And there is imagination and poetry in the cinematic world created by the Bergmanns, the Antonionis and the Lelouchs.

Earlier, James Joyce sounded this need to penetrate the catacombs of language and customs to catch the sound of the elemental. Freud, too, had argued for this strategy, taking as a motto to his *Interpretation of Dreams* the line from Virgil's *Aeneid*: "Flectere, si nequeo superos, Acheronta movebo" (If I cannot bend the Higher Powers, I will move the Infernal Regions.).

The Ghost's words "Remember me" echo throughout Hamlet's journey, and we noted that in Greek mythology, Memory was the Mother of the Muses. One such memory issues from the Chthonic realm and it contains the springs of inspiration and creative vision. And, there is another which reminds us that, in the beginning, was the Word, the *Logos* and the Act, that is, the necessary condition for order, reason and harmony. Together, they remind us that man is the desiring and wishing, as well as the speaking, thinking and symbolical animal.

Nietzsche noted that the more a tree grows towards the sun, the deeper do its roots reach into the earth. And Freud reminded us that the Latin *altus* means both "high" and "low." The mythopoeic prototypes examined in this study move in a synergic rhythm between the dark pits and the sun-lit heights. To reach upwards, they lie on the heap of ashes with Job, stand on the Crossroads with Oedipus and Dante, go down into the Caves of the Mothers with Don Quixote and Faust, expose themselves to the ravages of primitive sensualism with Mitya Karamazov and the oceanic terrors with Captain Ahab, traverse the lonely regions with Joseph and Adrian Leverkühn. Transfiguration calls for going *through* the rites of passage—the recurrent motif in mythology and mythopoesis.

Much as we may place our faith in the continuity between the past and the present, and great as is the promise contained in our mythopoeic chain, we cannot rely on its power alone to meet the contemporary juggernaut which is threatening to burn up the fruits of Demeter. This is the awareness of our distinguished writers—Nexö, Gide, Camus, Malraux, Thomas Mann, and among our poets, Robert Lowell. They have urged that artists and writers cannot rest with symbolic depiction, but need to become involved in the social demands of the hour by the act as well as the word. Their voices are the counterpoints to the entropic currents of the day. Theirs is the quest for a re-creation of the human heritage towards an approximation of a world of unity in dynamic interplay. As a whole, mythopoesis from the Book of Job to Mann's Joseph story helps keep alive the memory of man's genius and nobility.

This quest depends on favorable social and historic conditions. And hence, the task of cleansing the Augean stables of society is never-ending. In this process, the hero is forever mangled and the inevitable sacrifice places mythopoesis on a tragic plane.

The present contains the possibility of approximating the Third Act of mythopoesis, the integration of fraternity and freedom. The first is in the center of Eastern, the second of Western mythopoesis. The living myth depends on the coalescence of equality and excellence, directed towards One World—the *Grundbass* of mythopoesis. It will not eliminate tragedy. Yet, it could transpose our trials into the plane where they arise, not from avoidable historic pressures, but from the nature of things and of man. It can temper tragedy by mobilizing our powers towards fulfilling ourselves within human limits.

NOTES

1. Cf. Jerome D. Frank, *Society and Survival. Psychological Aspects of War and Peace* (New York, 1967).
2. Cf. my article "Eros and the Trauma of Death," *American Imago*, Vol. XXI, Nos. 3-4 (1964).
3. Ihab Hassan, *The Literature of Silence* (New York, 1967). Hassan sees in its negation of art a necessary condition for an apocalyptic rebirth of art.
4. Norman O. Brown, *Love's Body* (New York, 1966).

Appendices

I. Primitive and Oriental Mythology

PRIMITIVE MYTHOLOGY

MODERN ANTHROPOLOGISTS recognize that primitive life was not devoid of individualistic expression. Still, in the food-gathering stage, land was held in common; tilling of the soil, fishing, and hunting were carried on by the group. The organization of primitive life approximated a large scale family in which men and gods, the animal and vegetable kingdom, as well as the elements, formed what Levy-Bruhl calls a "mist of unity."[1] This sense of belonging was organized by myth and its rituals. Ancestor worship and other rites supported the feeling of the individual that he was, first of all, part of his tribe or clan, that his function was to play *a* role, not *the* role.[2]

It is now established that in primitive culture the myth was not a Romantic hypothesis, but operated as a living principle. The research of scholars, from Frazer, Malinowski and Paul Radin to G. Thomson, Henri Frankfort and Margaret Mead, shows that, while the origin of myth is emotional, its function is practical. The point is summed up by Bronislaw Malinowski. His *Myth in Primitive Psychology* (New York, 1926) states that myth is not

> an idle rhapsody, not an aimless outpouring of vain imaginings, but a hardworking, extremely important cultural force . . . not merely a story told, but a reality lived.

In his studies of a typical Melanesian culture, Malinowski found that its myth was not a symbolic fiction, historical speculation, or mere amusement, but "a warrant, a charter, and often even a practical guide to the activities with which it is connected." Myth is regarded as sacred, expressing and justifying belief and action. It serves as a precedent which determines and shapes the practical day-by-day life and the fate of mankind. For the primitive, the myth is an

> everpresent, live actuality . . . a statement of a bigger reality still practically alive . . . in that its precedent, its law, its moral still rule the social life of the natives . . . a vital ingredient of human civilization.[3]

For the primitive, the myth shaped work, ritual and play into a single whole.

The Seasonal Ritual

Primitive man depended for his existence on the elements and the seasonal changes. He felt them to be divine powers which spelled drought or deluge, an arid or fertile soil—that is, death or life. They were not regarded as automatic events, but had to be adjured by elaborate ceremonies. The seasonal rituals were at once commemorations of what had happened and incantations that they happen again. The succession of the seasons represented a *crisis*, and the entire community was engaged to meet this crisis by rituals of propitiation.[4] The promise that such propitiation would be successful rested on the feeling that man stood in a *familial* relation to these powers. The primitive anthropomorphized the elements and the seasons, thinking of them as fathers, mothers and siblings.[5]

Of the four elements, the Earth was generally regarded as the Great Mother who gave birth to man, to whom he returned and from whom the cycle of birth began once more. Water often shared equal prominence as the source of creation and invigoration. It too was often a mother figure, standing for the mother-breast and cradle.[6] In some Hindu hymns, the waters gave birth to gods who were conceived as mothers or young wives. The Egyptian God Atum arose from the primeval waters, begot the first pair of gods and began the creation of the world. In Greek mythology, the River Ocean was the all-enveloping source of existence, and the philosopher Thales raised water to a primary substance. This idea was revived by the nineteenth century Romantic nature-philosopher Oken who declared that everything living came from the sea.[7]

In contrast to the passive nature of earth and water, fire was conceived as dynamic. In his chapter on "The Interpretation of the Fire-Festivals," (*The Golden Bough*, I [New York, 1929] 641 ff.), Frazer speaks of fire as a productive and reproductive energy. Hence, the widespread custom of kindling great bonfires and of processions with blazing torches. The ambivalent function of fire is particularly stressed in mythopoesis.[8]

Myth, Ritual and Initiation

Anthropologists and ethnologists are agreed that myth and ritual are intimately related.[9] In the case of primitive tribes who have no developed mythology, ritual ceremonies are the only means whereby we can study their mythic attitudes.

Modern pragmatism tends to belittle the function of ritual. But John Dewey's statement that rites are mere "embroidery," actions performed for fun, applies to ceremonies in our own era in which myth often degenerates into mimicry. However, when the myth is alive, rites are expressions by which man tries to secure and adapt to his world and in which the individual finds collective identification. Ritual performance is the group's formalized dramatization of an emotional state. And, through the identical repetition of the ceremony, a past event is commemorated as a permanent "It is."[10] Primitive initiation rituals had a more specific function. They were the way by which the individual moved into adulthood and the candidate gained magical control over the crops and over the welfare of the community.[11]

ORIENTAL MYTHOLOGY

The mythology of the primitive stemmed from his cooperative organization. On the other hand, that of the Oriental Kingdoms—around 3000 B.C.—derived from a hierarchical structure, dominated by a priestly caste. Beginning with the monarchic eras in the second half of the Iron Age, "ideology" enters, and the function of mythology was to preserve the social divisions among the king, the priest and the slave. The rulers were invested with *mana*-power, and existing power-relations were mythicized into sacred institutions. History was immobilized and fixed to the past, becoming a kind of eternal spatial present.[12]

In the *Poetics*, Aristotle stated that the ancient religious myths did not acquire *meaning* until Greek tragedy endowed them with form and structure by means of a unified plot and a "single action." The Hindu *Vedas*, epics, the Egyptian *Book of the Dead*, the Persian *Zend-Avesta* are the products of multiple authors, resulting in amorphous overgrowths of legends, maxims, liturgy and ritual. The Oriental Kingdoms did not produce mythopoesis, such as the Book of Job or *Prometheus* because their social structure did not sanction a rebellious hero. Except for Babylon, their mythology taught that things were to be brought back to the beginning. This ideal was symbolized in the Egyptian myth of the Phoenix who rearises in the identical form of its previous existence, in the Hindu notion of the Four Ages which begin and end with "Nirvana," and in Confucius' ancestor cult. Only in the relatively democratic conception of kingship in Babylon do we get an approximation of the mythopoeic hero in Marduk and Gilgamesh.

Egypt: The Permanence of Osiris

The center of the Egyptian myth was the idea of spatial permanence, with the annual rise and fall of the Nile serving as a paradigm for the eternal static order of things.

This idea shaped Egyptian art and religion. The geometric forms of its sculpture, pyramids, graves and embalmings expressed the lastingness of bodily existence, with the dead celebrated as forever alive. (Breasted notes that the word "death" does not occur in the Pyramid texts, except when referring to the enemy.) Egyptian wordly immanence stood in contrast to Hindu spiritual otherworldliness; its static optimism differentiated it from the sense of conflict and crisis in Mesopotamian and from the temporal futurism of Persian and Hebrew mythology.

At the head of the Egyptian hierarchy stood Amon-Re, who, Phoenix like, was "the half-begotten youth." Amon-Re was the sun-god who created dry land within the primeval waters and whose regular solar movements assured eternal order, justice, victory and immortality. Rebellion against his divine status, such as that by Hathor and Isis, constituted violation of the heavenly order.

This constellation was transposed into the myth of Osiris. The son of Nut (the sky) and of Geb (the earth), Osiris was the God of the Nile and of the grain. He was the dead ruler who was ever alive. Frankfort states that the vitality of the earth was one of the manifestations of Osiris. He dies when the Nile recedes and is "found" when the waters begin to rise and fertility returns.[13] The Osiris myth also introduced the motifs of patricide and incest: In some versions, Osiris castrated his father Sebk and is in turn killed or castrated by his brother, Seth, who throws the pieces of his corpse into the Nile. Isis, his sister-wife, retrieves the body, and, with Osiris' resurrection, nature and vegetation revive.

The oedipal theme appears in a thinly disguised form in the folklore version of the Egyptian *Two Brothers*. Bitiou is tempted by Anoupu, the wife of his older brother. Bitiou rejects her, saying that she and his brother are like mother and father to him. When she tells her husband that his brother had attempted to attack her, Bitiou castrates himself to prove his innocence. We have here an early form of mythic decomposition in which the father and mother appear in the guise of other figures.[14]

Hindu Mythology: From Maya to Nirvana

Of Oriental mythology, the Hindu is most "Eastern" in its derogation of action, individuality and striving, which are viewed as belonging to the illusory world of "Maya."[15] According to the *Gita*, only he attains peace "who lives devoid of longing, abandoning all craving, without the sense of 'I' and 'mine'."[16] Where Egyptian mythology stressed the prolongation of life in death, where the Confucian saw value in practical ethical acts, and the Iranian saw promise in the future, Hindu mythology held that the world of time and activity was chimerical and that the goal was withdrawal from the world.

In Hindu mythology, the world began with "nothing," and the aim was to return to "nothing" or "Nirvana." Between the two lies the three-fold cause of suffering: "thirst for existence, thirst for prosperity, thirst for pleasure." The Four Ages start with the Golden Age of Krta of which the Creation Hymn in the *Rig-Veda* says:

> Then was non-existent, nor existent . . .
> Death was not then, nor was there aught immortal . . .
> That one Thing, breathless, breathed by its own nature:
> apart from it was nothing whatsoever. . . . (X, 129)

Desire, individualism and action arise in the Ages of Treta and Dvapara, when virtue declines and ceremonials increase. In the Fourth Age of Kali, religion disappears, castes become confused, leading to universal destruction by fire and flood. This is followed by rebirth into the original Golden Age where the wheel of time is broken, its stream flows no longer and suffering comes to an end.[17] Here, action, history, striving are of no avail, in that the new Age is identical with the old.

Vishnu represents the creative principle of Brahma and battles against man's ancient adversary, the ten-headed evil spirit Ravana.[18] One of Vishnu's incarnations is Krishna, whose story follows the lines of the Rankian hero: King Kamsa orders all of his nephews killed after he is warned by a voice from heaven that one of them would put him to death. But Krishna is saved and reared by a shepherd in a cave. Later, he kills his uncle Kamsa, becomes king and clears the land of monsters.[19]

Krishna plays a decisive role in the *Mahabharata*. It tells of the war between the Kurava Brothers, who represent the evil principle, and their cousins, the Pandava Brothers, who stand for the good principle. The conflict is brought on when the old, blind Kurava king chooses a Pandava to be monarch, regarding him as superior to his own nephews. In this war, Prince Krishna sides with the Pandavas.[20] However, in the *Bhagavat Gita* Krishna tells one of the Pandava warriors that it was his *duty* to fight for his caste, even if that meant fighting against one's own cousins. The *Gita* thus contributed towards support of the Hindu caste system. On the other hand, it combated the derogation of worldly life, declaring that if one did his caste-duty, one could be saved and enjoy life. In Hindu mythology as a whole, reincarnation higher up was not possible for "outcasts," except for those who were *good* slaves. Later, Buddha (563-483 B.C.) attempted to counteract some of these elements, preaching the Middle Path and the avoidance of all extremes, both those of pleasure and of fleshly mortification. And he was unsympathetic to the caste-system. But is was his challenge to the ancient Indian social system which was successfully met and ritualized in the *Gita*.

Babylon: Legends of Marduk and Gilgamesh

Henri Frankfort distinguishes between the relative serenity of the Egyptian festivals and those of Mesopotamia which were never free of anxiety. He connects this phenomenon with the contrast between the protected isolation of the rich Nile valley and the exposed position of Mesopotamia, which was "periodically robbed and disrupted by the mountaineers on its east or the nomads on its west." He further contrasts the never-failing rise of the Nile with Mesopotamia's uncertain rainfall and its unaccountable, turbulent Tigris. Frankfort also relates these factors to the aristocratic conception of kingship in Egypt and the democratic in Mesopotamia. Thorkild Jacobsen's studies established that the oldest political institution in Mesopotamia showed traces of "primitive democracy," harking back to an age which knew no kings. The Mesopotamian king was not a god, as was the Pharaoh, but a member of the community. Even the gods Anu and Enlil made decisions only after a general council.

This social situation is the basis for the Babylonian myth of Creation and the Gilgamesh epic which approximate Western mythopoesis in which the hero's unrest and rebellion are legitimized. Marduk successfully turns against his parental authority; Gilgamesh dares reject the goddess Ishtar, and he would find the plant through which man might become immortal.

The Myth of Creation: Tiamat-Marduk

In contrast to the Egyptian myth of a creator who rules the world for all time, the Mesopotamian myth speaks of the world as beginning with chaos and with conflicting authorities. The Babylonian Creation myth (*Enuma Elish*) deals with Tiamat's war against her son Marduk (Tiamat is a prominent example of the "Devouring Mother" in mythology).[21] The oedipal theme is suggested in Marduk's motives for subduing his mother. Marduk sends word to her:

> "Thou hast exalted Kingu to thy spouse . . .
> Thou has followed after evil,
> And against the gods my fathers thou hast contrived
> Thy wicked plan
> Stand! I and thou, let us join in battle."[22]

The Gilgamesh legend (about 2000 B.C.) is the first major story which explicitly sounds the motif of unrest in the hero's quest. When Gilgamesh is about to set out on his mission to kill the monster Khumbaba, his mother prays to the sun-god Shamash:

"Why hast thou for my son Gilgamesh
Provided a heart
Whose stormy unrest findeth no peace?"[23]

The twelve tables tell how Gilgamesh frees the nation from the Elamites, and relates Ishtar's passion for the hero. Attracted by his beauty and achievements, Ishtar, the Babylonian goddess of love and vegetation, proposes marriage. But Gilgamesh declines, for he has heard of the fate which had overcome her previous lovers:

"Which of thy husbands didst thou love forever? . . .
For Tammuz, thy youthful husband, thou causest to weeping every year. . . ."

She appeals to her father, the mighty god Anu, who sends a bull to kill Gilgamesh; but the hero vanquishes the animal.

Ishtar's unrequited love is preceded by the story of the friendship between Gilgamesh and Enkidu. Enkidu eats grass, lives with cattle and seems to be the nature-complement to Gilgamesh. After Enkidu is humanized by contact with a harlot, Enkidu and Gilgamesh become close friends and together they overthrow the tyrant Khumbaba. When Enkidu dies, Gilgamesh descends to the underworld to find his friend.[24]

Langdon, Jack Finegan, Morris Jastrow, Henri Frankfort, Thorkild Jacobsen and others stress the conservative social factors involved in the Babylonian myth of Creation and in the Gilgamesh story. According to Finegan, the "one purpose of the creation epic is to show the prominence of Babylon over all other cities in the country. . . ." And Langdon states that the lesson taught by the Babylonian myths of plants and floods (the "plant of birth") was that kings are appointed by the gods, and are the source of all civilization. In Frankfort's formulation, "man's position in the state of the universe precisely paralleled that of the slave in the human city-state."[25]

NOTE ON CHINESE AND PERSIAN MYTHOLOGY

The central note in ancient Chinese writings is the heavenly origin of tradition which is to be accepted as an unchangeable order, thereby ensuring tranquillity of soul. Confucius regarded himself as a transmitter of the past. His maxim was to honor the spirits of one's ancestors and to "act as though they are ever-present witnesses of thine actions, but seek to know nothing further about them." Yet, the Chinese idea of the past was oriented towards its practical, moral bearing on the present. In this spirit, Confucius' *Analects* placed less emphasis on immortality.

338

It opposed the divinity of the caste system, held that the law was above the state, and that there was no place for priestly castes. However, in the later teachings of Buddhism (which entered China from India about 70 A.D.) and in the Taoism of Lao-tse, the stress is on faith, inactivity and tranquillity, which bring vision of the one immovable order.

Of Oriental mythology, only the Iranian points to a futurism, similar to that in the Hebrew myth. In it, the priestly order is not privileged, and salvation comes not only through god, but also through man. The older polytheism is reduced to the duality of Ormazd, the god of light and clarity, and Ahriman, the god of darkness and evil. At the end, the power of evil is broken.[26] In its humanistic concept of individual morality, Persian mythology forms a bridge to later mythopoesis. Iran also contributed the story of Sohrab and Rustum in the tenth century *Book of Kings* by Firdausi, a version of the Oedipus theme of Greek mythology and the Old High German legend of Hildebrand and Hadubrand.

II. A Note on the Prometheus of Shelley and Goethe

Milton's Satan is an "Arch-Angel ruined" by his rebellion. Shelley's Prometheus becomes "the Champion." Echoes of Shelley's attitude towards the French Revolution are sounded in Prometheus' initial irreconcilable attitude towards "the Oppressor" Jupiter, whose tyrannical rule marks the end of the Saturnian golden age, brings suffering and strife into the world, "fear and self-contempt and barren hope" to man. Yet, although Shelley's Jupiter does not give up his tyranny, Prometheus renounces his rebellion, wishing "no living thing to suffer pain." Unbound by Hercules, he finds his gentle words "sweeter even than freedom long desired." He dethrones the tyrant by his spirit of love, which augurs the third age of an "unclassed" future when men are free, equal and fraternal:

> And behold, thrones were kingless, and men walked
> One with the other even as spirits do,
> None fawned, none trampled . . .
> The loathsome mask has fallen, the man remains
> Sceptreless, free, uncircumscribed, but man
> Equal, unclassed, tribeless, and nationless,
> Exempt from awe, worship, degree, the king
> Over himself: just, gentle, wise: but man

> Passionless?—no, yet free from guilt or pain,
> Which were, for his will made or suffered them,
> Nor yet exempt, though ruling them like slaves,
> From chance, and death, and mutability.

Shelley's Prometheus moves from absolute intransigence to absolute love, and his scene from absolute disharmony to absolute harmony. This lends the work (apart from the first act) a non-dramatic quality and makes it a lyrical pageant which familiarizes the reader, as Shelley himself put it, "with beautiful idealisms and moral excellence."

Yet, the poem contains traces of Shelley's hidden reservations about his idealized Prometheus. They appear in the charge of the Furies that he has weakened man by awakening desires in him which he can never still:

> Then was kindled within him a thirst which outran
> Those perishing waters; a thirst of fierce fever,
> Hope, love, doubt, desire, which consume him for ever.

These lines sound the Renaissance theme, found in *Hamlet, Faust, Moby Dick, The Brothers Karamazov*, that the very gift of an open, unlimited universe makes for a world in which man is incessantly driven from object to object:.

> The good want power . . .
> The powerful goodness want . . .
> The wise want love and those who love want wisdom;
> And all best things are thus confused to ill.

In contrast to Shelley's drama, Goethe's poem *Prometheus* remains impious to the end. If Shelley's work expresses both the rebellious mood of the French Revolution and its vision of harmony, Goethe's youthful poem is the voice of Germany's *theoretic* revolutionism claiming that he has created and maintained himself and the world—this at a time when the German "shopocracy" was a passive, obedient tool of the German state. The point is developed in the chapter on the Faustian myth.

III.   A Note on Virgil's Aeneid

In the Middle Ages, Virgil was regarded as a Christian poet and Dante makes him his guide in *The Divine Comedy*.

The central motif of *The Aeneid* is Piety. Aeneas' heroism lies in his obedience to the demands of his Roman authority. He is brave, fearless, persistent, but always within the framework of his public duty.

Aeneas falls in love with Dido. He tells her that he would rather stay with her and admits that he was going to Italy, not by his own volition ("Italiam non sponte sequor"), yet he leaves her. Aeneas is essentially "driven" by his duty to Rome, which he conceives as the bearer of the chosen people. *The Aeneid* is the first mythopoesis which apotheosizes a national idea in the guise of an international order.

The overt aim of the epic was to sanction the imperialism of Augustus by a myth of the divine Roman mission. Tribal Troy was to be replaced by an universal empire in peace (Pax Romana), with Aeneas as its prince. But we must note the reservations which are contained in Virgil's art. The poet pictures Aeneas as a man who never questions the mission with which he has been entrusted, and behaves somewhat like an unbending soldier. Virgil begins his epic with the word *arms* (*arma*) and ends it with the word *death* (*ombras*). These terms convey the mood of the poem and suggest Virgil's underlying feeling about the cruel war which was carried on in the interests of Augustus' imperialism.

IV. A Note on Eissler's Goethe

K. R. Eissler's monumental book, *Goethe: A Psychoanalytic Study 1775-1786* (2 vols.; Detroit, 1963), published after this chapter on *Faust* had been written, examines Goethe's life through his Italian journey and discusses *Wilhelm Meister, Iphigenia* and many poems and lesser known works which bear on the decade of Goethe's life centering in his relation to Charlotte von Stein.

Eissler regards Goethe as a genius and as "an ideal type of creativity" (p. 1353). The pivotal thesis of his book is that the necessary condition for such creativity is that the genius may not permit himself fully satisfying object-relationships. He must live under the condition of maximum tension combined with maximum frustration. However, Eissler adds that the creation of great art requires that the ego function remain uninjured even as there is an interplay between the ego and the repressed (p. 1165). His over-all view of Goethe is that he is an example of a "constructive or organizing" disease (p. xxxiii). For a discussion of the relationship between genius psychopathology and creativity, see *American Imago*, Vol. XXIV, Nos. 1-2 [1967].

In his examination of Goethe's biography, Eissler indicates that Goethe was able to circumvent the oedipal relationship to his father, partly by being nearer in years to his mother than she was to her husband. This made possible Goethe's near-identification with his mother.

Eissler sees Cornelia as focal for Goethe's problem. He shows that Goethe was incestuously fixated on his sister. Apart from an early love affair, Goethe could not fall in love so long as Cornelia remained unmarried. Her marriage to Schlosser brought Goethe close to suicide, an impulse partially sublimated in his *Werther*. Goethe's deepest guilt stemmed primarily from his relation to Cornelia. At the same time, this fixation helped save Goethe from a full-blown psychosis and from overt homosexuality (a tendency, evidenced in his relation to Behrisch, Merck, Karl August, Lavater) in that he was able to act out towards her the roles of both mother and father. She provided the condition which drove him from one achievement to another (both real and symbolical).

The most startling, ingenious—and, on the whole, persuasive—of Eissler's contributions to the understanding of Goethe's life-work is his painstakingly worked out thesis that Charlotte von Stein enacted the role of a proto-analyst in relation to Goethe for a crucial decade of his life, 1775-1786 (similar to that which Goethe himself attempted with F. Plessing). To begin with, she came to represent all his past love-objects, including those of the infantile period. She thus acquired "a unique and exclusive position comparable to that of the analyst" (p. 1091). Furthermore, she fulfilled the analyst's function by consistently holding up the reality principle. She made no demands on Goethe in love or marriage, and thus constituted no threat to him in his feeling of identity (p. 183). She stood for duty, adjustment to work, and her refusal to surrender to him helped stem his drive towards heedless acting out. Goethe's attraction to Charlotte is seen as the derivative of his past attachment to Cornelia (both were frigid) and thereby helped him overcome his fear of incest. Acceptance of resignation became the principle of Goethe's relationship to Charlotte. (Discharge of homosexual libido towards the Duke made it less difficult for Goethe to tolerate celibacy with respect to Charlotte.) Eissler believes that the ten years with her "preserved him from a catastrophe that would have severely interfered with his creativity" (p. 683). He also believes that this relationship led to the clinical removal of Goethe's sexual defect (p. 1091), resulting in his ability to have sexual intercourse for the first time in his life while in Rome. Summarily, she influenced him towards a change "from relying predominantly on the primary processes in artistic production to invoking increasingly secondary ones" (p. 1069).

To be sure, Eissler notes the unavoidable limitations in Charlotte's function as Goethe's analyst. In the transference, Charlotte could not become the target for his expression of hostility and aggression. Nor could she help him "dissolve the transference."

Christiane Vulpius, like Charlotte von Stein, is viewed as a sister image, even as Christiane was the antitype of Charlotte. He needed the latter's insistence on sexual renunciation in his pre-Italian period. In the post-Italian phase, Goethe found compensation in enjoying that which Charlotte had disallowed.

Eissler's study is a mine of original, highly stimulating observations (especially in the appendices of Volume II). It is based on most careful and minute consideration of voluminous data which should be the envy of the most scholarly "Goethe-Forscher."

V. A Note on Mark Twain and Walt Whitman

Melville's *Moby Dick* appeared at a stage in our history when America was still economically and intellectually attached to its European heritage. Writing in a later and industrialized era, Mark Twain, Walt Whitman and Carl Sandburg have sought for a tradition rooted in America's own experience, created more indigenous American figures and situations, expressed in an idiom which is more characteristically American.

Mark Twain rejected the European feudal legacy which took form in Southern slavery with its primitive vendetta and fake chivalry. At the same time, he warred against the industrialism of the North, its gilded values, its splitting up of the personality and its exploitation of man.

Huckleberry Finn continues Melville's theme of the foundling's quest for his sources. Melville's Pacific Ocean becomes the Mississippi river and his primitive international crew is transposed into the American boy. In him, Mark Twain saw America's native qualities of fraternity and cooperation, coupled with the desire for freedom. His heroes are either boys, such as Tom Sawyer and Huck Finn or child-like grown-ups, such as the Negro Jim. All rebel—Tom in a romantic manner, creating an imagined world gleaned out of *Don Quixote*, Huck and Jim in a practical realistic way. Through their fantasy, daring and non-pragmatic outlook, the boys manage to outwit their adult-world. They repudiate the lords of the earth, their counterfeit idealism and their social-economic enslavement. They secede from their parental homes, go on a river journey which becomes their initiation by water.

Yet, Twain's American myth is an idyll, away and apart from the ruling centers of American society. In Huck and Jim, Mark Twain pictures America as a child adrift, without a guide or destination, seeing only omens and portents. They are the hunted and, at times, the haunted children, never reach sex-maturity, and experience no homecoming. This gives point to Twain's later pessimistic determinism where he spoke of the "damned mangy human race." In *The Mysterious Stranger* and *What is Man,* he saw the future in terms of more and bigger wars determined by small cliques leading men like sheep. Still, in Tom Sawyer and Huck Finn, Mark Twain pointed to the American promise in the union between bold imaginative adventurousness and its fraternal friendship.

Walt Whitman attempted to enlarge Mark Twain's brotherhood to encompass all men, races, nations and tongues in what he called an oceanic form. His poem "Great Are The Myths" evinces a child-like interest in and acceptance of everything.

> Great are the myths—I too delight in them;
> Great are Adam and Eve—I too look back and accept them;
> Great the risen and fallen nations, and their poets, women, sagas, inventors,
> rulers, warriors, and priests . . .
> Great is Youth—equally great is Old Age—great are the Day and Night;
> Great is Wealth—great is Poverty—great is Expression—great is Silence.

Whitman's exuberant delight in life includes its terminus, death, which is viewed as continuous with it and passing over into a new creative existence.

Whitman's ideal goes back to what George Santayana called "the innocent style of Adam, when the animals filed before him one by one and he called each of them by its name." His world is a totalitarian pageant, an indiscriminate classlessness of people and their experiences. This vision of absolute democracy, of identical "leaves of grass," was "the song of the pioneer," who bypassed the complexities and fixities of modern America. Whitman's universe is Melville's world without its hero. In his fear that democracy has been "so retarded and jeopardized by powerful personalities," Whitman thought it necessary "to reduce everything to a dead level." It was his hope that this might be the preparatory stage "for grander individualities than ever."

Mark Twain and Walt Whitman celebrate the American mythic values of fraternity and freedom which Melville spoke of in his "Knights and Squires." In his Preface to the first edition of *Leaves of Grass* (1855),

Whitman declared that the genius of the United States is "always most in the common people. . . . Their deathless attachment to freedom . . . their good temper and open-handedness." He felt that differences do not make for classes "any more than one eyesight countervails another." He saw in the average American the virtues of the traditional aristocratic hero:

> The ranges of heroism and loftiness with which Greek and feudal poets endow'd their god-like or lordly born characters—indeed prouder and better based and with fuller ranges than these—I was to endow the democratic averages of America.

Contemporary writers, such as John Steinbeck, Carl Sandburg, Mark VanDoren, Alfred Kreymborg, William Carlos Williams and Benjamin Appel have refined this theme. In Carl Sandburg's lines from *The People, Yes*:

> The People sleep
> Ai! ai! The people sleep
> Yet the sleepers toss in sleep
> And the sleepers wake.
> Ai! ai! The sleepers wake.

VI.   Freud's Analysis of A Katya-Figure in Zweig's Story

In his essay "Dostoyevsky and Parricide" (St. Ed., Vol. XXI [London, 1961]), Freud does not mention Katya. And, he obviously refers to Grushenka when he writes that Mitya's motive of sexual rivalry with his father is openly admitted.

Careful scrutiny discloses, however, that Freud does sense Katya's role in the novel. This appears in Freud's discussion of Stefan Zweig's story "Four-and-Twenty Hours in a Woman's Life," which he includes in his essay on Dostoyevsky. His manifest purpose here is to illuminate Dostoyevsky's gambling mania and its connection with his onanistic burden. But what Freud says about the woman in Zweig's story applies—with allowance for digressive "free association"—to Dostoyevsky's Katya.

In his essay on Freud's "Study of Dostoyevsky," Theodor Reik pays tribute to it, making only some minor criticisms. One of these is that Freud's summary of Zweig's story is "an error in proportion" (*From Thirty Years with Freud* [New York, 1940]). In a letter (cited in Reik's

345

essay), Freud grants "that the parenthetical Zweig analysis disturbs the balance." Yet,—as though Freud felt that this digression *was* somehow relevant—he continues: "If we look deeper, we can probably find what was the purpose for its addition." Freud's discussion is "an error in proportion," if we limit ourselves to his avowed intention. But, as Freud suggests, if we "look deeper," that is, if we examine it for clues to Freud's unconscious "purpose," it is not "parenthetical," but central.

Freud summarizes the Zweig story in the following way:

An elderly lady of distinction tells of an experience she had more than twenty years earlier. "She had been left a widow when still young and is the mother of two sons, who no longer need her." In the gambling rooms of Monte Carlo, into which she wanders aimlessly, she is attracted by the hands of an unlucky gambler, who evidently leaves the gambling rooms in the depths of despair, with the evident intention of ending his hopeless life.

> "An inexplicable feeling of sympathy compels her to follow him and make every effort to save him . . . she . . . finds herself obliged, in the most natural way possible, to join him in his apartment at the hotel, and finally to share his bed. She "exacts a most solemn vow from the young man . . . that he will never play again, provides him with money for his journey home . . . is ready to sacrifice all she has in order to keep him." But instead, "the faithless youth had gone back to his play. She reminds him of his promise, but, obsessed by his passion, he calls her a spoil-sport, tells her to go and flings back the money with which she had tried to rescue him. She hurries away in deep mortification and learns later that she has not succeeded in saving him from suicide." ("Dostoyevsky and Parricide," p. 192)

Transposed into the relationship between Katya and Dmitry:

Katya's father dies while she is still young. She tries to be a mother to two of Fyodor's sons, Mitya and Ivan. Katya learns that Mitya has been leading a "gambling" life and that he is in despair. After the death of her father (who is analogous to the woman's husband in the Zweig account), she comes to Mitya's room. She does not share his bed, except in Mitya's phantasy and perhaps also in her own. Katya attaches herself to him, gets his promise to reform and gives him money, expressing her readiness to sacrifice everything to save him. But, here too, the hero surmises the woman's actual motivation and goes back to his "play." He is now seized with the obsession to return the money to her, who would interfere with his gambling life. At the end, Katya learns that she did not succeed in saving Mitya.

In the course of his analysis of Zweig's story, Freud writes:

> The equation of the mother with the prostitute, which is made by the young man in the story . . . brings the unattainable within easy reach. The bad

conscience which accompanies the phantasy brings about the unhappy ending. (pp. 193)

The woman wants to save the young man's soul. But this is a disguised
facade. To be sure,

> faithful to the memory of her husband, she has armed herself against all sim-
> ilar attractions; but—and here the son's fantasy is right—she did not, as a
> mother, escape her quite unconscious transference of love on to her son, and
> fate was able to catch her at this undefended spot. (pp. 193-194)

Earlier, Freud speaks of

> "Dostoevski's burden of guilt" which "had taken a tangible shape as a burden
> of debt, and he was able to take refuge behind the pretext that he was try-
> ing by his winnings at the tables to make it possible for him to return to Rus-
> sia without being arrested by his creditors." (p. 190)

Most of this applies to Mitya's relation to Katya.[1]

Freud's Martha and the Matriarchy

The question arises: How to explain Freud's omission of a central
figure in the oedipal situation? A thorough answer would entail a detailed analysis of Freud's life and work. But perhaps some light may be
thrown on this problem by considering briefly one element in Freud's
life.

As is well known, Freud's oedipal scheme centers in the patriarchal
cycle of human history. It has little to say about the matriarchy beyond
noting that "the maternal inheritance is older than the paternal one"
(Footnote to "The Savage's Dread of Incest" in *Totem and Taboo*). In
his essay, "The Heart of Freud" (Haldeman-Julius Publications, 1951),
A. Bronson Feldman suggests that this may be connected with the fact
that in his own life, Freud "had never experienced a mother's dictatorship." In his biography of Freud, Ernest Jones speaks of Freud's mother
as "indulgent." Where "the father stood for the reality principle," Jones
states, the mother stood for "the pleasure principle" (p.7). Freud's conception of what women and mothers are or should be corresponds
roughly to the nineteenth century German conception: the soft, giving,
noncompetitive figure.[2] He writes to his wife:

> Nature has determined woman's destiny through beauty, charm, and sweet-
> ness. Law and custom have much to give women that has been withheld
> from them, but the position of women will surely be what it is: in youth an
> adoring darling and in mature years a loved wife. (Jones, p. 176).

Ironically enough, we learn from Jones' account that Freud did experience some measure of a "mother's" dictatorship. The most promi-

nent women in Freud's life were, aside from his mother (about whom Jones gives very little), Martha Bernays, who became his wife, and her mother. Martha's mother was the head of the family and, according to Jones, Freud found in her "too masculine an attitude." Freud himself says of her that she "exacts admiration" (Jones, p.116). Freud had some bitter quarrels with this strong-willed woman and even threatened to break with Martha unless she defied her mother. Later, however, Freud got on quite good terms with the mother.

Now, Freud wanted to think that Martha was not like her mother. "If, for instance," he writes to his wife

> I imagined my gentle sweet girl as a competitor it would only end in my tell-ing her, as I did seventeen months ago, that I am fond of her and that I im-plore her to withdraw from the strife into the calm uncompetitive activity of my home (Jones, p. 176).

And again: "I seek similarities with you (and her mother), but hardly find any." (Jones, p. 116).

"Hardly any," yet some. For, referring to a photograph Martha sent him, Freud sees in her face "an almost masculine expression, so un-maidenly in its decisiveness." Jones adds that Freud was painfully to discover that "she was not at heart docile and she had a firmness of char-acter that did not readily lend itself to being molded" (p. 102).

Actually, Freud's courtship was no simple idyll. There were years of separation; passion alternated with resentment and with torturing doubts about Martha's love for him of which Freud needed repeated reassurance. It, too, was at first a "secret" relationship, jeopardized by the displeasure of Martha's family. In his first letter to her, shortly be-fore their betrothal, Freud would assure her "of a relationship which perhaps will have for long to be veiled in secrecy.—How much I venture in writing that!" (Jones. p.106). Only once did Freud allow himself to express some public resentment against his fiancée. This happened in connection with the Cocaine Episode in which Freud held her indi-rectly responsible for the delay in publishing his manuscript on co-caine. In his Autobiography, Freud would explain

> how it was the fault of my fiancée that I was not already famous at that early age . . . but I bore my fiancée no grudge for her interruption of my work.

Jones comments that Freud's excuse is "somewhat disingenuous," that "it does not tally very closely with the facts," and that it "must cover a deeper explanation" (p.79).

According to Jones, Freud thought of Martha as a truly noble character in whose presence one could not have a mean or common thought. He refers to Freud's feeling of being in "debt" to Martha:

> When he said he would be in her debt when he died he had more than one reason for his gratitude. She protected him from any kind of meanness, and he would do nothing improper or unworthy even in order to gain her in marriage (p. 125).

This feeling of "debt" should be considered along with what Jones calls Freud's "great dislike of helplessness and his love of independence." Yet, Jones observes that "in all major personal issues," Martha "proved stronger than Freud and held her ground." He speaks of "a remarkable concealment in Freud's love life," and that in his relation to Martha, Freud "often needed to express some hardness or adverse criticism before he could trust himself to release his feelings of affection" (pp. 129, 122, 124).[3]

However, Martha was not only "masculine." Jones notes that "Martha's tact and sweetness," again and again, "succeeded in smoothing things over." Thus, it was possible for Freud to see in Martha that which he wanted: "the gentle sweet girl." But the competitive, "masculine" strain was there, in Martha and more so, in her mother. It constituted a threat to Freud's ideal conception of woman, and he tried to keep it out of his sight. Here may be one of the roots for his failure to appreciate the historic function of the matriarchy. And here may be the explanation why Freud did not consciously recognize Katya's dominating personality as a mother-figure.

VII. Conclusion:
Related Philosophic Attitudes

Analogous to this outlook are those approaches which renounce the quest for certainty and for a firm tradition. Here belong the philosophies of Hans Reichenbach and John Dewey, of Logical Positivism and Existentialism, as well as Spengler's and Toynbee's philosophy of history.

In Hans Reichenbach's *Rise of Scientific Philosophy* (Berkeley and Los Angeles, 1951), the new scientific philosophy does not look to the past. "The glorification of the philosophy of the past . . . has undermined the philosophic potency of the present generation." (p. 325) Similarly, for John Dewey, "consequences, not antecedents, supply meaning and truth. . . . Change rather than fixity is now a measure of reality," and "the only *ultimate* result is the result that is attained today, tomorrow,

the next day, and day after next." In this view, the world is open at both
ends, firm principles are dissolved into liquid operations, and tradition
becomes the ashcan of history. Morris Raphael Cohen (*American
Thought* [Glencoe, Ill., 1954]) has characterized this approach as one
in which one is concerned with being on the go.

> We in America are especially in need of realizing that perpetual motion is
> not the blessed life and that the hustlers may not be the only ones, nor per-
> haps even the first, to enter the kingdom of heaven. (p. 301)

The philosophies of history which correspond to this temper are the
spherical *Untergang* of Oswald Spengler, the linear "shipwreck" of the
existentialists, and with a mixture of both, Arnold Toynbee's "Transformation."

Spengler's philosophy may be termed the cartel-view of history in
which the "Faustian" cartel is the final phrase. Existentialism counters
by what may be termed the free enterprise view of history. Both are
based on the idea of self-creation—the various autonomous cultures in
the one and the undetermined individual in the other. In neither, is
there a reference to a derived tradition, and hence, neither can find a
basis for a recreated tradition.

Toynbee rejects Spengler's biologic analogy of final disintegration,
Henry Adam's law of entropy, as well as the existentialist picture of
man doomed to the free and useless Sisyphus labor. He would replace
them with his theory of the anthropological process of growth issuing
from successful response.

In the section "The Mythological Clue," in *A Study of History*, Toynbee makes the point that physical science by itself cannot explain the
genesis of civilization and suggests that the language of mythology
offers an alternative clue. The story begins with what he calls a perfect
state of Yin. It is followed by "an adversary," who instils

> distress or discontent or fear or antipathy. This is the role of the Serpent in
> Genesis, of Satan in the Book of Job, of Mephistopheles in *Faust*, of Loki in
> the Scandinavian mythology, of the Divine Lovers in the Virgin myths. (p.
> 63)

The Yin-state passes over into Yang-activity or the "withdrawal" of the
individual which makes it possible for him to realize his powers which
might otherwise remain dormant.

The elemental rhythm in the alternating beat of Yin and Yang is
"Victory by defeat, creation by destruction, birth by death." This movement is not vain repetition, for

the Wheel of Existence is not just a devilish engine for inflicting everlasting torment on a damned Ixion. On this showing the music that the rhythm of Yin and Yang beats out is the song of creation. (p. 557)

Toynbee assigns the highest place in this process to the idea of the second coming of the historical Christ. Here, as in Dante, the symbolic nature of the mythic journey is fixed to a particular historical occurrence.

Toynbee does see the possibilities of growth for the personality. Here, growth depends on the hero having no organic tie with the social mass which is capable only of imitating the heroic person. Toynbee thinks that "the growths of civilizations are the work of creative individuals or creative minorities. . . . The superior personalities, geniuses, mystics or supermen. . . ." Ordinary humanity is the common clay which can learn something from the action of the genius through a mechanical social imitation.

It has been pointed out that on the basis of this sharp separation, Toynbee cannot account for the culture myth and epic in which the hero identifies himself with the higher levels of his social group. Toynbee states that our civilization need not die, provided "we have the grace to kindle the divine spark of creative power." This can come about if we reject "archaism" and "futurism" and adopt an Oriental "detachment" from wordly affairs. This is the method of "Transfiguration" which would produce the "Universal Church." As in the case of existentialism, the free creative act appears to spring full-headed from a miraculous agency. Both attempt to counteract the effects of the technological and political machine in which the gadget and the committee would replace the cult of the personality.

NOTES

APPENDIX I

1. In its earliest forms, there were no rulers or ruled, only the leadership of the most able, and relations were expressed in terms of kinship, not territory or possession. Whether the mode of reckoning kinship was patrilineal, matrilineal or bilateral, each sex contributed its respective share. In this stage, Frazer writes, "the world is viewed as a great democracy." To be sure, this was a limited democracy. The primitive had no concept of universal humanity and, with the growing scarcity of fishing and hunting grounds, conflicts developed among different tribes. This situation probably contributed to the rise of taboos and prohibitions, such as endogamy, incest and patricide. See the perceptive study by Joseph Campbell, *Masks of God: Primitive Mythology* (New York, 1959).
2. According to Elsdon Best (cited by Ernst Cassirer), when a primitive says "I defeated the enemy," the "I" may mean his tribe many generations earlier.

351

3. Malinowski calls attention to the fact that natives have no abstract word for Being, but instead words of action, such as to lie, to stand, etc.

4. According to Frazer, the ceremony told the story of a young and beautiful god who is beloved of a goddess. He suffers a tragic death and is then restored to life. In *Kingship and the Gods* (Chicago, 1948), Henri Frankfort argues against Frazer's formulation, pointing to important differences among the gods: Adonis is a youth who dies before his prime, whereas Tammuz was a mature and virile figure; in the cult of Adonis and Tammuz, royalty played no part. In any case, most of the gods were original vegetation deities (the title of Marduk was "Plougher of the Field"). In time, the physical and material advantages which the gods bring were extended to cultural benefits, and Jessie Weston indicates that, in the case of the Christian ritual, they were converted into spiritual and religious values: Christianity identified "the deity of vegetation, regarded as Life Principle, with the God of the Christian Faith." Weston's study also shows that the origin of the Grail legend lies in the vegetation ritual, treated from the esoteric point of view as a Life-cult. Jessie L. Weston, *From Ritual to Romance* (New York, 1957).

5. This idea was carried forward in the so-called "sacred marriages" of the Oriental fertility deities (Marduk and Sarpanitum in Babylon, Osiris and Isis in Egypt, Attis and Cybele in Asia, and, later, Zeus and Hera in Greece). They were a guarantee for the fertility and growth of nature and of the human community.

6. In the hierarchic thought of Egypt, the earth (Geb, Osiris) and the primeval ocean (Nun) have male character, but in Greek mythology, despite the reign of Zeus, creation came from a mother-goddess. In Hesiod (*Theogony*, 116), Gaia (Earth) came after primeval Chaos. In Aeschylus' *Prometheus* and *Oresteia*, the earth is the mother of Prometheus and the "primeval prophetess." The name "Delphi," the site of the Greek oracle, was connected with fish and means mother-body. Yet, Homer's Oceanus, Poseidon-Neptune, and the Tritons are male.

7. Water as nourisher and purgator appears in Hebrew mythology (Micah 7, 19) where we are told that God will cast our sins into the depths of the sea—a notion ritualized in the "Tashlich" ceremony, when, on the first day of the Hebrew year, sins are thrown into the water.

   In medieval literature, water stands for milk, the mother-milk by which the Virgin works the miracle. In the Eucharist, it appears as wine (combined with bread). Robert Greer Cohn has pointed out the ambivalence of water in the old French word "amer" (to love) which combines "mer" (the sea), "mere" (mother), "amere(e)" (bitter) and Marie (the bitter sea). See Robert Greer Cohn's *L'Oeuvre de Mallarme un coup de des*. (Paris, 1951).

8. In Aeschylus' *Prometheus*, fire is a useful and a dangerous tool; in Dante, it appears as hell-fire, but also as purging and heavenly; in Goethe's *Faust*, we have the fire in which the Earth-Spirit appears and the fire which consumes Philemon and Baucis; in Wagner a fire forges Siegfried's sword, protects Brunhilde, and consumes the world.

9. There is argument over which is temporally prior: The Boas school holds that ritual derives from myth; Robertson Smith thinks that myth is a later, artistic interpretation imposed on ritual. Similarly, Jane Harrison and the Cambridge anthropologists see myth as the spoken version of the ritual act. According to Clyde Kluckhon the issue over priority is largely spurious, something like "the hen or egg" question. Ritual centers in action; myth moves into meaning. The two are interdependent.

10. Theodor Gaster writes that the function of ritual within the scheme of the seasonal ritual is "to translate the punctual into terms of the durative. . . . What the king does on the punctual level, the god does on the durative." *Thespis* (New York, 1950), pp. 5-6. Cf. Mircea Eliade's concept that the ritual enacts primal time. See his *Birth and Rebirth* (New York, 1958), pp. 6-7 and passim.

11. According to George Thomson (*Aeschylus and Athens* [New York, 1950], pp. 97 ff.), the rites took various forms: The initiate was swallowed by a spirit, underwent a surgical operation, amputation or injury to a part of the body, scorching by fire, etc. Following a long period of seclusion, the candidate received a new name. Sometimes, he returned in a state of temporary insanity, possessed by his guardian spirit which had entered his body. The ritual was usually carried out by a secret fraternity and its mystery revealed to the uninitiated only in its outward form.

    The hero in mythopoesis reenacts some of these phases, particularly injury to a bodily organ: Job's skin, Prometheus' liver, Oedipus' ankles, Ahab's leg. More prominent is the inner injury, taking the form of "insanity": the frenzy of Io, Orestes, Medea and Pentheus, the "madness" of Don Quixote, Hamlet, Ahab and Mitya Karamazov. Their "madness" follows contact with a "guardian spirit" who possesses them: Io by Zeus, Don Quixote by his chivalric heroes, Hamlet by the Ghost, Ahab by Moby Dick. Some also receive a new name.

12. In Egyptian mythology, the archetypal waters of chaos from which life emerged were regarded as eternally present in the Nile waters which annually revived the fertility of the Nile valley. See H. and H. A. Frankfort *et al.*, *The Intellectual Adventure of Ancient Man* (Chicago, 1946).

13. *Kingship and the Gods*, pp. 185 ff. This discussion is based largely on Frankfort's studies.

    Osiris was identified with Seth and with his son Horus whom he had with his sister-wife Isis. Seth and Horus were perennial antagonists, yet both were embodied in Pharaoh, and in the end were reconciled. "Reconciliation, an unchanging order in which conflicting forces play their allotted part—that is the Egyptian's view of the world and also his conception of the state." The Egyptian community "sacrificed all liberty for the sake of a never changing integration of society and nature." (pp. 6, 22)

14. Oriental legends abound in the union between the mother-goddess and the husband-son: Ishtar-Tammuz, Astarte-Adonis, Isis-Osiris, Cybele-Attis, Maja-Agni, Iznani-Iznagi, etc.

15. The esoteric formulation of Hindu mythology is contained in the *Vedas* and its commentaries (*Brahmanas, Puranas, Sutras, Upanishads*), whereas the great

epics, the *Ramayana* and *Mahabharata*, present some of the myths through stories of battles and adventures.

16. Quoted in *Vedanta for the Western World*, ed., Christopher Isherwood (Hollywood, 1945), p. 216. Hindu thought was revived by Schopenhauer and Wagner in the nineteenth century and in our day by Aldous Huxley, Gerald Heard and Christopher Isherwood.

17. In Hesiod, the Four Ages account for all time; in the Hindu account, they recur eternally.

18. Here, too, the gods are associated with the elements and the seasons. It has been suggested that the victory of the storm-god Indra over Vrtra pictures the bursting forth of the rainy season.

19. A cosmological version of the oedipal theme appears in the story of the Vedic Dasyu, the night-demon, who is doomed to be destroyed by his solar offspring.

20. The conflict is over a woman, Krishna, who is married to five Pandava brothers.

21. The Babylonian myth begins with a dual principle—the male Apus (the primeval sweet water ocean) and Tiamat (the primeval salt water ocean). In his attempt to subdue the unruly and over-ambitious sons, Apsu is slain by the God Ea. Tiamat then spawns monster-serpents and asks one of them, Kingu, to revenge the parents. But Kingu is also killed and the gods fashion mankind from his blood. Cf. Alexander Heidel, *The Babylonian Genesis* (2d ed.; Chicago, 1951); also his *The Gilgamesh Epic and Old Testament Parallels* (2d ed.; Chicago, 1949).

    The Babylonian story of Creation was associated with the spring equinox, and the annual death of the Sumerian god at midsummer with the drought of the Mesopotamian valley. The battle between Marduk (who controls the wind) and Tiamat (who created the waters) was based on the annual storms and the spring floods which turn the plains into a watery chaos, until the winds dry up the waters (in the legend, the winds carry away Tiamat's blood). Cf. Morris Jastrow, "Babylonia and Assyria," in *The Sacred Books and Early Literature of the East*, Vol. I (New York and London, 1917); Thorkild Jacobsen, "Mesopotamia," in H. and H. A. Frankfort, *Ancient Man*, p. 180.

22. The point is reinforced by the manner in which Marduk subdues his mother: He catches her in a net, drives winds into her mouth and belly, pierces her belly with a spear, splits her in two halves, forcing "his way to the midst of Tiamat" becoming "the Seizer of the Midst."

23. One legend about Gilgamesh suggests features of the Rankian hero. Cf. S. H. Langdon in *Mythology of All Races*, V (Boston, 1931), 234.

24. Later, Gilgamesh goes to the land of Utnapishtim in quest of the plant of rejuvenation. Here, he is told the story of the Flood and learns that immortality is not for man. See the translation of the Creation epic *Enuma Elish* and of *Gilgamesh* by E. A. Speiser in *Ancient Near Eastern Texts*, ed., James B. Pritchard (Princeton, 1950 and 1955).

25. Morris Jastrow (*An Old Babylonian Version of the Gilgamesh Epic* [New Haven, 1920]), suggests that there may be some relationship between the twelve tablets of the Gilgamesh story and the twelve months of the year:

"Thus in the 6th tablet, the rejection by Gilgamesh of the advances made by the goddess Ishtar, the goddess of love and vegetation and general fertility, is probably a reflection of the decline of vegetation after the summer season had reached its height; and again the story of a destructive deluge, related in the 11th, is clearly associated with the 11th month, in which the rains and storms of the wintry season are at their height." (p. 187)

Cf. Langdon, in *Mythology of All Races*, p. 166; J. Finegan, *Light from the Ancient East* (Princeton, 1946), p. 51; Jastrow, *Gilgamesh Epic*, p. 187; Frankfort, *Ancient Man*, p. 149. There is also a rhythmic use of the numbers six and seven, suggesting the crisis which came to the valley towards the end of summer; Gilgamesh spurns Ishtar in tablet six, accusing her of instability; Engidu dies in the seventh tablet—the beginning of the rainy season. The crisis element in the numbers six and seven also appears in the following episodes: Engidu loves the priestess for six days and seven nights; Gilgamesh laments Enkidu's death for seven days and nights; he tells Ishtar of the "seven and again seven pitfalls" she dug for those she fell in love with; the deluge lasts six days and nights.

26. For specialized studies of Oriental mythology, see E. O. James, *The Cult of the Mother Goddess* (New York, 1959), and his *The Ancient Gods* (New York, 1960); Joseph Campbell, *The Masks of God: Oriental Mythology* (New York, 1962); R. T. Rundle Clark, *Myth and Symbol in Ancient Egypt* (New York, 1960).

APPENDIX VI

1. Freud's letter to Reik contains a sentence which is a kind of quick summation of the Katya-Mitya relation. Dostoyevsky, Freud notes, "really only understands either crude, instinctive desire or masochistic submission and love from pity."

2. Interestingly enough, in Teutonic mythology, women are distinguished not by their beauty or softness, but by their bravery and warrior-role, e.g., the Walküre.

3. Did Martha's firmness and nobility represent a concealed threat to Freud's love of independence (similar to that which Mitya felt in Katya)?—A possible clue may be contained in Freud's dream of the Botanical Monograph (*The Basic Writings of Sigmund Freud* [New York, 1938], pp. 241-46). In his analysis of the dream, Freud writes that he reproaches himself for remembering so seldom to bring his wife flowers, "as she would like me to do," and is reminded "that we often forget in obedience to a purpose of the unconscious." His next association is the monograph on the coca plant. (We know that he indirectly blamed Martha for interruption of his work on this subject). He further notes that the Genus Cyclamen which Freud remembers having seen next morning is "my wife's favorite flower." And he associates his dreaming of the "dried

specimen of the plant, as though from a herbarium" to his having become "a *book-worm* (cf. *herbarium*)." Erich Fromm would seem to be on the right track in commenting that "the monograph about the cyclamen stirs up his feeling that he fails in that aspect of life which is symbolized by love and tenderness" (*The Forgotten Language* [New York, 1951], p.92). Might one further suggest that Freud's desire for "independence" appears in the dreamer seeing a "dried specimen of the plant" instead of a "blooming" cyclamen? In his analysis of the dream, Freud twice mentions the fact that the cyclamen is "my wife's favourite flower."

Index

Abraham, Karl, 281
Albee, Edward, 328
Albright, William F., 63, 66
Anders, Günther, 308
Appel, Benjamin, 225, 242, 345
Aquinas, Saint Thomas, 104, 110, 129, 130
Aristophanes, 93
Aristotle, 40, 70 *Poetics*, 94, 97, 161, 334
Arlow, Jacob A., 34, 35, 44
Art, 35; form, 30; integrative function, 27-28
Asch, Sholem, 64
Aeschylus, 68-69, 72-73, 74, 75, 80, 97-99; Prometheia, 75-82, 99. *See also* Mythopoesis
Auden, W. H., 147, 153, 244, 245, 299
Auerbach, Erich, 110, 116, 117, 128
Augustine, Saint, 104, 109, 129, 185, 215

Babylonian Job, 47, 63
Bacchae, The. See Mythopoesis
Bacon, Francis, 35
Bacon, Helen, 101
Beckett, Samuel, 328
Benardete, M. J., 129
Berdyaev, N. A., 249
Bergler, Edmund, 26, 28-30, 43
Bergson, Henri, 42
Bergstraesser, Arnold, 221
Bickerman, J., 141, 150
Blake, William, 19, 42
Bloch, Ernst, 41
Boas, Franz, 19, 23, 42

Böhm, Wilhelm, 210
Bonaparte, Marie, 26
Borgese, G. A., 121
Bronislawski, J., 29
Brothers Karamazov. See Dostoyevsky. *See also* Mythology, Mythopoesis
Brown, Norman A., 328
Bunyan, Paul, 241
Butler, E. M., 185, 215
Buttenwieser, Moses, 63, 66
Byron, Lord, 150

Campbell, Joseph, 243, 245, 351
Cassirer, Ernst, 17, 20, 29, 31, 33, 43, 44, 64, 70, 105, 219
Castro, Americo, 147
Cather, Willa, 50
Catholic Vision, 103. *See* Dante, Mythopoesis, Cervantes. *See also* Don Quixote
Christianity and Myth, 103-105. *See* Mythology
Claudel, Paul, 168
Cohen, Morris Raphael, 350
Cohn, Robert Greer, 352
Corneille, Pierre, 155, 291
Creativity, 13-17
Croce, Benedetto, 105, 198
Culture Hero, 15, 24, 32
Curtius, Ernst, 129

Dante Alighieri, 103; Beatrice and sex-love, 111, 121; deviations in theology and art, 107; mythic crime, 113; pattern of the *Inferno*: Paolo and Francesca, 115; practical import, 116;

357

Harry Slochower is Visiting Professor at Drew University,
and Adjunct Professor at Syracuse University, 1969-70.
Dr. Slochower is Editor-in-Chief of *American Imago*
and also a psychoanalyst in private practice.

The manuscript was edited by Sandra Shapiro. The book was
designed by Mary Jowski. The type face for the text is Caledonia
linotype designed by Stanley Morison in 1931 and the dis-
play face is Weiss Roman designed by E. R. Weiss about 1928.

The book is printed on Bradford Book paper and bound in
Holliston Mills' Roxite linen over binders board.
Manufactured in the United States of America.